THE OGONI OF THE EASTERN NIGER DELTA
An Economic, Political and Cultural Analysis from Settlement to the Present

THE OGONI OF THE EASTERN NIGER DELTA
An Economic, Political and Cultural Analysis from Settlement to the Present

SONPIE KPONE-TONWE, PH.D

Published by
Safari Books Ltd.
Ile Ori Detu
1, Shell Close
Onireke
Ibadan.
Email: info@safaribooks.com.ng
Website: http://safaribooks.com.ng

© 2021, Sonpie Kpone-Tonwe, Ph.D
First Published 2021

All rights reserved. This book is copyright and so no part of it may be reproduced, stored in a retrieval system, or transmitted, in any form or by any means, electrical, mechanical, electrostatic, magnetic tape, photocopying, recording or otherwise, without the prior written permission of the author.

ISBN: Paperback - 978-978-57696-8-5
             Cased   - 978-978-57696-7-8

Dedication

To the Historian

Table of Contents

Dedication	v
Glossary	xv
List of maps	xix
List of tables	xix
List of figures	xix
List of abbreviations	xxi
Foreword	xxiii
Preface	xxv

CHAPTER ONE
Data Collection and Methods ... 1

1.1		*The Methodology of Oral Tradition*	1
1.2		*Ogoni Oral Tradition*	3
1.3		*Informants*	3
1.4		*Procedure at Interviews*	5
1.5		*Transcription and Translation*	7
1.6		*Analysis, Synthesis and Interpretation*	7

CHAPTER TWO
The Ogoni ... 9

2.1		*Geographical Location*	9
2.1(a)		*Climate*	9
2.1(b)		*Vegetation*	10
2.1(c)		*Occupations*	12
	i.	*Agriculture*	12
	ii.	*Fishing*	12
2.2		*Language*	13
2.3		*Culture I*	14
2.3(a)		*Religion*	14
2.3(b)		*The Gbene*	15
2.3(c)		*Concept of Time and Space*	16

2.3(d)	Marriage..	18
2.3(e)	Divorce	23
2.3(f)	Adultery...	25
2.3(g)	Life, Afterlife, Funerals....................................	26

CHAPTER THREE

Culture II: Origin of the Gbene Title **29**

3.1	Introduction...	29
3.2	The Distinction between the Gbene Title and the Gbenemene Title	30
3.3	The Importance of the Gbene to the Traditional Society..	32
3.4(a)	Prerequisites for the Gbene Title..................	34
3.4(b)	Preparation for the Pilgrimage......................	35
3.5(a)	The Journey to Nama.....................................	36
3.5(b)	Supernatural Challenges and Encounters.......	37
3.6	The Rite of Kpa Bina......................................	40
3.7	Conclusion...	41

CHAPTER FOUR

Culture III : The Yaa Tradition and Social Classification **47**

4.1	Introduction	47
4.2	Economic Activities......................................	50
4.3(a)	The Family System	52
4.3(b)	Mode of Inheritance	53
4.3(c)	Definitions	54
4.4	Youth Training in Ogoni	55
4.5	Pilgrimage to the Ancestral Homes.............	58
4.6	Field Activities	60
4.7	Presentation to the Yaa Totem and Mullet Banquet	62
4.8	Baptism and Separation Dance	64
4.9	The Yaa Marathon, Ritual Cleansing and Tree Planting...	65

| 4.10(a) | Conclusion | 68 |
| 4.10(b) | Recommendations | 71 |

CHAPTER FIVE
Origin and Identity of some Niger Delta Place-Names I: Pereira's Very Large Village 73

5.1	Overview	73
5.2	Early Study of Niger Delta Place-Names	74
5.3	Early Description of Niger Delta Coasts	75
5.4	Data Provided by Early European Travelers	78
5.4(a)	Geographical and Commercial Evidence	78
5.4(b)	Demographic Evidence	79
5.4(c)	Linguistic and Cultural Evidence	81
5.4(d)	Evidence from Local Traditions	84
5.5	Conclusion	86

CHAPTER SIX
Origin and Identity of some Niger Delta Place-Names II: "Moko" "Kuleba" "Others" 89

6.1	Introduction	89
6.2	Origin and Identity of Dapper's "Moko"	90
6.3	Origin and Identity of Dapper's "Kuleba"	92
6.3(a)	The Towns of Kwuri	92
6.3(b)	Effect of the Baan Wars on Kwuribue	93
6.4	Origin of the Duplication of Place-Names "Old" and "New" Calabar	94
6.4(a)	Effect of the Smallpox epidemic and the Baan Wars	95

CHAPTER SEVEN
Traditions of Origin 97

7.1	Traditions of Autochthony	97
7.2	Traditions of Ibibio Origin	98
7.3	Tradition of Old Ghana Origin	104
7.4	Linguistic Evidence	108

7.5	Archaeological Excavations at Nama	109
7.6	Archaeological Dating from other Niger Delta Communities	110
7.7	Conclusions	111

CHAPTER EIGHT

Settlement of Nama and Kugba... **113**

8.1(a)	Settlement of Nama...	113
8.1(b)	Settlement of Kugba	117
8.1(c)	The Proto-Sii Settlers	118
8.1(d)	The Founding of Wiisoro and Gure	118
8.2	Expansion from Wiisoro and Gure....................	120
8.2(a)	The Founding of Kónò.......................................	121
8.2(b)	The Founding of Sii Town.................................	122
8.2(c)	The Founding of Gwaara...................................	123
8.2(d)	Why the Traditions of Kónò are of Sii..............	124
8.3	Eastward Expansion	125
8.4	Northward Expansion	129

CHAPTER NINE

Settlement of Kpong and Outlying Districts **127**

9.1	Settlement of Kpong	127
9.1(a)	Kpong in the Early Age	128
9.1(b)	Kpong as a Watershed of Expansion	129
9.2	Settlement of Tee	129
9.3	Settlement of Gokana	132
9.3(a)	Emergence of the Names "Tee" and "Gokana".....	135
9.3(b)	Emergence of a New Language I......................	136
9.4	Settlement of Luekun and Bangha...................	138
9.4(a)	The Founding of Ko...	140
9.4(b)	The Coming of the Ebani..................................	141
9.5	Settlement of Eleme..	141
9.5(a)	Migrations from Gokana and Tee to Eleme......	143

9.5(b)	Emergence of a New Language II............................	147
9.6	Settlement of Boue..	148

CHAPTER TEN

The Emergence of Kingdoms **151**

10.1	The Kingdom of Nama	151
10.1(a)	Matrilineal Succession...	154
10.2	The Old Kpong Kingdom.....................................	156
10.2(a)	Atee's Migration from Tee to Kpong.................	160
10.2(b)	Establishment of a New Dynasty at Kpong.......	161
10.2(c)	Background to Atee's Ascendancy.....................	161
10.3	The Kingdom of Kwuribue.................................	163
10.3(a)	The Towns of Boue and Kwuri..........................	164
10.3(b)	The Founding of Kónò Boue..............................	165
10.4	The Causes of the Baan Wars............................	166
10.4(a)	Rumours of Assault on the Northern Women Traders	166
10.4(b)	Kwuribue and the System of Coastal Trade in the Sixteenth Century.....................................	168
10.4(c)	The Course of the War..	172
10.4(d)	First Use of Firearms	174
10.4(e)	The Change to Patrilineal Monarchy and Succession...	175
10.5	The Kingdom of Gokana	176
10.5(a)	Giokoo	177
10.5(b)	Unitary State	179
10.6	The Kingdom of Tee	181
10.7	Bangha, Luekun and Eleme	184

CHAPTER ELEVEN

Economic Activities **185**

11.1	Methods of Reckoning and Accumulating Wealth	185
11.1(a)	Investing in Land Livestock and Poultry	186
11.1(b)	Investing in Canoes (Transport)	192

11.1(c)	Investing in Permanent Tree-Crops and Plants	194
11.1(d)	Acquisition of Manilla-Type Bronzes (Kpọrọ)..	196
11.2	Agricultural Production	197
11.3	Crafts and Manufactures	203
11.3(a)	Pottery	203
11.3(b)	Smithing	229
11.3(c)	Carving	231
11.3(d)	Weaving	233
11.3(e)	Salt Making	234
11.4	Trade and Markets	236
11.4(a)	Commodity Trade	236
11.4(b)	The City of Bangha as Centre of Long-distance Trade	238
11.4(c)	Long-distance Trade and the Trade Routes	240
11.4(d)	Impact of the Transatlantic Slave Trade	243
11.5	Conclusion	244

CHAPTER TWELVE

The Canoe Industry at Ko and Long-Distance Trade 245

12.1	Introduction	245
12.2	Long-distance Trade and Canoes	246
12.3	Sources and Supply of Canoes	251
12.4	The Ko Canoe Industry Organization and Production	254
12.5	Implications for Economic Development	257
12.6	Conclusion and Recommendation	260

CHAPTER THIRTEEN

Early use of Money as Medium of Exchange in The Niger Delta 263

13.1	History of Money in the Niger Delta	263
13.2	Origin of the Manillas	266
13.3	Early Application of Money in Ogoni Economy...	273
13.4	Definitions	273

13.5	Investing in Land...	274
13.6	Investing in Transport...	276
13.7	Investing in Permanent Tree-Crops and Plants...	277
13.8	Acquisition of the Kpǫrǫ..	280
13.9	Conclusion..	280

CHAPTER FOURTEEN

Diversification of Social Organization **283**

14.1	Social Stratification	284
14.1(a)	The Rulers	284
14.1(b)	The Ordinary Citizens	285
14.2	Evolution of Political Institutions	293
14.2(a)	Social Organization and System of Governance..	294
14.2(b)	Emergence of the House of Hunters	297
14.3	Formation of the House of Elders	300
14.3(a)	Constitutional Changes and Membership of the House of Elders	302
14.3(b)	The Role of Assobienee	304
14.4	Functions of the House of Elders	306
14.4(a)	The Qualifications of an Elder	307
14.4(b)	The Powers of the House of Elders	308
14.5	Emergence of the House of Lieutenants	312
14.5(a)	Functions of the House of Lieutenants	313
14.5(b)	Qualification and Membership of Pya Zuguru...	314
14.6	Summary	315

CHAPTER FIFTEEN

The Transatlantic Impact **317**

15.1(a)	Ogoni at the End of the Slave Trade (1800-1900)...	317
15.1(b)	Trade Monopoly by the Delta States....................	318
15.2	Ogoni at the close of the Legitimate Trade	323
15.2(a)	The British Colonial Conquest	323
15.2(b)	Aftermath of Conquest: Ogoni under Colonial Rule	326

CHAPTER SIXTEEN

16.1   Conclusion and Recommendation 331

Appendices.. *333*
Bibliography... *359*
Index *377*

Glossary

Aan Zua	The New Year or New Yam feast celebrated in August with bounties of the year's harvest.
Akuu-ban	Ogoni pottery trade mark.
Apaan	Beach seines or fish-trapping beach fence.
Baraba	A large ceramic vessel found in ancient shrines.
Bàrì	Ogoni name for the Supreme God.
Bari-Bue	A town deity and guardian of governance.
Bari-Asaan	Earth deity and god of agriculture.
Damgian	Ogoni highest title for bravery.
Degene	A type of light wood for canoe making.
Eeri	Ogoni week of five days.
Enoo	The Lunar month.
Ereba Edo Khana	The "Seven Multitudes of Khana". This is the seven ancient political divisions of Ogoni
Etabajo	An extinct clan who occupied the coastal strip between Onne and Alesa.
Gbene	The highest military title in ancient Ogoni, used as a prefix to the bearer's name.
Gbenekwaanwaa	Great grand ancestor and first Queen of Ogoni people.
Gbeneyaaloo	Great Leader of the early Ogoni ancestors and founder of Nama Kingdom.

Gbenemene	The title for a king or paramount ruler of Ogoni.
Gberegbe	A spirit-mask used on the battlefield by ancient Baan people to neutralise the impact of the enemy's missiles and weapons.
Giokoo	A military base used by the Ogoni ancestors during the conquest of Gokana.
Gooh	An autochthonous people who occupied the areas of Tee and Gokana, who were conquered by the Ogoni ancestors.
Ikosi	Ogoni name for the British Consul's warriors, who fought their colonial war.
Iyiinayo	A refugee, or one who takes asylum under the protection of a god.
Jongo	Originally an autonomous town or village but now it is a political division of a town. The former word *Luu* is now archaic.
Kaan Zua	The lean feast celebrated in July, during which the elders and mediums eat no new crops until the New Year or yam feast opens in August.
Kawa-Bari	God the Mother-of-Mankind.
Koogian	An annual war dance by warriors and elders, which takes place during the feast of war or *Yonwidam*.
Kobege	Ogoni traditional knife used as insignia of status.
Korokoro	A war camp used by the Ogoni ancestors during the conquest of Tee.
Kónò	The volute which is the totem symbol of Kónò Boue kingdom.
Kpòrò	The class of large bronze currencies, of which the plain type was reckoned to be worth a million (*ezi*), and the decorated type, a billion (*pu*) of the standard currency.

Kpugi te mii	Traditional fee for the ancestors, paid at a marriage or at a social or religious ceremony.
Kue yo	A sacred forest belonging to a deity.
Kuna	A heavy iron tool used by ancient Ogoni farmers for cutting and slashing the bush.
Kwiri	Archaic name of an ancient currency.
Lah-Bue	The second highest office in Ogoni polity to that of the king or chief.
Laadem	Ogoni turn-table or potter's wheel.
Mana	Ogoni name for the eastern Igbo.
Mbulee	An extinct people who lived in Onne.
Mènè	A metal or wooden jingle worn on the neck of a hunting dog.
Nyo eba fah	"On a broken canoe". The name was given by the Ogoni ancestors to the Teenama rocks during their arrival in Ogoni, when their canoe ran on the rocks and broke off a piece.
Nubien	A feast of meat held in August to mark the end of training in hunting and war for boys.
Opuoko	Ibani name for the Ogoni town of Ko on the Imo River.
Pie-Koe	A period of day from 10-12 noon used by wine tappers for treating palm wine with a natural flavouring and colouring agent called *Lee*.
Poro-edon	A devil or evil spirit.
Saga	Ogoni name for the ancient *Asa* people, who lived in a region much farther north than where they are at present.
Sauwe	A king of the Etabajo, who waged a long war against the Khana and Gokana immigrants in Eleme.

Taa	A class of wicked spirits that live apart from human societies in evil forests; but they claim the corpses of wicked men at death and cause trouble if such corpses are buried in a society of decent people.
Uwegbo	Ogoni name for corporate hunting.
Wa Gbenebalikina	"Wife of Gbenebalikina". This was the hunter's idiom or praise name for the gun.
Wu Kon	The sacred act of an agreement, or arbitrament, or initiating an arbitration by solemnly pinning the point of the sword into the ground.
Yiike Beka	The "Gbenebeka interlude". It was a three months period of respite from strenuous activity, covering September to November, which was observed between the end of the Ogoni agricultural year and the beginning of a new farming session. During this period, Gbenebeka, the goddess of Ogoni sent out her emissaries to all parts of the nation to collect taxes and tribute.
Yonwidam	The annual feast of war, which takes place in March with a re-enactment of past war actions by the youths and the elders.
Yokurezogomo	An autochthonous diety/spirit discovered and worshipped by the Ogoni ancestors during their early settlement at Kugba. This spirit later became the god of Sii Town.

List of Maps

Map 1   The Niger Delta
Map 2   The Seven Cultural/Political Divisions of Ogoni
Map 3   Early Migrations of Ogoni
Map 4   Internal Migration and Expansion
Map 5   The Kingdoms/Chiefdoms of Ogoni
Map 6   Inter/Intra-Ethnic Trade Routes & Markets
Map 7   Battle Sites and Military Strategies of the Baan Wars
Map 8   Trade Routes from the Hinterland to the Ogoni Coast

List of Tables

Table I: Ogoni Division of Time in a Day
Table II: Khana and Gokana Place-Names in Eleme
Table III: Composition of a House of Elders
Table IV: Indigenous Words for Money in the Niger Delta and South-Eastern Nigeria
Table V: Some Niger Delta Place-Names Misread in the Writings of the Early European Travellers
Table VI: Archaeological Dating of Nama

List of Figures

Figure I: The Kporo Currencies
Figure II: Nama Pottery
Figure III: Kónò Boue Pottery

List of Abbreviations

AL	Anthropological Linguistics
BP	Before the Present
Calprof	Calabar Provincial Papers
CO	Colonial Office (London)
CSO	Chief Secretary's Office (Lagos)
FO	Foreign Office Papers (London)
IJAL	International Journal of American Linguistics
IJAHS	The International Journal of African Historical Studies
JAH	Journal of African History
JAL	Journal of African Languages
JAS	Journal of African Studies
JHSN	Journal of the Historical Society of Nigeria
JRAI	Journal of the Royal Anthropological Institute
NAE	National Archives, Enugu
NAI	National Archives, Ibadan
OG/SK	Ogoni Oral Texts recorded by the author
RLJ	Rhodes-Livingstone Journal
SOAS	School of Oriental and African Studies (London)
SWJA	South-Western Journal of Anthropology

Foreword

It is a privilege to receive *A History of Ogoni* into the growing body of books on the Niger Delta. Each contribution is unique because it deals with a part of the region that has not been previously studied in detail. *A History of Ogoni* fits into this pattern, being the first full-scale historical study of the Ogoni people by a professional historian from the inside.

Rev. Dr. Sonpie Kpone-Tonwe has come a long way, and has worked long and strenuous hours, days, months, and years to produce the book before us. The long list of acknowledgements tells the story of his long journeys to many places, and communing with many people over these years.

For my part, I have come to respect Rev. Dr. Sonpie Kpone-Tonwe, as a man of great integrity and humility, who has taken advice and admonishment in good faith. Through the most difficult circumstances, he has maintained a steadfast resolve and commitment to strive for the best scholarly standards he could attain.

In my view, Rev. Dr. Sonpie Kpone-Tonwe has brought together the largest collection of data on the early history of the Ogoni people so far. A great deal of this data is completely original, and he has interpreted older data in new ways to lay the foundations of future work in the history of the Ogoni people of the Niger Delta.

E.J. Alagoa
Professor of History
University of Port Harcourt, Port Harcourt.
16 May, 2015

Preface

Two factors stimulated my interest in this work. The first was my family background and a rich cultural environment in which at an early age I observed my maternal grandfather, elder Kuwete, who was a medicine man and a member of the House of Hunters. Incidentally, my paternal ancestor, Gbenekiri, was also the founder and ruler of Uwegwere Town in Boue. At the end of the Baan wars in the 17th century, Gbenekiri became the first *Gbenemene* of a greater Boue, with its centre at Kónò Boue. Following his movement from Uwegwere to Kónò Boue to assume the office of *Gbenemene*, two political groups emerged in Boue, known as *Nobana Uwegwere* and *Nobana Kónò*. At the root of it were the members of his lineage. Those who continued to rule at Uwegwere retained his lineage name, *Nobana Uwegwere*, while those who ruled after him at the centre in Kónò Boue became known as *Nobana Kónò*.

Gbenekiri was later deified as the *Yomii* (god of wine) and honoured with a perpetual feast by the same name *Yomii*, which was celebrated throughout Ogoni every year in May, in recognition of the importance of the raffia palm and the palm wine industry which he introduced. After Gbenekiri's death, his descendants followed his footsteps, among whom were Tonwe I (d.1943), who ruled as Gbenemene of Boue, and Tonwe II, who ruled as Gbenemene of Boue and Babbe until his death in 1975.

As a youth in the royal compound during the reign of Tonwe II, I had the privilege of hearing and observing the performance of many aspects of Ogoni historical traditions. This early exposure in a centre of Ogoni cultural activity affected and influenced my study interest in later life.

The second, and perhaps the most important factor that intrigued my interest was the series of publications, which have come out on the Niger Delta and its mainland region during the last two or three decades. This began with the publication of K.O. Dike's pioneering work, *Trade and Politics in the Niger Delta* (Oxford, 1956), followed by G.I. Jones', *The Trading States of the Oil Rivers* (Oxford, 1963).

Since then, many publications with concentrations on specific peoples of the delta and its hinterland region have appeared. For instance, E.J. Alagoa's *History of the Niger Delta* (Ibadan, 1972) concentrates on the *Ijo* kingdoms of the delta, their culture and their polities; similarly, A.E. Afigbo's *Ropes of Sand* (Nsukka, 1981) and Elizabeth Isichei's *Igbo People* (1976) and *Igbo Worlds* (1977), have revealed so much information about the Igbo of the hinterland, Ogoni's northern neighbours; and David Northrup's *Trade Without Rulers* (Oxford, 1982) has x-rayed the Ibibio, eastern neighbours of Ogoni to the reading world. Even more recently, N.C. Ejituwu has published *A History of Obolo (Andoni)*, who live to the south of Ogoni.

Reviewing these publications, it became clear to me that in the literature of the entire region, only Ogoni was left, as it were, an "Island". Apart from passing references, no concentrated study has been done on Ogoni to give information about this important section of the Niger Delta region to the outside world.

Considering these facts, I found that there was no alternative except to confront the problem, not only as a duty but, much more as a challenge. This book is therefore, the outcome of that resolve, namely to reconstruct a history of Ogoni by the use of oral traditions and other methods of modern research, such as the interdisciplinary approach. The reconstruction traces the experience of the Ogoni from the period of their initial settlement at Nama through centuries of internal migration and expansion to 1947/48, the year of effective British colonial presence in Ogoni. If this effort is considered worthwhile, then I would have succeeded in bridging that old gap which existed in the Niger Delta in the Ogoni region; and this book would have come into being as a useful contribution to Niger Delta studies. But be that as it may, there is still a lot to be done on the history of Ogoni.

For instance, this book was consciously designed to concentrate only on the internal developments within Ogoni itself. Not much has been touched about the external relations of Ogoni with the early Europeans and some of her neighbours over the centuries. Such an attempt would have made this work very unwieldy. Even in the case of the internal developments, there are still many rich sources that are yet to be tapped. Many questions, issues and subjects have been raised in this work, for which further investigations are required. It is hoped that other scholars will take up the challenge to pursue such issues and subjects from where this writer has stopped. In that way, some of the shortcomings of this book will be corrected and the world will get to know more about Ogoni, her culture and her environment.

I cannot complete this preface without mentioning some individuals whose contributions and encouragement made this work possible. To this end, I am profoundly grateful to Emeritus Professor E.J. Alagoa of the Faculty of Humanities, University of Port Harcourt, who both encouraged me and personally supervised my doctoral dissertation from which this book has now become a reality. My thanks also go to the late Professor Kay Williamson of the Department of Linguistics and Communication Studies, who taught me the method and the use of lexico-statistics as well as the use of the botanical names from some Food Plant Names in the Niger Delta, which enabled me to construct a lexico-statistical table for comparing the relationships between the Ogoni languages; and to Professor W.R. Horton, of the Department of Philosophy and Religious Studies, who offered me valuable suggestions and encouragement. I am also grateful to Professor P.D.S. Kinako of the Department of Plant Science and Biotechnology, University of Port Harcourt, who supplied the botanical names of the local plants; to Professor A.A. Derefaka, Curator of the University of Port Harcourt Museum, who granted me permission to study some artifacts he excavated from the site of Nama, the traditional first settlement of Ogoni.

I am especially thankful to the former Vice-Chancellors of the University of Port Harcourt, Professor S.J.S. Cookey, under whose tenure the university granted me the initial funds with which I started my fieldwork on Ogoni. My special thanks also go to Professor S.N. Okiwelu of the Faculty of Science, University of Port Harcourt, for his encouragement and moral support.

I am especially thankful to Professor M.A. Onwuejeogwu of the Department of Anthropology, University of Benin, who as my External Examiner, made useful suggestions for the improvement of this work. My thanks also go to Professor J. D. Fage of the Centre of West African Studies, University of Birmingham, who also read through the manuscript and made useful suggestions for improvement; to Professor G.I. Jones of Jesus College, University of Cambridge, who gave me some materials on the *Andoni* and the *Asa* and offered me useful suggestions; and to Dr. Sue Martin of the Department of History, School of Oriental and African Studies, University of London, who at an earlier stage read through the manuscript and made some valuable suggestions. I am also thankful to the curator and staff of the Ethnographic Department, Museum of Mankind, London, who gave me permission to visit their store, where I was able to identify some ethnographic items which had been taken from Ogoni, especially the Mogho iron money, described by Dapper. Similar thanks are also due to the staff of the National Archives, Enugu and to the staff of Rivers State Archives, Port Harcourt, for giving me the benefit of their professional expertise and co-operation during my research.

Perhaps this work might never have been written at all but for the great interest and co-operation I received from my informants. I should have liked to list all of their names but this is not possible for obvious reasons. I therefore wish to express my warmest gratitude to all of them. In this regard, I am pleased to mention His Royal Majesty, J.P. Bagia, the Gbenemene of Gokana; His Royal Majesty, G.N.K. Gininwa, the Gbenemene of Tee; His Royal Highness, M.A.M. Tonwe III of Boue; His Royal Highness, Edward Nwebon Kpea of Mogho; His Royal Highness, D.D. Deemua, the Mene Bua Boue; His Royal Highness, Isaiah Bekanwaa, the Mene Bua Luawii; His Royal Highness Chief Hon. Dr. J.D. Osaronu, Paramount Ruler of Onne; Chief O.O. Ngofa of Aleto; Chief M.F. Mpeba of Nyongo; Prince F.B. Teedee of Gure; Prince Inatura Inayo of Boue; Chief M.D. Nwikogbara of Sii; Chief J.P. Tigiri of Bien; Chief E.B. Nyone and the Elders of Lewe; Chief Dominic Anderson of Kpong; Chiefs J.B. Yomii and G.N. Loolo of Ko; Chief M.N. Akekue of Kpuite; Chief

Nnaa Kpugita of Keneke Boue; Chief Frank Iwerebe of Uwegwere; Mr. D.L. Ejor of Egbeta; and Mr. A'ean Gbigbo of Kwaakwaa.

Last but not the least, I am especially grateful to my wife, for her care and encouragement throughout the period of the project, and to my daughters, Leyo and Lebeabu, who assisted me with the secretarial aspects of the project; more especially, I am thankful to these two daughters of mine for paying the cost of dating the four charcoal samples excavated from Nama at Beta Analytic Inc. Miami, Florida, USA.

Finally, I give my thanks to the Almighty God, who gave me the guidance, the sustenance and the hindsight I needed to accomplish this work. I acknowledge that it is He who has made it all possible. This book is therefore dedicated to God, because it is He who is the historian, and my greatest and best informant.

SONPIE KPONE-TONWE, PH.D
Department of History and Diplomatic Studies
University of Port Harcourt.
May, 2015

CHAPTER ONE

DATA COLLECTION AND METHODS

1.1 The Methodology of Oral Tradition

Before I started my fieldwork, I had already become very conscious of the fact that the writing of an Ogoni history would depend largely on the use of oral tradition. With this consciousness, I settled down to study the methodology of oral tradition for historical reconstruction. I read every available literature on the subject. In the process, I became acquainted with the well-known specialists in the field, whose writings sharpened my mind and enabled me to grasp a considerable depth of the subject. Before I realised, I had already fallen in love with oral tradition. I stopped worrying about lack of written sources. I soon learned that most of the great writers of past ages achieved their feats by using oral traditions – famous writers like Homer, Herodotus, Josephus, Thucydides, Polybius, etc. (cf. Henige, 1982). Armed with this awareness, I began to enquire deeply into the nature of oral tradition. What is oral tradition? I asked. In the view of Professor E.J. Alagoa, oral traditions are "testimonies concerning the past transmitted from one person to another over time" (Alagoa, 1987). And Jan Vansina describes it as "verbal messages or statements reported from the past beyond the present generation" (Vansina, 1985:27). J.C. Miller on the other hand, defines oral tradition as "a narrative describing or purporting to describe eras before the time of the person who relates it" (Miller, 1980). But Miller's perception of oral tradition has been criticised because of his emphasis on the narrative aspect of traditions. Similarly, Henige's description of oral tradition as "those recollections of the past that are commonly or universally known in a given culture," has also been criticised because of its emphasis on universal historical consciousness (Henige, 1982).

For instance, in some African societies, knowledge of particular traditions is the special preserve of persons occupying certain positions in the society. Among the Bemba, for example, oral tradition is not universal knowledge. Such knowledge belongs to the social group known as "priest councillors" (Roberts, 1973). Among the Yoruba, such groups were the ballard singers of the Obas (Biobaku, 1956). In Ogoni, certain messages were communicated by means of talking drums. To the ordinary ear, such messages were mere sounds, but to the trained ear, they were messages from past generations to the present, between the spirit world and the world of living people, and between the ancestors and their living descendants. Such messages have become a part of the oral traditions. By this wider application of oral tradition, Daniel McCall's definition becomes potent. According to this definition, oral tradition is "any lore of whatever nature that is passed down verbally from one generation to the succeeding generation" (McCall, 1970).

In Ogoni, oral tradition includes other areas of culture besides the spoken word. In some cases, it is a matter of specialised expertise rather than universal consciousness. Because of these considerations, it will be appropriate and relevant for the purpose of this work to define oral tradition as the corpus of cultural transmissions of a people from generation to generation, mainly by word of mouth. The primary mode of transmission is by word of mouth, but besides the verbal transmissions, there are also transmissions by means of periodic performances or re-enactments of past actions and events in the form of rituals, ceremonies, festivals or feasts, and the use of certain materials in connection therewith.

For example, among the Boue of Ogoni, the "feast of *yonwidam*" held in March every year is a traditional dramatisation or re-enactment of battle actions and movements which took place during the Baan wars, a war which was actually fought in the sixteenth century. Thus the "history" of that event has been transmitted from generation to generation for four centuries, not only by word of mouth but more so by periodic dramatisation or re-enactments.

1.2   Ogoni Oral Tradition

The Ogoni have a knowledge of history. They know and remember their past. They remember a certain war which took place in the past between them and their neighbours. They remember why the war was fought and the leading men who took part in it. The term *doonu keneke* (poorly translated "traditions") has a more significant meaning than the English word "history." Literally, *doonu keneke* means the "doings" or the "customs of the land." The "doings" is a record of the "goings on," in the land from the time of the ancestors till the present. It includes names, actions, and events; as well as a "history" of all the ceremonies, rites, and rituals; and the sacrifices connected with each event.

Parents were expected to teach their children about the local traditions. The teaching of some traditions was the responsibility of the whole clan. Such traditions were those connected with war, which were collectively rehearsed annually in the form of festivals. Knowledge of the traditions was regarded by the people as wisdom or intelligence. Thus the saying was spoken, *"Nwi aa ton loo te a da kam"* meaning, "a child who stays close to his father understands the proverbs." The proverbs or deep sayings, were the accumulated knowledge and experiences from the past. There are no special persons designated as traditional historians. Oral tradition as a body of cultural transmissions consists primarily of rites, rituals, ceremonies, festivals, place-names, old sites, fortifications, certain food plants, shrines, tools, weapons, titles, certain marriages, proverbs, etc. These materials have particular origins or events connected with them.

1.3   Informants

My access to the right informants was due to two factors. First, my family background was well-known in Ogoni. Gbenekiri, my ancestor, was a holder of the *Gbene* title and a ruler in Ogoni. Tonwe

I, (d. 1943) my grandfather and a descendant of Gbenekiri, was a paramount ruler or Gbenemene of Boue, and Tonwe II, (d. 1975) my uncle, was the Gbenemene of Babbe. As a young man in the ruling house during the latter's reign, I got to know many important men in Ogoni. I also witnessed and became acquainted with many of the traditional practices described in the corpus of Ogoni traditions, which became the main source of this book. Moreover, many of the chiefs and elders also got to know me personally, having seen me with the late Gbenemene or met me within Tonwe's compound in Kónò Boue.

The second factor that enhanced my research was the social status of my field assistant. Apart from the fact that his mother was married from Tonwe's compound, he had been initiated into the highest secret society in contemporary Ogoni traditional/socio-political ethos, the Amanikpo Secret Society. This was important because it gave him a prerogative which was Ogoni-wide, since once a person was admitted as a member in one town, such membership right extended to all parts of Ogoni. Consequently, his membership had brought him into contact with the elders and chiefs of Ogoni in the course of attending functions organised by the society in different towns.

With this kind of background, it was possible for me to secure the right interviews, sometimes at very short notice and sometimes without prior notice at all. The informants were very pleased to welcome me and to discuss the traditions freely with me. On the basis of information previously gathered, the type of informants believed to possess the information included ancestral spirit-mediums, traditional rulers, titled men, ancestral priests, land priests, yam priests, lineage heads, heads of secret societies, royal wives, occupational heads, such as palm wine tappers, canoe makers, blacksmiths, hunters, medicine men, pot makers, pot traders, etc.

To locate this type of informants throughout the fieldwork area, I divided the field into six zones, namely Boue, Babbe, Nyokana, Tee, Gokana and Eleme. I then visited each of these areas to make enquiries about the oldest villages in each area. With the help of some local persons, usually the chiefs, I located the informants enumerated above. The first period of the research covered from June to November 1981. During the second phase which was from October 1983 to April 1984, I collected the bulk of the material used in this book.

Several re-visits were made thereafter mainly for the purpose of cross-checking some information or to interview a few persons on matters which became relevant during the period of analysis and writing.

The fieldwork was not without its own problems. The main problem during the first phase was that of mobility. During the rainy season, the roads to the villages were very bad; some were flooded and impassable for days. There was also no public transport by car or bus to the villages. Consequently, the major means of transportation to the villages was motorcycle. But most motorcyclists did not want to go out because of the rains, especially because of the bad condition of the roads. On days that the rain stopped for a brief period, the people would not be available at home, as they used that time to go out to farms to collect their foodstuffs or to gather in their crops. Thus, apart from the other aspects of the fieldwork, most of the actual interviews during the first phase took place towards the end of the period.

The second phase was very successful. This was in the dry season and the roads were good. It was possible to travel by motorcycle to any village within Ogoni territory. The only problem during this period was that it was the farming season. Most villagers were not available to hold interviews during week days. Thus interviews were mostly fixed for weekends and Sundays.

1.4 Procedure at Interviews

Interviews were recorded by tape and, only in a few cases, by hand. I used a small high fidelity tape recorder which, with respect to the illiterate villagers, had the advantage of minimising detractions as I had earlier learned that when informants were confronted with a large recording gadget, their consciousness of being taped increased negatively. They became inhibited and tended to speak to the machine rather than to the researcher, with the result that they purposely omitted some aspects of the traditions, especially those which modern influences have condemned, and narrated only those aspects which, in their judgment, would be acceptable to the researcher.

Further safety and privacy measures were taken by having a respectable person of the community to do proper introduction before the interview began. He was to explain to the people the fact that the purpose of the interview was to recover and preserve the memory of the past, especially the memory of the ancients and the work of the ancestors.

Once the interview had started, all variants of the traditions were recorded. As already stated, details about each informant were noted before the interview began.

These included his social status, social group, occupation, title (if any), how regarded in the community, etc.

The interviews were conducted in an informal and relaxed atmosphere. As the Ogoni do not have the type of formally structured traditions, such as exist among the Bakuba, or among the Yoruba, or like those of the Malinke griots, the success of the interviews depended largely on the degree of preparation and the level of acquaintance the researcher had had with the culture of the society before starting the fieldwork. One factor that helped me a great deal was a large handwritten book which Tonwe III handed to me at the beginning of the fieldwork. The book contained a description of traditional government in Ogoni, showing the functions of the chief and the elders, as well as those of the town-crier, and many miscellaneous customs and practices.

From the contents of the book and from what I had known personally, I drew up a questionnaire containing a set of 276 questions covering many aspects of Ogoni historical traditions and customs. Of course, some of the questions were repeated many times but each time a question was repeated, it was reframed to deal with new matters and new situations. Having gone over this number of questions, and the subjects they treated, coupled with my theoretical preparations, I felt sufficiently equipped to embark on the interviews. Some of my informants after the interviews felt more confident, happier, and more mentally exercised than when they started, having learnt quite a few new things, especially things which they had taken for granted or regarded as unimportant.

1.5   Transcription and Translation

As already stated, my advantage lay in my being a speaker of the Ogoni languages and one whose roots rested in the centre of the culture and in the traditions of the people. These credentials were for all practical purposes a great asset to me in my transcription and translation of the texts. I tried as much as possible to transcribe and translate the actual words and meanings of the informants. I was strictly mindful of David Henige's remark in which he stressed the point that translation is much more than mere references to dictionaries for possible meanings of terms and phrases (Henige, 1982). Since the Ogoni languages are tonal languages, a good understanding of the culture and the languages were vital for accurate transcription and translation. Fortunately, Kay Williamson's work on *Practical Orthography for the Ogoni Languages* was handy (Williamson 1984). The transcripts and the translations, together with the tapes are now deposited in the archives of Niger Delta Studies in the University of Port Harcourt.

1.6   Analysis, Synthesis and Interpretation

The material thus assembled together, transcribed and translated, could now be properly called the corpus of Ogoni historical traditions. But in the form it now exists, it cannot be called a history of Ogoni. This is because oral traditions by themselves are not taken as complete historical truth. They are regarded as historical source – materials to be used along with other sources. Such other sources have been used in this book in conjunction with oral tradition to produce authentic results, through analysis, synthesis and interpretations. These other sources include written sources, ethnography, linguistic and archaeological evidence.

CHAPTER TWO

THE OGONI

2.1 Geographical Location

Ogoni territory forms the easternmost extension of the mainland fringe bordering on the Niger Delta (Map 1). It covers an area of approximately 1,300 square kilometres and lies between latitude 4°30' and 7°C' and 7°35'E. It is bounded on the north and east by the Imo River, on the south by Bonny and Obolo (Andoni) and on the west by Port Harcourt. By the 1963 census, the population was 233,000 and by the projected figures for 1988, on the basis of 2.5% annual growth, the population is over 500,000.

The topography of the territory is a gently sloping plateau, the central part of which is about a hundred feet above sea level. The soils are derived from sandy material from oligocene to pleistocene age and are suitable for the growth of both annual and permanent crops (Ndiomu, 1980; Hartoungh, 1966).

2.1(a) Climate
Climatic data for Ogoni are based on data recorded for the entire Niger Delta region, particularly the Eastern Delta; and are usually recorded at Bonny and Port Harcourt on the southern and western borders of Ogoni respectively.

MAP 1 - The Niger Delta

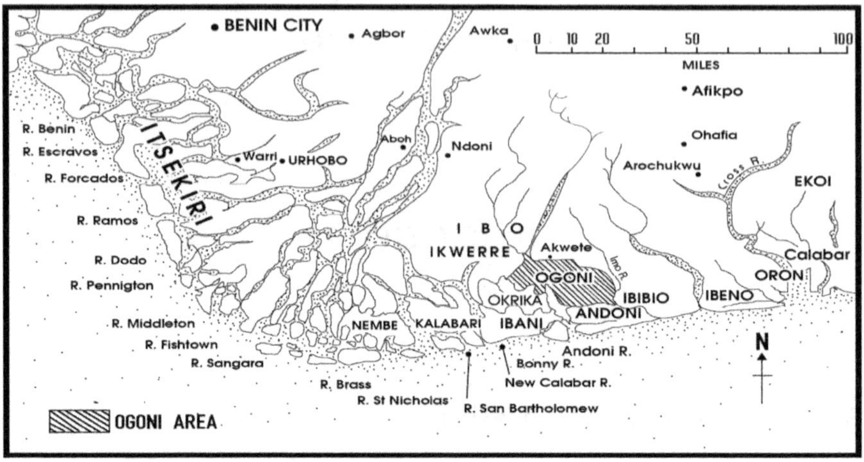

The rainfall in the area is about 178 inches. The wettest months are June, July and September, while the driest months are December, January and February. But even in these months, at least between one and five inches of rainfall is often recorded. In December and January, a local wind known as harmattan blows from the northeast across the Sahara desert as far as the Atlantic coast. It is a cool dry wind laden with a cloud of fine dust particles which absorbs the sun's heat and greatly reduces its intensity over the area during these months.

The highest temperatures usually occur in February when the mean daily maximum for the month is 32.3°C (90.2°F). The lowest maximum is recorded in July at about 27.9 °C (82.3 °F). The mean monthly maximum does not depart much from 21.1°C (70°F). Winds are normally from the south-west and are light, except for occasional line squalls associated with thunderstorms. The skies are often cloudy and the relative humidity is high, about 84.3°C (Hartoungh, 1966; Ndiomu, 1980:4).

2.1(b) Vegetation

Ogoni lies within the tropical rainforest zone. It is therefore within an area of heavy rainfalls and high humidity. The character of the vegetation is marked by the existence of large tall trees, comprising some valuable tropical timber. Most of the forests, however, have been cleared through felling of trees for firewood and for timber, and through clearing for agriculture. A few patches of the tropical forests can still be seen along the rivers and streams. Some of the important species of timber include iroko, mahogany, abura, black afara, camwood or edo, the African oil bean, etc. Many of these trees are almost extinct due to constant felling for building, furniture, carving and for canoe making. The oil palm, the coconut palm and the raffia palm are especially important tree-crops. The oil palm produces vegetable oils and kernels. In the nineteenth century, during the period of 'legitimate' trade, Ogoni was one of the areas which supplied these products for export. Material from its boughs were used in making brooms and packing baskets, essential for packaging and carrying agricultural produce to the market centres. The raffia palm produced palm wine which was the favourite drink of the masses. In recent years, palm wine has also been used in the manufacture of gin. The raffia palm also produces building materials such as poles (for rafters) and roofing mats, as well as raffia for making raffia mats, bags, and cloth; and piassava for making hard brushes and strong cords from which climbing ropes were produced.

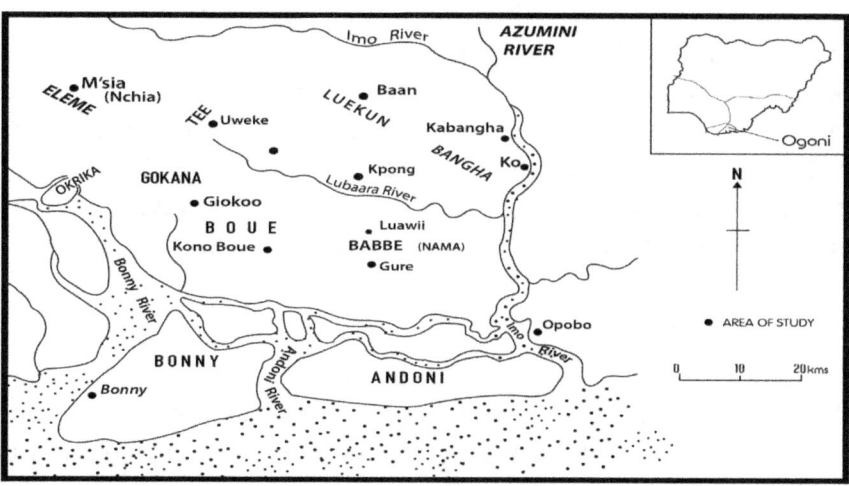

MAP 2 - *The Seven Cultural/Political Divisions of Ogoni*

2.1(c) Occupations

(i)   Agriculture

The Ogoni are both farmers and fishermen. Initially, farming operations in the area were very difficult because of the high rainforests. Farm clearing and cultivation was very labourious and needed many hands. Cultivation was done mostly on flat grounds as the making of mounds in-between large, interwoven tree-roots was very difficult. The main crops were yams, plantains, peppers, bananas, cassava, sugarcanes, vegetables, etc.

The common method of agriculture was by shifting cultivation or land rotation system. The suitability of the climatic condition and soil type encouraged the growth of permanent economic tree-crops such as raffia palms, oil palms, coconut palms, plantains, bananas, rubber, cola, walnut, cashew, etc. Some domestic animals were kept by the traditional method by which the animals were allowed to roam about the homestead and the countryside fending for themselves. Such animals included a few cows, goats, sheep and poultry. These animals were constantly in demand as ritual goods by people wanting to make various kinds of sacrifices and rituals. Thus in the context of traditional Ogoni society, such animals were kept primarily as wealth or source of income and only secondarily as additional food for the family.

Palm wine tapping and palm fruit cutting were specialised occupations. Other specialised occupations included carving, canoe making, blacksmithing and weaving. Pot making was a very important occupation for women until about the 1950s. The decline of pottery industry followed the introduction of plastic and aluminum industries in Nigeria which produced substitute products. The decline of the pottery industry also resulted in the collapse of a lucrative pot trading business by canoes on the inland waterways and along the coast.

(ii)   Fishing

All Ogoni towns along the Imo River and the coastal sea board along the Andoni and Bonny Rivers are farmers as well as fishermen. Bodo, for example, is the largest fishing town on the coastal sea board along the Bonny River (Scott, 1966:30).

Ogoni fishermen use various fishing techniques and methods. The most popular method was by the use of cast-nets. Other methods include the use of gill-nets, lines, traps, bag-nets, beach seines, etc.

They use fairly large canoes carrying four to six persons and five to six cast-nets. The important fishing grounds are on the Bonny River and on the Imo River. Large numbers of Ogoni fishermen also migrate to the Tiko area of the Cameroon Republic in October each year and return the following April bringing good earnings from the rich fishing grounds in the Cameroons.

The Ogoni also specialise in fishing for mudskippers, using batteries of conically-woven raffia-basket traps.

> They "go as far as the Santa Barbara River in search of the fish which, when smoked, are very popular in the inland markets" (Scott, 1966).

2.2 Language

Three languages are spoken in Ogoni viz Kana, Gokana and Eleme. The Kana language is spoken by the largest number of people mainly in the eastern half of the territory. The Gokana language is spoken in the west-central part and Eleme in the western part. The Ogoni languages have been classified and are said to belong to the Benue-Congo branch of the Niger-Congo family of African languages (Greenberg, 1966).

Hans Wolff who did a comparative study of Niger Delta languages also concludes that the Ogoni languages are a distinct group within the Benue-Congo branch of the Niger-Congo language family (Wolff, 1959). Some years later, after a further comparative study of the Ogoni languages, Wolff stated that the three Ogoni languages were inter related but at the same time they were mutually distinct from the rest of the Niger Delta languages (Wolff, 1964).

In another comparative study of the Niger Delta languages, Kay Williamson distinguished seven main linguistic groupings in the area four of which were from the Kwa branch of the Niger-Congo family and three from the Benue-Congo Branch. Each of the main linguistic groupings was further broken down into their component sub-groupings.

MAP 3 - Early Migrations of Ogoni

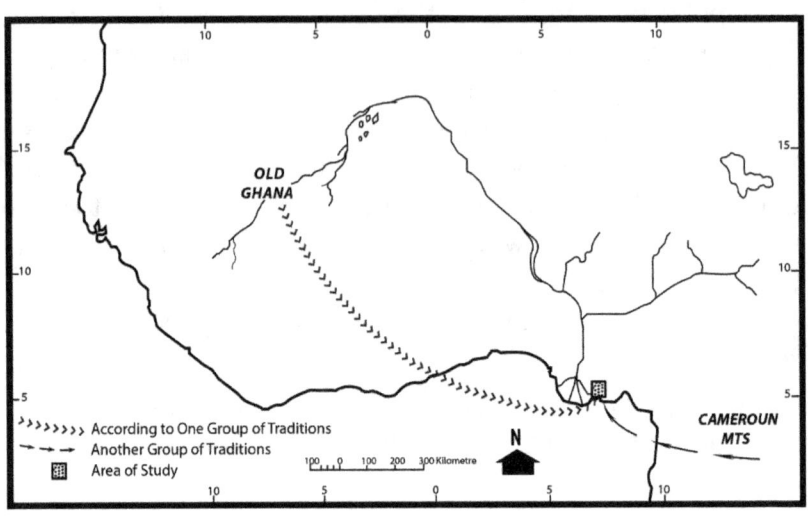

Accordingly, the three Ogoni languages were classified as a distinct language group or cluster within the Benue-Congo branch (Williamson, 1968:126). But in her latest study, Kay Williamson classified the Ogoni languages as a distinct group within the Delta-Cross sub-branch of the Cross-River branch in the New Benue-Congo family of the Niger-Congo phylum (Williamson, 1988:68,71).

2.3 Culture

(a) Religion

In pre-colonial Ogoni, as in most societies before the dominance of scientific thought (Horton, 1967:56), every aspect of culture revolved around a religious base. The role of the supernatural in social, economic and political life was crucial. Religion was polytheistic, since it combined belief in a Supreme Being and belief in a complexity of supernatural spirits.

The Supreme God was called *Bari*, the Creator of the sky, the earth and all things. But to the Ogoni, God was by gender feminine. Accordingly, God was also called *Wa-Bari* (Woman-God) or *Kawa-Bari* (Mother-God). The term *Wa* means "wife" or "woman" depending on the context. Similarly, the term *Ka*, means mother. Thus *Kawa* refers to a woman who is a mother of children. Accordingly, when the Ogoni use the term *Kawa-Bari* (Mother-God) they describe a God that is not only the Creator but also the Mother of mankind. Significantly, however, there is no reference in Ogoni oral tradition to any male relationship with the Supreme God. Thus in Ogoni worldview, the concept of God is twofold:

(i) God is the Creator or Maker of all things, i.e. the physical world and the world of nature, excluding the world of humanity.

(ii) God is the Mother or Bearer of all mankind. To the Ogoni, mankind, unlike the world of nature, was born out of "God's womb," not made. A similar concept of God has been recorded among the Ijo of the Niger Delta. "To this group," professor Alagoa notes, "God is not merely Creator but pro-Creator" (Alagoa, 1989:1).

The Ogoni believe that the Supreme Creator lives in the sky, from where "she" focuses on the earth and knows everything that man does.

2.3(b) *The Gbene Title and Ancestor Worship*

The cult of ancestor worship and the *Gbene* title are related institutions in Ogoni polity. It is a well-known fact that the *Gbene* title existed since the settlement at Nama. All the known ancestors who founded the first settlement at Nama bore the *Gbene* title as a prefix to their names. It is said that a large number of warriors, spirit-mediums and medicine men accompanied them at the initial settlement.

Since that time, the institution of spirit-mediums and ancestor worship have continued to dominate Ogoni society. All sections of the society seem to depend on their services for all sorts of problems. Whether as individuals or as a community, no major undertaking was embarked upon without consulting the ancestral spirit-mediums. Their services were particularly needed in times of emergency such as war, famine, flood, epidemics, etc. David Lan has described a similar practice among the Shona of Zimbabwe (Lan 1985:187). On occasions of national celebrations, festivals, or the performance of a traditional rite, ancestral spirit-mediums were invited to offer their services (cf. Lan 1985:157).

Most informants emphasise that only those ancestors who achieved the *Gbene* title at Nama attained the spiritual power which enabled them to perpetually possess their descendants. Nama remained the only place where the *Gbene* title was granted. Along with the title was received the power which enabled the recipients to transcend after death into a possessing spirit, able to come back to earth to possess their descendants from generation to generation. All such ancestors are worshipped as gods (for details see chapter four).

2.3(c) Concept of Time and Space

In Ogoni, short periods of time(s) were reckoned in days, weeks, months and years. A day was reckoned from a period in the morning indicated by the first cock crow to the first cock crow of the next morning. According to Onwuejeogwu with respect to Nri Igbo, this period was marked from one twilight to the next twilight (Onwuejeogwu 1987:60). As in Igbo, the Ogoni divided a day into a number of periods which may be designated by approximate clock time as on the following table:

Table I: Ogoni Division of Time in a Day

Period	Designation	Approximate Clock Time
Bee Loole	Top of the morning	4 a.m-6 a.m.
Loole	Morning	6 a.m.-10 a.m.
Pie-Koe	Treating the raffia palm	10 a.m-12 noon
Sonpie	"high" sun	12 noon-3 p.m.
Adodee	"low" sun	4 p.m-6 p.m.
Nyon-Uune	Fore night	6 p.m-7 p.m.
Uune	Night	7 p.m-10 p.m.
Tua Son daa	First period of sleep	10 p.m-12 midnight
Era-son	Period of completion	12 midnight-2 a.m.
Bae son daa	Second period of sleep	2 a.m. — 4 a.m.

A week *(Eeri)* consisted of five days, namely *Deemua, Deebom, Deezia, Deeson* and *Deeko*. Six *eeri* or weeks was approximately one month. The month *(enoo)* was the lunar month, and one lunar month was the period from one new moon *(Daa-enoo)* to the next.

The year was calculated on the basis of the lunar month and the Eeri. According to my informants, the beginning of the Ogoni year coincided with the calendar month 'of December'. The Ogoni utilised a number of natural phenomena in the calculation of their agricultural year or lunar year. Such natural phenomena were the regular departure and return of certain migratory birds such as the kites; and the shedding of foliage by certain deciduous trees. Accordingly, the Ogoni agricultural year began in December and ended in August but with an additional three months of respite (September to November inclusive) known as the "Gbenebeka Interlude" *(Yiike Beka)* intervening before the beginning of the next agricultural year.

A year was divided into periods marked by a number of major feasts. The first major feast was the feast of *yonwidam* (feast of war) which took place in February and the last was the feast of *Zua* (or yam) which was celebrated in two stages, a lean feast in July and the great end-of-year feast in August.

Time in the past was expressed in relative terms. For example, an incident "A" might be said to have taken place "after the smallpox epidemic." Another incident might be said to have taken place "before the Ikosi war" (colonial conquest), or that the father of "B" died "during the Ikosi war" or "two cultivations" (i.e. two years), before the Ikosi war.

Long ago or distant past was expressed as "ancient time" *(sonkere)*, and recent times as "new times" *(aanson)* or "new days" *(aandee)*.

Not long ago or short durations of time were expressed in terms of linear time or in relative distances. For example, if a woman came home from the market to find that her husband had gone out to town or to the village, if she enquired from her daughter how long ago this was, she might get one of these answers:

(a) About the time it takes to walk to the market place and back; or
(b) About the time it takes to walk to (or from) the village "x".

Geographical directions and distances were not expressed by the cardinal points but in relation to the speaker and with the perception of "up" *(nyon)* and "down" *(ke)* or right *(le)* and left *(kie)*. Up *(nyon)* was north and down *(ke)* was south. The sun rises on the right and sets on the left. In other situations, "down" is where the speaker is or where we are, and "up" is where those people or those things are.

Positions and directions were expressed in terms of either on the right or on the left or ahead. Things located nearer were said to be located to the "down part" or "on the way down" *(deeke)*, and things located farther away were said to be located to the "up part" or "on the way up" *(deenyon)*. But things located midway or in the middle were said to be located in the middle part *(TeeYee)*. Unknown distances were expressed as "far" *(ebani)*, or as "not far" *(naabania)*.

2.3(d) Marriage

(i) The Early System of Marriage (Before c.1600)

Evidence from oral tradition and by extrapolations from the beginning of the 20th century, indicate that marriage practices in

Ogoni have undergone some radical changes. Before the seventeenth century, marriage in Ogoni was based on endogamous matrilineal system. Under this system, women were not married out of their mother's compounds, and no dowry or bride-wealth was required. A family having a girl of marriageable age looked out in the community for a suitable husband. When such a young man had been identified, the procedure for the marriage involved several steps.

First the family of the girl made enquiries into the moral background of the young man, including his family and relatives. Similar enquiries were made about the young man's personal character, that is, his reputation in the community, whether he was dependable and hard working.

The next step consisted of courtship, during which the young man was gradually courted into close relationship with the family of the girl. Such courtship took several forms. For example:

The mother of the girl might confront the young man at a convenient opportunity with a problem and a mild request. She might tell him that there is a nagging leakage in the roof of her house and that she had no one to climb up there to mend it. She would then ask whether he knew how to do such a thing, and whether he would be willing to do it for her. Alternatively, she might tell him that her grandmother's coconut tree is full of mature fruits and that it is wasting because there is no one to climb up to cut the fruits down. She might add by asking whether he had ever climbed a tree like that and if he would be willing to do it for her. The type and form of these requests or confrontations are numerous and unpredictable. In each case the young man's response was expected to be positive.

On every occasion when the young man had performed these tasks, he was lavishly praised and showered with thanks. If the young man was properly educated from his palm wine camp, he would from that point seize the initiative by offering his services to the most senior brother of the girl's mother (i.e. the girl's most senior maternal uncle) at the beginning of the new farming season. The uncle, of course, would not have to notify the young man when he was going to clear his farm or plant his yams. It was the duty of the young man to be on the lookout and to be ready on the spot with his tools on the day such an event was to take place.

The period of courtship continued for some time (perhaps a year or two). Eventually on a convenient occasion, the young man was formally confronted with the information that their daughter loves him and that they wished to give her to him "for him to take care of her as his wife." From the day of this formal announcement, the young man would restrict his visit to the house until he was ready to do the marriage. He would go home to confer with his friends and patrons *(tebe)* about the matter. The latter would advise him on the necessary preparations. The young man's actual parents had little or no role to play in this type of marriage. The period of preparation could take several months or even a year, depending on whether the young man had got an apartment of his own or not, or whether such was one of the projects he had to take care of before the marriage.

When he was ready, a particular evening was set aside for the marriage with advance notice to the family of the girl. The marriage itself was very simple. All that the young man needed to carry along were a large calabash of the best palm wine available, a bottle of good quality traditional gin and twenty manillas called "prop money" *(Kpugitemii)*. The amount varies in different parts of Ogoni. In Eleme for instance, the amount was four manillas (Ngofa, 1988:58). These things were carried to the girl's compound at night.

The girl's most senior maternal uncle (i.e. her mother's eldest brother) presided at the ceremony as the priest. When all was set, the young man was called upon by his *Yaa* (patron) to carry the items and place them one at a time into the hands of the priest, who announced the receipt of each item, beginning with the calabash of palm wine and ending with the "prop money."

After that, the priest poured libations to the ancestors, inviting each of them by name. Finally, he placed the girl's right hand into the young man's hand and enjoined him to take good care of her as his wife. Similarly, he enjoined the girl to be faithful to him only as her husband. From the moment of this ceremony, both the man and the woman became socially recognised as wife and husband, the news breaking out the following morning.

However, in this type of marriage, all the children born belonged to the girl's family and lineage. But the maintenance of the woman, her children and their training remained the responsibility of the woman's mother and her maternal uncles.

(ii) The Later System of Marriage (or Exogamous Marriage (c. 1600 to present)

From Nama oral tradition, we learn that the leaders who founded the towns needed human victims to sacrifice to the earth god *(Asaa)* for the foundation of the new towns. Similarly, those who aspired to the *Gbene* title needed human victims; and cows, goats, tortoise, etc. to sacrifice at Nama as a requirement for the title. These demands encouraged men to travel far into the hinterland to buy slaves, (usually condemned criminals) to use for these purposes. Consequently, there developed a trade in ritual victims between the hinterland and the coast. Towards the end of the fifteenth century, the Portuguese mariner, Duarte Pacheco Pereira reported the transportation of such ritual "goods" by canoes from the hinterland to the coastal markets (Pereira, 1956:147).

In the course of this trade, some of the men married wives from the hinterland; some converted their slaves into wives. The children born by such wives remained in their father's compounds and became their direct heirs. Since only the rich could afford this long-distance marriage, it became a marriage of the upper class, specially associated with titled men. However, during the sixteenth and seventeenth centuries, the change became more dramatic and widespread following the termination of matrilineal monarchy in Ogoni by the overthrow of the Bariyaayoo dynasty at Luawii during the Baan wars.

According to Boue oral tradition, as a result of the crisis, most men began to exercise direct protection and control over their own families. Women-headed families which lacked men were exposed to danger and needed direct protection by their own husbands. Thus, the experience of that crisis quickened the pace of the transition from endogamous matrilineal to exogamous patrilineal marriage.

The evidence shows that several methods were adopted. One method was that the families which had both grown-up sons and daughters exchanged daughter-for-daughter to be the wife of the son of the opposite family in lieu of bride wealth. That is, the daughter of family A was given in marriage to the son of family B, and the daughter of family B to the son of family A. This method was common among the poorer classes who did not have enough money or land for the bride wealth. A reference to this earlier or transitional method is evident in the following marriage dialogue:

> What money do I have to give to you? And if I had a
> Mature virgin such as you demand in exchange for
> Your daughter, I should have given her..." (Ngofa, 1986:62)

The second method was that families which owned land gave land as bride wealth in lieu of cash payment. But the amount of the bride wealth was put on the land, which could be redeemed at a later date. The third method was by cash payment of sums of money carried in cradles (Ngofa, 1988:62). The amount of bride wealth ranged from about 400 manillas to 1,200 manillas. Only the wealthy could pay the higher amount and for the best and most beautiful women in the community.

Despite the dramatic change, vestiges of the earlier endogamic matrilineal system of marriage have survived into the present. For example, Chief G.N. Loolo describes a relic of it as concubinage (Loolo, 1981:27).

Under the exogamic patrilineal system of marriage, the methods and procedures were completely reversed. In this system, instead of the girl's family, it was the family of the young man who were constantly on the lookout in the community for a suitable girl to marry for their son. Instead of the young man, it was the girl who was courted by the parents and relatives of the young man. It was the girl's character, morality and family background that were secretly investigated. In the new system, the parents of the young man, instead of remaining on the side lines, took the initiative and played the leading role throughout the marriage process. On the day of the marriage proper, instead of the girl's senior maternal uncle, it was the girl's actual blood father who presided and acted as the priest at the final ceremonies. Moreover, the children of the marriage became members of their blood father's compound and lineage, and heirs of their blood father.

During the nineteenth and twentieth centuries, the increase in money income, as a result of earnings from cash crops sales and from wage labour, enhanced the capability of large numbers of men to engage not only in long-distance marriage, but also in direct local exogamic patrilineal marriages. One result of the increased marriage capability was a steady rise in bride wealth. In recent times, education has added more to the value of wives. Thus between 1600 and 1948, the bride wealth in Ogoni has risen from between 400 to 1,200 manillas in 1600 to between ₦1,000.00 to ₦5,000.00 in 1948.

2.3(e) Divorce

Although the oral traditions do not refer directly to divorce cases, there is unconscious evidence which show that divorce existed among the Ogoni from very early times. Such evidence appears in reports about marriages in which a woman was said to have been married together with her child by a previous husband. According to Chief Keekee, Gbeneatee of Kpong did such a marriage.

In another report, an incident is said to have occurred around the seventeenth or eighteenth century, in which a man named Asobienee, because of his physical strength and courage, was employed by the paramount chief and the elders of Boue to be their "policeman." His duty was to summon to appear before the Council of Elders any person wanted by them or any person against whom a report was lodged before them. It is said that he was given the power to compel such a person to appear before them and, if the person resisted, to disable or render him incapable of escaping by breaking one of his limbs, usually his leg. His salary was to be a consolidated amount of three manillas charged on revenue derived from each divorce case settled by the council of elders. According to the informant, this amount became permanent statutory revenue payable to the House of Asobienee till today (Asoo, tape 12, 12th Jan., 1984).

From these pieces of information, we are able to draw a certain conclusion that marriage and divorce were a regular feature of Ogoni social life from very early times. But evidence from the nineteenth and twentieth centuries indicate that the rate of divorce was limited by the number of children already born in a marriage. The custom was that children were not separated from their mother. A new husband was required to marry the woman together with her under-aged children born in her previous marriage.

When divorce was granted, the new husband was required to refund the bride wealth paid by the previous husband and all capital expenses made on the woman by him or by his relatives. Expenses on food, cosmetics and jewelry or anything that went for the make-up of the woman's beauty, was not refunded. According to the elders, "the beauty of the woman was for the pleasure of the husband." However, if any of such items of beauty like cloth, dress, jewelry, etc. were still in good condition at the time of divorce, they were to be returned to the previous husband before going to the new husband. If this was not done, the value of such items was refunded to him. Moreover, if by any means the woman acquired some property like land or permanent tree crop, while she was with the previous husband, such property were not to be taken to the home of the new husband. They remained the property of the old husband.

Since by custom, children were not to be separated from their mother, in a divorce, the new husband was required to pay a prescribed amount for each child already born by the woman in the previous marriage. Usually, the amount payable for each child was about one-third of the total refund bride wealth. That is, for each child, he was to pay about 33 1/3% extra of the total refundable bride wealth.

These conditions seemed to have curbed the incidence of divorce among the Ogoni. Thus divorce was rare in marriage in which children were already born.

Where either the dissolution of marriage or reconciliation was impossible, separation was allowed. In that case, the woman returned to her parent's compound with her children or lived separately in a rented or purchased house, where she fended for herself and her children. If during separation she got additional children by another man, such children remained legally the children of the separated husband.

If at the time of separation, the woman had not got any child, she would be free to live with any man of her choice as concubine *(ga)*. But if during that relationship, she got any children, such children remained legally the children of her separated husband. When a separated woman died, her remains were returned to her separated husband's compound and buried there.

2.3(f) Adultery

Adultery was a serious offence among the Ogoni. An adulterous man was treated like an outcast. He was despised by the elders, shunned by his age group and avoided or dreaded by married and unmarried women alike, lest he should tarnish their reputation. An adulterous woman was treated in like manner, particularly by married women for the same reasons.

A safety-valve for maintaining face socially was for the man involved to step forward and declare his intention to marry the woman concerned. But only the wealthy could do so. When such was the case, the matter was then treated as a case of divorce. However, if the husband of the woman was a strong man, he would press for the payment of the fine for adultery before the proceedings for divorce could start.

Such a submission was usually upheld by the council of elders, provided that the man could successfully establish a case of adultery prior to the declaration of intent by the man to marry the woman. Once a case of adultery was established, the fines were awarded which include a goat, one hundred manillas (or ₦1000.00), one schnapps (or one bottle of homemade gin). If the settlement concerned only adultery and payment of fine, an oath was usually administered by the judges that the man should not commit adultery with the woman again and that none of the two men should seek the life of each other or of the woman or of her children.

2.3(g) Life, Afterlife and Funerals

(i) Life

The Ogoni have a series of beliefs about life. They believe that this life is not the end of everything. There is another life after this life. For this reason, there was training to prepare for life. It was believed that every evil action of man has retribution in this life and after this life; and the person who does the retribution is God *(Bari)*. Thus, there was a demarcation between a holy life and a profane life. A holy life would be successful but a profane life would be doomed. A holy life avoids evil such as stealing, witchcraft, adultery, etc.

Sexual intercourse was believed to be unholy hence, a man going to war or embarking on an important mission must avoid sex or contact with women, unless it was a young virgin. It was believed that a boy who indulged in early sex would shorten his growth and become a mature man prematurely. He would be a man much smaller in size and shorter in height than his parents.

Accidents, misfortunes, sicknesses, etc. were believed to be unnatural. They were supposed to be caused by wicked spirits variously called *taa, poro-edon* or *yo*. But these wicked spirits were often induced into the society by evil men. Misfortunes or sicknesses caused by ancestral spirits were supposed to be corrective, not destructive or fatal. Mediums were consulted, the causes revealed and sacrifices made for appeasement.

The Supreme God *(Bari)* does not afflict men with misfortunes. If the Supreme God wants to give warning or draw attention to some evil in the society, he would cause a tree in the townsquare to fall or lean to one side, or break down a branch or cause a building in the townsquare to collapse on one side without loss of life. When such was noticed, the spirit-mediums were consulted, reasons or causes revealed and the appropriate sacrifices made.

The Supreme God was not represented by any object or altar. Therefore, such sacrifices were not made to the Supreme God but made to purify, cleanse or remove evil from the people. Accordingly, such sacrifices were placed on palm fronds and dragged on the ground round the extremities of the community and finally dumped into a river or sea, or scattered at a distant road junction if a river or sea was not near.

(ii) After-Life

To the Ogoni, death was not the end of life. The death of an elder was only a transition or translation into spirit life in a wider world. Those ancestors who achieved the *Gbene* title at Nama would still come back "visibly" into this world by possessing their descendants from generation to generation, and thereby through their spirit-mediums participate actively in the affairs of this life.

Death itself was not natural, it was caused by the wicked spirits, and are induced by human enemies. Thus when death occurred, spirit-mediums were often consulted to explain the 'cause' of death. Even the death of children and infants were said to be caused by enemies. But such children were said to still be alive in the spirit-world, stronger and more powerful than the enemies who "murdered" them.

Stories are told of children and infants seen to be twisting the neck of the wizards who 'killed' them when they were in this life; and the latter are said to be groaning helplessly in their hands. Thus at the burial of young persons and infants, messages and instructions by parents and relatives are often heard saying, "Hold him tight, never let go your hands from his throat."

The death of young persons and adolescents are regarded as a calamity to the society. It meant an early termination of a fruitful life. If several of such persons die within a short space of time, appeals are usually made to the Supreme God to intervene; and cleansing or purification sacrifices are made for the whole community to remove the evil that caused the deaths of young persons. Such purification sacrifices are also made in times of natural disasters such as epidemics, flood, famine, bad harvests, crop disease, etc.

(iii) Funerals

The funeral of an elder was elaborate and expensive. It involved the slaughtering of goats, cows, tortoise, etc. and many rituals. An elder with the *Gbene* title was buried inside his house with a shrine set up on his grave. A youth who had performed the *Yaa* traditional rite was buried in front of his father's house. An unmarried girl of similar status was also buried in front of her mother's house.

Young persons who had not performed the appropriate traditions were buried at the back of their parents' houses. An adult man who had not performed the *Yaa-ge* traditional rite, irrespective of his age, was buried at the back of the house.

Persons who died accidental deaths were buried outside the town. These included women who died during childbirth or during pregnancy, or during labour with child in their womb. Persons who died of swelling or of an evil disease such as smallpox, leprosy, etc., were not buried at all, because it was believed that their bodies would defile the earth (soil) and prevent it from yielding its fruits. Their bodies were thrown into an evil forest and covered with leaves to rot away.

Similarly, the remains of a person who was known to be a wizard or murderer, was treated in the same way. His body was thrown into an evil forest.

For all these cases, namely deaths by accidents, bad disease, or murderers' deaths, there were no cries or mourning, but for pregnancy and accident deaths, people wept or grieved in their hearts.

CHAPTER THREE

CULTURE II:
ORIGIN OF THE GBENE TITLE

3.1 Introduction

The institution of the *Gbene* title and ancestral spirit-possession has been a part of the Ogoni culture from the time of the initial settlement. In central Africa, for instance, it is said that ancestral spirit-possession and medium consultancy has been in existence for at least four hundred years (Lan, 1985:44).

Bourdillon (1976:298) notes that among the shona of Zimbabwe, the belief is that the spirit of a deceased chief first takes possession of a young lion and wanders about in the forest before it finally enters and possesses a medium. Whether in central Africa or in Ogoni, evidence shows that the main function of ancestral spirit was the control of land, a territory or chiefdom. And the exercise of their power was reflected in their ritual and public activities as protectors of the land.

Although some fundamental differences existed between titles in central Africa and titles in Ogoni, the politics of titles and ancestral messiaship is common in the culture of both regions. A crucial question, therefore is, how did the early ancestors acquire possession powers? Most studies on this subject are yet to come to grips with this question. A great deal of research has been done on the authenticity of ancestral spirit possession, only very little attention has been given to the question as to how a particular ancestor began before he acquired possession powers.

This chapter seeks to answer this question by a study of the process of acquiring the *Gbene* title in Ogoni, the attainment of which enables an individual not only to become a possessing ancestral spirit, to be worshipped or venerated by the people, but also to become a source of political legitimacy and authority. We shall begin by explaining the differences between the *Gbene* title and other titles within the Ogoni polity and by nothing their respective roles within the social and political structure.

3.2 The Distinction between the Gbene Title and the Gbenemene Title

The titles '*Gbenemene*' and '*Gbene*' are distinct in all respects. Although in pre-colonial times, both referred to the occupant of the highest political offices, each was distinct and the manner of their attainment was also distinct.

In the Ogoni social structure, the smallest political division or unit was the compound or house *(Be)*; and the political head of the house was called *Menebe*. He was a titled man and a member of the upper social class called *Kabaari* (Chief or Elder), who must have performed the *Yaanwii* tradition. A number of such houses in a contiguous geographical area constitute a larger political unit called *Luu or Jongo*; and the ruler of a *Jongo* or *Luu* was called *Mene-Jongo* or *Mene-Luu*.

The *Jongo* or *Luu* was originally an autonomous village town or community with its own identity. *Luu* or *Jongo* was applied when several such autonomous towns were merged to form a bigger town under one leadership for purposes of effective defence (ef. Horton, 1969:2). A number of *Jongo* in a contiguous geographical area was called *Bue* (Town), and its ruler bore the title *Menebue*. Accordingly, the term *Pya Mene-Bue* (lit. 'the rich of the town,'), referred to this political class. A number of such towns consisting significantly of large populations in a contiguous geographical area was called *Adonyon* or *Edonyon* (lit. country or multitudes abroad or beyond).

The ruler of such an area bore the title *Gbenemene* meaning the great rich/wealthy one, which appropriately translates as "king".

Before the colonial conquest, there were seven of such political divisions in Ogoni, namely Babbe, Baen, Baan, Boue, Gokana, Tee and Leme (Eleme). After the British conquest, the rulers of the Boue kingdom were punished because they resisted the British, so they recognised the six kingdoms which 'co-operated' with them. Thus in the Rivers State house of Traditional Rulers today, Ogoni has six First Class seats, whose history goes back to very distant pre-colonial times. Evidently, this is the largest and most legitimate representations in that house by any ethnic group. Most other representation there are of recent creation by government in response to pressures by the ethnic groups.

It is pertinent to note that from the term *Mene-be* (House head) to the term *Gbenemene* (Great Ruler), the operative word or root is *Mene*, which means rich or wealthy. Thus in pre-colonial Ogoni, wealth was reckoned principally by the amount of land or territory a person owned or possessed (Kpone-Tonwe, 1990: 169;1997:135). It follows then that in pre-colonial times, those who possessed the largest land and livestock were the founders of kingdoms, towns, and communities. They and their descendants and associates owned the bulk of the land. They also formed the governing body of their towns and villages. Accordingly, they were variously called pya-*mene* bue or *pya bee bue* (lit. the rich of the town or the rulers).

Consequently, the man who controlled the largest land and livestock bore the title *Gbenemene* (Great Ruler or King).

All these were titles of the political class or political offices. The holders or occupiers of these offices still bore their personal names distinct from their political titles. In pre-colonial and colonial times, these political titles or offices were hereditary, hence, they were transferrable from father to son or from incumbent to successor or descendant.

In contrast, the *Gbene* title was both political and spiritual or divine. It referred to the person or individual who bore the title. For that reason, the title was inseparably prefixed to the personal name of the bearer of the title. The *Gbene* title was, therefore, not hereditary or transferrable from person to person, or from father to son, or from a bearer to his descendants. Each *Gbene* title was original, unique and distinct.

However, the relations or descendants of the *Gbene* did enjoy perpetual benefits, such as succeeding to the seat of rulership though without the *Gbene* title. Moreover, the outcome of the achievement of the *Gbene* title was the emergence of a line of political offices, ancestral spirit-media, priests and generations upon generations of worshippers or devotees.

In terms of rank, the *Gbene* was by far greater than the *Gbenemene*. The *Gbenemene* derived legitimacy and authority from the *Gbene*. Moreover, both the *Gbenemene* and his subjects venerated the *Gbene* as a messiah and poured libation (or said prayers) to him. Chronologically, the *Gbene* preceded the *Gbenemene*. The former related to original conquest or founding of the domains of rulership, such as kingdoms and towns, while the latter emerged in periods of political coalitions and consolidations against external attacks. During the preceding periods, however, the positions later occupied by the *Gbenemene* were held by the *Gbene*, who at that time were not called *Gbenemene*. Examples were *Gbenesaakoo*, king of Gokana, *Gbenekuapie,* king of Tee; *Gbeneyaalo,* king of Nama; *Gbenekiri,* king of Boue; *Gbeneakpana,* king of Kónò; (including Bean areas); *Gbenetiginagua,* king of Luekun (including Baan, Taabaan and Kpong areas); and *Gbenesaagba,* king of Ko (including Bangha areas).

3.3 Importance of the Gbene to the Traditional Society

To the traditional society, the *Gbene* title was the epitome of achievement, which only very few could attain. In pre-colonial times, communities which could boast of a *Gbene* were considered great. There was need for such men then, because that was the age of frequent wars. Many communities had to fight constant wars in order to survive. There was always the fear of surprise attacks or raids by aggressive neighbours. Quite often, such raids took place during the funerals of their heroes or during the celebrations or worship of their national gods (cf Jones. 1963: 115).

According to the elders, the way to the *Gbene* title was rough and dangerously hazardous. Consequently, the men to fill such positions of great leadership were rare, unlike in modern times, when men struggle for such chiefly positions in air-conditioned courtrooms and from rug carpeted palaces. In pre-colonial times, such leadership was jointly cultivated. For example, during the performances of the *Yaage* tradition, the elders took notice of youths with exceptional abilities. Such youths were gradually drawn closer to the elders by special recognition and favours. In times of emergency, they were sent on important secret missions into the enemy territories. In times of war, they led their community against the enemy.

Through years of association with the elders and engagement in war-like activities, such men acquired the knowledge of different kinds of war medicines, some of which had been put on them by the elders; and others they had acquired by their own initiatives. Eventually, they became war mongers so that even when their own communities were not engaged in any war, they had the urge to go to wherever there was war to hire themselves out as mercenaries in order to satisfy their desire to own human trophies. Moreover, engagement in such 'foreign' wars provided the opportunity for them to test their own war medicines.

This was necessary because the success of a great warrior, which a candidate for the *Gbene* title was, depended on his possession of large resources, which would enable him to practice or to make 'experiments' with different kinds of ritual elements or combination of elements to produce effective war medicines. In the view of the elders, frequent sacrifices and experiments with new ritual elements led to the discovery of new supernatural powers. For this reason, as soon as a recognised warrior made a bid for the *Gbene* title, he became not only the focus of attention, but also the target of all other warriors, both living and dead! Because of this, the warrior's success at Nama was seen as a national achievement and an honour to the community which produced him and a pride to the entire ethnic nationality. That was why such warriors became cultural heroes, who were venerated by whole communities and held up in social lore as examples for emulation by succeeding generations. Gbeneakpana of Kónò, Gbenesaakoo of Gokana, and Gbenekiri of Boue are good examples; the latter is still being worshipped annually throughout Ogoni under the pseudonym of *Yomii* (god of wine) (Chief Tonwe, III, 70, tape 25, 21.1.84; Chief Menewa 47, tape, 4,21 10:81; Chief Iwerebe 36, tape 18, 22. 1. 84).

After his death, the *Gbene* reappeared in the society as a possessing ancestral spirit *(Zim)* by possessing one of his sons or descendants. This possession power, which continued from generation to generation, was the ultimate goal of the candidate for achieving the *Gbene* title. As possessing ancestral spirits, they became the guardians of the society. Their spirit-media were consulted on important national matters (cf. Ian. 1985; 47; Gulfand, 1973; 134). In times of emergency, they made potent medicines against the enemy and provided advance warning about the approach of the enemies by suddenly possessing their media, who under such influence alerted the people by yelling round the communities calling upon men to take up arms against the enemy and giving information about the enemy's position and direction of approach. Because of the nature of their activities, especially in this regard, the institution of the *Gbene* title and the existence of the *Gbene* in a community was regarded as a source of strength.

3.4 (a) Prerequisites for the Gbene Title

Certain pre-requisites were vital before a person could aspire the *Gbene* title. An aspirant to the *Gbene* title was a person who must have performed all the important traditional rites, including *Yaage, Yaanwii, Yaabe,* etc. He was one who could pay the prescribed traditional dues and customs to the ancestors (Gbigbo, 23, tape 21,27.12.83). Such a man must be a *Kabaari* (Chief). Above all, he must be an outstanding warrior, who had spent most of his life in hunting and war-like activities. The expression *"doo kiri doo be"* (done all sorts of deeds") must fit his character. In other words, he must be known to be the type of person with a strong will to do both good and evil without any qualms or scruples.

The implication is that the candidate for the *Gbene* title was expected to be the sort of person who could willfully break statutory norms and taboos, the sort of person who had the will power to set aside all restrictions of morality, and able to do some of the things forbidden in the society's moral codes, like Friedrich Niezsche's "superman" (Tr. Zimmorn, 1886). Because such men were rare, only very few could attempt the title in several generations.

As Chief Nwikogbara noted, in early times, the requirements for the title were probably not as stringent or brutal as the rivalry was, because a candidate for the *Gbene* title was of necessity required to possess powerful medicines and charms for specific purposes. This led to experiments with different kinds of ritual elements and sacrificial objects, as well as performing all kinds of actions. In such circumstances, what might have originally involved the sacrifice of simple animals at Nama, later developed into an elaborate and extravagant ritual system, involving not only the sacrifice of animals, but also of human victims.

3.4 (b) Preparation for the Pilgrimage

The following testimony by an informant gives us a potent illustration of how an aspirant to the *Gbene* title went about pursuing his objectives: an objective whose ultimate goal was to become a possessing ancestral spirit.

> Gbenebaara was a human being who had father and mother like all men have. But he initialed himself into many supernatural affairs. Finally, he went to Nama, where he did all the things and got the Gbene title. When he died, the first person he possessed was Gwerre, his son (Ipaan 34, tape 20, 9.1.84).

As elucidated in the above passage, before a candidate for the *Gbene* title went on pilgrimage to Nama, he must first of all get himself well prepared spiritually from home. This involved the preparation of many medicines and charms for different purposes, and the performance of numerous sacrifices and rituals. All the informants affirm that at that level in the quest for supernatural power, the sacrificial elements or ritual goods which the aspirant used were not prescribe for him by any one. He himself must experiment with different ritual elements or combination of elements as he was motivated and influenced by his own supernatural forebodings toward particular goals. Examples of such ritual goods were chameleons, bats, vultures, eagles, tortoises, ants, wasps, bees, lizards, scorpions, cows, sheep, goats, sharks, mullets, hens, cocks, frogs, toads, vegetable goods, etc. Some of the elements consisted of males and females. In later periods, human victims were added to the list. The title aspirant performed most of the sacrifices at his personal shrines at his home and at other appropriate places over a period of years before the actual pilgrimage to Nama.

Having performed all the necessary rituals and sacrifices, and having equipped him supernaturally as a top medicine man and warrior with the ability to conjure supernatural phenomena against a target, etc, the title aspirant then made the ultimate journey to Nama. First, he had to give a formal notice to the priest of Nama about his intending pilgrimage. This formal notice was called *"kpaana bu Nama"* (opening the door at Nama). According to Chief Kpugita, this involved carrying wine to the priest of Nama and saying that they should "open the door" at Nama for him, because he wanted to perform the traditions.

After the necessary rituals, they 'knocked' at the door and opened for him. Then they took the wine which he brought and poured libation to the Nama spirits saying, "this man is coming to perform the traditions" (Kpugita 42, tape 10, 2.1.84). After that, he returned home to prepare for the full pilgrimage, which must take place on a date fixed by him and confirmed by the priest and the Mene (chief of) Nama. The *Mene Nama* then circulated the information to all men who had successfully made the pilgrimage to Nama, both living and dead. These then got ready to test the ability of the intending pilgrim by supernatural means.

3.5(a) The Journey to Nama (Si Nama)

Among the sacrificial victims which the pilgrim must bring along were two human victims – a male and a female, one of whom must be his beloved son or daughter both already hypnotised. Other sacrificial requirements were cows, sheep, goats, fowls, tortoise, yams, plantains, palm wine, gin, fish (shark), etc.

The warrior/pilgrim was dressed in a new red cloth *(Kabe)* on his loins, knotted and smartly tucked on his waist, a red cap *(miimii tũn)* on his head, held firmly by a circular crown to which were fixed on the left side at an angle, four or seven white eagle feathers and one vertically on the right side, and charms on his waist and arms. On his waist also he wore a sword with decorated hilt packed in a sheath and held by a leather belt. In his right hand, he held a bundle of charms and medicines and in his left a bottle of gin for libation. His entourage included friends, supporters, and attendants, bearing ritual goods and money.

3.5(b) Supernatural Challenges and Encounters

As the pilgrim drew near to Nama, he began to experience supernatural encounters launched against him by those who had been waiting to challenge him. Some of the medicines they 'threw' at him by remote control were those called *Bun koo* (rib-bow), because they twisted the ribs of the human target and paralysed his waist and legs. The aim was to knock him down, and thus be declared incapable or unable to take the title. But if he was spiritually strong and masterly in the supernatural arts, he resisted by warding off or neutralising the attacks by his supernatural means or medicines. Meanwhile, his companions could be hearing loud incantations and pronouncements issuing from his mouth as the supernatural attacks and encounters intensified, just as it would happened in actual battle situation.

All these attacks were aimed at terminating his journey to Nama by the intrusion of natural and supernatural forces. The supernatural forces included the simulation of hazardous weather, hords of dangerous reptiles and insects, alteration of the terrain with fearful obstacles, etc. According to Chief Nwikogbara, the supernatural confrontations were aimed at preventing the warrior pilgrim from reaching his goals. Such an occurrence was interpreted to mean that his hand had failed to 'reach' the title.

There are four stages of the supernatural confrontations, each leading to the point of particular ritual sacrifices. Chief Iwagbo, who at the time of interview, was himself the priest of Nama, explains that the ritual stations were located some distance from each other on the route to Nama in ascending order of importance. The first was called *Akom Kuru*. At this station, the chief ritual element for sacrifice was the tortoise. Here, a tortoise was hung on a stake to the spirits and gods of the *Gbene* title in that place.

From this station, the warrior pilgrim pressed on through the many supernatural hazards towards the second ritual station called *Akom pee*. At this station, the pilgrim hanged a live goat to the spirits. Meanwhile, the supernatural confrontations intensified. The title candidate summoned his utmost courage while at the same time reciting the appropriate incantations and recalling and recounting the brave deeds which he had done, which qualified him to embark on the journey to Nama. This in traditional parlance or idiom was called *"kaaga gian le kue-amue"* (lit. "brave utterances and self-citation").

By the time the pilgrim had advanced towards the third ritual station called *Akom Nam*, the supernatural attacks reached their climax, such that only the very stout hearted and spiritually invulnerable could survive. On arrival at this station, which is at Kugba, the title bidder made a higher sacrifice by hanging a live bull which has been already hypnotised.

After a successful arrival and performance of rituals and sacrifices at this station, the chief pilgrim and title bidder was then led solemnly by the *Mene Nama* and the priest to the fourth and final station called *Akom nee*, located in a forest at Nama. There, he performed his highest ritual and sacrifices, which included the hanging of the male partner of the two human victims, and the planting of a live tree call *Zue* in commemoration of his successful pilgrimage to Nama.

Having done that, the title pilgrim, led by the *Mene Nama* and the priest, returned with their attendants to Kugba, where the female of the two human victims together with the females of the animals were slaughtered on his medicine and their flesh, including that of the female human victim, used in preparing a feast for the guests who had gathered there for the occasion. The ceremonies came to a climax with the conferment of the *Gbene* title on the pilgrim by the *Mene Nama*.

According to Chief Kpugita, at the end of the ceremony, the recipient of the title was asked to perform the valedictory ceremony of "closing" the door at Nama *(Kpae bun Nama)*. With the performance of that action or ritual, the 'door' was deemed 'closed' and remained closed until the day someone else came to say that it should be 'opened' for him (Kpugita 42 tape 10,2.1.84).

While the chief pilgrim and recipient of title remained behind to perform this last ritual, all the guests departed. Consequently, the new title holder had to depart Nama last. Thus, if his journey to Nama had been difficult, his return alive from Nama with the title was now even more difficult. All the supernatural warriors who had set themselves to test the supernatural strength of the new title holder were now more determined to prevent his return with the title. Actual battle situations were now simulated against him, including attempts to ambush and kill him but with his own fresh medicines aflame with the blood of ritual and fortified with the power of new discoveries in supernatural 'journey'; he detected, countered and evaded them.

On arrival at his home town, he proclaimed his victorious return from Nama by a processional parade round the town. Meanwhile, special emissaries sent out from the *Mene Nama*, went from town to town and from village to village throughout Ogoni, proclaiming that such and such has become *Gbene*. Chief Iyoro explains that the proclamation was accompanied by the blowing of two solemn instruments–the *Pumbu* and the *Gbon*. The latter was a round, low-keyed, wind instrument, sounded only on occasions of momentous contemplations. The *Pumbu* (Trumpet) was a horn instrument with a high velocity and robust sound, blown in times of war or on a great national occasion. Both instruments were blown on this occasion to proclaim the attainment of the *Gbene* title. This was done at night in the period known as *Bee Loole* (Top of the morning), i.e. from about 4:00 am.

Chief Kpugita explains that once a man had achieved the *Gbene* title, he automatically became lord over the land on which he settled, and ruler of the section of the town where he lived. He could also establish a new town for himself. His children and descendants ceased to answer the name of their former ancestor. He became the founder of a new lineage and was venerated by all citizens as an ancestral spirit *(zim)*.

3.6 The Rite of Kpa Bina

A year or two after one had received the *Gbene* title and had successfully retuned from Nama, one was required to perform a final ritual at Gure. This was called *Kue-suu*. The *Gbene's* entourage on this occasion consisted of his priests, spirit-media, and medicine men. These dignitaries accompanied him to Gure on an appointed date.

At Gure, they took him to a sacred forest called *kue-suu*, and gave him a piece of land to cultivate. Seven yam seedlings were given to him. He cleared the land and planted the yams. They grew supernaturally and also matured the same day. He harvested the yams, cooked and ate them on the same day. Once he had eaten that meal, it became ominous that his time of transition was near. The authority of his *Gbene* title was ratified and confirmed.

Chief Nwikogbara explains that a *Gbene* who died without reaching this stage was said to have partially failed. But he still became an ancestral spirit after transition and was able to possess his descendants. Nonetheless, he possessed female descendants instead of males (Nwikogbara 57, tape 9, 8.3.84). According to Chief Iyoro, a *Gbene* title holder who reached this stage prepared his shrine in advance before the ceremony at Gure, and after the performance at Gure, another solemn proclamation was made throughout Ogoni land from town to town that such and such has passed into his shrine *(e yira loo)*, that is to say, he has become an ancestral spirit (Iyoro 37, tape 12, 5.2.84).

At his home, the *Gbene* entertained his ancestors and the spirits of all past great men of the area by the highest traditional rite in Ogoni known as *Kpa Bina*. This was a very expensive rite which required the slaughter of many cows, goats, fowls, etc. with an overflow of wine and drinks for numerous guests from all over Ogoni. The *Bina* was a sacred band consisting of eleven drums of graded sizes, and accessories. It was not accompanied with vocals; it was music of spirits which entertained the soul and the mind and relaxed emotions.

After this great ceremony, it did not take much longer before the *Gbene* passed into transition. Evidence shows that some had passed away within a few months or weeks after this ceremony. A'ean Gbigbo explains that when such men were translated, their remains were buried inside their houses, under the shrine which they had prepared beforehand (Gbigbo 23, tape 21, 27.12.93). Soon after their translation, they began to possess their sons and descendants. Tobina Ipaan informs us that his own ancestor named Gbenebaara began to possess his son named Gwerre before he actually passed into translation (Ipaan 34, tape 20,9.1.84). This, however was not peculiar to his own ancestor. Many informants confirmed that it often happened like that, where the individual concerned was exceptionally brave and powerful in the supernatural arts.

3.7 Conclusion

We have shown in the *Gbene* title of Ogoni, one of the greatest arts of an ancient indigenous African society, whose history may be traced back to B.C. times. We have also shown that the *Gbene* title was the ultimate achievement of a renowned warrior in the society. The fact that this tradition has survived into the present is a strong testimony of its importance to the society. That importance may probably elude the perception of the modern observer, owing to the fact that the conditions and the environment have changed so greatly. Under the changed conditions, the *Gbene* title institution began to decline. Thus, it was seen that by the turn of the nineteenth century, when British colonial rule was imposed, the *Gbene* title institution had already lost its values.

According to the informant, A'ean Gbigbo, the last attempt at the title took place in the nineteenth century by a man named Gbosi, who did not succeed in getting the title. Another tradition mentions Gbeneteenwaawo of Luawii, who made his pilgrimage about the late eighteenth century.

It seems that one of the causes of the decline of the *Gbene* cultural title was a change in moral values. There appears to have been a general recognition of the absolute value of human lives. This was first manifested by a shift in the choice of ritual victims, which saw an increasing use of the cow as a substitute for human beings. According to Chief Kiriki, the cow was seen to be similar to human because it carries its foetus for nine months, just like human (Kiriki *et al* 74, 17. 2. 90).

Another factor which contributed to the decline of the *Gbene* title was a change in the marriage system and in family relations. Before the seventeenth century, the marriage system in Ogoni was matrilineal endogamous. Under that system, a man was not responsible to this wife or family. Men had no children of their own to cater for, since the children they begot belonged to the families of the women. Men were therefore completely free and detached from the obligations of a nuclear family. Accordingly, they spent their time and energies in hunting and warfare and in acquiring charms and titles.

About the seventeenth century, however, as a result of the Baan wars, the marriage system in Ogoni began to change from matrilineal endogamous to patrilineal exogamous. Under this system, men became responsible to their own wives and children and had the obligation of a family whose membership comprised their own heirs and successors. The bond of family became stronger than traditions. The urge to engage in traditions whose rituals demanded the sacrifice of one's own blood relations and heirs gradually weakened.

Thus in about the late eighteenth century when Gbeneteenwaawo made what was traditionally regarded as the last attempt at the *Gbene* title, he did not sacrifice his own heir in the ritual at Nama. Instead, he sacrificed the child of another woman (probably an endogamous wife). When the matter was discovered, a public outcry was raised against Gbeneteenwaawo, who was immediately seized by the people and publicly tried and condemned to death for murder.

According to the account, when the executioners were about to carry out the execution of Gbeneteenwaawo at a town square in Luawii, two of his associates, Gbeneguasoo and Gbeneakata intervened supernaturally by conjuring into the arena some 'demons' which appeared in the form of a pack of wild pigs. These attracted the attention of the executioners. In the confusion that ensued, Gbeneteewaawo slipped from the townsquare and disappeared. He later made his appearance at Sii, where he was received by Gbeneteetagana, who gave him a part of Nyowii Sii to rule (Nwikogbara 57, tape 9, 8. 4.84. 17.81; Bekanwaa 77, tape 34/B, 7,4,90). Although Gbeneteenwaawo escaped death by the use of supernatural agents, the incident of his trial and condemnation reflected a standard of morality among the people at that time, which condemned ritual murder.

Perhaps the most significant factor which contributed to the decline of the *Gbene* title in Ogoni was the introduction of the gun as a weapon of war in the seventeenth century. Prior to that date, the sword was the most important weapon of war. The great importance attached to the sword in the *Yaage* tradition emphasised that fact. With the sword, however, a man needed to be extra brave and highly efficient to be successful in war, especially in hand-to-hand combat. Men, therefore, had to seek the aid of supernatural agents to supplement the sword and man's abilities.

With the gun, however, a man needed no supernatural aid to fight well in battle. People saw the gun as a tremendous step forward in their search for war power. The gun became a source of power in itself. Instead of struggling to acquire supernatural powers, men therefore, sought only to possesses the gun. Thus with the introduction of the gun as a weapon of war, the need to go to Nama for the *Gbene* title was no longer necessary.

In the nineteenth and twentieth centuries, the impact of the Christian missions, the colonial rule, and the colonial economy, was very effective as factors of change, which combined to force the final collapse of the *Yaage* traditions and the *Gbene* title institution in Ogoni land. Christian teachings forbade traditions that required sacrifices to spirits and supernatural forces. They condemned ritual murder and ancestral worship. They preached against the practice and use of magical powers and initiation into secret societies.

Instead, the Christian missions provided substitutes by opening literacy schools and by introducing Western education. As a result, a new class of elites, based on western education began to emerge (Ade Ajayi, 1965:172f). The old social structure based on the *Yaa* traditions gradually disintegrated. By the 1950s, the *Yaa* traditions as a means of social differentiation had virtually ceased to exist. More and more parents recognised the benefit of sending their sons and daughters to school, rather than initiating them into traditional institutions.

The development of urban centres of the colonial administration, the introduction of wage labour, the poll tax, and an export economy, further undermined the traditional society. Many young men began to move away from the traditional societies to work in the urban cities, in order to earn the money needed not only to pay their taxes, but also to buy some imported goods pay bride wealth, and acquire membership of elite social clubs.

In the 1970s, however, following the experiences of the Nigerian civil war (1967-70), there was a frenzied effort to revive the *Yaa* and the *Gbene* title traditions. For example, in 1976, the installation of Chief Birinee of Kónò was moved from Kónò to the old site of the ancient town of Kugba, the site of the award of the *Gbene* title. In 1979, Chief Appolus of Sii was installed the *Gbenemene* Nama. During the same period, His Majesty, King G.N.K. Gininwa of Tee performed the *Yaanwii* and *Yaabe* traditions. And between 1982 and 1988, Chief Dike Iyoro of Boue performed the *Yaanwii* and *Yaabe* traditions and made a token pilgrimage to Nama.

Nonetheless, these efforts towards a revival of the old traditions, were largely futile. The tide of change in the direction of modernity could not be abated. The youths have gone to school and to the urban centres. This has brought utter frustration to the elders who see the youths of today as a disappointment. They are too soft and greatly estranged from the tenets of the traditional society.

Perhaps the elders may not be altogether wrong. There exists a veritable vacuum between the traditional society and the modern youth. This vacuum needs to be filled. This can be done by a deliberate policy involving the adoption of the useful elements of traditional culture into the modern school system. Such useful elements should include traditional music, oral literature, certain traditional dances and sports, and traditional art and occupations. Such a blend of cultures would in the short or long run yield a fuller and richer reward by creating a strong, culture-based society, with a civilisation that is firmly balanced on its roots, able to reach out to the future with penetrating vision and self-reliance.

CHAPTER FOUR

CULTURE III: THE YAA TRADITION AND SOCIAL CLASSIFICATION

4.1 Introduction

There are three different titles in the *Yaa* tradition. The first and second titles, *Pya Gbara* and *Kabaari*, are dealt with in this chapter. The third and highest title in Ogoni, known as Gbene has been treated elsewhere (Kpone-Tonwe, 2000). These three titles constitute the soul of the Ogoni personality. They contain a history and philosophy that goes back to the very origins of Ogoni society.

The first stage in the *Yaa* tradition was called *Yaage*. *Yaa* meaning a rite and *ge* – a sword or machete. Thus *Yaage* literally means the rite of bearing arms. As will be shown in this chapter, the *yaa* tradition provided a means for steady recruitment and training of Ogoni youth for the defence and preservation of their society. A youth who did not undergo *yaa* training would suffer social isolation and be treated as an economic and political underdog in adult life.

The *yaa* tradition has steadily declined from late nineteenth century on, and is virtually nonexistent at present. Few people are alive today who have performed the tradition. In the 1950s when this writer took part, the tradition was still being performed frequently. The interval between two performances then was not more than three to four years, depending on the level of prosperity among the leading men of the society.

The next time it was performed was about the mid 1960s. The last two performances was in the late 1970s and again in 1983. The last two performers, Chief Dike Iyoro, who performed the *Yaanwii* tradition in 1983, was interviewed in February 1984, and Chief Gbenegbara Gookinanwaa, who took the *Gbene* title in the 1970s, was interviewed in March 1984. Both have since passed into the realm of spirits. It is ominous that no performance has taken place since 1983, and there is little likelihood that a performance will take place in the foreseeable future.

Many factors have contributed to the decline of this great tradition. Beginning in the early 1900s, Christian missionaries forbade a number of traditional practices. These had a negative impact on the principles and practices of the *yaa* tradition. Given the relatively small percentage of Christian converts among the Ogoni, the impact of Christian teachings should have been minimal, but there were other factors as well. Ogoni is very near Port Harcourt, a port city and an oil centre; and from the 1970s on, Onne, a south-western Ogoni town, has also become an ocean terminal and industrial base. The population of these places has become cosmopolitan and their modern influences have adversely affected the *yaa* tradition.

The greatest of these modern influences was western education, which changed the norms of social stratification in Ogoni, as a certificate in western education became the means of social recognition and a passport to a better life. The school teacher replaced the house-father of the *yaa* tradition and the village school replaced the palm wine camp. Youths were gradually estranged from the local traditions and drawn to the wider world of the city. More parents were persuaded to send their children to school rather than spend their resources on the *yaa* traditions.

Other factors that contributed to the decline of the *yaa* tradition included changes in lifestyle, in social values, and in the economy. Since the early 1900s, the Ogoni lifestyle has changed significantly. People now value such luxury goods as chieftaincy gowns, shoes, hats, and walking sticks more than permanent wealth. The changes in values have also affected the fabric of the economy. People now prefer wage labour to owning and working on a farm. As a result, the level of agricultural production has fallen, aggravated by the effects of oil exploitation.

Perhaps the most insidious of all these influences has been the advent of military rule. During the last thirty years, people from all sorts of background have used their personal connections to advance in the society without regard to legitimacy or achievement. Thus, all sorts of people have acquired the title of chief without appropriate qualifications. This has bastardised the traditional titles and values. Because of this, people are no longer prepared to go through the rigours and the hardship that tradition required before one could earn the title of *Kabaari* (Chief). Taking all these factors together, we find that the forces of change against the *yaa* tradition have been overwhelming. It is against this backdrop that this writer decided to collect the information about the *yaa* tradition in an attempt to rescue it from obscurity.

Thus in September 1991, I proposed to Ken Saro-Wiwa that we make a major literary documentation of the *yaa* tradition, based on my research. He was very optimistic about the proposal after reading my papers. At that time he had just completed work on Ogoni folktales and was considering the possibility of documenting Ogoni proverbs. He saw that a combination of my work with his work on folktales and proverbs would give us a full picture of Ogoni culture and worldview, and would therefore form the basis of a literary documentation. So he wrote to say, among other things,

> Your work, the folktales, the proverbs, together will prepare the way for a possible novel... Let us pray for life and the gift of the gods.[1]
>
> ***Personal communication from Ken Saro-Wiwa***
> ***18 september 1991***

While the plan was being developed, the crisis struck that ultimately led to his murder, Saro-Wiwa's tragic and untimely death was therefore a serious setback to the project. Our idea was to produce a historical novel in which the characters described in my work would be made to speak and act out the episodes and events described. We wanted to invite other writers, artists and intellectuals to come forward to take up this challenge. We believed that the *yaa* tradition provides suitable material for such literary or artistic adaptation. It is interesting, educational, creative, dramatic, historical, original, youth-oriented and colourful. Such a useful piece of culture should not be allowed to disappear. Instead efforts should be made to incorporate it into our educational system as part of the creative art of humanity.

The *yaa* tradition provides useful material for character formation in our youths by its discipline and by discouraging such anti-social behaviours as theft, drug abuse, sorcery, idleness, truancy, and disrespect for elders. Instead, it inculcates a positive attitude to life by inducing a desire for hard work, excellence, creativity, and respect for human dignity.

4.2 Economic Activities

Ogoniland is a fertile plateau rising to about 100 feet above sea level. From very early beginnings, agriculture had been the Ogoni's chief occupation, with yam as the principal crop. Other occupations such as palm wine tapping, palm fruit cutting, long distance trade and fishing were special occupations for which selected individuals were trained. Fortunately, Ogoniland was a fertile territory endowed with abundant water supply. Forest resources such as oil palms and raffia palms were well tapped. The Ogoni established a canoe industry at Ko on the Imo River and became the distributors of both the small fishing canoes and the large transport canoes throughout the eastern Niger Delta (Kpone-Tonwe, 1998). They supplied their Ijo neighbour who depended on canoes but did not make them.

They also established a large pot industry at the town of Kònò Boue, which supplied water pitchers and pots of various descriptions to their Ijo, Igbo and Ibibio neighbours. The distribution of pots became an important aspect of long distance trade using large canoes and providing jobs for a sizeable crop of men. In addition to yam cultivation and yam export, all these produced a class of wealthy men who began to use their money to acquire titles, marry foreign wives, and promote cultural activities such as the *yaanwii* tradition. Thus economic well being was instrumental in promoting and sustaining the *yaa* tradition. This was very evident in that those who were poor could not perform it, and because they could not perform, they lacked status in society and become second class citizens. By the sixteenth and seventeenth centuries, yam cultivation had become a competitive occupation attracting classified chiefly titles for the best and most successful farmers (Kpone-Tonwe, 1997). This period also marked the rising tide of the trans-Atlantic slave trade, and large quantities of yams were exported for use in feeding the slaves.

The class of titled yam-chiefs controlled agriculture and yam production. They produced yams both for home consumption and for export. They established a yam club and a yam house *(to zia)* or a shrine manned by a yam priest in every village. They gathered at the yam house every year to perform rituals and sacrifices before the start of every farming season. The titled chiefs gradually became the owners of the largest farms in some of the best farming areas. People who owned land but were in financial need would pledge their lands to those wealthy men for a loan of money. As a result of this process, coupled with the high density of the population, agricultural land became a scarce commodity in Ogoni (Kpone-Tonwe, *ibïd*).

Moreover, as evidence of wealth and social status, and as part of the requirement for the award of titles, those chiefs were required to marry a number of foreign wives in addition to their local ones. This necessitated the appointment of agents from the class of long-distance traders, who secured such wives from the Igbo, and Ibibio hinterlands via the Imo or Cross River water ways (Daryll Forde, 1964).

Because they were hard working and had accumulated wealth, those men earned chiefly titles, married many wives, and established their own compounds. It was this class of men also who were able to put their sons forward to perform the *yaage* tradition. It will be seen also that it was from this class of men that those who performed the yaanwii (the rite of sons) tradition emerged. Viewed from another angle, it will be seen also that the *yaage* tradition was promoted by this social group because it ensured the perpetuation of their own class. The youths who performed the *yaage* tradition also constituted the elite class in Ogoni society.

4.3(a) The Family System

There has been no anthropological study of Ogoni kinship system and culture. Consequently, no systematic classification of the Ogoni family system and mode of inheritance has been documented. Unfortunately, the present writer is not an anthropologist and the use of terms in this section is likely to be inadequate. Nonetheless, our main concern is to explain the historical changes in the Ogoni family system from the sixteenth century until the present that has affected the *yaa* tradition.

Evidence from oral traditions and by extrapolation from the beginning of the twentieth century indicates that the family system in Ogoni has undergone some radical changes. Before the seventeenth century, marriage in Ogoni was based on matrilineal endogamous system. As I have explained elsewhere (Kpone-Tonwe, 1990), the first ruler of Ogoni was a woman named Kwaanwaa. After the death of Kwaanwaa at Gure, the succession did not pass to her son but to her first daughter, Za; after the death of Za, succession also passed to the latter's first daughter, Bariyaayoo, who ruled at Luawii. After Bariyaayoo, the succession went to another daughter, a great granddaughter of Za named Gbeneyana, who ruled at Ka-Gwara. The last of these royal ancestresses was Gbenebeka, who succeeded to the Ka-Gwaara stool in the sixteenth century and whose name is mentioned in the colonial intelligence reports:

> Mr. Jeffery refers in detail to a belief in a common ancestress of divine origin, Gbenebeka, but I am unable to confirm the fact that this belief is universal among all the clans of the tribe. At the same time, there can be little doubt that the name Gbenebeka is one of very significance, and her shrine at Gwaara possess even today a very real importance as being the most important place of sacrifice throughout the country (Gibbons, 1932).

This shows that the early kinship system was matrilineal. By the sixteenth century, however, the marriage system in Ogoni had changed from matrilineal endogamous to patrilineal exogamous. Several factors contributed to this early change. The most important was the practice of wealthy men marrying "foreign wives" as required when they took war titles or yam titles. Another factor was the insecurity suffered by women during periods of crisis. For example, in the sixteenth century, during the civil war known as the "Baan wars", non-citizen wives who lived closer to their husbands were better protected.

Moreover, the wealthy men desired to have their own heirs who would inherit their estate, a desire partly satisfied by the children of their foreign wives. Consequently, some of the citizen wives and their children also demanded rights in their husbands' and fathers' estate. In the early twentieth century, Daryll Forde noticed the beginning of a similar development among the Yako (Daryll Forde *ibid*). These factors stimulated the early change from matrilineal to patrilineal virilocal system of marriage in Ogoni. The reason this change took place among the Ogoni before the other parts of the Delta is that important economic changes occurred first among the Ogoni (see Kpone-Tonwe, 1998).

4.3(b) Mode of Inheritance

Before the sixteenth century (i.e. during the period of matrilineal succession), inheritance also went to the firstborn daughter *(sira)*. A lesser part was distributed among the other daughters. The daughters inherited things like cloth, household property, domestic animals, equipment, farms, plantain groves, money, offices, and coconut and other fruit trees. Mothers' brothers took charge of raffia palm and oil palm bushes. The sons inherited nothing directly from their blood mothers and nothing from their blood fathers. When they were grown up and had been trained by their maternal uncles (mother's brothers), and perhaps had become fathers themselves, they began to inherit the raffia palm and oil palm bushes that were under the control of their mother's brothers, as the latter grew older.

After the sixteenth century when Ogoni changed to patrilineal virilocal system, the mode of inheritance also changed radically. By that time, wealthy titled men had established their own autonomous compounds, where their wives and children lived with them. At the death of such a man, his firstborn son succeeded him as head of the compound and inherited the bulk of his father's wealth. Part of this wealth was distributed to the firstborn sons of other wives, however, the daughters inherited their mothers' property, the bulk of which went to the firstborn daughters. As noted above, the firstborn daughters were not married out. The other daughters were married out, and they moved to their husbands' compounds or homes.

4.3(c) Definitions

I have tried to present a bird's eye view of the environment and background of the *yaa* tradition. Before we proceed to the *yaa* tradition itself, however, a few terms should be defined to avoid ambiguity. In this chapter, the word patrilineage *(gan)* refers to the father's line of descent, the lineage of the legitimate father. To that extent, it excludes all illegitimate fathers, such as a father by adultery, by concubinage, or by the old matrilineal connection. All such fathers are called *tɛgbọọ*, meaning "father-outside-the-gate". They are not legal fathers because they did not marry the mothers and did not pay the recognised bride wealth. Patrilineage in our context has a genealogical tree known as *gan* and a historical origin that dates back to the fifteenth or sixteenth century when wealthy, titled men began to establish autonomous families and compounds by marrying foreign wives. The autonomous compounds were ruled by a line of accredited successors of firstborn sons called *saro*.

Similarly, the term matrilineage *(bua)* is used here to refer to the mother's line. It does not imply a notion of double descent, as practiced among the *Yako*, nor does it suggest membership of a localised lineage organisation or citizenship of a chiefdom in which a mother's lineage is legally domiciled, as among the Ashanti of Southern Ghana (Meyer Fortes, 1950:252-84). In our context, the term matrilineage has a more religious or ritual undertone than political or economic. Its root is based on the Ogoni worldview and on a belief that blood or essence passed from mother to children and with the divine order of governance (Audrey Richards 1950). They believed that the Supreme Creator is feminine; and that although the world of nature was created, man was not created but born out of God's womb. God is therefore seen as the Great Mother *(KawaBari)* of mankind, from whom all authority and governance emanated.

This divine essence and authority had been passed on to the woman and is manifested in childbearing. All mothers in turn passed this divine essence and authority to their daughters, particularly the firstborn daughters. Thus, succession and inheritance passed to the firstborn daughters during the matrilineal era.

To maintain the continuity of this divine essence and authority after the transition to a patrilineal system, the firstborn daughters were not married out. They remained in their father's compounds, where they held the office of priestesses. Owing to the strong belief in the divine endowment of matrilineal priestesses and the spiritual power they were believed to impart, pilgrimages were made to them during the performance of the *yaa* tradition. Apart from these religious functions, no inheritance or other obligations were involved.

4.4 Youth Training and Ogoni Society

There is abundant evidence that the Ogoni adopted youth training as a fundamental aspect of social organisation earlier on. Oral traditions suggest that children born into the society were observed from childhood until they became responsible leaders. The early Ogoni social system had a system of organisation and training that enabled youths of ability to gain necessary political and economic experience from the grassroots till they grew up to occupy positions of leadership.

Ogoni society was structured into social classes and categories. Overshadowing the society was the class known as *Pya Bɛɛ Bue* (the rulers) which comprised the *Gbenemene* (king or paramount ruler), *Pya Kanee* (the elders) *Pya Kabari* (the chiefs), and *Pya Zuguru* (the lieutenants). Below the class of Pya Bɛɛ Bue was the general class known as *Pya Kebuɛ* (the commoners). Within this class of *Pya Kɛbue* were the following categories.

- *Pya gbara*   elites or gentlemen
- *Pya kune nee*   commoners or ordinary free men
- *Pya kporowa*   unmarried poor
- *Zooro/gbon*   slaves
- *Pya saa nee*   strangers

The social category called *pya gbara*, the elites or "gentlemen" were the closest to the rulers *(pya Bɛɛ Bue)*. In fact, it was from the rank of *pya gbara* that candidates for the class of *pya bɛɛ bue* were recruited. The question then arises, who were the *pya gbara* in Ogoni society? How did they attain this social distinction? It was through the *yaa* tradition that young men who constituted the elite were organised and produced.

The title *pya gbara* was the first social title in Ogoni applied to every young man who had performed or undergone the traditional training and discipline called *yaagɛ*. The term means the rite of bearing arms, the suffix *gɛ* means sword or machete. Accordingly, a man or a youth who had performed the *Yaagɛ* tradition was by custom allowed to wear an insignia publicly at any time. This was a short decorated two-edged sword called *kobɛgɛ*, packed in a sheath and worn around the waist on a leather belt. The *kobɛgɛ* served a dual purpose, both as a weapon and as the insignia of social status. All young men from adolescence to full adult were expected to undergo the *yaagɛ* training before they could be recognised in society. In later times, younger boys have been initiated because parents were anxious to have their sons perform the tradition while they were still alive. This assured them that their sons would not lapse into the lower social class called *kune nee*, men who had not performed the *yaagɛ* tradition.

Men or women who had not undergone the traditional *yaagɛ* training were thought to be physically and spiritually or mentally deficient. They were considered incapable of leadership or making decisions for others. Consequently, they were not listed as fighting men for the community or as soldiers in time of war. A warrior's spiritual soundness was believed to be vital, a spiritually weak person could easily be led astray and "entrapped" by the enemy. Since the *kune nee* lacked the benefits gained from the physical and spiritual discipline and military training provided under the *yaa* tradition, they were considered to lack the essential ingredients that equipped a man to fit well in an active society.

Moreover, the *kune nee* had vital political limitations and could not take part in a political debate or deliberations. According to Chief Nii:

> If an important matter occurred in the community and they wanted people to meet to discuss it, only those who had performed the *yaagɛ* tradition could enter the house where the matter was being discussed. Those who had not performed the *yaagɛ* tradition would sit outside and listen from outside. They could not take part in the discussion.

Prince Teedee tells us that such persons were restricted from entering certain places in the community; when they died, they were not buried in the front but at the back of houses. (S/No.67, Tape No.Og/sk/15-16,18th March 1984). Since eligibility was by no other qualification except the ability to pay the cost and the fact that the candidate must be a free citizen, the *yaagɛ* tradition might be seen therefore as a primary means of social stratification between rich and poor.

The *yaagɛ* tradition was not exclusively performed by youths. The youths performed the tradition under a rich, wealthy, and popular leader. This began when such a leader declared his intention to perform the *yaanwii* tradition in order to earn the title of *kabari* (chief), as the leader or commander of the fighting force (or army) for his town or community.

The term *yaanwii* is a combination of *yaa* ("a rite") and *nwii* (a child), hence, *yaanwii* means the rite of raising sons or warriors. Consequently, the man performing the *yaanwii* tradition must by custom be a person who possessed good leadership qualities and unblemished character. He must also be a good fighter and a charismatic leader. In addition to his wealth, these qualities guaranteed the elders' approval and inspired the confidence of parents to entrust their sons to him for training in the performance of the *yaagɛ* tradition.

Once such a man had received the go ahead from the elders, parents from all parts of the district brought their sons to enroll under him in order to perform the *yaagɛ* tradition. From that moment on, the man began to be known and addressed by all as the *tɛ-yaa (yaa* father), and the youths so enrolled under him became known as *pya dam yaa* (the *yaa* men). Each *yaa* man could then choose two men from the community who had previously performed *yaagɛ* tradition, whom he appointed as his *tɛ-be* (house-fathers). The choice of the house-fathers was usually made by the youths' parents. These men become the day-to-day companions and trainers throughout the period of the traditional performance, which lasts for about two years.

4.5 Pilgrimage to the Ancestral Homes *(si bu zim)*

After the youths' registration, the first series of activities consisted of performances called *si bu zim*, which were formal homage or pilgrimage to the ancestral shrines of the *tɛ-yaa's* ancestors.

The first called *si bu zim te* (pilgrimage to the sacred shrine of the patrilineal ancestors) took place at the patriarchal compound of the *tɛ-yaa*, i.e. at the compound of the founder of the *yaa* father's patrilineage. All the chiefs, elders, and principal men of the district were invited to this occasion. Goats and chickens were slaughtered and food and drinks served throughout the day. Many sacrifices and rituals were performed and libations poured to the ancestors. One of the features of this occasion were the presentation of cash gifts to each of the titled patriarchs or firstborn sons *(saro)* of the patrilineage *(gan)*, as their names were recited beginning with the earliest. According to Chief Kiriki, the cash gifts varied from three to four manilas each. Without this formal way of informing the ancestors about the title taking, tragedy might occur that could terminate the whole project. The aim of the *te-yaa* was to prevent any tragedy such as sickness or death of the candidates.

Therefore, all the *yaa* men *(dam yaa)* were required to be present on such occasions. For this occasion, each *yaa* man was required to pay a prescribed fee in support of the *yaa* father for the cost of the rituals. The traditional fee was four manillas and seven yams each. Where the *dam yaa* was a firstborn son *(saro)*, the payment was thrice the prescribed amount, plus seven yams. A second born son paid twice the amount, plus seven yams. Where all the three sons of one family were performing the tradition, payment by the last born son was waived.

The second homage or pilgrimage called si *bu zim ka* (homage to the matriarchal shrine), was to the *te-yaa's* matrilineage house *(bua)*. In preparation for this occasion, the *te-yaa* sent money in advance to the head of the matrilineage house for them to make ready all food and drinks for the entertainment of the guests. On the appointed date, all the principal men of the district and all the members of the matrilineage gathered at the matriarchal house. As on the first occasion rites, rituals and libations were performed amidst a great reunion of people.

As at the patrilineage, cash gifts were also presented to all the matriarchs or firstborn daughters *(sira)* of the matrilineage as their names were recited. As before, all the *yaa* men were required to take part and pay the prescribed fees, following the pattern described above.

Next, the *te-yaa* visited all the important places in Ogoni to perform the rituals and to pay the traditional fees. Among such places were the houses of the founders of the towns, the war shrines, and the matriarchal house of Gbenebeka at Ka-Gwaara, the last of the original women ancestors and universal rulers of Ogoni people.

Finally, the *te-yaa* went to his ancient matrilineage or the home of his great-great-grandmother *(si bu zim nama-kaama)* to perform the rituals and to pay the required fees. As usual, he sent money in advance in preparation for the occasion. On the appointed date, ceremonies proceeded as at the matrilineage. The climax of the rituals on this occasion was a holy bath or baptism performed on the *te-yaa* by the priestess of the matriarchal house. This baptism was supposed to give him his greatest spiritual insulation against external negative forces and endow him with wisdom and a sense of direction in the spirit world, which according to the elders, was the basis of proper behaviour and actions in the natural world.

While the *te-yaa* was performing the above traditional actions, the *yaa* men also went to their different patrilineage and matrilineage houses to perform similar rituals and to pay the prescribed fees. But their rituals were private and low-keyed. Nonetheless, they served the important purpose of giving formal notice to their relatives about their participation in the on going performance.

4.6   Field Activities

After the ceremonies at the patrilineage and matrilineage compounds, the traditional performance moved full swing into the field stage. This began with a ceremonial banquet called *Ataadee Gɛɛrɛ* at the compound of the *te-yaa*. This was really a huge open air picnic by the *yaa* men. Each *yaa* man or *dam yaa* was accompanied by his house-fathers, who were supposed to bring along a cock, a hen, yams, plantains, palm wine, pots, condiments, and wood. They set up their cooking positions on both sides of the road leading from the compound of the *te-yaa,* forming two rows of cooking extending as far as possible into the near by streets. There was a wide space in-between for people to pass through. The banquet began about 5:00pm and continued into the night.

To secure good positions, participants came earlier in the day to plant a wild cocoyam plant (colocasia anti-quoum) at the position of their choice. Once that was done, no one else occupied that position. It is significant to notice that the banquet name, *Ataadee Gɛɛrɛ* had evolved from the rows of wild cocoyam plants that lined the streets used for the banquet. The name comprised several component words: *ataa* (a row), *dee* (a road or street) and *gɛɛrɛ* (cocoyam).

One of the aims of the banquet was to foster a *sense of brotherhood* and friendship among the *yaa* men. Other young men who had previously performed the tradition came to join in the festivities. Men who had not performed the tradition were forbidden to eat the dinner. According to the elders, if any such person ate the dinner, the person would die within days. In recent years, several youths and men who had not performed the tradition have been reported dead after eating the dinner.

Each *yaa* man gave a share of his dinner to the *te-yaa*. According to Chief Kiriki, each *yaa* man gave one chicken leg, two yams, and the upper segment of the plantain bunch to the *te-yaa* or *yaa* father. The latter in turn shared his collection with the chiefs and the elders of the town the following morning.

After this banquet, all the *yaa* men withdraw from public appearances and from their parents and relatives and retired into a confinement known as *bogoyaa,* during which their mothers were forbidden to see them. This confinement lasted for about three weeks *(taa-εεri)*, during which they underwent a spiritual rebirth and holiness. Consequently, they were not supposed to have any physical contact with women. Men who had slept with women the night before were forbidden to come into their presence. A phenomenon called *pah-yaa* was believed to issue from their bodies and cling to any female who came into physical contact with them. The *pah-yaa* was said to have undesirable and unpleasant consequences for such a woman unless a ritual or sacrifice was performed to remove it.

The *yaa* men remained with their house-fathers and ate only the food they provided. They could associate with each other, however, a virgin boy (i.e. a page called *gian-yaa*) was attached to each *yaa* man and acted as his messenger. When the *yaa* man moved to another location, the *gian-yaa* accompanied him, carrying the carved stool called *tan-yaa* for him to sit on. The *dam yaa* was not supposed to sit on a common seat during this period of personal holiness. They slept on special mats called *bui-yaa* and kept their skins smooth and fresh by a nightly rubbing of a skin-toning preparation called *doh*, which they washed off in the morning.

Among the instructions the *yaa* men received during the performance of the tradition was that they should regard their bodies as holy or sacred. Accordingly, they were expected to live a disciplined life, especially with respect to food, drinks and sex. Second, they were taught that in spirit life, they had taken precedence over persons who had not performed the tradition, irrespective of age. Consequently, they were not supposed to take advice or instructions from such persons or to let themselves to be led by them. According to the elders, to do so was to act contrary to the spiritual order. They were told that they were spiritually wiser and stronger than anyone else who had not performed the tradition, and that proper behaviour in spirit life was the basis of success in the natural world.

Throughout the initiation period, which lasted for about two years, the *yaa* men also received instructions in the art of swordsmanship or fencing in the leading occupations such as yam cultivation, tree climbing, palm wine tapping, and oil palm cutting; and instruction in traditional music, art, and sports. This way, the *yaa* men became imbued with a high degree of self-confidence, a positive attitude to life, and a sense of leadership and obligation to their communities.

4.7 Presentation to the *Yaa* Totem/Deity and Mullet Banquet

At the end of the period of confinement, all the *yaa* men and their house-fathers dressed in fine cloths with bells on their waists and assembled at the compound of the *yaa* father. They were all dressed in traditional pageantry, with each man bearing an iron weapon called *ega-yaa*. This was a long pointed shaft, which was borne on the left shoulder with its pointed end knobbed and held high. It is presumed that this was the type of iron weapon first used by the Ogoni ancestors. Accompanied by the elders and all the principal men of the district, they proceeded in a gorgeous processional parade through the important streets of the town, being led by an ancient dancing club called *Soosoo*, amidst great cheering by crowds of admirers, parents, relatives, well-wishers, and friends. This was the occasion on which the *te-yaa* and his *yaa* men presented themselves before the *yaa* totem or deity known as *ku* or *yo-uweyaa*.

The ritual requirement for this occasion included the presentation of a puppy dog by each *yaa* man as a sacrificial offering to the deity. The animals were not killed with an instrument. The puppies were dashed against an object, usually a tree, but the *yaa* father sacrificed a lamb by "boxing" it with his fists until the animal died. This practice was called *bog-pee* and was supposed to give him a healthy long life.

As each *yaa* man received his blessings from the presence of the deity, each returned joyfully to his home. As they went, they gave gifts to the various groups of people they met, especially to groups of farmers *(ataa wii)*, to groups of traders *(ataa du)*, and to groups of domestic servant such as water carriers *(ataa maa)*. It would seem that this aspect of the tradition was created to give practical expression to the culture of generosity that was one of the pillars of the *yaa* tradition.

After the conclusion of the presentation to the *yaa* deity, the *te-yaa* announced the date for another banquet. This was called *Egara Aka* (lit., scattering the mullets), probably reflecting the fact that mullet was the principal fish eaten at this banquet. According to Chief Kiriki, each *yaa* man or *dam yaa* was required to bring a specific number of mullets. A firstborn son was required to bring 60 mullets, plus one large fish, usually a shark *(tae)*, while a second born son was required to bring 50 mullets and a shark. In addition, each *yaa* man also brought yams (usually, seven), plantains and palm wine. As usual, the last born of three or more sons of a family participating received free dinner.

On the appointed date, all the *yaa* men and their house-fathers or patrons assembled at the compound of the *yaa* father at about 5:00pm. Unlike the previous banquet, the cooking of this dinner was done centrally by attendants.

The mullet banquet was another great occasion in the performance of the *yaagɛ* tradition, featuring a great deal of sharing and fellowshipping among the *yaa* men. Other young men who had performed the tradition were welcome to attend the dinner. As custom required, each yaa man gave a share of the fish to the *te-yaa* and a share to the representatives of each of the ancient patrilineages present at the banquet.

After the banquet, the *yaa* father fixed the date for a grand parade of himself and his lieutenants or *yaa* men through the main streets of the town. The occasion gave the *te-yaa* the opportunity to give a speech on his successful performance of the *yaanwii* tradition. Chief Iyoro who himself performed the tradition in 1983, explains that the day of the parade was the day the *yaa* father demonstrated in public, the fact that he had become one of the great men of the area. According to the chief, on this occasion, the *yaa* father dressed in his chiefly apparel, adorned with costly ornaments.

The first stop of the parade visited was the local war shrine. The *yaa* father was accompanied in the parade by chiefs and elders and by all the *yaa* men. They walked in a grand procession through the major streets of the town and visited the important places and centres. All along the route, the *te-yaa* constantly dipped hand into his purse and scattered handfuls of money to cheering crowds of admirers. When the parade approached an important road junction or the gate of a chief or titled man's compound, people barricaded the way and demanded payment of tolls. As soon as money was paid, the barricades were quickly removed and the procession continued until all the important places and streets had been covered.

4.8 Baptism and Separation Dance

After the parade, the traditional performance entered its last phase. The *yaa* father sent money to the house of *pɛɛ*, an ancient musical society, to hire them to play for him and his *yaa* men. To get ready for this baptismal ritual, each *yaa* man slept alone in the house of his patron or house-father the evening prior to the holy bath. About 4:30am, each house-father took his *yaa* man to the nearest running stream for the holy bath. This was a running bath.

The *dam yaa* or *yaa* man dipped his feet into the water and ran as fast as he could towards the village or town. As soon as he caught a glimpse of the village, he turned and ran to dip his feet into the stream again. He repeated this until seven times. At the seventh time, he threw himself into the water and took a quick bath and ran straight back to the home of his house-father. The whole bath must be completed before twilight, and no fly should perch on his body during the ritual.

All the while one of his house-fathers was running with him and keeping the count until the seventh time. The *yaa* man must be completely nude, his cloth being in the possession of his house-father. At the seventh time when the *yaa* man throws himself into the stream, the house-father left him and ran home with the cloth. Thus, the *yaa* man had no choice but to run home nude. He stayed that way at the home of his house-father until about 8:00 or 9:00pm, the next night when the "separation dance" (*pɛɛ*) commenced.

There were two musical societies. One was called the elders' *pɛɛ* (*pɛɛ pya kanee*). This *pɛɛ* was sacred and was played for honourable men. Young men who were virgins were to dance this music. The dance took place at night, starting roughly from between 8:00 or 9:00pm. The musicians were inside a house but the *yaa* men gathered outside. The *yaa* men danced in turn to the music from outside into the house and placed their hands on a sacred instrument and then danced from the house to the outside amidst cheers by spectators and well-wishers.

The second dance at a separate location, was called *pɛɛ izan*. This dance was not sacred and was open to all men who had lost their holiness or "wholesomeness" before performing the *yaa* tradition. According to Chief Iyoro, the *izan* were men who could not keep themselves holy, such as men who had had extramarital sex or carnal relations with a twin mother, or with a strange woman, and boys who had had sex before performing the *yaagɛ* tradition. Chief Nwilabba explains that youths of this category were dubbed *elo* ("deviants") and were eliminated from the society or sold into slavery (tape no. og/sk/24, 15:3.84). Chief Iyoro states that if such a youth concealed the truth, danced the holy *pɛɛ*, and touch the sacred instrument, he would drop dead instantly (tape no. og/sk/12, 5.2.84).

It seems that the *yaa* tradition had within it a machinery meant to purge society of such deviant youths. This may explain why at certain stages in the traditional performance; parents (especially mothers) were forbidden to see their sons. In effect, this was a method of conditioning the mothers of such young men for such an eventuality. Meanwhile, the virgin *yaa* men who danced the holy *pɛɛ* were acclaimed successful, and were received with great joy by their parents and sponsors. Gifts were given to them by parents, relatives, friends and well-wishers.

4.9 The *Yaa* Marathon, Ritual Cleansing, and Tree Planting

Finally, about 5:00am the following morning, the *yaa* marathon (*teera yaa*) began. This non-competitive race began with the *izan* men, i.e. those who had danced the unholy *pɛɛ*. They wore around their waists a mini raffia cloth called *igwa*. They began the race early in order to cover the local areas when most people, especially the women and girls, were not yet a wake to line the routes.

The virgin *yaa* men began their race about six o'clock that morning and ran their race almost nude. On their waist they wore a leather girdle to which was attached a bronze figure called *gɛɛn yaa*. On their heads was a circular crown called *igia yaa*, with a strap passed under their chin to keep it in place. To the crown was attached one or two eagle feathers. Each *yaa* man was armed with two short swords called *kobɛgɛ*, one in the hand and the other on the waist, packed in a sheath and held by a leather belt.

Each *yaa* man ran between two guards, his house-fathers, who wore their cloths knotted, gathered, and tucked. The *yaa* man's page *(gian yaa)* wore a leather girdle with a bronze figure attached and carried the *yaa* man's carved stool *(tan yaa)* in one hand and sword in the other.

Dressed in this way, each *yaa* party marched to the compound of the *yaa* father. There in the open court, each *yaa* man stood on his mat ready to start the race. When everything was set, the *yaa* man's virgin sister and firstborn daughter came forward carrying a little bowl of oil-chop made from *gɛɛrɛ* (old cocoyam) and put a sop of the stuff into the *yaa* man's mouth. As soon as the sop entered his mouth, the "warrior" set off with his guards and page, the guards running slightly abreast him, one on either side and his page running behind. As they ran, they followed specific routes through the towns and communities and only stopped briefly at important places.

The *yaa* marathon marked the climax of the *yaa* traditional performance. All along the routes were crowds of people, especially women and girls, who cheered with great enthusiasm at the sight of so many young men taking part in this traditional exercise. As the race progressed, the public made comments on the individual runners. Characteristics such as swiftness in motion, trim figure and brave looks attracted favourable comments. Other characteristics such as plumpness provided vents for light-heartedness and joy. The two guards or patrons protected the *yaa* man and gave him direction at appropriate points along the route.

As the race moved from the local areas into the neighbouring towns and communities, the exercise became truly war-like. People in those places attempted to snatch the eagle from the *yaa* man's crown. In such circumstances, the guards and the *yaa* man brandished their swords and forced their way to safety. According to tradition, if the *yaa* man's eagle was taken, that was tantamount to taking the warrior prisoner. In such circumstance, the patrons negotiated to recover the eagle by payment of a ransom before the race continued again.

At certain friendly places, they rested briefly, during which the *yaa* man sat on his carved stool.

Throughout the race, each *yaa* party kept chewing a certain watery plant called *ating (costus afer)* in order to prevent exhaustion, husky voice, and dry throat. This was necessary because as they ran, they kept voicing certain words intermittently punctuated with loud shouts and ululations, as shown in the following illustration of the *yaa* "chorus" repeated frequently:

One – *Tow..............................Tow..........................*
All – *................................Whoa....................Whoa.......*

The race ended at about 5 o'clock in the evening with the traditional cutting down of a plantain plant at the outskirts of the town. The plantain plant should be cut down with one stroke of the *yaa* man's sword (in later periods, when boys of younger age were initiated, the stem of the plantain plant was thinned down to a suitable size). Cutting the plantains probably symbolised an act of war, such as the execution of an enemy or a prisoner of war. This is explained by the fact that it is done at the end of the race and on the outskirts of the town.

Early in the following morning, a simple ritual was performed to remove the *pah-yaa* from each of the *yaa* men. Chief Iyoro commented that the *pah-yaa* was a negative influence or spirits of war, which tended to cling to the *yaa* man after the performance, having been attracted by the activities of the *yaa* tradition. A special ritual was therefore performed to remove such influences and to banish them to the sea. Without this ritual, the *yaa* men would behave abnormally and might have constant nightmares. Prince Isaanee Nii explained that a similar ritual was performed on warriors when they returned from battle before they were allowed to return to their families (S/No.53.Tape No. Og/sk/4,29/2.83). This emphasises the fact that the *yaa* tradition was originally a war-related activity.

Finally, at the end of the whole performance, the *te-yaa* received the title of *Kabari* and was admitted to the ranks of rulers as chief. His compound became classified as one of the notable compounds or "houses" in Ogoni. As an insignia, a certain live tree variously called *te-Bari* (tree of God) or *te-mene* (tree of wealth) was planted in the centre of his compound. With that, his compound became recognised as one of the compounds to be visited by public dances, outing ceremonies, public processions, and masquerades. Moreover, the passage or road through the front of the compound became a tribute or toll collecting point during processions and public outings or performances.

4.10(a) Conclusions

This chapter has traced the origin and background of the *yaa* tradition introduced at the initial settlement by the Ogoni founding ancestors. The *yaa* tradition was part of a military culture and discipline in which the Ogoni ancestors were familiar in their former homeland before they migrated to their present domain. They left their former country in a period of extreme civil strife and became a wandering army. Of necessity, they held firmly to the *yaa* tradition, the soul of the Ogoni cultural heritage, for their own survival. This interpretation is strengthened by the fact that no similar tradition has been found among any of Ogoni's neighbours.

The class of titled chiefs who were great yam farmers and traders and had accumulated wealth put their sons forward to perform the *yaagɛ* tradition. The yaa tradition was promoted by this social group partly because it ensured the perpetuation of their own class. The youths who performed the *yaagɛ* tradition constituted the elite in Ogoni society.

The introduction of foreign wives into title taking had important ramifications for kinship system and inheritance. A truly nuclear family system developed, where wives lived with their husbands in the husband's compounds for the first time, husbands and wives also began to have children whom they called their own and who lived with them in their own homes as future heirs. This consciousness encouraged such men to plan for the future of their heirs, which includes enrolling their sons and financing their participation in the *yaagɛ* tradition. The matrilineal system began to disintegrate as a result. Daughters moved away to live with the men they loved. Mothers' brothers now demanded monetary payment at the marriage of their sisters' daughters so they could use the money to marry foreign wives and an exogamous virilocal marriage system developed. The attention and care of mothers' brothers was diverted from their sisters' sons to their own children.

I have placed these broad changes in the fifteenth and sixteenth centuries here, but they could have began much earlier. Use of the later date is based on the written reports of Portuguese and Dutch travellers, who described the people, culture, language, and economic activities in the town that has now been identified as Ogoni. My own view is that the Portuguese and the Dutch described practices that were already the results of centuries of development.

I have shown elsewhere that when similar changes occurred in other parts of the Niger Delta, they resulted from the trans-Atlantic slave trade, which can be dated from the seventeenth to nineteenth centuries (Kpone-Tonwe, 1996; 1998). Although the Ogoni had been in the vanguard of innovations in the Niger Delta in the pre-colonial period, their resistance to colonial rule meant that they had to suffer both the effects of conquest and the consequences of being marginalised in the large scheme of colonial development.

In many African societies (including the Igbo, the Ijo, and the Ibibio, for example), age is a determining factor in social classification. Society is divided into age-sets and political power is vested in the elders. In Ogoni, age is not a determinant of political power. A person could be quite old and yet have no political power. The determinant of social classes and political power is the *yaa* tradition.

The *yaa* tradition prepared a young man for leadership and for life. Through its teachings and discipline, it inculcated attitudes of hard work, self-discipline, integrity, generosity, friendship, and good character. Our house-fathers were not only our teachers but they were also our idols and our examples. They took us daily to the farms, or to the palm wine camps, *nuloo,* where at certain times of the day, elderly and experienced men retired to relax from their work. There, we listened to them as they talked about almost everything under the sun.

They talked about sea travel, how one could come out of one's house at night and look into the sky and know whether there would be a storm at sea for the next two weeks, or whether it would be safe to cross a certain sea at certain period of the day or night. They talked about how to look at the shape and position of the moon and know whether the fishermen would make a good catch during the week. They talked about how to study the flight of birds and know whether a storm was eminent. They talked about the behaviour of animals at different times of the day and night and in different seasons. They talked about how to detect the footprints of animals and recognise the animals involved.

We listened to experts compose songs and oral poetry and discussed good prose. They freely composed satire about the behaviour of certain individuals and laughed heartily. They discussed politics, economics, and love. They discussed biographies and talked about certain great warriors or medicine men, how they behaved, and what they did in certain emergencies. They demonstrated the different ways of using tools and weapons. They showed us how to identify a raffia palm that would mature in the next two or three months. They showed where we should tap a mature raffia palm tree to get the full amount of its sweet juices.

These experiences continued on an almost daily basis until we completed the *yaa* tradition. By the end of it, we knew we had learned a lot and could do many things. We behaved in certain respectable ways with self-confidence and self-assurance. Moreover, during training, if a certain youth was found to be a budding genius, information about him was quietly passed on to the elders and to the authorities of the appropriate secret societies or clubs, where his talents would be properly utilised. Before long, he was discreetly lured or encouraged to become a member or associate member, despite his young age. Each time the *yaage* tradition was performed, a number of such talented youths were identified and they became the foremost leaders in their generation. Thus, it can be seen that the *yaa* tradition acted to stratify Ogoni society, and the prospects of poorer youths whose parents could not sponsor them were limited.

4.10(b) *Recommendations*

In the early 1970s, there was some talk in Nigeria about abandoning bad traditions. At that time, many people mistook the phrase to mean abandoning everything traditional. Then in 1977, Nigeria hosted a Festival of African Arts and Culture, christened "FESTAC 77", which opened many eyes to the value of culture.

Compared with other traditions, the *yaa* tradition is a classic in its contemporary setting. Today in Ogoni, less than 20 per cent of the population know about the *yaa* tradition because it is no longer performed and nothing has been written about it. The *yaa*tradition deserves to be preserved and to be made known. This will require the combined effort of scholars, artists, actors, film makers, photographers, and above all, the provision of funds and materials.

A literary documentation is necessary now because the older generation who knew about the *yaa* tradition are fast disappearing and, although the density of the population of Ogoni is high, the average life span is getting shorter and shorter. Right now, it is probably less than thirty-five or forty years. Thus, we can see that the day is fast approaching when no one will know anything about the *yaa* tradition. But they can know and re-learn these things if there is a book they can read or a film they can see.

CHAPTER FIVE

ORIGIN AND IDENTITY OF SOME NIGER DELTA PLACE-NAMES I: PEREIRA'S "VERY LARGE VILLAGE"

5.1. Overview

In this chapter, effort is made to utilise the benefit of oral tradition and linguistics to uncover the mystery which for centuries has surrounded the origin and identity of some place-names in the Eastern Niger Delta. Among such place-names are Duarte Pacheco Pereira's "very large village" and Olfert Dapper's *'Moko'* and *Kuleba'*. In this chapter, we shall argue that the early European travellers had described actual towns and settlements and had also provided sufficient data for the identification of the towns. Unfortunately, however such data have not been sufficiently utilised. This chapter enunciates the fact that any worthwhile effort towards unravelling the mystery surrounding the identity of the place-names must corroborate all the data provided by the early European travellers. Such data, for example include geographical, commercial, linguistic, demographic, and cultural evidence. By a somewhat nostalgic analysis of these categories of data, this writer has revealed the existence of an extinct city named Bangha, which was located on the coast of Gokana in the Ogoni region of the Eastern Niger Delta. By all standards, this city appeared to have satisfied the data provided by Pacheco Pereira. The city became deserted and extinct following the introduction of a smallpox epidemic into it by the Portuguese.

We shall conclude the chapter by noting that the identification of Bangha as the 'very large village' described by Pereira, only points to the beginning of a whole new idea and direction in Niger Delta studies. Consequently, the expertise of artists, archeologists, linguists, historians, ethnographers, etc. will be needed to search into this regions past, in order to bring out more information not only about the people of Bangha but also about a fuller history and culture of the entire region.

5.2 Early Study of Niger Delta Place-Names

One of the earliest attempts at the study of Niger Delta place-names was by William Balfour Baikie who, as a member of the Niger/Benue expedition of 1854, took up residence at Bonny from where he conducted his research on the geography, economy, and culture of the Niger Delta region. Among other things, Biakie compiled a list of Niger Delta peoples, occupations and place-names. A remarkable aspect of Baikie's work was the manner he recorded information about the different peoples of the region. He tried as much as possible, to identify the changes that had taken place as a result of the way each ethnic group pronounced the name of its neighbour or the names of particular places and things. For example, Baikie recorded that at Bonny, Bonny people called themselves *Bani* but that Kalabari people called them *Ibani,* while Igbo people called them *obani* and the European traders called them *Bonny*. In another place, Baikie recorded thus:

> There is plenty of palm oil in Ozuzu, an abundance of cocos and yams. To the north or north-west of Ozuzu lies 'Mbohia' called at Bonny :Ikpofia: There are few towns here, it being chiefly a bush country. The derivation being from *Mba* country, and *Ohia* bush. There is but little oil made here, and the people are war like. Close to it is another similar district and with inhabitants of like propensities. It is named *Ogone* but at Bonny, it is known as *Egane*. (Baikie, 1856)

From the above, we can see that up to the middle of the nineteenth century, Bonny was being called and identified by four different forms, namely *Bani, Bonny Ibani* and *Obani*, each by a different ethnic group. We can see also that the simplest form Bani was the one by which Bonny people identified themselves. It is, however, noteworthy that it is not this simple or original form that has survived. Rather, it is the form adopted by the most articulate or literate groups, the European traders, which has survived or has become prominent. Similarly, we can see that up to the middle of the nineteenth century, Ogoni was also being identified by at least three forms, namely *Ghana*, *Egana* and *Ogone*. What is the origin of all those forms of ethnic identity and place-names? What about other confusing and unidentified ethnic names or place-names in the Eastern Niger Delta or Bight of Bonny such as *'Moko' 'Kuleba'*; the "very large village", *Kalbarch*; *Caabool*, *Maneba*; *'Kalbanges*, "New Kalabari", *'Old Kalabari'*; *'Okoloba'*, etc? Did Ogoni have any connection with any of these forms? How have these names come to be?

5.3 Early Description of Niger Delta Coasts

One of the earliest descriptions of Niger Delta coast was by the Portuguese Mariner Duarte Pacheco Pereira in his book, *Esmeraldo de Sitis Orbis*, whose publication is generally placed between 1505 and 1508. According to Professor J.D. Fage, the *Esmeraldo* is the first comprehensive account that has survived to our time. In it, Pacheco Pereira described the actual coast line with considerable and generally recognised details. Throughout, he gave detailed information about sailing directions, navigational features including hazards, bearings and distances between landmarks, etc.

> except for stating the principal commodities involved in trade with them, relatively little tends to be said about the peoples who live there. In his *Esmeraldo*, therefore, he was writing a practical navigational manual for his colleagues and successors' (Fage, 1980).

With the above explanations, we may now be better disposed to grapple with Pacheco Pereira's use of place-names in the Eastern Niger Delta.

At the mouth of the Rio Real, in a creek off its eastern arm (otherwise called Bonny River), Pacheco Pereira described the existence of a "very large village". Based on Mauny's translation,

Pacheco Pereira said in part:

> Eight leagues beyond Rio Pequeno to east is found a very big river called Rio Real, which is five leagues wide at its mouth between the first points of its mouth, point to point; and further inside the width is one and a half leagues. This river in our time had two entrances one of which runs in a north-south direction and is in the middle of its mouth between two sand-spits.

> When you must have crossed this sand-bank going towards the hinterland, you'll watch out for (or be headed to) a sand-spit located on the right. Within this sand-spit you can anchor right in front of the mouth the arm (of the river)which takes off from here, in twelve fathoms you'll be a quarter of a league from the shore at the mouth of the Rio Real, within the arm we have spoken about above, is located a very large village of about 2000 household and in this place are found the biggest canoes ever known in the whole of Ethiopian Guinea and made out of a single tree trunk... the blacks of this area go about naked, around their necks they wear copper necklaces as thick as a finger. They are warriors who rarely live in peace (Mauny, 1956).

Based on George Kimble's translation

> The people of this river (Rio Real) are called Jos, being the same as those (of Forcados River) of whom we spoke above... At the mouth of this river within the creek above mentioned, is a very large village... where much salt is made. The people of this area have bigger canoes capable of carrying up to eighty men. And they came from a hundred leagues or more up this river bringing yams in large quantities. They also bring many slaves, cows, goats, and sheep. Sheep are called "bozy". They sell all these (merchandise) to the native of this village for salt, and our ships buy these things for copper bracelets, which are here greatly prized more than those of brass... they carry daggers like those of the white Moors of Berbery. They are war-like and rarely at peace (Kimble, 1937).

Up till now, the identity of the "very large village" is not known. Professor Fage regrets the fact that Mauny left this question unanswered, while Kimble only suggested that it could have been Bonny (Fage, 1980). Dapper made no reference to the "very large village" neither did Barbot. G.I. Jones was also worried about Pacheco's failure to give the name of the "village". Nonetheless, Jones suggested that it could have been Bonny, but it could also have been

Iyankpo, the traditional home of Tombia, "which became the Finima of history" (Jones 1963). In a recent work, N.C Ejituwu asserted that the "very large village" was Andoni. According to him,

> "the Obolo (Andoni) settlements stretched from the present location of Andoni to the present site of Bonny (Ejituwu, 1991).

So far, the mystery surrounding the identity of Pacheco Pereira's "very large village" has been the subject of wide-ranging speculations. There has been no definitive proof or concrete evidence put forward. Consequently, it has become necessary that certain factors hitherto ignored be brought into focus. There is no gain saying the fact that Pacheco Pereira was very meticulous and precise in his description of the "village" in terms of the culture of the inhabitants, the geographical location of the "village" the nautical information and commercial activity of its market, including salt production. The cultural, linguistic and geographical information have been largely ignored or neglected. Another important factor which has been given little or no consideration is the long stretch of mainland coastal fringe dotted by heavily populated towns. For example, right next door to the site of Pacheco's description of the "very large village" is the Ogoni coastal lands extending from the eastern arm of Rio Real (or Bonny river) all the way to the Imo River which constituted the eastern end of the Eastern Niger Delta (see Map 8).

According to numerous evidence from Ogoni oral tradition, before the coming of the Europeans, the coastal towns of this mainland were the centres of population and business activity. The islands were places where men alone went periodically to hunt, while their families were left behind at places close to the sources of food, the mainland. A careful reading of Pereira will show that such temporary, hunting settlements were often described by him as non-business areas because of lack of trade. Before the coming of the Europeans, most fishing was done close to the shores because the main tools then were beach seines and traps. Deep sea fishing was rare, if not non-existent. It was the introduction of cast nets, gill-nets and lines by the Europeans in the nineteenth century that encouraged deep sea fishing. Similarly, it was the European ships anchored off the coast which encouraged permanent settlement on the islands and at distant out-posts in the estuaries, because from there, they served as suppliers and contractors to the ships. A good example is the settlement of the Cross River estuary in the sixteenth and seventeenth centuries (Forde, 1956, Waddell, 1863 and 1970).

It has to be recognised that any worthwhile effort towards discovering the identity of the "very large village" described by Pereira, must, as a matter of principle, make use of all the data provided by him. As already stated, such data include cultural, linguistic, geographical, demographic and commercial evidence. So far, these data provided by Pereira have not been seriously investigated. A lesser but equally vital factor which may assist in the discovery of the "village" is an analysis of the pattern and chronology of settlement in the region. And last but not least factor towards the same end are evidences from local traditions. Again, this vital source of information has not been adequately exploited. In view of the foregoing, the present effort will seek to explore each of the above-stated category of evidence.

5.4 Data Provided by Early European Travellers

5.4 (a) Geographical and Commercial Evidence

Paecheco Pereira located his "very large village" in a creek off the eastern arm of Rio Real (or Bonny river) but on the coast to the north of Bonny Island, there existed many populous Ogoni towns in the creeks off the Bonny river. The most notable of these were *Bangha, Kwuribue* and *Mogho* (see map 8). I shall return to the last two-named towns in chapter seven.

Pereira gave an account of the trading activities at the market of the "very large village". Traders from far away hinterland came in large canoes bringing yams, cows, goats, sheep and slaves. Pereira also reported the making of salt in the "village" and that this salt became and important item of exchange between the people of the "village" and traders from the hinterland. Another important item which Pereira observed in connection with trade was that the people of the area possessed the largest canoes ever known in black Africa. However, the mention of salt making has induced some scholars to suggest that Bonny was the "very large village". But this assumption has generated a considerable debate. It is argued that Bonny was not the only town which made salt in pre-colonial times. Several other towns in the Bight of Bonny have also claimed to have made salt in the past (see Ejituwu, 1991, Noah, 1980; Alagoa, 1970). In Ogoni, the coastal towns of Gokana (located directly north of Bonny Island) were the greatest salt-makers on the mainland coast (Kpone-Tonwe,1990). Nonetheless, salt making was not the only data Pereira provided for the identification of the "very large village". Other data provided by him will be corroborated.

As for the reference to the large canoes, it is clear from Pereira's report that the canoes were made within the immediate locality of the "very large village" since their type were not frequently seen else where outside the region. Pereira's description of the large canoes was confirmed by later European travellers (see Barbot, 1732; Dapper, 1680). The question arises, who made and used the large canoes in the Eastern Niger Delta? Baikie states that Bonny did not make canoes (Baikie, 1956). Alagoa points out that the Ijo of the Eastern Niger Delta did not make canoes because the mangrove forests did not provide suitable timber (Alagoa, 1970). Although Robert Smith has done an extensive work on the canoe in West African history, his work did not cover the Ogoni area (Smith, 1970). This writer has done an extensive research on the canoes in the Eastern Niger Delta and found that the Ogoni were the makers of some of the largest canoes known in the region. They made and distributed the product not only in the Eastern Niger Delta but also as far as the Cross River Basin and the Cameroon (Kpone Tonwe, 1998).

5.4 (b) Demographic Evidence

Professor Kay Williamson has done an important study on the chronology of settlement in the Niger Delta. According to that study, the ancestors of the Ogoni reached the Eastern Niger Delta from an easterly direction before 2000 years ago. Starting from 1985, when Kay Williamson did the study as the base date, and counting backwards, this would show that the Ogoni had been settled in their present location before 15 BC. According to the same study, the ancestors of the Obolo (Andoni) arrived in the delta from the east "somewhat less than 1500 years ago" (Williamson, 1988). Alagoa explains that the ancestors of the Ibani and the Okrikans migrated from central delta through overland routes and re-entered the delta in the east at points directly opposite their present locations (Alagoa, 1967). Besides, Bonny, Okrika, Andoni and Ogoni oral traditions corroborate the point that the Ogoni were already settled in their present location before these neighbours arrived in the region (Porter, 1933; Mackenzie, 1933 Alagoa, 1972; Kpone-Tonwe, 1990). The implication is that the Ogoni had had some centuries of settled life, economic, cultural and demographic growth before their neighbours settled in the region.

These strands of evidence tend to give the necessary backing to Pereira's demographic and cultural data which are vital for the identification of the "very large village". According to Pereira, the "village" contained about 2,000 *Vezinhos*, 'households' (Mauny, 1956). Fage recommends Mauny's translation of *Vezinhos* as "household" against Kimble's translation of it as "inhabitants" because Mauny best represented Pacheco Pereira's meaning (Fage, 1980). It may be pointed out that in Ogoni, as in most African societies, heads of houses did not normally reveal the actual number of persons contained in their houses or compounds, not only for security reasons but also because it was considered arrogant, indiscreet, undiplomatic and in bad taste. The expression "few children", a "couple" or a "handful of men", were preferred. Moreover, for political purposes (to which the information given to Pereira belonged), actual households (i.e. *to* or *nu-to*) were not normally counted. What were counted were houses or compounds *(be)*; and before a compound or house was classified as such for political purposes, it must have attained a certain social level in terms of manpower and wealth. It must have attained a population figure of about fifty or more able-bodied men and women and its head or spokesman must have been a titled man (Kpone-Tonwe, 1992).

Notwithstanding the above explanations, to obtain a conservative population figure for the "very large village", Fage has suggested that the number of *vezinhos* (household) should be multiplied sevenfold (Fage, 1980), which gives a conservative figure of 14,000 for the population of the town. It is doubtful whether Bonny had attained that size of population by 1500 AD, given the fact that about a century later, John Barbot described Bonny as a modest village of mere three hundred houses, even though by that date, Bonny had already started to enjoy some economic benefits from the trans-Atlantic slave trade (Barbot, 1732). It is also noteworthy the fact that Barbot found nothing specifically attractive about Bonny, except to observe that they were engaged in the on going (slave) trade and some fishing like the people of new Calabar (Barbot 1732).

Then in 1846, Hope Masterton Waddell, a presbyterian missionary and traveller, visited Bonny and recorded his impression of the town as follows:

> The town was a confused assemblage of mean houses, without order, on a mud bank, with winding foot tracks for streets huge iguanas, four or five feet long, sleeping in the sun or crawling about the houses as domestic animals. They were harmless or unharmed, being juju, or sacred. The houses we saw were small, dark and dirty, without a window, confused buildings, all gables and wings constructed of wattle and doub. The king's was like the rest (Waddell, 1970).

Again, like Barbot, Waddell did not show any indication that the population of Bonny was impressive, and there is no tradition that a natural disaster was visited on an earlier population of Bonny.

5.4 (c) Linguistic and Cultural Evidence

Pacheco Pereira also gave an unmistakably linguistic evidence as another clue for the identification of the "very large village". He explained that the people of the " village" called sheep 'bozy'. All attempt to identify this word with the languages of the various ethnic groups in the Eastern Niger Delta and the surrounding hinterland have proved unsuccessful. Only Ogoni has come more than 50% per cent closer to identifying with the word. The word is an Ogoni word of the Gokana language. Evidently, there was a misreading of the word. Nonetheless, a diligent student of Ogoni languages cannot fail to recognise that it is a distortion of the Gokana word *ból* which means goat or sheep (cf. "Wolff, 1959). The misreading of the word might have been an error of Pereira himself or his editors. It seems that the error was detected at some point but, evidently, they could not correct it. This may be the reason (in order to alert readers), the word was printed in inverted commas instead of italics, the usual way of indicating a foreign word. There are many examples of such errors in the writings of the early European travellers. The following table shows that there have been margins of errors of this kind as widely divergent from the original form as 60 per cent, 75 per cent and even 100 per cent. In the case of *'bozy'* (sheep) the margin of divergence from the original form *ból* (sheep) is only 50 per cent (Table V).

Table V: Some Niger Delta Place-names Misread in the Writing of the Early European Travellers

Original form of word	Early European travellers version	Percentage of of divergence from original	Reference
Igbo	Hackbous	75	Barbot, 1752
Ijebu	Geebuu	50	Fage, 1980
Awusale	Agusale	17	Fage, 1980
Ughoton	Huguatoo	38	Fage, 1980
Igo	Iguou	25	Fage, 1980
Oghene	Hoogunee	55	Fage, 1980
Oghene	Ogane	20	Fage, 1980
Nupe	Obuu	60	Fage, 1980
Warri	Oueve	55	Fage, 1980
Bo'l	Bozy	50	Kimble, 1837
Bani	Bonny	40	Dapper, 1676
Mogho	Moko	20	Dapper, 1676
Kabangha	Kalbarch	40	Ardener, 1968
Kabangha	Calbangos	33	Dapper, 1676
Kalabari	Kalbarien	33	Dapper, 1676
Bangha	Calborgh	60	Ogilly, 1670
Bangha	Kalbanges	50	Ardenr, 1968
Kwuribue	Kuleba	20	Dapper, 1676
Bile	Belli	50	Barbot, 1752
Menebue	Moneba	20	Ardener, 1968
?	Mumu	100	Fage, 1980
?	Teebuu	100	Fage, 1980

Next, Pacheco Pereira described a very notable eye-catcher in the culture of the people of the "very large village". He said, that they carried daggers, the like of which was not found anywhere else known to him, except among the white Moors of Berbery (Kimble, 1937). This is another very vital piece of data provided by Pereira for the identification of the "very large village" as in the case of the linguistic evidence, no ethnic group in the Eastern Niger Delta and in the surrounding hinterland has been identified with this piece of cultural data, except Ogoni. Apart from Ogoni, no other ethnic group in the region has an ancient tradition linked with life-long wearing of "dagger" as an insignia of social status.

In Ogoni, all young men and adult were required to perform the *yaa* tradition. The first stage of the *yaa* tradition was called *yaa-ge* (the Yaa of bearing the sword). The suffix *ge* means sword or machete. Accordingly, all the young men and adults who had performed the tradition were required and authorised to wear or bear the traditional sword or weapon called *kobɛgɛ* at all times, as an insignia of their social status. The *kobɛgɛ* was a short curved, two-edged sword with a decorated hilt. It was usually packed in a sheath and held firmly to the waist by a leather belt. Pacheco Pereira made his observations with considerate accuracy when he noted that the people were "war-like". This is because part of the training which the *yaag* participants received during the one or two years the rite lasted was military, for examples, they were taught the art of fencing. In society, those who had performed the tradition were given the title of *Pya-Gbara*, meaning "gentlemen" and they occupied the upper social classes. For this reason, men who had not performed the *Yaag* tradition could not join the peoples, fighting force and they had no political rights or privileges, as this testimony shows:

> If an important matter occurred in the community and they wanted people to meet to discuss it, only those who had performed the *yaagɛ* tradition could enter the house (or venue) where the matter was being discussed. Those who had not performed the *yaagɛ* tradition would sit outside and listen from outside. They could not be able to take part in the discussion (Nii, 53, tape 4, 29th Dec. 1983).

Thus from the above analysis, it can be seen that the people Pacheco Pereira described in the "very large village" were the *Pya Gbara* social class of Ogoni. Their appearance, bearing, and traditional attire unmistakably attracted the attention of the observant visitor. An engraving of the *kobɛgɛ*, the Ogoni insignia of social status has been identified by this writer in James Barbot's "Abstract of a voyage" in John Barbot, *A Collection of Voyages and Travels* Vol. V (1752), p. 462, plate 26 item "E" (see also Kpone-Tonwe, 1990: 337-40).

In view of all the above explanations, the question arises, where on the Ogoni coast was the "very large village" located? What happened to it? What was the local name? Where did its inhabitants go? Do the Ogoni have a tradition about this city? We shall endeavour to answer these questions.

5.4 (d) Evidence from Local Traditions

According to Ogoni oral tradition, there was a very big city called Bangha on the coast of Ogoni in the Gokana area. In 1984, during my field work in the Gokana area, I visited the site, which is now covered by forest but parts of it have becomes farmlands. There are many signs of previous settlement as old sea shells are plentiful in the area. The site is at the head of a creek branching northward from the Bonny river. It is about five kilometres east of Mogho and Bomu. A village by the same name Bangha stands a short distance from the old site. This village was founded in the 1940s by a man named John Gbo, a preacher of the Christ Army Church. He founded the village as a healing home for the sick and named it after the old city.

According to tradition, the old city of Bangha was founded by a brother of Gbene Saakoo named Boonen. Gbene Saakoo himself was the founder of Gokana, after conquering the autochthonous Goo people who inhabited the area. Gbene Saakoo established his headquarters at Giokoo in the heart of Gokana. While at Giokoo, a bitter quarrel broke out between him and his brother, Boonen, who was accused of infidelity with one of his wives. There was separation between the two brothers. Boonen moved away and founded the town of Gaagaa about four kilometres east of Giokoo. Not long afterwards, the 'curse' of Gbene Saakoo attacked Gaagaa and scattered the town. Some of the inhabitants migrated northwards and founded the town of Yeghe located on the Port Harcourt –Kónò express way. The majority moved southwards towards the coast and founded the town of Bangha at the head of the creek mentioned above (Map 8). Bangha grew to become a large, prosperous city. Its large market attracted traders and goods not only from all parts of Ogoni but also from the Igbo hinterland, Ikwerre, Ibibio and the riverine areas, including Kalabari (Map 8). One informant explained that as the city of Port Harcourt did not exist then, Bangha was what the city of Port Harcourt is today. The account states that white men from across the sea frequented the Bangha market. Undoubtedly, those white men were the early Portuguese who came from the island of Equatorial Guinea (formerly Fernando Po) (cf. Ryder, 1977; Ardener, 1978).

According to the account, a white man who was attacked by the deadly epidemic, smallpox, died in the market. As smallpox was not known in Ogoni at that time, nobody knew anything about its precautions. The epidemic spread like wild fire and almost wiped out the population of the city. At first, the people tried to bury their dead, but they soon observed that after burying their dead, those who buried them also caught the disease and died. So they realised that the power of the disease was active in the entire environment. Thus they called the disease *Poro-efop* (evil breeze). There upon, the surviving inhabitants of Bangha deserted the city in all directions.

Majority of the survivors from Bangha founded the early towns of Boue, which includes *Kwuribue, Lee, Barike, Gaen, Yaara, Gbamene, Toga, Kako,* and *Baraboue*. They named this group of new towns *Boue* from the Gokana word *bo-ól*, meaning "on Land" as against *Bódo* (on shore) which was the previous topographical location of their former city. The prefix *bo* is the Gokana prepositional root or stem, which means "on" and the suffix *ue* is the Kana equivalent of the Gokana "ól" both of which mean "land" or "bush". I had explained elsewhere that although this people originally spoke the Gokana language, but by moving eastwards, they came more in contact with the pure Kana speaking peoples. This affected their language as can be seen in the above analysis. Nonetheless, some of their family names still reveal their Gokana origins. For examples, Kpone-Tonwe Kpone (Gokana: *Kponen*) meaning, Energetic, resourceful human; and Tonwe (Gokana: Tonwe) meaning "rearguard" or "protector" (see Kpone-Tonwe, 1990: 139).

Some of the survivors from Bangha moved north-west into the heartland of Gokana. This group relocated the Bangha market at a site near Giokoo, the capital of Gokana and re-named it *Ki-Bangha*, meaning "Bangha market" after their former city. A remnant of *Ki-Bangha* market has survived until this day.

5.5 Conclusion

What I have done in this chapter is to present a whole new scope and direction of research in Niger Delta studies. It is a preliminary effort, but it shows that it is still possible to gain more knowledge about the past of the region. By making proper use of the trickling of information that has come to us from the past through oral traditions and by reading with care and objectivity the fragmentary reports handed down by the early European travellers. This chapter has only succeeded in pinpointing the site of Duarte Pacheco Pereira's "very large village" on the coast of Gokana in the Ogoni area. A lot more work still has to be done in the area. We need to know about the language, culture, and lifestyle of the people of Bangha. At the time of my visit to the site in 1984, it was relatively intact. It is not known, however, whether since then the oil companies which are stripping the environment in the area have destroyed the sites. With the availability of funds, the next preliminary stage should be to do some test excavations on the site.

The demographic data given by Pereira although underestimated, appears to have been more than vindicated by the testimony from oral tradition. The very fact that the survivors from Bangha were able to found so many towns, "simultaneously" suggest that the population of Bangha was large indeed. More than that, there is also the fact that a remnant Ki-Bangha (Bangha Market) existing today in Gokana which is not bearing the name of its host location but that of an extinct ancient coastal city. In fact, the name of the town where this ancient market is now located is *Nwe-ól*, which is also the town where the ancient *Giokoo*, the traditional capital of Gokana is located.

Owing to the conquest of smallpox by the World Health Organisation (WHO), it will not be possible for the twenty-first century man to fully comprehend the scale of the tragedy the people of Bangha suffered at the time they did. For example, in 1949, despite the existence of the benefits of medical science, this writer as a primary school boy, witnessed a terrible smallpox epidemic in Ogoni land. The epidemic started in the writer's own town, Kónò Boue. A certain stranger who was a prostitute and who lived alone, caught the disease and died in her house with the door shut. As she lived alone, nobody took notice until it was too late. Unfortunately, her house was situated by the big Kónò Boue market (Du-kónò), which was attended by people from all parts of Ogoni and by people from the riverine area. People who came to the market from those places caught the disease and carried it to their own towns. The disease spread like wild fire throughout Ogoni. In Kónò Boue itself, it killed more than half of its population. Whole families were completely wiped out within a day or two. It is hard to conceive of a foreign army which could cause such a wastage of human lives. During my field work in 1984, I discovered that the chief of the town and his elders had kept a record of this tragedy in the town's statute book. Even the very name of the prostitute woman and her place of origin were recorded.

With that first hand experience, when I read in the oral traditions that the survivors from Bangha founded so many towns, as mentioned above, it did not take me a much stretching of the imagination to realise that the population of Bangha must have been really very great. It underscores the relative accuracy of Duarte Pacheco Pereira and the reason this particular aspect of the town did not escape his attention. It also underscores the fact that there can truly be a real corroboration between oral tradition and written records, especially when the two are treated with integrity and objectivity.

As earlier stated, because of the volume of information involved, the subject matter in this chapter cannot be dealt with in one installment. We shall therefore continue this discussion in chapter six, where we will discuss the origin and identify of other place-names in the Eastern Niger Delta, including Dapper's *"Moko"*, and "Kuleba" and the unexplained duplication of others such as "old" and "new" Calabar.

CHAPTER SIX

ORIGIN AND IDENTITY OF SOME NIGER DELTA PLACE-NAMES II: *"MOKO", "KULEBA,* AND "OTHERS"

6.1 Introduction

This chapter is a continuation of the discussion of the subject matter of chapter five. Therefore, in order to fully grasp the trend of the discussion in chapter six, it is recommended that the reader should also read chapter five, where the groundwork for the arguments are set.

It is important to note that the events discussed in chapter five were the events that took place during the Portuguese era in West Africa, which are placed in the fifteenth and early sixteenth centuries. During this period, the Portuguese were mainly concerned with getting some new products of Africa, usually referred to as exotic goods. Any slaves that the Portuguese got from West Africa during this period were in the category of exotic goods to provide domestic servants to the rich in Europe. The Portuguese took their cue from what they saw in the Eastern Niger Delta at the Bangha market, where the Ogoni chiefs were contracting for high class distance marriages as a component of the requirements for the *Gbene* title taking for the purpose of establishing their independent lineages. They were also contracting for banished or condemned criminals from the hinterland to be used as human victims for the rituals connected with the *Gbene* title taking at Nama.

During the sixteenth century, however, the Portuguese lost control of the trade in West Africa to the Dutch as a result of events happening in Europe during the mercantile period, when the Dutch began to dominate the commerce of Europe on the high seas, including West Africa, particularly the Gulf of Guinea and the Eastern Niger Delta. Because the transition was so abrupt and the time gap great, vital connections and communication links were lost. Fortunately, however, Duarte Pacheco Pereira had made a cartographic description of the Niger delta coasts in his book, *Esmeralado de Situ Orbis*, which supposed to be a manual or guide for his Portuguese successors (Fage, 1980). It is uncertain whether the Dutch had access to this book. This is because Olfert Dapper, who described the Dutch expedition in West Africa did not mention the "very large village". However, the Dutch also made some discoveries of their own in their own time, among which were the discovery of the Iron money in *"Moko"* market and the discovery of the influential town of *"Kuleba"*, whose king he described as the lord of the Eastern Niger Delta coast.

6.2. Origin/Identity of Dapper's *"Moko"*

Dapper described the geographical location of Mogho *("moko")* in the following manner: "the district of Krike (Okrika) is about twenty miles up the Rio Real (i.e the eastern branch or Bonny river) and borders on the north-west of Mogho *(Moko)* while the district of Bani (Bonny) borders on the south of Mogho *(moko)* (Dapper, 1668, 1676:135; Barbot, 1732: 380; Jones, 1963:36).

By this geographical description, Dapper precisely identified Mogho, a south-western Ogoni town in the Gokana area, whose market was located at Gbee (Gia, 26, Tapes Og/sk/27-28, 8.2.84).

A glance at map 6 of this book will show that Dapper's description was very precise for an easy identification of his *"Moko"*. By that description, it was clear that Mogho, a coastal Gokana town in the south-west district of Ogoni was the place that the Europeans (i.e the Dutch) first saw an iron money in circulation at Gbee market.

However, by some unexplainable mystery, some scholars have completely ignored Dapper's geographical data and have relied on speculation. For example, Northrup thinks that Dapper's *"Moko"* refers to Ibibio (*ibid* 1978:159), and Noah states that *"moko"* is Ibibio (*Ibid* 1980:3). Others have speculated that Dapper's *"Moko"* should be somewhere in southern Igboland (Jones, 1963:36).

Assuming that *"Moko"* is *"Ibibio"*, that "Ibibio "is not a market place, and not bordered (or contiguous) on the north-west by Okrika and was not bordered (or contiguous) on the south by Bonny, only the town of Mogho in Gokana in the south-west of Ogoni, satisfies this description. On the other hand, the term *"Moko"* in general is not a proper name of Ibibio people. According to G.I. Jones, the term *"Moko"* was an abusive word by the eastern Igbo against the Ibibio, which the Ibibio detested and rejected. The abuse was intended to mock the sound of their speech. The eastern Igbo person would say, *"Nwam Moko"*, meaning *"Moko"* child or *"Moko"* person (Jones, 1963). Such derogatory expressions did not exist at the time of Dapper, so, reference to such derogatory expression in the context of Dapper's geographical data is ahistorical.

According to Chief Edward Nwebon Kpea of Mogho Town in Gokana, the Ibibio farm labourers used to come to their town every year at the beginning of the farming season to do farm work. Some of them used to stay on after the farming season had ended in order to do other kinds of labour, such as oil palm cutting. When they had stayed too long, they asked for land where they would build their own labour camp or village, which they were given. Because Gokana people did not know their names individually they called them *"Mogho-Mana"*. The term *"Mana"* is the Ogoni name for the eastern Igbo people, such as the Abriba, Abam, Arochuku, Ohafia, Bende, etc. In the nineteenth century when these peoples spread all over south-eastern Nigeria, the Ogoni did not know their different local names, so the Ogoni identified them by the general name, *Pya Mana*, meaning Eastern Igbo peoples.

Whereas, the Gokana knew that the general Ogoni name for the Ibibio is *"Bibi"*, but in the case of the farm labourers, the Gokana identified them by the geographical area from which they came. So the Gokana called them *"Mogho-Mana"*, meaning "those Ibibios whom the "Mana" called "Mogho". Over time the name passed to the settlement where they stayed. According to the chief:

In the early times, Gokana people used to call Ibibio people *"Mogho-Mana"*. The men were migrant job seekers. When they had stayed too long, they asked for land to stay, which they were given. Their real names where not known, so they called them *"Mogho-Mana"*. Later that name was passed to the town (S/N.4o,Tape No. Og/sk/27,7.2.84.)

Our purpose in citing the above oral evidence is to show that, even the Gokana in Ogoni land knew that the term *"Moko"* was not the proper name of the Ibibio people, but a derogatory name applied to them by the eastern Igbo.

Therefore, Dapper's *"Moko"*, by virtue of its identifiable location and on the basis of the geographical data supplied by Dapper himself, is no other place other than the town of Mogho on the coast of Gokana in the south-west of Ogoniland.

6.3   Origin/ Identity of Dapper's "Kuleba"

(a)   The Towns of Boue and Kwuri

Kwuri towns were located on the coast. The principal town among them was Kwuribue (Dapper's *"Kuleba"*). Other towns in the area were *Barike, Gaen, Lɛɛ, Iloolo, Iboori, Keneke,* and *Nookwuri*. The men did fishing as well as long distance trading by canoes along the coastal waters and on the rivers and creeks. They also practised some agriculture. The women traded on fish and on various kinds of sea foods such as shell fish, crabs and lobsters.

The women of Kwuribue particularly specialised in the making of fine pottery. Kwuribue potters supplied ceramic wares to the peoples of the hinterland as well as to the riverine peoples.

Immediately beyond those coastal towns were a group of inland towns located in the Boue area. Among the towns grouped in this area were *Baraboue, Kako, Keon, Gbamene, Kaboo, Toga, Uwegwere,* and Gbam. The economy of these towns was mainly agricultural. They cultivated yams, cocoyams, aerial yams, peppers, plantains, oil palms, raffia palms, walnuts, and varieties of vegetables, the best known of which were the fluted pumpkins (telfairia). Besides cultivating the minor crops, the women traded on smoked fish, foodstuffs, camwood, and "industrial barks" used for treating palms wine.

Kwuribue ruled all these towns and controlled their trade. Dapper described the role of Kwuribue by saying that it is "the principal town in the area, having about eight or nine sub-towns under it and ruled by a governor, who boasted that he controlled the coastal trade as far as Sangama" (Dapper, 1676:135; Jones,1963:36). Dapper's description corroborates with the oral tradition. For example, one oral source states:

> There were many great men in Kwuribue. Men like Gbenegarakara, Gbenetigina, Yoko, Genegoo, Gbenekarayoo, etc. Gbenegoo was from Kwuri. Those who founded towns and owned the land were Gbenekanayoo, who founded Tego; Gbenegarakara, who founded Eepie; Gbenetigina, who founded Kwaakwa; and Gbenetibarakaan, who founded Nobana (Inayo, S/No 33, Tape No 0g/sk/5, 7.3.84.).

Thus, Dapper's *"Kuleba"* was Kwuribue

(b) The Effect of the Baan Wars on Kwuribue

During the 16th century, a long drawn civil war broke out in Ogoni between the towns north of the Luubaara River and the towns south of it. In the south, the war was called the "Baan wars". The northern forces over-ran the south. Many southern towns were deserted, especially those that lay on the coast and on the ancient trade routes from the north. Even Kwuribue was severely threatened, as the northern armies came by land and by sea via the Imo River. Eventually, Kwuribue was evacuated to a new site further inland in the Boue area.

One of the defence measures adopted during the war was the digging of deep trenches round the towns. According to Chief Kpoko Kinanwii, every man and woman in Boue was tasked to dig the trenches, and anyone who failed was fined severely.

From these reports, we gathered enough hints that the natural defences of Kwuribue was badly inadequate. For example, there is a reference to being "in a mighty sea". It would appear that the flat, sea level nature of the site of Kwuribue did not permit the digging of deep trenches for defence purposes.

We have suggested the sixteenth century, possibly the latter part of the sixteenth century, as the date of this war because of information contained in the oral tradition, which we have corroborated with a written document. The oral tradition states that the one single event that finally brought the war to an end was the introduction of firearms into Bonny at that time by the Europeans. From Bonny, the Boue leaders obtained the firearms and won the war (Kinanwii S/No.39, Tape No.og/sk/11-12 5.1.84.) K.O Dike has dated this event to the sixteenth century (Dike, 1956: 105.).

6.4 Origin of the Duplication of Place-names: "Old" and "New" Calabar"

The name "new Calabar" was given by the early European travellers to the Kalabari town of Buguma on River Rio Real, and the name "old Calabar" to the Effik town of Calabar on the Cross River estuary. According to G.I. Jones (1963), and E.J. Alagoa (1972), the Europeans first established trade on the Rio Real before they established trade on the Cross River estuary. If that was the chronological order, why then did they call the Kalabari town "New" (instead of "old") Calabari? And the Effik town "old" (instead of "New") Calabar? And why did they give the two trading towns the same name "Calabar"? It is clear that a confusion occurred. This confusion, therefore, is what we intend to clear.

As explained in chapter five, the early Portuguese first traded with Ogoni town of Bangha, where they saw real market system in existence.

According to Pereira, most places they saw along the Guinea coast were empty spaces except for a few fishing locations. At that time, the town of Buguma (new Calabar), Okrika and Bonny did not exist, as Pereira did not mention or describe them. By the sixteenth, seventeenth century, when the Dutch displaced the Portuguese on the Guinea coast, Buguma, Okrika and Bonny had come into existence, having been attracted by the anchorage of European ships in the region.

Thus when Dapper described the location of Mogho *(Moko)*, a Gokana town in the south-west of Ogoni, he used Okrika and Bonny as reference points. Similarly, when describing Kwuribue *(Kuleba)*, another Ogoni town on the coast, Dapper referred to all other towns in the region, including Bonny and Okrika as sub-towns under Kwuribue *(Kuleba)*, whose governor controlled the sea coast from the Bight of Bonny to Sangama (Dapper, 1676:135; Jones, 1963: 36).

Another Ogoni town with which the early Portuguese did business was Kabangha on the great bend of the Imo River.

According to Ardener, the Portuguese described Kabangha as the "people who live at the back of the river" (Ardener, 1968:97). Significantly enough, the Portuguese knew the name of Kabangha, though they did not pronounce it right. They variously called *"Kalbarch"* (Ardener, 1968:97), *"Calbanges"* (Dapper, 1686:316), *"Calborgh"* (Ogilby, 1670:483), and *"Kalbanges"* (Ardner, 1968:96) (see Table V).

(a) Effect of the Smallpox Epidemic and the Baan Wars

It will be recalled that both Pereira, Dapper and the Barbots described Ogoni people as "war-like" "rarely at peace". Thus, while the early Portuguese traded with these Ogoni towns, the Baan wars disrupted Ogoni society. Earlier on, the smallpox epidemic had decimated Bangha market and society (see chapter five). Then the Baan wars caused Kwuribue *(Kuleba)* to be evacuated. It will be recalled that it took a long while (perhaps several years) for the Portuguese or the Dutch to make a return trip to the Niger Delta markets. In the sixteenth century also, the mercantile rivalry in Europe saw the Dutch in ascendancy in which they displaced the Portuguese in West Africa, particularly in the Niger Delta. The English followed suit in the seventeenth century as indicated by the appearance of the Barbots in West Africa. Meanwhile, the Kalabari town of Buguma (New Calabari) had emerged in the region as a market. The Dutch called the Kalabari market *"Kalbarien"* but it did not match the description laid down by Pereira for the "very large village" (Bangha), so they were not satisfied with the Kalabari market. They continued to search toward the east of Rio Real, particularly east of the eastern arm (the Bonny River) for the "old" markets. (Bangha and Kabangha on the coast of Ogoni). In the process, they came to the Cross River estuary and discovered the Effik market. There upon, they assumed the Effik market to be the "old" Bangha and Kabangha markets (on the Ogoni coast). So they called the Cross River market the "old" market and the Rio Real market in Kalabari, "new" market. Because of the physical presence of the Kalabari at this time, they adapted *"Kalabarien"* (Kalabari or Calabar) as the common name for the two markets, without knowing that they had passed the "old" (or Bangha and Kabangha) markets on the Ogoni coast, which were then no longer functioning as a result of the smallpox epidemic and the Baan wars.

The above is the explanation of the confusion which arose among the European trades in the Niger Delta that resulted in the duplication of the place-name "Calabar" and the use of qualifying adjectives "new" and "old".

CHAPTER SEVEN

TRADITIONS OF ORIGIN

Ogoni traditions of origin are few. Most of the traditions refer to settlements and migrations within Ogoni itself. Only few of the traditions make references to external places of origin. These fall into two groups:

(1) Those that refer to a Ghana origin, and
(2) Those that refer to an Ibibio origin.
(3) The third category of traditions of origin are the traditions of autochthony.

These three categories of traditions constitute the Ogoni traditions of origin. We shall discuss these sets of traditions in order, beginning with the traditions of autochthony.

7.1 Traditions of Autochthony

The great majority of Ogoni traditions of origin belong to this category of traditions. In this type of traditions, there are no references to migrations from any place outside Ogoni territory. When they say that their ancestors came from such and such a place to found a community or town, they do not mean that they migrated from somewhere outside the immediate area. Such traditions are rightly designated as traditions of autochthony. A typical example is given by A'ean Gbigbo, who claims that:

> Gbeneitekina was one of the original ancestors who first came into this world. He first settled at Baraboue, having cleared part of that area. They did not come from a different part of the world into that place. They were naturally there from the beginning of the world. No other people had settled at Baraboue before them. They were the only people who ever settled at Baraboue (Gbigbo, tape 21, 27 Dec., 1983).

Examining the traditions of autochthony, we notice that these traditions are held by those who no longer remember their place of origin. They have come to believe that Ogoni was settled from the beginning of the world, as there is no indication of migration from anywhere outside the area. To them, the ancestors did not come from a different part of the world into Ogoni territory.

It has been observed that this type of tradition is an indication of long settlement. The people have been settled in the area for so long that "they have completely lost all memory of earlier migrations from anywhere outside the general area in which they now live" (Onwuejeogwu, 1979).

7.2 Traditions of Ibibio Origin

Several informants narrated a number of traditions which might be regarded as traditions of Ibibio origin. One informant gave two radically contradictory versions of this tradition; one in 1981 and another in 1984. This was Benedict Yomii, who claimed that two men from Ibibioland crossed the Imo River and founded the town of Ko (Opuoko) on the west bank of the river. In an interview in 1981, he gave the following version:

> The origin of Ko (Opuoko) began when two brothers came from Ibibio and crossed the Imo River. One of them settled at Baene, the other at Ko. The man who settled at Ko built a hut by the river. While there, he met another man who had settled on the land. When the man who had settled on the land demanded to know who he was, he introduced himself as a "friend," which in Kana language means "Koo." The two men lived together. Gbenesaagba was the name of the man who had settled on the land. As they settled together, Gbenesaagba continued to call the man on the bank of the river "my friend" *(Koo)*. (Yomii, 21st Oct., 1981).

When he was interviewed again in 1984, it was observed that his version has undergone considerable changes.

> Two friends who were hunters came across the Imo River and settled on this side. One of the men settled at Ko (Opuoko), the other at Baene. The friend who settled at Ko was called "Konee," while the one who settled at Baene was called "Baenee." When they first arrived, they did not see any person in these parts. Some Ko people can speak Ibibio language and dance their dances. Similarly, some Ibibio people can speak Kana language and dance Kana dances. Kana people marry wives from Ibibio but the Ibibio do not marry wives from Kana (Ogoni). Apart from these two men who migrated to this side in the earliest times, no other Ibibio people migrated to this place.... It seems that those who first settled on this side did not allow other Ibibios to settle here. Even those who crossed over and attempted to settle here were driven back (Yomii tape 24, 15th Mar. 1984).

In 1981, the informant spoke about two brothers; in 1984, he tells us that the settlers were two friends. In 1981, their names were not known, but in 1984, their names are given as "Konee" and "Baenee," and the names of the towns were said to have been derived from their personal names. In 1981, the informant told us that when the two men arrived, they discovered that one called Gbenesaagba had already settled on the land. In 1984, however, the position is that when the men arrived, they did not see or find anybody on the land. If these contradictions were given by different informants, they would probably be regarded as variants.

The informant maintained that there were no contradictions in the two versions. He claimed that there were two separate settlements by two different groups. The 1981 account dealt with the group of settlers which settled at Ko, while the 1984 account had in view the group that settled at Baene. According to him, the two groups later established contacts and agreed among themselves that Ko should be their centre or bond of unity (Yomii tape 23/B, 2nd Dec. 1990).

Another version of the traditions of Ibibio origin is given by J.B. Obuh concerning the founding of Kabangha, another Ogoni town located on the west bank in the great bend of the Imo River. According to this version:

> The founder of Kabangha was Gbene Oleghere. Oleghere was his father. He lived in Ibibioland, where he was a hunter. He crossed the Imo River from Ibibioland by canoe. After he had found a good land for settlement, he went back to take his wife. On a certain day, he saw smoke in the forest. When he approached the place he saw a man named Namayo, who had settled there. Namayo told him that he came from Kugba Sii. Namayo told the story that he fled from his town because they accused him that he was a sorcerer. The two men became the rulers of Kabangha, and they caused the town to grow and expand. Gbene Oleghere became the "leader" and Namayo became his second or deputy. If they decided on something to do in the town, Namayo was the person who appointed those to carry out the tasks. Today, it is the members of the lineage of Namayo, who control or bear the town's basket (Obuh tape 24, 15.3.84).

The name Gbene Oleghere is really Gbeneoleghere. It is a titled Ogoni name. The informant gave it as separate names. Ibibio names do not bear the *Gbene* title and are not so constructed. The *Gbene* title suggests that the bearer had been to Nama or that he came originally from there or from Kugba.

The statement that Gbeneoleghere went back to Ibibioland to "bring" his wife, is probably a reference to a long distance "marriage." This type of marriage or slave trade was common among titled men.

The name Namayo is Ogoni. The evidence suggests that he was the first to settle at Kabangha. The fact that there is no title in his name seems to confirm the story that he was a fugitive running away from accusations of witchcraft and sorcery at Kugba. This problem handicapped him from assuming the full control and rulership of the territory in which he was the first settler. His problem was that he could not go back to Nama to perform the traditions for the *Gbene* title which could have given him the authority to be the ruler of the territory. In ancient Ogoni, one could not become the founder or ruler of a territory or town without the *Gbene* title. On the other hand, a person who was not a founder of a town or territory, on achieving the *Gbene* title at Nama, automatically became a ruler in the town in which he lived and owned and ruled the piece of country where he lived.

MAP 4 - Internal Migrations and Expansion of Settlements

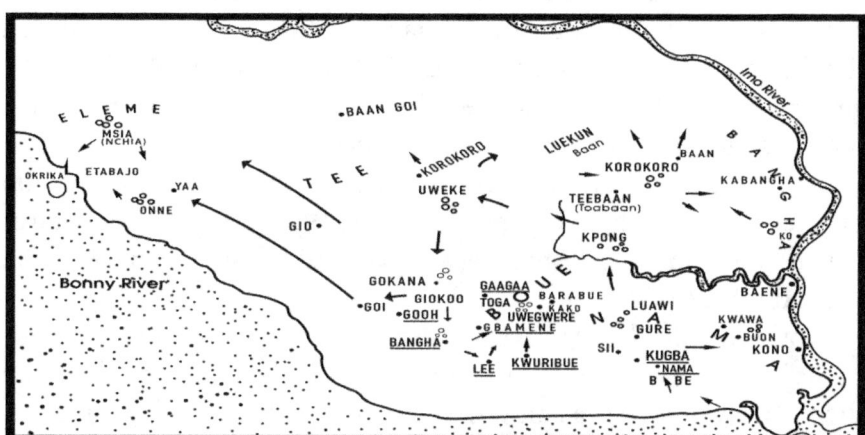

It appears that an agreement was reached between Namayo and the newcomer, Gbeneoleghere so that the latter performed the founding traditions and rituals and received the rulership while Namayo occupied the second but powerful position of *La-Bue* (prime minister) and had the control of agriculture and revenue as land priest (or keeper of the town's basket). It is important to point out here that in Ogoni polity, the post of land priest was usually reserved for an autochthonous lineage. The fact that Namayo holds this position in addition to the town's basket confirms that he was probably the first to settle in the town.

The next tradition of Ibibio origin to be considered is the one by Edward Kpea who claims that he heard from the old people how the town of Mogho in Gokana was founded:

> According to what I heard from the old people, certain two men on their journey, came to Gbenesaako, having come from Ibibioland *(Bibi)*. The two men were brothers. Gbenesaako brought the two men to this place (Mogho). He gave the land of Mogho to one and the land of Kpoo to the other. Because they came from Ibibioland, they called them "Mogho-Mana." That was how this town came to get the name "Mogho". In the early times, Gokana people used to call Ibibio people "Mogho-Mana." The men were migrant job seekers *(pya sitam kpugi)*. When they had stayed too long, they asked for land where to stay, which they were given. So they called them Mogho-Mana. Later the name was passed on to the town (Kpea, tape 27, 7 Feb., 1984).

It is not certain that the Gokana used to call the Ibibio "Mogho-Mana" at that time. The general name by which the Ogoni called the Ibibio from very ancient times is *"Bibi."* The term *"Mana"* is the general name the Ogoni called the Eastern Igbo peoples, which includes the Aros, the Abiriba, the Ohafia, etc.

But the term "Mogho" was a term given by these Eastern Igbo peoples to their Ibibio neighbours (Jones, 1963:32), but it was a term which the Ibibios detested because it was abusive (Baikie, 1956; Simmon, 1956).

Now why did the Ogoni call the migrant farm workers "Mogho-Mana" instead of Bibi? It is here suggested that they did not call them *"Mogho-Mana"* as an ethnic name or ethnic identity but as a geographical description of their place of origin, namely, that they came from that part of Ibibioland which the Eastern Igbo people (or the *"Mana"*) call *"Mogo"* (Mogho), i.e. the *Mogho* of the *Mana (Mogho-Mana)*.

If these men were migrant farm workers, it means that they came annually during the period of heavy farm work, especially during the bush clearing period. Those of them who could not return annually settled in a camp in the suburb of the town and engaged themselves in other jobs such as palm fruit cutting. Such a settlement of Ibibio migrant farm workers would be called *"Mogho* camp," or *"Mogho-Mana* camp."

Eventually, the place became a town, although not a town of Ibibio settlers but of Gokana people, who absorbed the small Ibibio settlers. In the mean time, the name *"Mogho"* or *"Mogho*-camp" had become permanent. Thus when we examine the king list of *"Mogho,"* we notice that the term *"Mogho"* does not appear in the list. Accordingly, Gbenekpegbara is listed as the first ruler of Mogho.

The coming of the migrant farm workers is placed in the time of Gbenesaakoo. Is it possible that there could have been contacts between Ogoni and Ibibio in the time of Gbenesaakoo? This question could be answered in the affirmative because of certain evidence in the oral traditions. First, we noticed above in the founding of Kabangha, that one of the founders, Gbeneoleghere was said to have gone to "marry" a wife from Ibibioland. Secondly, it is reported in Gokana oral tradition that there was a bitter quarrel between Gbenesaakoo and his brother, Boonen, because it was alleged that the latter committed adultery with the former's wife. When the incident was discovered, Boonen was said to have escaped to Ibibioland. However, the location of Ibibioland at that time was probably not the same as what it is in the twentieth century. According to Ogoni oral tradition, Ibibioland was more to the north of Ogoni than to the east, and Igboland, in particular Asa, was still much more to the north than where it is today.

Our final consideration for traditions of Ibibio origin is the account of John Tigiri, who states that the founders of Gwaara towns (Map 4) came from Ibibioland across the Imo River. According to him, the Imo River at that time was a very small river so that people could wade across it on foot. He states:

> I will tell you what I heard and how I heard it. I heard that the founders of the three Gwaara towns and some others came from Ibibio. When they came they crossed the Imo River. At that time the Imo River was not big, so that they could wade across it on foot into the land which we know today as Ogoni, and into this part known as Babbe. The first place they settled was at Nama, where they stayed for many years. After they moved from Nama, they advanced into the hinterland and there they spread to all directions. Thus, Nama in Babbe was the first settlement of Ogoni people. Nama was situated on the coast very near to the present site of Sii Town (Tigiri tape 14, 10th Mar., 1984).

This tradition accepts the traditions about the settlement of Nama as a historical fact. Nevertheless, our examination of the names of the founding ancestors of Gwaara towns does not reveal any Ibibio origin.

The notion that Ogoni was settled at a time when the Imo River was a little stream which could be crossed on foot, suggests age. It could also refer to a period when the bed of the river was filled or raised in certain places and narrowed and deepened in others, due to the geological structure of its terrain. A similar view has been noted in connection with the settlement of some autochthonous groups in Igboland (Afigbo, 1974).

7.3 Traditions of Old Ghana Origin

Concerning the traditions of old Ghana origin, Doonee Nwigbue Fogho had this to say:

> The founders of Bara Sii were two brothers, Gbeneguasoo and Gbeneyaanwaaka. The latter was the second son. According to the tradition, they came originally from "Ghana" and settled at Nama.
>
> Their occupation was hunting and agriculture. The first of them to arrive in Sii was Gbeneberezi. Later, Gbeneteetagana took over the leadership of the government of the town because Gbeneberezi had become deformed in the nose, and could no longer give the leadership. Gbenesirakinaebia was the next person who joined in the founding of Sii.
>
> He founded a separate town which later became part of Sii. The part he founded was called Ebia Sii. Gbeneteetagana founded Nyowii Sii. Gbeneyaanwaaka and Gbeneguasoo were co-founders of Bara Sii. Later, Gbeneyaanwaaka moved to found Yeghe Sii. Gbenemene Nama was the highest ruler in Nama. He ruled with a council of chiefs. Among others who also came from Ghana were Gbeneyaanwaaka, Gbenesaakoo, Gbenekuapiedam and Gbeneyaaloo. Gbeneakpana moved to Kónò and founded the town of Kónò (Fogho, 21st Oct., 1981).

Apart from the details about the founding of Sii, the most important piece of information in the above account is that part of the narrative which states that these leaders came originally from Ghana and settled at Nama. Another important information in the account is that which says that their occupation was hunting and agriculture.

Finally, we noticed that others, including Gbeneyaanwaaka, Gbenesaakoo, Gbenekuapiedam and Gbeneyaaloo, were also mentioned as having come from Ghana. Gbenesaakoo was mentioned in other traditions as the founder and ruler of Gokana. Similarly, Gbenekuapiedam was mentioned in connection with the founding of Tee. Gbeneyaaloo is generally acknowledged in Nama and Gure sources as the general leader and founder of Nama, Kugba and Gure (Map 4). In this account, the informant simply mentioned him as one of the leaders who came from Ghana.

And Tuanee Birinee gave his own version as follows:

> Gbeneyaanaa was among the early Ogoni ancestors who migrated from Ghana to settle at Nama. They migrated from Ghana because of civil war. The men were hunters and medicine men. They were also warriors and spirit-mediums. From them the institution of priests, spirit-mediums and medicine men was established and propagated in Ogoni (Birinee 18th Oct., 1981).

In his own account, John Iwagbo describes an incident which occurred at the arrival of the ancestors on Teenama River en-route to Nama:

> When they came, they came by sea in canoes. As they approached Teenama, they saw a rock which grew out of the water and hung above it. There was a passage through the rocks. As they piloted their canoes through the little passage, the bow of the canoe hit against a rock and broke but the canoe did not capsize. Because of that incident they called that place *Nyo eba fah* ("on the broken canoe"). The place is near the village of Teenam. From there they continued their journey until they arrived at Nama. They disembarked at Nama and established their first settlement there. That rock is there till today (Iwagbo, tape 18, 24.3.84).

This informant mentioned other names in addition to the leaders named above by informant No. 16 (Mr. Fogho). It was this informant, Mr. Iwagbo, who told the story that Gbenegaragiri died en-route at sea, it was he who showed to the writer what he called the latter's grave at Nama. At Kugba, he visited the shrine of Gbeneyiranam in a farm where he poured libations. He mentioned two women who were among the group, one of whom became the mother of Gbeneakpana the younger, who was born at Kugba and who became the founder of Kónò Town (Map 4) on the Imo River.

He explained that the oldest man among the leaders when they arrived at Nama was Gbeneakpana, the elder, who was the maternal uncle of Gbeneakpana the younger, Gbeneyiranam being his blood father. According to him, the siting of the settlement at Kugba was at the instance of Gbeneakpana the elder who summoned a meeting in connection with the matter.

Furthermore, he explained that at Kugba, Gbeneyiranam discovered an autochthonous spirit indwelling a standing rock in the forest some distance away. The spirit spoke out of the rock and gave its name as *"Yogurezogomo."* The three leaders: Gbeneyaaloo, Gbeneakpana the elder and Gbeneyiranam secretly worshipped this deity in the forest. Thence Gbeneyiranam became its first priest. According to him since that time, this autochthonous deity has continued to possess people from generation to generation.

When eventually the forest was cleared and Sii Town was founded there, the deity became the town deity of Sii. Today, it is called *Bari-Sii* (God of Sii). According to the informant, his own father and grandfather, Kina, were possessed by the diety and at the time of interview, he himself was the spirit-medium of the deity and of the spirits of Nama and Kugba.

According to him, the details about the founding ancestors of Nama and Kugba have been revealed by this autochthonous spirit during possession sessions, and that he had heard a lot of the details narrated at such possession sessions and from his father and grandfather.

Finally, in the account of D.D. Deemua, we gather that his own ancestor, Gbeneitekina, was among the original settlers at Nama, having come from Ghana. He states:

> My father was Ikpuru. I heard words from my father, Ikpuru. Deemua and Ikpuru were brothers of the same father and mother. Their elder brother was Koo Deenwa. Ikpuru told me that he heard all these things from Koo Deenwa concerning the beginning of Gbam Boue. There was war between the peoples of Zaakpon, Wiiyaakara, Baan and Kpong. The war spread to Sogho and then to Boue. People scattered in every direction seeking places of shelter from the crisis. For all Ogoni people came originally from a place called Ghana. It was from there that they settled at Nama. From Nama, they began to spread. It was at that time that Gbeneitekina came from Nama and settled at Gbam Boue. The section he first settled at was called Keon (Deemua, tape 23, 5th Dec., 1983).

According to this informant, all Ogoni people came originally from a place called Ghana. Apparently, he does not have the slightest idea where the place is. He only provides a chain of transmissions through which he got his information and seems to have a certain conviction and certainty about his evidence.

Moreover as shown earlier under early system of marriage, the Ogoni were matrilineal; ancient Ghana also were matrilineal.

Intelligence report by the colonial administrators suggest that the transition from matrilineal to patrilineal system of marriage in Ogoni was not yet complete.

The Reverend Kingston, a missionary, was quoted to have observed that because the Ogoni languages lacked inflection and expressed possession by placing the thing possessed before the possessor in the genitive, they could be classified as belonging to the Sudanese group. Professor Watermann who was said to have discussed the Ogoni languages with Reverend Kingston in 1929, was reported to have found resemblances spoken on the former Gold Coast (now Ghana). The inference the intelligent report concluded is that the Ogoni migrated from an area much further north, probably at a time of expansion by the desert peoples (Gibbons, 1932).

Secondly, a cliché found in Ogoni oral tradition *(du Bari le nee* "the trade of God and men", i.e. the "Silent Trade") shows that the Ogoni ancestors had carried with them from their place of origin a story about the "silent trade", first described by the Greek historian, Herodotus, in the fifth century BC. According to Herodotus, the "silent trade" took place between the Carthaginians of North Africa and the Africans of the Upper Guinea Coast or old Ghana Empire (Rawlinson: 1862:144, 196).

Thirdly, in the fifteenth century A.D., a Portuguese named Duarte Pacheco Pereira, visited the Eastern Niger Delta and described a people (now identified as Ogoni) whom he saw there as "war-like", and noted that their weapon was not like any he had seen elsewhere, except that it was "like those of the white Moors of Berbery" (Kimble, 1937:31-32). It is most likely that the Ogoni ancestors obtained this weapon during the period they engaged in the "silent trade" with the Carthaginians of North Africa.

Fourthly, in an article titled, "A Reconsideration of the Mane Invasions of Sierra Leone" (*Journal of African History,* Vol. viii, 2 (1967), 219-246), Walter Rodney has described a similar story which took place in the same region of Old Ghana Empire. In the story, Rodney referred to a report by the Portuguese traveller, Dornelas, who collected it from the elders of Sierra Leone, as tradition handed to them by their grandparents. They told the story of invasions some centuries back, of a people of the Old Ghana Empire, whom they called the *"Manes"*, whose army was commanded by a woman. The account states:

> The original Chief of the *Manes* was a woman. She was a leading lady in Mandimansa, Marcarico by name, who offended the emperor and had to leave the city. She took with her large numbers of friends relatives and dependents, who were transformed into a conquering army. This army overran vast territories and many nations, and the ranks were swelled with recruits... When she reached the Atlantic, she divided the army into three parts: one part marched along the coast, the second part marched parallel to it some forty miles inland, the third part marched equidistant on the right flank (Quoted by Rodeny, 1967:224).

It is interesting to notice the close extent the above description corroborates with Ogoni oral tradition recorded by Sonpie Kpone-Tonwe (1990, 55-99; 69-71). This raises some pertinent questions: Were the Ogoni ancestors part of the *Mane* army? Who were the *Manes*? Was Kwaanwaa the commander of the Ogoni expeditionary army, the same woman as Lady Marcarico, the commander of the *Mane* army? When did these events take place? The answer to these questions will require a separate investigation, a task which is beyond the scope of the present enterprise.

7.4 Linguistic Evidence

In 1959, after a comparative study of Niger Delta languages, Hans Wolff classified Ogoni languages as a distinct language group within the Benue-Congo branch of African languages (Wolff, 1959:32, 1964:38).

Further comparative studies by Williamson resulted in her postulate that the Ogoni ancestors migrated from an easterly direction into the Niger Delta fringe before 2,000 years ago, and that they had been settled in the area for that long (Williamson, 1988:95). Furthermore in the same study, Williamson classified Ogoni as a distinct language within the Delta-Cross sub-branch of Cross River branch in the New Benue-Congo family of the Niger-Congo phylum (Williamson, 1988:68, 71).

However, historians have often raised the question, "Is language a sure means of determining the origin of a people?" (Afigbo, 1965). This question may perhaps be relevant for Ogoni in view of the overwhelming claim of the oral tradition to the contrary.

7.5 Archaeological Excavations at Nama

Some archaeological excavations were done at Nama in 1985 by A.A. Derefaka. The finds excavated consisted mainly of numerous potsherds, a few pieces of burned bricks, a decorated smoking pipe and a bead. Professor A.A. Derefaka sent four charcoal samples from the Nama sites to Beta Analytic Inc. Miami, Florida, USA, for radiocarbon dating. The C14 dates obtained are shown in Table VI below:

Table VI: **Result of Archaeological Dating of Nama**

Sample Data	Measured Radiocarbon Age	13C/12C Ration	Conventional Radiocarbon Age
Beta – 355377 Sample: UPMN – SAD 0001	140+/-30BP	-25.0 0/00	140+/-30BP
Beta – 355378 Sample: UPMN – SAD 0002	190+/-30 BP	-27.8 0/00	140+/-30 BP
Beta – 355379 Sample: UPMN – SAD 0003	250+/-30 BP	-22.9 0/00	280+/-30 BP
Beta – 355380 Sample: UPMN – SAD 0003	360+/-30 BP	-27.4 0/00	320+/-30 BP

For more details see Appendix VI

In Table VI above, the result of the first two samples show the earliest date of 140+/-30, which gives a date of 110A.D. In archaeological terms, this date should be regarded as the earliest date of settlement of Nama. Also, this date is closer to the linguistic dating by Professor Kay Williamson, in 1985, when she stated that the Ogoni ancestors entered Ogoni territory from an easterly direction before 2000 years ago. Counting backwards from 1985, we arrived at a date of before 15 B.C. (Williamson, 1988:95).

Based on Williamson prognosis, we may suggest that the Ogoni ancestors did not settle in Ogoni territory in the first instance after they moved from their country of origin and arrived in the Bight of Bonny, but that they first settled somewhere in the east, probably in the Cameroon region. And that after some years, they moved again as a result of some crisis. This time, they traced steps back and settled in Ogoni territory at Nama. If this prognosis is correct, then their stay in the east affected their language somewhat, but it did not alter or absorb it. That is why the Ogoni languages are classified as unique in their present location.

However, the likelihood exists that the Ogoni ancestors settled at Nama earlier than 110 A.D. for the following reasons: first, because linguistic evidence puts Ogoni settlement at Nama to a date before 15 B.C. (Williamson, 1985); second, because the Ogoni ancestors carried on their oral tradition of the classic story of the "silent trade", which was first reported by the Greek historian, Herodotus' writing in the fifth century B.C.; and third, because the charcoal samples now dated might not represent the earliest charcoal burned at Nama by the Ogoni ancestors. For these reasons, more archaeological excavations will be needed, especially at Kugba, Nama.

7.6 Archaeological Dating from Other Niger Delta Communities

Dr. N. Nzewunwa did some excavations at Okochiri located on the southern borders of Eleme in 1976 and 1977. Radiocarbon dating for the site puts the earliest date of settlement in the ninth century A.D. (i.e. A.D. 940 ± 80), or about 850 A.D. (Nzewunwa, 1980:238).

In 1974, F.N. Anozie excavated some test pits at Ogoloma, Okrika. The radiocarbon dating for this site showed the earliest date of settlement in about 1250 A.D. Among the finds were 100 smoking pipes (mainly locally made), brass and ivory bangles, pots, bowls, arca shells, manillas, etc. (Anozie, 1976; Nzewunwa, 1983:105).

Dr. Anozie had earlier done excavations at Onyoma and at Ke

in 1973. Radiocarbon dating for these sites put the earliest date of settlement at Onyoma to A.D. 1335 ± 85 or about 1250 A.D., and that of Ke to 965 ± 150 B.P. or about 815 A.D. (Anozie, 1973:4; 1976:89). So far, Ke is the oldest Ijo settlement in the Niger Delta; and both Ke and Okochiri are shown to have been settled in the ninth century A.D.

A comparison of the artifacts from these sites do not indicate any connection with Ogoni. Not even one of the hundred smoking pipes excavated at Ogoloma showed any resemblance to the single Nama pipe.

7.7 Conclusions

In studying the origin of a people, a number of factors come into consideration. Factors like language, culture and ethnography must be identified. In our study of the traditions of origin of Ogoni, we dealt with these factors of origin. Three categories of traditions usually linked with the origin of Ogoni were identified. Each tradition in each group was carefully studied and analysed. Our study revealed no trace of Ibibio custom or culture in Ogoni traditions. Consequently, these traditions cannot be jettisoned.

Of the traditions of autochthony, the conclusion is that this type of tradition is common among peoples who have been settled so long in a territory that they hardly can remember having migrated from anywhere else. These traditions therefore suggest long residence of Ogoni in their present territory.

The traditions of Old Ghana origin provide abundant evidence about the ancestors – their names, compounds, descendants, etc. – even their graves are known, and the marriage system was also matrilineal. They gave war as the reason for leaving Old Ghana Empire and described their occupations as hunters, warriors, spirit-mediums, priests, medicine men, etc. Evidence of these descriptions is manifested by their establishment of the war-related institution of the *Gbene* title at Nama, the discovery and adoption of the autochthonous spirit at Kugba and the installation of one of the leaders (Gbeneyiranam) as the priest and medium of that spirit.

The fact that these institutions developed at Nama and Kugba apparently without any indication of transmission or diffusion from outside, appear to confirm the claims of the oral traditions that the ancestors were already the practitioners of these customs and institutions before they arrived in Ogoni.

The possibility exists that these institutions and customs could have developed at Nama. Nonetheless, another explanation for the Old Ghana-related traditions, is that when the Ogoni ancestors migrated from Old Ghana Empire, they first settled somewhere in the region beyond the Cameroons. Then after many centuries, they migrated back again towards the Niger Delta region and settled in Ogoni territory. At that time, the entire Niger Delta region was still a vast uninhabited waste land. That explains why the radiocarbon dating for Nama (110 A.D.) is the oldest in the entire Niger Delta region, older than the oldest Ijo settlement (Ke, 815 A.D) by more than seven centuries.

The linguistic evidence which suggests migration from an easterly direction and affiliation with the New Benue-Congo linguistic family may prove to be the most potent explanation for an earlier settlement of the Ogoni ancestors in the region beyond the Cameroons after migrating from Old Ghana Empire.

CHAPTER EIGHT

SETTLEMENT OF NAMA AND KUGBA

8.1(a) Settlement of Nama

According to studies by Kay Williamson, the Ogoni may have settled at Nama before 15 B.C., counting from 1985 backwards. According to Nama sources, the Ogoni ancestors arrived by sea in canoes. They entered through the Teenama River, a small river flowing south-east into the sea. The direction from which they came is not known. An account in the oral tradition describes an incident which occurred at a point near the present village of Teenama. Here, they saw a rock projecting out of the water and standing high above the surface. They berthed their canoes near the rock and took shelter under it for some days.

The account states that when they left the rocks at Teenama, they attempted to pilot their canoes through a narrow passage between the rocks, as they did so, the bow of the canoe struck against the rocks and a piece of the canoe was broken off, so they named the place *"Nyo eba fah"* (On a piece of canoe). This has since become the name of the place till today.

(i) Some Names of the Founding Ancestors

Certain names were mentioned among the early Ogoni ancestors. Gbeneyaaloo was mentioned as their leader. An old man named Gbeneakpana was mentioned, and a third leader named Gbeneyiranam was also mentioned. Two women were specifically mentioned. The first was called Kwaanwaa or Gbenekwaanwaa. It is said that she was the ruler of their former country before they fled from there during a war. She commanded the expeditionary party until the position was taken over by her son, Gbeneyaaloo, after he attained the age of maturity. The other woman mentioned was called Yaagunwaa. Kwaanwaa was described as the mother of Gbeneyaaloo and Za. Za later became famous in Ogoni oral tradition for child-bearing. She received the praise name of "Mother of Ogoni people."

Yaagunwaa was also mentioned in connection with child-bearing. She was reported to have given birth to Gbeneakpana the younger at Kugba. One report said that Gbeneakpana the elder was the father of Gbeneakpana the younger. Other reports assert that Gbeneyiranam, the second man in command of the expedition, was his blood father. However, from his family name and from what we know about the marriage system at that time, we think that Gbeneakpana the elder was his maternal uncle and that Gbeneyiranam was really his blood father. The mention of these women and the role they played emphasised the matrilineal character of their polity.

In childhood, Gbeneakpana the younger was reported to have been very wild and troublesome - "a child who gave much trouble to the people at Kugba." However, as an adult, he was cited in the oral tradition as a fierce swordsman and a brave warrior. He is credited as the founder of the town of Kónò on the Imo River.

(ii) The Early Society

The Ogoni colonists appear to have settled down immediately to create a community at Nama. Agriculture seemed to have been their immediate pre-occupation. Evidence from oral tradition which states that they carried *ega* (pointed iron weapons or javelins) was confirmed from test excavations at Nama which revealed fragments of iron tools and weapons. With such tools and weapons they were able to create a settlement in the immediate place of disembarkation. The contrary would have forced them to depend solely on gathering for survival. In such circumstances, they would have wandered far and wide from their point of disembarkation. For they would have soon exhausted whatever existed in the immediate vicinity. Being a relatively small group, they would have eventually become extinct in the harsh environment or become completely absorbed by the autochthonous groups with whom they later came into contact. The fact that they possessed sea-worthy canoes was an indication that they had the tools and the technology for making them.

With such tools they cleared the forests and cultivated the land. Yam must have been one of their first root crops. With their weapons, they defended themselves against wild beasts, such as pythons and other dangerous snakes, leopards, wolves, elephants and gorillas. According to Nama and Kugba sources, these creatures abounded in the area in the early times.

They also established their religious centre at Nama. This religious system was probably carried over from their country of origin. This appears to be the case because the religious system at Nama was militarily-oriented. According to the oral tradition, the Ogoni ancestors fled their country in a time of war. The account states that when Kwaanwaa, who was the ruling monarch of their country of origin abdicated and fled, a large number of warriors, priests, mediums and medicine men accompanied her. It is to be assumed that some of the religious-cum-military practices which they introduced at Nama were practices connected with war as they knew it in their country of origin. The most important of these rites were those connected with the ultimate title, the *Gbene* title.

One of the important contributions of this religious system was its tendency to unite the Ogoni people culturally from the very early period. For instance, the final rituals for the *Gbene* title was performed only at Nama. This meant that every important Ogoni leader who aspired this title had to make at least one pilgrimage to Nama. Those who succeeded, received the title only at Nama. The result was that a strong cultural and political link was maintained between Nama and all the other parts of Ogoni at the highest level. Besides, under their polity, there developed an organised social system in which men and women of ability enjoyed special status. Firstborn daughters in particular enjoyed special privileges based on the system of succession and inheritance which was matrilineal.

(iii) Oral Tradition and Archaeology

Effort was made to corroborate evidence from oral tradition with the results of test excavations at Nama. Ogoni oral traditions assert that their ancestors had iron tools and weapons; and that they knew about the cultivation of some food crops. Also from oral tradition we gather that the movement from Nama to Kugba and later from Kugba to Wiisoro and finally to Gure (Map 4), was due to rapid population growth and the need for better security.

The period of this evidence probably synchronises with the layers excavated at Nama, which showed the existence of numerous decorated potsherds, fragments of iron tools, quantities of land and sea shells such as oyster shells, cockle shells, Vass shells, arca shells, snail shells, etc. The implication is that with iron tools, they were able to practice agriculture to produce sufficient food to feed their population. The quantity and quality of shell foods they consumed, in addition to bush meat, fish, birds, etc. indicate that they had ample access to rich supplies of protein resources for part of their diet. On the other hand, the presence among them of a large number of trado-medical practitioners (i.e. medicine men, priests and spirit-mediums), meant that there was a measure of healthcare for the population.

These factors accelerated population growth as reported in the oral tradition. The quality and fabric or texture of the ceramic industry at Nama, as indicated by the type of decorations and designs, suggest a level of cultural development which was not merely rudimentary.

As the population of Nama increased, the need for a better site was commonly felt. It was in this connection that it is reported in the oral tradition that the old man, Gbeneakpana, summoned a meeting of the people. Gbeneyaaloo was one of the presiding leaders at this meeting, at which the issue of founding a new settlement was discussed. Gbeneyaaloo was probably the youngest among the leaders at this time. The fact that he did not summon the meeting suggests that his position as "commander-in-chief" at this stage was merely formal. However, he seemed to have assumed full and practical leadership during the settlement at Kugba, as we shall see shortly.

8.1(b) Settlement of Kugba

Kugba was eventually selected as the site for the new settlement. It was located about two to three kilometres north-west of Nama. The movement from Nama to Kugba thus marked the beginning of a process of internal migration and expansion within the Ogoni territory. Kugba seemed to have been a good location. Agriculture continued to be their major occupation.

As life flourished at Kugba, the ancestors continued to maintain their religious links with Nama. Several reasons accounted for this. Nama was the place where they established their religious rituals and ceremonies when they first arrived in Ogoni. Nama became a type of religious holy land to them. It became a memorial place where the memory of the ancestors was kept alive. According to the oral tradition, while they were on sea voyage, an important leader and member of the royal family died and when they arrived at Nama, a "funeral" was held for him.

When I visited the Nama site in 1984, one of the things they showed me was a small shrine covering what was supposed to be that man's grave, which might not have been the original grave. His name was given as Gbenegaragiri. From his name, it is evident that he was a titled man and a member of the ruling class of that society, other members of the expedition may have died also at sea but his own was remembered because of his rank and because he was a member of the royal family. He was said to have been a brother of Gbeneyaaloo, the royal commander of the expedition. Perhaps he was the actual blood father of the royal family or their maternal uncle.

These things made Nama a memorable place in the lives of the ancestors. Nama continued to be a sacred centre for war traditions until recent times. Wherever they migrated, the ancestors returned to Nama to perform some rituals and sacrifices, especially those who became founders of new towns or candidates for the *Gbene* title. Thus Nama remained the only place in Ogoni where the highest title and "power" could be obtained.

As the community at Kugba increased, the need for expansion was again felt. The oral tradition states that Gbeneyaaloo told the people that the town had become too crowded. The report went on to say that the town of Kónò on the Imo River was founded at this time by Gbeneakpana, the younger who was born at Kugba.

The desire for population increase seemed to have dominated the interests of the ancestors in this period. This was only natural for a relatively small group of immigrant colonists in an empty foreign territory.

Contingent on population increase was the issue of territorial expansion, which also dominated the minds of the ancestors. As the population of Kugba increased, individuals and groups were encouraged to found new settlements. This was necessary to obviate any tendency by the people to congregate in one single location. The founding of Kónò by Gbeneakpana within that period was one of the notable responses to this desire.

8.1(c) The Proto-Sii Settlers

In the course of searching the forests for a suitable site for a new town, one of the leaders, Gbeneyiranam, discovered the existence of a "spirit" indwelling a rock in the forest at a place which later became the site of Sii Town. This discovery was kept secret between himself and Gbeneyaaloo. The oral tradition records that the two leaders made this spirit-being their secret object of worship, to which they often resorted for succour and power. The control of this part of the forest by the two men delayed the effective founding of Sii Town until a later date. Some of the ancestors who migrated from Kugba settled in a camp in the neighbourhood of this forest deity. They became the proto-Sii Settlers.

8.1(d) The Founding of Wiisoro and Gure

One of the notable incidents that sped up the urge for founding new towns was a flood which killed some children at Kugba. The flood incident became the immediate cause for the founding of wiisoro by Gbeneyaaloo. With the founding of Wiisoro, a gradual movement of people from Kugba followed. Kwaanwaa now very old, was probably among the first group to move to Wiisoro. There at Wiisoro, the oral tradition reports that Za gave birth to many more children.

While at Wiisoro, Gbeneyaaloo discovered that the site where Gure now stands was even better than Wiisoro. He again took the initiative to clear the site, which was about two kilometres still further inland. Other versions give more reasons for founding Gure. One of such reasons was a prohibition of the women folk by the land deity from giving birth within the town. Pregnant women under labour had to leave the town to a bush where they gave birth under a tree. After delivery, they went back to Nama for a purification bath before they returned to wiisoro with the newborn baby.

As stated earlier on, Za the heir of the royal family, was still bearing children. Gbeneyaaloo, her brother and guardian of her children, was anxious to see that she did not continue under that difficult condition.

According to the account, one of the children born during this period was Gbeneatekina. It is said that he was born at Gure. In another account, Gbeneatekina was mentioned as one of the three leaders who joined Gbeneyaaloo to establish the town of Gure. Given the marriage system in this period, this was probably the elder Gbeneatekina, a maternal uncle of the younger Gbeneatekina, born either at Wiisoro or at Gure. As Gbeneakpana was biographically mentioned in his generation at Kugba, so was Gbeneatekina mentioned in a subsequent generation. The implication is that these families were not only the founding families but they were also the families of significant achievement, whose members became the subjects of the biographical tradition of this period.

Thus, a Gbeneatekina is mentioned as born at Wiisoro and a Gbeneatekina is also mentioned as one of the three notable persons to be associated with Gbeneyaaloo in the establishment of the traditional government at Gure.

> When I had settled down, three other leaders joined me, following my back. These were Gbeneatekina, Gbenetiginagua and Gbeneakaka. They all joined hands together and held the hilt of my sword. Together they planted its tip to the ground. This happened after I had established the town deity and the land deity. Thereupon I appointed Gbeneatekina to be my right-hand man to act as the land priest (Gbeneyaaloo's spirit-medium during possession tape 17, 12.3.84).

This ceremony provides an early information about a traditional public ceremony. Joining hands together on the hilt of a sword and planting it into the ground, is still practised in Ogoni as the sealing of a sacred agreement between two or more parties, especially when one party is a god(s) and the other party men. Usually, when an agreement was sealed in this way, the implication was permanent peace or a stay of action to allow mediation leading to permanent peace. On this occasion, the agreement was between Gbeneyaaloo and three others who were presumably younger leaders. They jointly acknowledged his leadership and authority and solemnly pledged their loyalty. In return, he distributed to them certain positions of leadership and power. The ceremony has within it elements of an arrangement for smooth distribution and transfer of governmental functions in the traditional system. We notice, here the mention of some of the key offices in the Ogoni traditional system. It is pertinent to notice that these three names later appear in the Luawii account as being responsible for the conferment of authority on the Bariyaayoo dynasty at Luawii.

8.2   Expansion from Wiisoro and Gure

In the account of John Tigiri, we gather quite a bit of information about the early internal expansion of the ancestors. According to him, they settled for a long time at Nama (and Kugba) before they moved inland and established at Gure. The latter place became the first watershed of expansions from which "they spread out to all directions" – to Kani-Babbe, Luawii, Gwaara, etc.

Not all the people who moved from Wiisoro settled at Gure. Some of them took other directions and founded other towns. A group from the Wiisoro-Gure nucleus moved west to the Gwaara area and founded the towns of KaGwaara, Luuyo, Bien, Kapyon and Eeke. In the case of Sii Town, the founding did not take place until much later – after the deaths of the top two leaders – Gbeneyaaloo and Gbeneyiranam. As noted earlier on, while at Kugba, these two men discovered an autochthonous spirit which indwelt a rock in the forest. They adopted the spirit and declared the forest a sacred area

(Kue Yo). Gbeneyiram who became the first priest of the deity did not move from Kugba. If, and when he moved, he did not go to either Wiisoro or Gure but to a position nearer to the abode of the deity.

Another person who did not emigrate to Wiisoro or Gure was Gbeneakpana. He stayed closer to help his father, Gbeneyiranam, who was now very old. His maternal uncle, Gbeneakpana the elder, had already died at Kugba and he had inherited his "medicine bag" His father also was the priest of this new, powerful deity. So he kept very close at hand. By now, he himself was already a medicine man.

8.2(a) The Founding of Kónò

In the days of his youth, Gbeneakpana was described as wild and troublesome. But he was also noted as a skilful swordsman. By the time he founded Kónò, he had become older and more experienced. Because he was a man of energy, drive and very ambitious, he frequently went afield to the east hunting. As he went, he discovered a beautiful site in the forest there, which was very good for settlement. He cleared the site and eventually founded the town of Kónò on the Imo River.

By this time, a rumour had already circulated concerning him. When they saw him living so far apart in that forest, they suspected that he was engaged in head-hunting and cannibalism. On the day of "laying the foundation" of the town, he made a speech in which he made an allusion to the rumour-mongers. In the speech, he was quoted to have said:

> When I was going about this business, they said that I was walking the walk of cannibalism. Now here it is. This is the cannibalism *(Kónò)* (Fogho, 21st Oct., 1981).

So from that day, the name of the town was called Kónò (cannibalism). After the founding of Kónò, Gbeneakpana began to concentrate his effort in developing the new town. By this time, his father, Gbeneyiranam had died; so had Gbeneyaaloo of Gure. It is very likely that Gbeneakpana also inherited the "medicine bag" of his father, Gbeneyiranam. From now on, he was to concentrate his effort at Kónò in order to make the new town successful.

8.2(b) The Founding of Sii Town

While these things were taking place at Kónò, something dramatic happened at the place which is now Sii Town. With Gbeneyiranam and Gbeneyaaloo dead, and Gbeneakpana himself also out of the way to where his interest lay, the way was open for some strong-willed individuals to move into the forest of the "secret cult" of the late leaders to take possession of the area and to clear it for settlement. The plan to do this must have been hatched at the funeral of one of the two leaders. It is not known which of the two men died first. Most likely Gbeneyiranam died first because in relative age, Gbeneyaaloo was the younger of the two.

The question of succession to the priesthood of the deity must have been raised secretly at the funeral of Gbeneyiranam. Gbeneakpana was no longer a suitable candidate because he was now the priest of *Yokono,* the deity of his town. Thus, succession to the priesthood of *Yogurezogomo* as the deity was then called, became open to rivalry. But this rivalry seems to have been suppressed until the last of the two leaders had died. Owing to the audacious manner the sacred forest of the deity was invaded and cleared, the action was described as "daring" *(Sii)*. The word became the name of the town, meaning a "daring" or "venturesome" people.

The men were part of a small group who, like Gbeneakpana, did not migrate to Wiisoro or to Gure. They remained in the peripheral area called Nyowii, which was not far from where the priest of the forest deity was staying. Evidently, they were ambitious but they managed to keep up a low profile, waiting patiently for their opportunity. Thus after the death of the last of the two leaders, and the third man had also moved away, they could not delay any longer but to wade into action to take possession of the area.

This explains why the founding of Sii was done by so many persons at the same time like a city invaded by an army from different fronts at the same time, each founder carving out a section into a separate town, with himself as its ruler.

> They first settled at Nyowii. From Yowii they cleared all other parts of Sii. They then divided the area into separate towns with each one of them becoming the founder and ruler of one town. Gbeneanwaaka took Bara and became its ruler.

Gbenesirakinaebia took Ebia and became its ruler. Another leader, Berezi, founded an additional town called Tem and became its ruler. Then Gbeneakaratee cleared another area known as Korogbere and became its ruler (Nwikogbara, tape 9, 8.3.84).

Gbeneteetagana, their leader at Nyowii, which was the peripheral location where they all first settled, not only became the ruler of that place, but he was also given the pride of place as the paramount ruler of Sii. Other names mentioned as having taken part in the action were Gbeneguasoo, in connection with Bara; and Gbeneteenwaawoo, who was said to have settled with Gbeneteetagana, having migrated from Luawii. There are some slight contradictions or variants in the reports. For example, one report states that the first man who settled at Nyowii was Gbeneteetagana, who had two brothers, Gbeneanwaaka and Gbenesirakinaebia. Another report states that the founders of Bara were two brothers, Gbeneguasoo and Gbeneyaanwaaka. Notice that Gbeneanwaaka and Gbeneyaanwaaka are likely to be the same person. Apart from these slight contradictions, the foregoing analysis seems to present a coherent interpretation of events. In terms of relative chronology, Sii appears to have been founded later than Gure, Luawii, Kpong, Gwaara and Kónò.

8.2(c) The Founding of Gwaara

The background to the founding of Sii explains the causes of the wars that took place during the founding of the Gwaara communities. As I have related above, when the movement from Kugba took place, the veteran leader, Gbeneyiranam, did not move completely from that vicinity. Gbeneyaaloo had to move because his aged mother was still alive and he had to take care of her. Besides, the well being of his sister, Za and her many children was his responsibility. In the case of Gbeneyiranam, he did not seem to have any dependents. This was one of the reasons he was the proper candidate to become the priest of the mysterious deity in the "sacred forest". So when the movement from Kugba began, he remained behind in the vicinity of the sacred forest in order to serve the deity in the forest. As would be expected, a small number of servants and attendants remained with him. This group or their descendants formed the nucleus of what might be called the Proto-Sii settlers.

It was this small group of people who rumoured about the movements of Gbeneakpana, that he was a cannibal *(Kónò)*, a term from which the name of the town later derived. It was the same group who attended the foundation ceremony of the new town at which Gbeneakpana was said to have made an allusion to them about their rumours in the speech quoted above.

Since as at that time, their settlement merely existed as a camp; for it had never been classified in the proper way as a town, it and its residents could not be identified by name as a town.

In the local idiom, they were referred to merely as people living "beyond the farmlands" *(Nyowii)*, i.e. the place was outside the farming area of the nearest village or town. But to people farther away, they were regarded as the remnants of Kugba. That was why when Gbeneakpana came from there to found Kónò, it was said in the oral tradition that the founder of Kónò came from Kugba.

> Gbeneakpana was the founder of Kónò. He came from Kugba, He was a priest and medicine man (Opusunju 4, 23.10.81).

Now when emigrants from Wiisoro and Gure moved westwards into the area to found the towns of Gwaara, they clashed with this people who had been there some generations back.

This was the essence of the series of wars between the various Gwaara groups and the Proto-Sii people. The latter, backed by their powerful deity, repulsed the Gwaara settlers and forced them to withdraw their settlements from Wiibara to Luulee and to their present location.

8.2(d) Why the Traditions of Kónò Are of Sii

In their oral tradition, the people of Kónò claim that the founder of their town came from Kugba, yet they also assert that their traditions, customs, and culture are based on those of Sii. The history of the founding of Kónò, as explained above shows why they make such contradictory claims. From the very beginning, the proto-Sii settlers had connections with Kónò through the influence of Gbeneakpana, its founder, who kept contacts between the new town and the proto-Sii people. One factor that kept these contacts alive was the forest deity. When Kónò was founded, the first immigrants were from the proto-Sii people.

As usual with all traditional towns of Ogoni, these immigrants kept contacts with their original home in proto-Sii, especially in connection with the powerful deity worshipped there. It was these proto-Sii people who assisted Gbeneakpana in establishing a town deity called Yokónò in the new town of Kónò. They also depended on the proto-Sii people for defence, trade and for protection. Because of these connections, the traditions, customs and culture of Kónò were bound with those of the proto-Sii and later with those of historical Sii.

8.3   Eastward Expansion

The oral tradition states that the people of Buan made war against Kónò soon after it was founded. Included in the Buan group of towns were Buan, Kpean and Kwaawa. They were a group of towns dotted on a line running eastwards from the Wiisoro-Gure axis. Like those who moved west from the Wiisoro-Gure nucleus to found the towns of Gwaara, they had been founded by those who moved east from the same centre.

They were the same people and knew about Gbeneakpana and about his connection with the powerful deity of the proto-Sii people. Accordingly, their chief invited him to make medicine for them so that his people might be united. The oral tradition states that the whole of that part was a thick forest. As a hunter and medicine man, Gbeneakpana penetrated the forest and discovered that the interior was suitable for settlement and proceeded to establish a settlement there. When the people of the Buan group of towns saw that a new settlement had been established there, they tried in vain to stop it.

From the preceding evidence, we come to the conclusion that the Buan group of towns were founded before Kónò, and Kónò before historical Sii; although Proto-Sii was already in existence when Kónò was founded. Thus in Proto-Sii, the forest deity was known as *"Yogurezogomo"*, the name by which the spirit was said to have revealed itself. In historical Sii, however, it became the land deity and was known as *"Bari Sii"* ("god of Sii"). It became the unifying factor of all the separate parts of Sii. At the time of this study, my informant, John Iwagbo was its priest and medium. And he told me that his grandfather, Kina, had been its priest and medium, and was popularly known as Kina Bari-Sii. (Iwagbo 35, tape 18, 24.3.94).

8.4　Northward Expansion

The greatest number of emigrants from the Wiisoro-Gure axis went northwards to Luawii and Kpong. The oral tradition (Nama and Kugba sources) place Luawii as the second oldest existing town in Ogoni after Gure; and Kpong as the next oldest existing town. According to the evidence, these towns maintained direct linkages connecting the founding ancestors of Ogoni. They stand on the main route of migration and expansion from Nama to Kugba and from Kugba northwards through Wiisoro to Gure and Luawii, and across the Luubaara River to Kpong.

All the towns discussed so far and their subordinate villages constitute the kingdom of Nama, controlled by the original rulers of Nama, Kugba and Gure. Gbeneyaaloo, the founder of Nama, Kugba and Gure, was alive after the founding of Gure. His mother, Gbenekwaanwaa, and his sister, Za, were also alive at the founding of Gure. They all died at Gure and their graves/shrines are all at Gure.

Because the system was matrilineal monarchy, after the death of Gbenekwaanwaa, the succession passed to Za, whose centre of rulership remained at Gure. Under that system, the principal role of sons at that time appears to have been that of the soldier/protector and provider. Gbeneyaaloo fulfilled this role for the royal family, which consisted mainly of his sister's children.

After the death of Za, the succession passed to her first daughter, Bariyaayoo, who established her dynasty at Luawii. From Gure and Luawii, the kingdom of Nama extended its influence to Kpong, which became a big centre of expansion in the area north of Luubaara River (Map 4).

CHAPTER NINE

SETTLEMENT OF KPONG AND OUTLYING DISTRICTS

9.1   The Settlement of Kpong

There are at least two variant accounts about the founding of Kpong. One variant states that the founder of Kpong was one Atee who came from Ban in Tee. It is said that he escaped from Tee after killing his brother. According to the tradition, he and his junior brother were working on a farm with their mother. When their drinking water was exhausted, he asked his junior brother to go and fetch water from the local source. His junior brother refused. He alone went and fetched the water and as soon as he brought the water, his junior brother took from it and drank. Atee became angry and beat his brother. In the fight which resulted, his brother fell on a stake in the farm which fatally pierced him so that he bled to death. When he saw that his brother had died, he fled from Ban. The account concludes that it was during that period that he founded Kpong.

Another Kpong source gives two separate origins of Kpong, one in Tee and the other in Gure. First of all, this source gives an almost identical version of the Atee tradition. Then it adds a statement which points to Gure. This states that Za was another founder of Kpong, but all Kpong sources assert that Atee was a dealer in the Atlantic slave trade. One of the sources tells the story of how Atee at one time contrived to sell his own stepson named Saa into slavery but the plan leaked at Baene and Saa escaped. The account concludes by saying that this incident created a relationship of permanent enmity between Atee and his stepson, Saa. The latter made the river port of Baene (Map 4) his permanent home. In another account, it is stated that Baene itself was founded by Atee, presumably as a slave port and that the population of the town was all colonists (slaves) sent there by Atee.

The reference to commercial slave trading places Atee's time in the era of the Atlantic slave trade, probably in the eighteenth century. It is therefore estimated that the Kpong associated with Atee in the oral traditions is the Kpong of the New Age. A broader discussion of this New Kpong or new dynasty in Kpong is taken up in Chapter 10. For now, we shall focus attention on the Kpong before the era of Atee, which refers to its Gure origins.

9.1(a) Kpong in the Early Age

One of the Kpong sources mentions that Za was another person connected with the founding of Kpong. According to Nama oral tradition, the founder of Kpong came from Gure. This evidence corroborates with the Kpong source which credits the founding of Kpong to Za. As already pointed out, Za was the successor to Gbenekwaanwa. After Za, the succession went to her first daughter, Bariyaayoo, who established her seat at Luawii. In Ogoni, it is generally acknowledged that Gure, Luawii and Kpong are the three oldest towns which have existed until the present.

The preceding evidence suggest that references in Nama and Kpong oral traditions point to an old Kpong chiefdom founded by the early ancestors or by the descendants of Za. Chronologically, this would have followed the founding of Gure and Luawii.

As we have already noticed during the period of the northward expansion, the greatest number of emigrants from the Wiisoro-Gure axis moved towards Luawii and Kpong. These towns maintained direct links with the early ancestors and lay on the main route of migration and expansion from Kugba through Gure and Luawii to Kpong. Kpong therefore became the big centre and the principal link between Nama and all the towns north of the Luubara River.

9.1(b)   Kpong as a Watershed of Expansion

As the population of Kpong increased, many sub-towns were founded in the adjoining territories. A major route from the Kpong nucleus went north-west along the northern banks of the Luubaara River into Tee area. More emigrants from the Kpong nucleus followed this route and settled first at Uweke. From Uweke they spread to other parts of Tee. During the same period, a branch of them moved southwards from Uweke central area into the part now known as Gokana and stopped at Giokoo. It was there at Giokoo that they organised their forces for the conquest of Gokana. The process of conquest and settlement of each of these areas will be discussed in detail as we study them area by area with a view to determining the direction of population movements and territorial expansion.

9.2   Settlement of Tee

Tee oral tradition states that the people of Tee came from northern Khana, particularly from parts of Lueku and Bangha (Map 4). According to one Tee source, the proof is shown in the similarity of place-names, language, tradition and customs between Tee, Bangha and Lueku. The source cites place-names such as *Bunu* in Tee and *Bunu* in Bangha; *Nonwa* in Tee and *Nonwa* in Bangha; *Korokoro* in Tee and *Korokoro* in Lueku. There is also similarity in speech between the two areas, such as tone, accent, common names and expressions, customs and traditions.

The question is, are these facts sure proof that the people of Tee migrated from Bangha and Lueku? Is there a possibility that there was multiple migrations from many places? As a matter of fact, our research reveals that a contrary hypothesis or tradition exists in the Lueku and Bangha areas. We have noted that during the period of expansions from the Kpong watershed, numerous emigrants from Kpong moved west then north-west into Tee and settled at Uweke. We noted that when the population of Uweke increased, and as more and more people arrived from the Kpong watershed into Tee area, subsequent expansions began in Tee. This brought the Khana immigrants into conflict with the autochthonous Gooh peoples who occupied parts of that area. Eventually, the strife between the newcomers and the autochthonous inhabitants resulted in war.

When the war deepened, the Khana leaders repeatedly retraced their steps to the religious centres at Nama and Kugba to "strengthen" themselves for the war. The practice of always going back to Nama for war power popularised the *Gbene* title in Khana, Gokana and Tee. It will be shown that all the great leaders of these areas had the *Gbene* title prefixed to their names. It will be shown also that the names of the leaders of these areas were well-remembered in Nama oral tradition. In contrast, the oral traditions of these areas did not recall the names of the leaders of Nama and Kugba.

Tee oral tradition corroborates with Nama sources that Gbenekuapie was the founder of Tee. The town of Uweke, where he settled is widely held as the oldest town in Tee (Map 4). One Tee source, however, holds a different view. It asserts that the founder of Tee was Gbenegininwa, and that Uweke and Korokoro were the oldest towns in Tee. This view lacks support as it is not supported by other Tee sources nor by the Nama sources. Even internal evidence within the text itself shows that Uweke was indeed the earliest Khana settlement in Tee. The source states:

> In Tee we usually have much argument concerning the first man who founded Tee, or concerning the first ancient town in Tee. Some people used to say that Uweke was the most ancient town in Tee. Some say that it is Korokoro. I know that Uweke and Korokoro were the two most ancient towns in Tee. There is no other town in Tee older than these two. All matters pertaining to Tee traditions are done in Uweke and Korokoro. These towns were two brothers. As I said earlier about *"Kpa,"* Uweke people have their own. They call it *"Bina."* Korokoro people have their own which they call *"Kpa"* (Gininwa, tape 16, 19th Mar., 1984).

The *Bina* was one of the great ceremonies performed by a great man as part of the requirements for the *Gbene* title. In Ogoni, the performance of this ceremony was called *"Kpa Bina."* The word "Kpa" is a Kana verb, meaning "to play a musical instrument." The *Bina* was a highly resonant musical set (or band) consisting of eleven drums of varying sizes, which were played at the ceremony with other accompaniments. Notice that the original word *"Bina"* which originated from and connected with the ceremonies at Nama was retained at Uweke but lost at Korokoro and perhaps lost also in other parts of Tee.

According to Uweke oral tradition, Korokoro was not a town during the time of Gbenekuapie. The testimony explains that during the time of Gbenekuapie, what is now Korokoro Town was then a forest behind the town of Uweke. Inside this forest, Gbenekuapie made a secret camp where he frequently retired with his elders to deliberate on important matters, unknown to the general public. The oral tradition further explains that the very name "Korokoro" was a functional derivative as a result of the functions which the place served during the time of Gbenekuapie. According to the statement:

> Gbenekuapie and all Uweke made Korokoro their secret place for consultations *(Ke bira-bira)*, their hide-out *(Ke goa)* their retreat *(Ke begia loo to)*, their sanctuary *(Korokoro ke)*. When they had a very serious matter to deliberate upon, they went there to discuss it. They also prepared "something" and kept there – things that would make the decisions that took place there firm and buttressed, things for national ceremonies and rituals. That was why whenever the tradition of *Yaa* was performed, they went there to the front of that sacred thing *(Akob)* inside their sanctuary to do certain ceremonies and rituals.... Gbenekuapie gave land there to one of his servants (a priest) to live there so that he could watch over the national things preserved there.... That was the reason they used to visit there with new plays and dances (Gookinanwaa tape 16, 19.3.84).

The time of Gbenekuapie was a time of war in Tee area, possibly under Gbenekuapie and the leaders of that time. What later became the town of Korokoro, was in fact a war camp, where important plans and decisions about the wars were made and executed. In ancient Ogoni, the *Yaa* tradition was an initiation or recruitment into the people's fighting force.

Virtually every *Yaa* initiate was a warrior, and its training was war-like. The location was a sacred place. References in the above tradition to the front or presence of the "Sacred thing" inside their sanctuary are made to the war medicines and to the symbol of the *Yaa* totem or deity. Because they were regarded as very sacred, they were kept secret or out of the way of evil men or profane persons who would rather use them for purposes dangerous to the society or to the individual. There were two of such things. One was called *Apapee;* in Tee, it was called *Akop.* The other, which was a sacred underground spot in a forest, was called *"Si Ku"* or *"Si yo-Uwe yaa"* "Abode of the totem" or "presence of the *Yaa* deity."

The historical origins of Korokoro therefore developed out of the special purpose for which the site was put in the early period of Tee during the era of Gbenekuapie. It will be shown later that when the wars of conquest shifted from Tee to Gokana area, Gbenesaakoo, the founder of Gokana, also adopted a similar strategy. Thus in Gokana, Gbenesaakoo's *"Giokoo"* was an improved version of Gbenekuapie's *"Korokoro ke"* in Tee.

After the era of Gbenekuapie, there was a period in Tee during which the forest of Korokoro was cleared and settled. This period could be designated as an era of peaceful consolidation and development, the conquest of the Gooh peoples having been over. Emphasis had shifted from war to culture and religion. The cultural, social, and religious aspects of the *Yaa* tradition became paramount. The military or war-like characteristics receded to the background. The existence of some national artifacts or relics created by Gbenekuapie in the forest of Korokoro, added impetus to the development of the place during the latter periods. It will be recalled that a similar example was noticed in the founding of Sii Town.

Some of the autochthonous inhabitants survived the wars. Some of them escaped into the peripheral forests to the north-west, where they became the remnants of such old outpost villages as Baan-Goi (Goyi), and Horo. Here their language is still different from that of the rest of Tee (Map 4,).

9.3   Settlement of Gokana

In Gokana area, the settlement process took a still more dramatic turn. Here, the Khana settlers met a much tougher resistance from the autochthonous peoples than they had encountered in the Tee area. A large proportion of the autochthonous people had escaped from Tee area during the wars of conquest there. All of these had concentrated in the area now called "Gokana."

Although the oral traditions do not make direct references to them, there is internal evidence in the oral tradition which refers to them. The first hint to their existence is revealed in the manner the settlement of Gokana began. It began in the form of an invading army with its base at Giokoo. According to one Gokana source, the man who began the conquest was Gbenegboro, the son of Saa and grandson of Fee. Gbeneboro was the father of Gbenesaakoo and Demedam. Although Demedam was the first son, Gbenesaakoo superseded him owing to his great personality and power. For the same reason, Gbenesaakoo's name became more popular than that of his father; and he almost completely eclipsed his father. Gbenesaakoo became the embodiment of the spirit of the conquering Khana forces. Accordingly, he was given the praise name *"ErebaMene EnebaGian"* (lit. "Great Seven, Brave Seven" or simply "Seven Sevens"). Gbenesaakoo took over and completed the conquest of Gokana and became its first king.

The second hint to the existence of autochthonous forces was a common element in the oral traditions which emphasises that all the Gokana towns had their origin from Giokoo. Under normal circumstances, this should not be the case. The area is a flat hinterland country and people could have entered it and settled wherever they wished without having to come to Giokoo first. Yet, the oral evidence throughout Gokana emphasises that every group that came into Gokana came to Giokoo first.

But the oral tradition also emphasises that Giokoo itself was not a town or settlement and it had never been a town or settlement. The word Giokoo is a combination of two words, each of which means a different thing viz *Gion* which means a "ward" or "section," and *Koo*, which means a "mate," "fellow," comrade" or "associate." As an idiom, the word could be translated "camp for fellows, associates, or comrades."

The consensus of Gokana oral tradition is that the founders of every town had to come to Giokoo first, and that they had to have the approval of Gbenesaakoo. The question thus arises, why was it that every comer into Gokana had to come to Giokoo? And why did they have to stay there until they had had the approval of Gbenesaakoo before they could even begin to search for a place to settle?

Evidently, Gbenesaakoo was a war chief or a leader of all the Khana forces which were set against the former inhabitants of the area, Giokoo was a war camp or military base from where Gbenesaakoo directed his command. That was why Giokoo was not classified or given the definition of a town, and it has no tradition of its own. There is no mention when it was founded or how it was founded, or who founded it. It is not even stated that Gbenesaakoo founded Giokoo. There is no account of its growth, no mention of children being born and no mention of women or wives as we found in other places.

The concentration and resistance of the autochthonous peoples appear to have been much greater in Gokana than in the Tee area. Consequently, the war against them in the Gokana area lasted for many years. During that period, the bulk of the would-be Gokana ancestors remained in the Tee area. Some of them even began to move slowly north-east into the area now called Lueku and Bangha. For sometime, the autochthonous people proved a serious threat to the Khana immigrants until Gbenesaakoo appeared on the scene as the leader of the Khana forces.

I have already referred to certain internal evidence in the oral tradition which point to the identity of the autochthonous peoples. One more example is the tradition which lists the names of the oldest Gokana towns. Apart from Giokoo (which is a class by itself), Gbee stands at the top of the list of oldest Gokana towns. Yet, Gbee oral tradition mentions that there was an older town which stood near to the site where Gbee was built. This town became extinct when Gbee was founded. The name of the town which was not a Gokana town, was given as "Go" or "Ko".

It is believed that this "Ko" or "Go" town belonged to the autochthonous peoples, who became extinct or were absorbed by the Khana invaders. Accordingly, it is believed that the names of such other old and, in some cases, extinct towns like Goi (in Gokana), Gio, Baan-Goi or Goyi, Horo (in Tee), were derived from these autochthonous peoples. Furthermore, from these facts and from the predominance of the "Go" root in their place-names, it is presumed that the "Go" augment or prefix in "Gokana" is a qualifying word derived from the same autochthonous peoples, i.e. the Khana who have become "Go" or who have displaced the "Go".

9.3(a) Emergence of the Names "Tee" and "Gokana"

There are numerous internal evidence which show that all Ogoni including Khana, Gokana, Tee and Eleme, regarded themselves as brothers and as one nationality. However, when particular areas were concerned, the Eleme man still referred to himself as Eleme, the Gokana man as Gokana, the Tee man as Tee, and the Khana man as Khana almost invariably not exclusively.

Again, the seven ancient political divisions of Ogoni known as *Eraba Edo Khana* (lit, the Seven Multitudes of Khana people) included all Ogoni, namely, Baan, Babbe, Baen, Boue, Gokana, Tee and Eleme.

In Nama oral tradition, reference is made to a conference of "all Khana (Ogoni) people held at Luawii under the auspices of Bariyaayoo to draw up a general calendar for Khana (Ogoni). According to the account, the list of attendance at that conference included Boue, Nyo-Kana, Ke-Kana, Gokana, Babbe, Tee, and Leme (Eleme).

From the above examples, it is evident that in the period before the conquest of the autochthonous peoples of the territory, the name "Khana" applied to all sections of Ogoni. However, in the period following the conquest of the autochthonous peoples, the names Go-Khana and Tee began to emerge. This was a period of social and political consolidation.

The names "Gokana" and "Tee" did not appear in the time of Gbenekuapie. These terms originated from the Khana of the eastern part of the territory in the period after the conquest. They used these terms partly to denote possession and partly to denote the relative geographical positions of their ethnic compatriots. The peculiar nature of the Kana language is that when possession is expressed, the thing possessed precedes the possessor. For example, *to Lebira* means Lebira's house. Thus during this period of consolidation, the eastern Khana began to use certain expressions to distinguish between the various sections of their compatriots in the territory.

First, they distinguish themselves from the rest by reserving for themselves the name Khana without qualification. Second, they distinguished themselves from the other Khana people who have taken possession of or occupied the former territory of the autochthonous peoples by adding a distinctively qualifying word. Thus they called them "Go-Kana" i.e., the Khana owning or possessing or occupying the Go's former territory (or Go land).

In the case of Tee, first, the Khana in the east of the territory distinguished those Khana occupying the central part from themselves. Second, they distinguished them from the Eleme of the west and from the "Go-Kana" of the west-central area. Thus, they called them "Middle" or "Central" Khana people *(Pya Tee-Yee or Tee-Yee Khana)*. Over the centuries, this has been shortened to the form we have today *"Tee-Yee"* or simply *"Tee."* In recent times, (i.e. colonial period), the name "Tee" has been corrupted from "Tee" to "Tai." This has happened as a result of increased trade contacts between Ogoni and her neighbours, particularly the Ibani of the coastland and the Igbo of the hinterland.

In the case of "Tee," the name reflected their relative position in the middle of the territory, while in the case of Gokana, the name was a possessive derivative expressing the fact that the Khana in that area had taken possession of the Go's land. It was also a sociological expression describing the mixed society of Go-Khana descendants or offsprings living in that area.

9.3(b) Emergence of a New Language I

The appearance of a generation of children born out of the union of "Go" mothers and Khana fathers marked the beginning of a new language in the Gokana and Tee areas. By the second and third generations, "Gokana" language had emerged in the area.

In Gokana, a great deal of the Kana language was still present in the new language which emerged due partly to continued contacts between the Khana to the east and the Go-Khana speakers to the west-central part of the territory.

The same linguistic transformations, though in a lesser degree, took place in the Tee area. This was because when war first broke out there, the bulk of the Go peoples were pushed to the Gokana area. Lexicostatistical comparisons give cognate relationships between Kana, Tee, Gokana and Eleme as follows: 98% between Kana and Tee, 82% between Kana and Gokana, 75% between Kana and Eleme, 84% between Gokana and Tee, 83% between Gokana and Eleme, and 73% between Eleme and Tee (see Appendix I).

A glance at the lexicostatistics shows that Tee is closer to Gokana by the same degree that Gokana is closer to Eleme. In the forthcoming section, it will be shown that a similar large number of the "Go" peoples also migrated from Gokana into Eleme. These migrations affected the pattern of linguistic transformations in these areas. In Tee area, the "Go" impact was considerably less because by their geographical position in the central area, they had more interaction with the standard Kana speakers than the Gokana, and still more than the Eleme. Moreover, the number of them which remained in the Tee area was relatively smaller than the number of the Khana men and women who moved into the area. Thus, their impact on the Kana language in that area was considerably less, but very noticeable.

Language studies in the area have provided more evidence in support of our hypothesis. In his preliminary studies in the area, Hans Wolff noted three mutually intelligible dialects in the Khana area, namely Tee, "Northern Kana," around Taanbaan (Teebaan), and "Southern Kana," "recognised as the standard and occupying the south-eastern part of the district, including Bori and the village of Kónò on the Imo River" (Wolff, 1964:38). This linguistic description within the Kana language area corroborates with our sketch of routes of expansion and settlement in the territory. The area described as the part where the standard Kana is spoken coincides roughly with the Kingdom of Nama. With regards to the dialectal areas pointed out in Tee and Northern Khana, we explained that a branch of the populations from the Tee area moved north-east then east into Northern Kana area after the people had already been affected by the linguistic impact of the "Go" populations there. And most probably, a remnant group of the autochthonous peoples also joined in the movements to that direction.

In some old isolated village communities like Goi, the linguistic accent is still markedly different from that of the general area, showing evidently that a remnant of the original inhabitants had survived there. Recently, Professor Kay Williamson discovered that the language of Goi was very distinct from that of the rest of Tee (Williamson, 1988:90).

9.4 Settlement of Luekun and Bangha

During the period of wars in Tee, some of the Khana immigrants endeavoured to avoid the wars by moving east and north-east into Luekun and Bangha areas. The emigrants from Tee carried with them memories of the culture and traditions of their original homes in Tee. In the new places, the immigrants from particular villages in Tee lived together in separate villages. Consequently, many of these villages or communities were identified by the communities or villages in Tee from which they emigrated. That is reflected in the fact that the names of certain towns in Tee are duplicated in Luekun and Bangha areas.

Thus the names of such Tee towns as Bunu, Nonwa, Bangha, Baan, Korokoro, etc. were duplicated in Luekun and Bangha. According to Luekun oral tradition, "Gbenetiginagua was the founder of Luekun. He came from Korokoro Tee and founded Korokoro Luekun. At that time there were no settlers in Baan and there was no Taabaan. Gbenetiginagua and Atee were contemporaries. Both of them came from Tee, and both of them married from Tee" (Mpeba 49, 1984).

In relation to Uweke, Korokoro Tee was at this time a new town, a popular cultural centre where newcomers to Tee preferred to settle. It was a different period and age from that of Gbenekuapie, the founder of Tee, Gbenetiginagua is mentioned as a contemporary of Atee, and we know from internal evidence that Atee was a slave trader. This would suggest a date of about eighteenth century for Gbenetiginagua's settlement in Luekun. We have already shown that Atee conquered the old Kpong chiefdom during this period, which was the period of the Baan wars.

Accordingly, Gbenetiginagua might not have been the first immigrant of Tee to settle in Baan or Luekun. Many emigrants from Tee and from Baan-Goi had migrated to Baan Luekun during the period of the conquest of the autochthonous peoples in Tee and Gokana. Atee might have invited Gbenetiginagua from Tee as a mercenary warrior to assist him in his overthrow of the old Kpong chiefdom during the Baan wars. He established his base at Korokoro Luekun, the war centre of Baan people; and probably assumed the leadership of the Baan forces in the war. This is evident from his title, perhaps this was how he became a ruler and was subsequently credited as the founder of Korokoro. We have a similar example in the Boue kingdom. The chiefs of Boue invited a warrior/medicine man named Yobue from Bonny during the same war. Through this man, Boue people obtained firearms from Bonny with which they won the war. Boue people honoured Yobue and elevated him to the rank of a ruler even though he did not have a title. He became the priest of the war gods of the Boue Kingdom.

The early immigrant settlers from Tee had continued to regard themselves as citizens of the towns from which they emigrated. Their new settlement in Baan or Luekun was to them a colony of Korokoro people, or a colony of Bunu people, or a colony of Nonwa people and so on.

In a similar vein, the settlers from Tee in Luekun, and Bangha continued to regard themselves as Tee citizens. They commuted frequently between the new settlements and their former towns in Tee, especially during the annual feasts or on the great religious occasions. In that way, the culture and traditions of Tee were gradually transmitted to the new areas.

A Luekun source recalls that one of the taboos of the Luekun national deity was the snail. For that reason, Luekun people did not eat snail. Furthermore, the source recalled that incidentally, the people of Korokoro Tee also did not eat snail. It may be noted here that E.O. Erim has made an effective use of totems of this kind in tracing the relationships between the Idoma of Central Nigeria, the Igala and the Yoruba (Erim, 1977:21).

The settlers from Tee in Luekun frequently went back to Tee to marry wives. Evidently, those wives were married from Tee at a time when the linguistic impact of the "Go" peoples of that area was already well-established in the culture of the area. It is to be observed that the practice of cross-marriages from Tee to Luekun area was one of the basic causes of the linguistic divergence in Baan area as pinpointed by Hans Wolff (Wolff, 1964:38).

9.4(a) *The Founding of Ko (Opuoko)*

The general consensus is that Gbenesaagba was the founder of Ko, and that he came from Tee. According to the oral tradition:

> Gbenesaagba was the founder of Ko. He was the leader of a group who came from Tee. At first they settled at Ko. After some time, Gbenesaagba told Gbeneiloo to move to another place because Ko would not provide sufficient space for all of them. Thereupon, Gbeneiloo moved to Buon and cleared the site of Buon (Nwilabba tape 24, 15.3.84).

Another Buon source states:

> The founder of Buon was Gbeneabee. In these parts, the name is pronounced Gbeneobia, but it is the same person. He was among those who came from Tee. Gbenesaagba and Gbeneiloo were the people who founded Ko. Gbeneoso and Gheneabee were the first founders of Buon-Ko before others came to join them (Dunwaa, tape 24, 15th Mrch, 1984).

Gbenesaagba probably moved from Tee along with others either before or during the war with the Goo peoples in Tee area. This was the era of Gbenekuapie in Tee. At that time, the linguistic impact of the Goo peoples had not yet taken root among the Khana in Tee. That would partly explain why Kana language is spoken in Ko and the surrounding areas and not the Tee dialect.

The second hypothesis is that Gbenesaagba came directly from Khana area; either from Gure, Luawii or Kpong. In that case, the group would have migrated east along the north banks of the Luubaara River and then turned north to Ko. This would have taken place during the period of the old Kpong Kingdom. If that is so, then it would explain why Ko and its surrounding towns retained the Kana language and traditions. One of such traditions was the isolation of twin mothers in separate villages. This tradition started in Ko from its early beginnings. It was responsible for the founding of the second town of Ko otherwise called Buon-Ko.

9.4(b) *The Coming of the Ebani*

Ko grew to become a prosperous market town on the west bank of the Imo River. It was during this period of its prosperity that the Ebani appeared at Ko (Opuoko). They settled for a while in Ogoni before they moved again on their way to their present location in the Eastern Niger Delta (Alagoa, 1972:3). But although the Ebani had settled in their own territory, the trade relations between the Ogoni and the Ebani have continued ever since.

The oral tradition at Ko reports that when the Ebani, who came in small batches, first arrived at Ko, they found that it was a large market town on this side of the river. Near to it was a smaller off-shoot town called Buon-Ko. The Ebani whose home at that time lay up the river either in Ndoki or beyond, traded with the Ogoni at the Ko waterside market. As they traded and interacted with the Ogoni, the Ebani left a bit of their linguistic characteristics on Ogoni place-names. For example, the name "Ko" the Ebani called "Oko." To that they added their qualifying words to distinguish between the bigger town and the smaller town since both towns bore the same "Ko." Thus they called the bigger town "Opu-Oko" and the smaller town "Kala-Oko". Over the centuries, these names have come down to us, especially in written form as single words, namely "Opuoko" and "Kalaoko" respectively.

The lesser Ko emerged as a result of the custom of isolating twin mothers and twin children from the larger community. Accordingly, it was called "Buon-Ko". The term *"Buon"* or *"Buu"* means "joined" or "double." Thus *"Buon-Ko"* means the *Ko* of the "double ones" or "twins."

9.5   Settlement of Eleme

Eleme oral tradition is full of many variants on how Eleme was founded. Some accounts tell the story of two brothers, Lenee and

Giokpee, who escaped from Gokana because Lenee's wife gave birth to twins and he was also to be killed because he was accused of having physical contacts with the mother and the babies. Lenee secretly escaped from Gokana at night being accompanied by his brother, Giokpee. Having escaped as far as possible, he sat down at a place and declared *"Msi-an?"* "Where am I going?" Other sources state that the place they first settled was *Agaelee* (Ogale). Still other sources narrate that when they escaped from Gokana, they first settled at a place called *Gboo-Msia* (Agbonchia).

There are also many variants about the identity of the original ancestors. As already mentioned, some sources stated that the original ancestors were Lenee and his brother, Giokpee. According to the account, the name Lenee was later corrupted to "Leme" and subsequently to Eleme. The two brothers later separated as a result of a quarrel, Giokpee moved south to a place now known as O'nee (Onne).

Another source states that the original ancestor was Msia (Nchia). Msia had four sons viz Agaelee (Ogale), Gboo-Msia (Agbonchia), Aleton (Aleto), and Aleesa (Alesa). The four sons founded the four original towns of Msia (Nchia).

Still other accounts assert that the original ancestor was Eleme. Eleme had two sons, Msia (Nchia) and Do-nyon (Odido). From the two sons, the Eleme communities were established. Msia (Nchia) produced six sons – Agaelee, Gboo-Msia, Aleeton, Aleesa, Alode, and Kpaajo – The six sons founded the six communities of Msia (Nchia). Do-nyon (Odido) had four sons – Bubuli, O'nee, Tee-ol and Kpora – Each of these also founded a town. Accordingly, the ten sons founded the ten towns of Eleme, with each town bearing the name of its founder.

Still other accounts state that the name Eleme was actually derived from the Gokana word *"Aleemame,"* meaning, "I like it." According to the source, this statement was made by Lenee when he was asked concerning his condition in the new place. The account concludes that Lenee's reply became a by – word or a proverb namely that he said, "I like it." Thus they twisted the meaning of his reply by alluding to the incident which brought about his exile, i.e., the matter of the twin mother and babies and his relationship with them.

9.5(a) Migrations from Gokana and Tee to Eleme

In studying the preceding evidence, certain questions become pertinent. Did the Eleme ancestors migrate from Gokana? What is the evidence of Gokana origin? Was Eleme settled by immigrants from Gokana?

We have seen above that Eleme and Gokana oral traditions are full of testimonies about the Gokana origin of Eleme people. Many versions explain the causes of the emigration from Gokana to Eleme. Some versions tell the story of bitter land disputes, such as happened at Lewe. In other accounts, references are made to bloody civil wars. According to the informant, one of such civil wars occurred at Gbee, following a masquerade dance during which a masquerader fatally wounded a man who died. The vengeful killings which followed, resulted in a civil war which forced many people to escape from Gokana to Eleme.

Evidence of such stories also occur in Eleme sources. Gokana sources do not mention the incident of the twin births directly, although the name of Lenee and that of his brother, Giokpee, frequently occur. This is probably because in the present dispensation, it has become unpopular to recall the bitter ordeal of twins and twin mothers.

For example, a Gokana source at Lewe recounts that a certain man named Kpui, the son of Gbara and grandson of Digi, had two sons Nteyoo and Lenee, all of the kindred of Giokpee in Lewe. A quarrel broke out between Nteyoo and Lenee over a plot of farmland. The trouble grew so big that Lenee had to quit the town and went into exile in Eleme. While there, he practised the customs of his ancestral patrilineage *(gan)*. When asked what those practices meant, he replied that they were the traditions of his ancestral patrilineage from his place of origin. When asked what the name of his ancestral patrilineage was, he replied "Giokpee." From there, it was known that he originated from the house of Gbara Digi in Lewe, Gokana.

The oral tradition adds that these immigrants from Gokana named one of their sons, Tetenwi (or Ntetenwi) after one of their ancestors. Eventually, the family of Tetenwi in Onne established contacts with the house of Gbara Digi in Lewe, where they made frequent visits, especially during the annual Zua feast, to pour libations of food and drinks to their ancestors. These annual pilgrimages from Onne to Lewe have continued until the present. Moreover, they also founded a kindred organisation whose membership included the descendants of Giokpee in Lewe and Tetenwi in Onne.

In February 1984, I visited the so-called Gbara Digi house in Lewe, where I recorded a statement from one Mr. Ndii Nteyoo, a descendant of that house who at that time was very ill. According to him, the founders of Onne came from their house. Lewe people troubled them and expelled them from Lewe after seizing their land and possessions. They escaped to Eleme. After a long time, a man from Nwe-ól, Gokana named Deera, discovered them when he observed that on the occasion of the Zua feast, they performed like Gokana people. And when they cut the palm fruits, they did like Gokana people also. On asking, they explained that their ancestors came from Gokana, and named the kindred of Giokpee as their *Gaan*. Having heard this, Deera knew that they came from Gokana (Nteyoo 55, 1984).

One conclusion that may be drawn from all these testimonies is that some emigrants from Gokana did settle in Eleme. But the causes of migration from Gokana to Eleme could have been much more than what the oral traditions say. War and the struggle for land were the strongest reasons. Harsh customs and traditions were some of the causes, such as the killing of twin mothers and their babies. In some parts of Ogoni, they were simply separated from the larger society; in other parts, they were not separated at all, only some rituals and sacrifices were made for their "purification." Perhaps the most important reason for migrations from Tee and Gokana to Eleme was that Eleme lay on the "path" of population movement. Ogoni was hemmed in on the south by the coastal forests and on the east and north by the wide Imo River and forest. The only open country suitable for settlement by an agricultural society was to the west in the direction of Eleme.

Linguistic evidence is very strong that Eleme was settled largely by immigrants from Gokana and Tee and even from Khana (see Table II; see also Wolff, 1964:38; Williamson, 1988:90-91). Emigration of large groups from Gokana and Tee began in the period of the "Go" wars. The "Go" wars seemed to have been longer and more bitter in Gokana area than in Tee area. The implication is that the "Go" peoples put up their strongest resistance against the Khana immigrants in the Gokana area. It will be recalled that during that stage of the war, only the name of Gbenesaakoo became outstanding. He was described as the embodiment of the "war spirit."

There are several explanations for this. It means that the conquest of the "Go" peoples was very difficult. It also suggests that the "Go" peoples were a strong people, who probably possessed some effective weapons. However, when they were finally defeated, their forces scattered in disarray. Many of them who were able to escape made it to Eleme area. In Eleme, some groups of them became the original settlers in that area. A certain number of them had earlier settled in Eleme area when the Goo wars first broke out in Tee area. These together with those from the Gokana area now formed a part of the autochthonous peoples in the Eleme area.

Later immigrants from Gokana encountered all these groups, which now included all the other autochthonous inhabitants of the area, such as the Mbulee, the Etabajo, the Oku, the Mgube and the Ebregu (Laaka 44, 1984; Osaronu 65, 1984; Ejo 15, 1984). The postwar immigrants from Gokana from the time of Lenee would include the Nchia (Msia) group, the Yaa (Eyaa) group, and the Onne (O'nee) group. At first, they all lived together as peaceful neighbours, as this brief statement indicates:

> The daughter of the traditional ruler of Alode had a friend who was the daughter of the traditional ruler of Etabajo (Laaka 44, tape 8, 6th March, 1984; Awala 5, tape 31, 4th March, 1984).

One reason for the initial peaceful co-existence among the various groups was the availability of sufficient agricultural land for all of them. During that period of peaceful co-existence and interaction, a gradual cultural and material synthesis began to take place. One dynamic factor in this cultural synthesis was the practice of intermarriages between the various groups. Often, the immigrants, who were mostly adventurous men, arrived without women or wives in their company. Accordingly, the women of the autochthonous peoples became their source of wives. In these circumstances, the language of the wives became the language of the children of the new households. A period of linguistic transformation began. This process continued for a long time without incident.

Then a period arrived when, as a result of the bloody civil wars in Gokana, large numbers of new immigrants (or refugees) began to arrive from Gokana. The "influx" of such numbers of people began to exert pressures on the social and economic order of the area. Soon, Eleme became another theatre of violence, strife and war, just as Tee and Gokana before it had been the new immigrants from Gokana fighting against the autochthonous peoples. Sometimes, the latter immigrant groups from Gokana fought against an earlier immigrant Gokana group, who had become like one of the autochthonous peoples.

According to the account, one of the most notable of the autochthonous peoples of Eleme area was the Etabajo people, who occupied the coastal strip of land between Aleesa and Onne (O'nee). Under their leader named Sauwe, they defeated all the Gokana immigrant groups who came against them in battle. They were eventually defeated and dispersed when the Onne (O'nee) and the Yaa groups joined in the war against them. This account gives a clear perception of the main cause of the conflict, which was the control of the best agricultural land:

> As Onne (O'nee) and Alode lived adjacent to the Etabajo territory, their land was divided between Onne and Alode.... The remnants of the Etabajo were scattered all over Eleme. They are in Onne, in Aleesa, in Alode, in Agbonchia, in Ebubu, etc. Wherever you find them, they are, always industrious and prosperous.... but there is no Etabajo town in Eleme today. The name "Ogosu" is a common Etabajo family name. Wherever you find this name in Eleme, know that the person is a descendant of the ancient Etabajo (Laaka 44, tape 8, 6.3.84).

We noticed again the go root in the term "Ogosu" in the above quoted passage. We noticed also that it is a common family name of the ancient Etabajo. We have already drawn attention to the predominance of the go root in the "Go" place-names found in Tee and Gokana areas. We have also drawn attention to the fact that during the wars of conquest in the Tee area, some of the "Go" peoples had moved or migrated to the Eleme area where they settled as part of the autochthonous peoples of that area, presumably, the Etabajo were part of that early emigrants from Tee and Gokana areas.

In Onne, the Gokana immigrants were very virile and energetic. Under their leader named, Yaa (Eyaa), they successfully organised all the scattered groups together to form one large community under a unified authority, with Yaa as the paramount ruler.

9.5(b) Emergence of a New Language II

As already explained, the earlier immigrants from Tee and Gokana lost their original language; the language of their autochthonous wives having become the language of their offsprings and descendants. The later immigrants from Gokana, from the time of Lenee and Giokpee to the conquest of Etabajo, spoke the Gokana language. By that time, the synthesis of the Go-Kana languages in the Gokana area had been consolidated.

In the Eleme area, these Gokana speakers settled in their own separate villages but they had free intercourse and association with the autochthonous peoples. Their settlements could be identified by their place-names, as shown in the following table:

Table II: Gokana and Khana Place-names in Eleme

Original Form of Name	Meaning	Origin	New/Corrupted Form of Name
Msia(n)	("I said) where am I going?"	Gokana	Nchia
Gboo-Msia	Foreground/ Gate of Msia's Compound	Gokana	Agbonchia
Agaelee	It'll be well	Gokana	Ogale
Aleesa	It's well already	Gokana	Alesa
Aleeto(n)	It's time (to act/ do something)	Gokana	Aleto

O'nee	(We are) your people	Kana	Onne
Yaa	Namesake of the Yaa tradition	Kana	Eyaa
Bubu	Deep inside (bush)	Kana	Ebubu/Ibudu
Tee-ol	In the middle/centre of the farmlands	Kana/Gokana	Eteo
Kpora	Separate/separated	Kana	Ekporo
Do-nyon/Do	From "Abroad"/"Foreigner"	Kana/Gokana	Odido

In contrast to the Tee and Gokana areas, the origins and meanings of the autochthonous place-names found in the Eleme area are unknown. These include *Mbulee, Etabajo, Oku, Mgube, Ebregu,* etc.

Just as we found in Tee and Gokana areas, after the conquest of these autochthonous peoples, their menfolk were completely scattered. The example of the conquest of the Etabajo people amplify this. However, their womenfolk became the source of wives for the intruders. The result was a further synthesis of the language by the fresh injection of more Gokana speakers into the area. Consequently, there was the emergence of a new language, the Eleme language, in which the impact of the Gokana language is conspicuously noticeable (see Appendix I).

9.6　Settlement of Boue

Boue oral tradition states that the founder of Boue was Boonen, the brother of Gbenesaakoo. It is said that he founded Boue after a bitter quarrel broke out between him and his brother. According to the account, the quarrel occurred because Boonen was accused of committing adultery with his brother's wife. This accusation resulted in a permanent separation between the two brothers and the introduction of a curse between them.

Having separated, Boonen went his own way and founded the town of Gaagaa. The account states that the curse of Gbenesaakoo attacked the settlers of Gaagaa and forced them to abandon the town.

Some of the men who fled from Gaagaa went to settle at a place now known as *Yeghe*. The great majority of them went towards the coast and founded the town of Bangha on the coast. The account states that Bangha grew into a very large town on the coast whose market was visited by white traders from across the sea. According to the oral tradition, during the period of trade with the white men, the latter introduced the deadly disease of smallpox into Bangha market. The plague spread like wild fire and devastated the population of the town. The survivors fled from the town in many directions.

Among the refugees from Bangha were the descendants of Boonen, who moved to the Boue area and founded the town of *Toga*. Others led by Gbenebalegboro settled at *Gbamene*. Prior to that, some emigrants from Kpong had moved into the north-eastern part of Boue and settled at *Kako* and *Baraboue*. A branch of those from Bangha moved east along the coast and founded the towns of Kwuribue and Lee.

From Toga, Gbenekiri moved further east and founded the town of Uwegwere in Boue. Later on, more immigrants came from Kpong area and settled at *Keon* and at Uwegwere. On the coast, the town of Kwuribue grew to become a large town like Bangha, having many able leaders. The oral tradition states:

> There were many great men in Kwuribue; men like Gbenegarakara, Gbenekarayoo, Gbenetigina, Yoko, Gbenegoo, etc., Gbenegoo was from Kwuri. Those who founded towns and owned the ground were Gbenekarayoo, who founded *Tego*; Gbenegarakara, who founded *Eepie*; Gbenetigina, who founded *Kwaakwaa*: and Gbenetibarakan, who founded *Noobana* (Inayo, Teera 33, tape 6, 7.3.84).

According to the informant, Kwuribue was the principal town of the district. Accordingly, most of the important men of the district resided at Kwuribue. In Chapter 10, the role of Kwuribue in the emergence of Boue as a leading state in Ogoni will be carefully analysed.

CHAPTER TEN

THE EMERGENCE OF KINGDOMS

10.1 The Kingdom of Nama

From available information, we have attempted to piece together the type of polity the Ogoni ancestors established at Nama. According to Nama oral tradition, Gbenekwaanwaa was the ruler at Nama. She continued to rule in the new town of Kugba and thereafter until her death at Gure. The type of polity which was matrilineal monarchy continued into the sixteenth century. After the death of Gbenekwaanwaa, succession passed to her daughter Za, who ruled at Gure. Za herself was succeeded by her first daughter, Bariyaayoo, who established her rule at Luawii.

Although the daughters succeeded to the stools, the actual exercise of governmental functions rested with the sons (men). Gbeneyaaloo the leader of the colonists and brother of Za, presided over the exercise of governmental functions. Under his leadership, the small colony prospered and expanded rapidly, as new towns and communities were founded. The political system was monarchy. Gbeneyaaloo was assisted by a group of leaders with whom he directed the affairs of the colony. At Kugba, his supporters included Gbeneakpana the elder and Gbeneyiranam. The latter became the priest of the autochthonous deity called *Yokurezogomo* and thus held office as the first Ogoni land priest and controller of agriculture.

During this early period, the functions of government were not elaborate. But there were consultations between the leader of government (i.e. Gbeneyaaloo) and his chiefs and elders. One instance of such consultations was when they decided to establish a new settlement at Kugba. Another instance was when as a result of a flood disaster at Kugba, Gbeneyaaloo summoned a meeting of the leaders and presented a proposal for establishing a new settlement at a site further inland. Gbeneyaaloo himself took the initiative by spearheading the establishment of a new settlement at Wiisoro; and from Wiisoro he founded Gure Town.

MAP 5 - Kingdoms & Chiefdoms of Ogoni

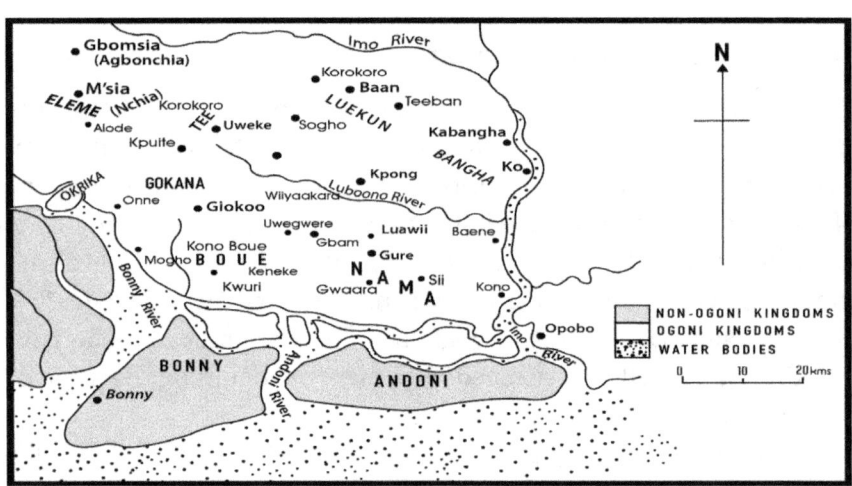

At Gure, there was a significant development in the structure of government. Here, Gbeneyaaloo made some specific appointments with specific functions. For example, he appointed Gbeneatekina to the post of *La-Bue*. By analogy, this was a type of chief minister. His functions included deputising for the Gbenemene (King) and acting as the spokesman of the chiefs and elders. In Eleme area, this office became known as *Óne-Mkporon* (Mackenzie, 1930:8;Ngofa, 1988:4). He appointed Gbenetiginagua to be in-charge of the area which later became Sii. The Gbenemene himself had the direct control of Wiizo area.

Prior to these appointments, Gbeneyaaloo had first established certain instruments of state-power at Gure. These were a state god *(Bari-Bue)* to which every citizen paid allegiance, and a land-deity *(Bari-Assan),* which provided the supernatural sanction for the control of land, agriculture and revenue. Special priests were appointed to administer these "state gods."

After this, it is reported that a ceremony called *wu kon* (planting the spear) was performed, in which all the establishments and appointments were permanently sealed by a joint planting of a sword into the ground at a sacred spot. *Kon* was the term for spear; and it was basically a weapon of war. When the point of a spear was ceremonially pinned to the ground, the signification was "cease-fire" or a "call for peace" or "for laying down arms." When it was done as an act of sealing an agreement, a decision or settlement, the signification was "permanent peace" such as "forever let it be as it has been said, decided or done." Even though what was pinned to the ground was a sword, the traditional term was *wu kon*, which means "planting the spear."

This is the earliest recorded statement about a state ceremony in Ogoni. Over the centuries, the offices mentioned in this ceremony have been passed down as hereditary positions in Ogoni polity. For example, the office of *La-Bue* is still the second highest office in any given community or town in Ogoni after that of the chief or ruler.

As new towns and communities were founded, such communities developed close ties not only with one another but also with Nama which became their metropolis from where they derived cultural, political, religious/ritual powers and authority. For example, a source from Kónò expresses this relationship thus:

> All the traditions of Kónò including all annual feasts are based on the traditions of Sii (Nama). Anything of traditional importance to be done at Kónò must first have approval from Sii (Opusunju 54, 23rd Oct., 1981).

According to the source, in 1975, Chief Birinee of Kónò was installed at the ancient shrine at the site of Kugba before he returned to rule at Kónò. As settlements expanded, local autonomous areas sprang up. Such autonomous areas retained some political powers in certain matters but in other matters such as murder, sorcery, war and the major feasts, they referred the decisions to the centre. Such autonomous areas included Gwaara, Boue, Buan, Kónò, Sii and Zaakpon.

10.1(a) Matrilineal Succession

After the death of Gbeneyaaloo, the oral tradition does not mention any male successor at Gure, instead the succession passed to the female line, the line of Za. Za herself was often called the "Mother of Ogoni." In some versions, she was even fondly called "Mother of the world." Among her great daughters were Bariyaayoo, Gbeneyana and Gbenebeka. Bariyaayoo was her first daughter but Gbeneyana and Gbenebeka were descendants or great great grand-daughters.

Each of these descendants of these great ancestors of Ogoni became dominant in different periods. Bariyaayoo, for instance, was dominant at Luawii in the period after the deaths of Za and Gbeneyaaloo. Under her dynasty, Luawii became politically and culturally powerful in Ogoni. The title, "Mother of Ogoni" suggests that Za had also been very influential in her own period. But it was under the Bariyaayoo dynasty that the political power of the women rulers appeared to have reached its highest. Under her dynasty, Luawii became the scene of a representative government. Representatives of local autonomous areas gathered at Luawii under the presidency of Bariyaayoo to deliberate on matters of government, religion and politics. They settled capital cases such as murder, sorcery, witchcraft, etc., and reviewed and confirmed the appointments of paramount rulers.

Bariyaayoo and Gbenebeka appeared to have extended their influence Ogoni-wide. One instance mentioned during the reign of Bariyaayoo was in connection with the formation of a general calendar to regulate trade and markets and the annual feasts. Representatives from all parts of Ogoni, including Nyokana, Kekana, Gokana, Babbe, Tee and Eleme (Leme), gathered at Luawii under the auspices of Bariyaayoo to plan an Ogoni calendar involving the numbering of days, weeks, the various markets and all the major ceremonies and feasts. These rulers also collected annual tribute from all these areas in the form of agricultural produce, fish and crafts. Funeral duties were also collected on all deaths of titled men. Such men were not buried until their representatives had gone to report the death at Luawii or Gwaara and paid the prescribed taxes or fees.

Like in most ancient polities, religion and politics were common bed fellows. Accordingly, most of the political and administrative actions of the Bariyaayoo and Gbenebeka dynasties were performed throughout Ogoni with the support of religious sanctions and regulations. According to D.L. Ejo, in Eleme, Gbenebeka (also called Ndowa) was deified as the goddess of land. All land disputes were referred to her or her representative for settlement. Annually, the elders of Eleme collected tribute and paid to Gbenebeka.

One characteristic feature of the Bariyaayoo dynasty of Luawii was the cordial relationship which existed between it and the Royal Houses of Gure. For example, during the annual *Zua* (or yam) feast, the celebrations began from the Gure Houses with the offering of ritual foods to the ancestral spirits of Gbeneyaaloo, Gbenekwaanwaa, and Za. The rituals began with the *Kaan Zua* ("Lean Feast" or "Old Yam") in July, followed by the *Aan Zua* ("New year" or "New Yam") in August.

After the new crops harvested that year had been offered in ritual foods to the ancestral spirits of the Gure Houses, the Elders and priests from these Houses went to Luawii to consult with Bariyaayoo concerning the proclamation of the New Year (or New Yam Feast). The proclamation was formally made with the ceremonial clapping of hands by Bariyaayoo or her representative in the full market session at Luawii on a Deeko. With that, the public celebrations of the *Zua* or Yam Feast began. The marketers carried the news to their various towns and villages. An important feature of these New Yam celebrations was the collection of the taxes or tribute throughout the area. The collections began at Duko market at Luawii, immediately following the formal proclamation by Bariyaayoo.

The Bariyaayoo dynasty lasted until it was dissolved during the Baan wars in the sixteenth century. Although thereafter, Gbenebeka appeared on the political scene as the last female ruler and royal descendant of the original ancestors, her political base was considerably eroded as a result of the Baan wars. But her religious and ritual influence continued unabated until the colonial period.

Meanwhile, Boue under the leadership of Gbenekiri, had emerged from the Baan wars as the leading political and military power in Ogoni. Accordingly, Gbenekiri as the king of all Boue and the new Babbe Federation, had to move from Uwegwere, his town to the centre at Kónò Boue.

One memorable result of that political action by Gbenekiri was the establishment of two branches of his *gan* (patrilineage), one at Uwegwere and one at Kónò. Prior to that occasion, his *gan* was known only by the name *Nobana* but from that time onwards, his *gan* became known by the dual name *Nobana Uwegwere, Nobana Kónò*. Thus in Ogoni, on ceremonial occasions, any notable descendant of Gbenekiri appearing in the arena, whether from Uwegwere or from *Kónò, must be greeted by the talking drums by the praise name:* "*Nobana-Uwegwere, Nobana-Kónò*".

To understand the part Boue, under the leadership of Gbenekiri, played in that crisis, it will be appropriate to acquaint ourselves with the background that led to the crisis. And it will be shown that a substantial part of the problem was not unconnected with political developments in the old Kpong Kingdom.

10.2 The Old Kpong Kingdom

During the era of Gbeneyaaloo, the Kingdom of Nama had extended its influence across the Luubaara River into Kpong. Kpong became a meeting point and a watershed between Khana, Gokana and Tee. Brief references to the beginnings of this old kingdom occur in Nama and Kpong oral traditions. In Chapter Nine, I quoted from some of the Nama sources which state that the founders of Kpong came from Gure and Luawii during the time of Gbeneyaaloo and Za; and that Gure, Luawii and Kpong are the oldest existing towns in Ogoni today. In this section, I will refer only to the references that occur in the Kpong sources with a view to examining them more closely. One of the Kpong sources states:

> The founder of Kpong was Atee. Atee came from Ban Tee. He escaped after killing his brother and took refuge in Kpong. At that time, there were no settlers at Kpong and no villages. Atee built a hut there. He married a woman named Yiranwaa. Before the marriage, Yiranwaa had had her first son by a previous marriage at Luubaara. That son was called Saa. Yiranwaa brought Saa to the new husband's place.... Gbeneakpong was a deity which existed in the area before Atee came there. It became the land deity of Kpong. Za was another name connected with the founding of Kpong... Atee was a slave trader in the trans-Atlantic slave trade. He sold Saa but Saa escaped and returned home (Keekee 38, 24th Oct., 1981).

Another Kpong source states:

> He (Atee) divided the territory and gave one part to Gbeneakpong, one part to Gurete, and one part to Yaakaragute. Then he sent colonists to Luawii and Baene. It was people from Kpong who went to settle at Baene... What was called a ruler, as far as the whole of these parts was concerned, was called Gbeneakpong. He was the ruler of the whole of this area and the first to be recognised even in matters of tribute (or taxation). Thus they used to say, "The ruler, Gbeneakpong; the ruler, Atee, the ruler, Gurete." Each one according to this order. When they offered food and libations to the ancestors during the time of feasts, they followed the same order (Menewa 47, tape 4, 21.10.81).

The two Kpong sources quoted above claim that Atee was the founder of Kpong. Apparently, they are not referring to the latter kingdom or dynasty but to the early settlement and the establishment of the early kingdom. One of the sources, however, mentions that Za was one of the founders of Kpong. This testimony which refers to the Za connection confirms the evidence from Nama sources.

Secondly, the Kpong sources claim that Atee came from Ba (or Baan) in Tee and took refuge in Kpong as a fugitive from justice, having committed the crime of manslaughter. Furthermore, one of the sources claims that when he first arrived there, he saw no houses and no people. Both sources refer to Gbeneakpong. In one, it is claimed that he was a deity, in the other, it is said that he was a ruler or king.

These claims and assertions must be examined critically. It is probable that Atee migrated as a fugitive from Ban (or Baan) in

Tee and settled in Kpong but it is unlikely that when he arrived in Kpong, the place was unoccupied. During the period of expansion by the Ogoni settlers, Kpong was the big centre of expansion north of the Luubaara River. It was from Kpong that the Ogoni moved west along the north banks of the river to occupy Tee and Gokana. From this early settlement, the old Kpong Kingdom emerged.

One of the Kpong sources states that when Atee came to Kpong, he divided the territory giving one part to Gbeneakpong, one part to Gurete, and one part to Yaakaragute. We notice here what might be called telescoping or anachronism, in that events of a later period have been pushed to the earliest beginnings (Henige, 1974:34). Nonetheless, the source appears to present an accurate picture of the situation when it asserts that Gbeneakpong, Gurete and Yaakaragute were human persons who were rulers of territories. In contrast, the other Kpong source contains serious distortions, since it makes Gbeneakpong a deity and Yaakara (Yaakaragute), a son of Atee.

Evidence from other versions suggest that these names belong to the rulers of the old Kpong Kingdom whom Atee conquered and either eliminated or reduced to subordination. Notice this statement in the above passage "what was called a ruler, as far as the whole of these parts was concerned, was called Gbeneakpong," and notice also the fact that in ritual order, Gbeneakpong was first and not Atee. However, in Ogoni, names of gods do not have titles as Gbeneakpong does, unless it is an ancestral spirit. Gbeneakpong was probably the name of the previous king, whose ancestors were among the founders of Kpong. In that case, he was closely connected with the sacred office of land priest, the functions of which he must have delegated to another person whose ancestors also contributed to the founding of the town. What appears to have happened is that Atee eliminated the previous king but spared and subordinated his land priest. In doing so, he intended to avoid the desecration of the land. The preservation of the land priest accounts for the third name in the ritual order, which now comes after Atee. This in a nutshell is the 'history.' What happened in later periods was that some versions of the oral tradition not being able to account for these earlier names have turned them into gods.

Yaakara (or Yaakaragute) was the founder and ruler of the town of Wiiyaakara on the Luubaara River. The name Yaakara or Yaakaragute refers to the same person. The suffix - *"gute"* is a Kana alliteration used in a praise name. It has no specific meaning by itself except for its sound. The story was told that when the man, Yaakara accomplished what was a near impossible task of clearing the thick virgin forest of that place, people marvelled at his industry and energy. They sang a praise of him using the sound of his name and the machete he used.

Yaa - Kara - gu - te

Ba - aga - ge – top

Ba means hand, *aga* means firm or strong; *ge* means sword or machete; *top* means sharp. Literally it means, "a firm or strong hand makes the machete sharp," which is to say that when an industrious and energetic person performs a task, he does it so well that the task appears easy to the onlooker. It is not certain whether this was the famous Yaakaragute who was captured alive by Boue forces during the Baan wars.

One Kpong version states that after Atee had arrived in Kpong, he married a woman named Yiranwaa, together with her first son by a previous marriage. The version further explained that when Atee became a slave trader during the trans-Atlantic slave trade, he attempted to sell his stepson, Saa into slavery but the latter escaped to Baene. Then Saa plotted to kill his stepfather; for which offence he was not given any inheritance in Atee. Other versions however assert that Saa was a son of Atee and that both Saa and Atee were alike in temperament, being professional head-hunters and warriors.

So far, we have noticed that the evidence presented about Atee in the oral tradition is fragmentary. To piece together a substantial body of facts in support of the evidence, we will need more evidence and ask the right questions. To that end, we need to examine closely the evidence contained in the following statement:

> When Atee went over (the Luubaara River) to the place (Wiiyaakara), he saw Yaakaragute, who had already crossed and planted his 'flag' there. So Atee told him to occupy that area and he named the place Yaakara. He then left that place and rushed to Luawii where he

stayed for sometime.... Then he left Luawii and went to clear the site of Baene. After that colonists from Kpong came and occupied the whole of Baene both men and women as you can see today (Menewa 47, tape 4, 21.10.81).

In the above passage, Atee's movements do not represent the movements of one engaged in the task of founding a town. The founding of a town according to Ogoni standards, was a life-long pre-occupation. Apart from Gbeneyaaloo which was a specific case, it is yet to be discovered in Ogoni, one who founded several towns in a life-time. Atee's movements in the above testimony represent the movements of a leader of an army engaged in a highly successful operation.

10.2(a) Atee's Migration from Tee to Kpong

In Chapter Nine, I explained that when the Khana moved west from Kpong, they settled first at Uweke in Tee. In that area, they met for the first time a new people known as the "Go". A series of wars broke out between the Khana and the "Go" peoples; first in Tee, then in Gokana areas, the last of these wars was fought in Eleme area against the Etabajo.

Now when the wars began in Tee, the Khana forces broke the ranks of the "Go" armies forcing the bulk of them to retreat to their haven in the Gokana area. A part of them retreated to the peripheral area in the extreme north-west of Tee, an area which at that time must have been an impregnable forest. A small number of them moved eastwards along the edges of the Imo forest and parallel to the Khana line of communication between Kpong and Tee and between Kpong and Ko (Opuoko) on the Imo River. This group quietly settled in the area now called Baan Lueku. Later emigrants from Tee area joined them. This latter group were concentrated in the area which was then known as *Tee-Baan*. This name was later corrupted in the colonial era to *Taabangh* and in more recent times to *Taabaa*. *Tee-Baan* was a name by which they distinguished the Tee settlement or community in Baan Lueku from the actual Tee territory.

Prior to the intrusion of Khana people in Tee area, there was a community of "Go" people living in Tee area called *Baan* or *Ban*.

When as a result of the wars the aborigines scattered, a group of people from this Ban (or Baan) community moved east to settle in Lueku as the *Baan Lueku*. This group and a later group of mixed immigrants from Tee area brought about the linguistic divergence in the Tee-Baan area of Khana. Part of this Ban/Baan community of "Go" peoples which had retreated into the peripheral forest to the north and north-west of Tee, had remained there. In course of time, it became necessary to distinguish between these two Ban/Baan communities, namely between the one in Lueku and the one in Tee. The one in Tee area was referred to as *Baan-Goi* (i.e. the Baan community of "Go" remnants in Tee) and that in Kana as Baan-Lueku (i.e. the Baan community in Lueku). As in Tee-Baan (Taabaa) area of Khana, there is also a linguistic divergence in the *Baan-Goi* area of Tee (Wolff, 1954:38; Williamson 1988:90).

The above explains how Atee migrated from Baan in Tee to settle in the old Kpong Kingdom sometime in the sixteenth century. This is probably the most likely date not only because Atee participated in the trans-Atlantic slave trade but also because the events which followed took place around this period.

10.2(b) *Establishment of a New Dynasty at Kpong*

In the sixteenth century (probably in the later part of the 16th century), a civil war broke out in Ogoni known as the Baan wars. It was during this crisis that Atee allied with his kinsmen of Baan-Lueku to overthrow the old Kpong Kingdom, presumably this is the event hinted at when it is said in the oral tradition that Atee "divided the territory."

10.2(c) *Background to Atee's Ascendancy*

Since it was customary that a newcomer to a community to be conducted to the chief or king for interrogation about his personal details and about his mission in the area, it would be expected that this was done to Atee when he arrived in Kpong. Without this formality, he could be in danger of being regarded as a foreign head-hunter or cannibal and could be killed before he had the chance to kill any citizen (cf. Horton, 1969:54). Undoubtedly, Atee was able to present his case in such a manner that he won the sympathy and support of the chiefs and elders present, who then decided that he should be enlisted in the king's service. This brought him into close contact with the king's households; for he was occasionally sent to the king's farms to perform some of the heavy tasks.

After some years in the king's service and in close relationship with the king's households, a scandalous thing happened. Atee was accused of having an affair with one of the king's young wives. This was Yiranwaa, whom the king had married newly from Luubaara. Following this accusation, Atee secretly disappeared from Kpong and went to his kinsmen in Baan-Lueku. At this time, all Baan people were engaged in a bitter war against all Ogoni towns south of the Luubaara River. Baan people had persuaded all the northern towns to join in the war against the south. Many northern towns had already joined the war because their grievances were the same.

Apparently, Kpong did not join in this war because Kpong was a vassal of Nama, being directly under the control of Luawii, the seat of Bariyaayoo. Atee's case now gave Baan people a cause to regard Kpong as enemy. With the help of Atee, they secretly planned an attack on Kpong and overthrew the old kingdom. The king and "many of his supporters were killed. Thereupon, Atee declared himself king of Kpong. The plan was to attack both Kpong and Luawii at once in order to prevent the latter from coming to the aid of Kpong. At the same time ,Wiiyaakara on the Luubaara River was held to prevent any attempt by Luawii to come to the aid of Kpong. Meanwhile, troops were "rushed" to Baene on the Imo River to block any movements by the South through the Imo River to cut them off from the rear. The plan was perfectly executed and Atee became the king of Kpong.

With reinforcements from Gure and other southern towns, Baan troops were later driven out of Luawii. But they continued to hold Wiiyaakara and Baene, where they were able to bring in constant reinforcements (colonists). Baan people were finally and completely defeated after Boue had entered the war. Because Kpong was cut off from the south, and because what happened there was in the form of a coup d'etat, people in the south did not know what actually happened at Kpong until a long time afterwards; and even then only very few knew the facts.

Atee now married the young woman Yiranwaa of Luubaara. By then, Yiranwaa had given birth to Saa. But Atee did not love Saa, probably because he did not beget him. When Saa grew up, he learned secretly from his mother and from his maternal uncles about what happened. This knowledge estranged Saa from the king. Having discovered this, Atee secretly arranged to sell Saa into slavery but the plan leaked at Baene and Saa escaped. For the greater part of his life, Saa remained an exile at Baene and never returned to Kpong, except when he unsuccessfully attempted to kill his stepfather.

On the basis of the evidence, it would seem that Atee spent the rest of his life engaging in the traffic of slaves, getting his subjects from the hinterland and using Baene on the Imo River as his depot, and the Bonny chiefs as his customers. This suggests a probable date for his existence between the seventeenth and eighteenth century.

Atee is remembered in the oral tradition for some of the developments that took place during his time. According to the account, he is credited with opening many roads. For example, he was said to have opened roads to Baene, to Koo, to Yoo and to other parts of the kingdom. He extended the kingdom to these places and planted colonists or settlers in them. Above all, he divided the state into administrative units. For example, such administrative units included Bara, Gure, Korogbere, Yaagobara, Keon, Taebara, and Uwegwere (Menewa 47, 1981).

One of the administrative units or towns was called Gure. Notice also in one of the passages quoted above that one of the rulers of the old kingdom at the time Atee took over was called Gurete, which means "father of the Gure community" in Kpong. The Gure community or town in Kpong was probably the location where the original founders from Gure settled.

10.3 The Kingdom of Kwuribue/Boue

The term, *Boue* does not refer to any particular town in the area. The term was used both to refer to the group of towns as well as to the inhabitants of the entire geographical area. Literally the term *"Boue"* means "on the land", "in the middle of the farming area" or "in the middle of the fields." Some variants claim that the name was derived from Boone, the traditional ancestor of Boue people. This claim is somewhat speculative.

In actual fact, the term came into use after the destruction of Bangha by a smallpox plague. The groups of people who dispersed from the city to found new settlements in the uninhabited country beyond the coast were referred to as "those on the land" or "in the middle of the fields" *(bo-ól)*, as distinct from "those on the lower ground at the sea coast." The word *"bo-ól"* ("on the land") is a Gokana word. As those who had moved up to settle in the inland country expanded eastwards and began to associate with the Kana-speaking communities from Kpong and Nama areas, they dropped the Gokana ending -*ól* and replaced it with its Kana equivalent -*ué*, both of which mean a "field," "bush" or a "piece of farmland"; but they retained the Gokana prepositional root *"bo"* which means "on." Thus the term *Boue* evolved. The implication is that the people of Bangha spoke the Gokana language.

10.3(a) *The Towns of Boue and Kwuri*

The Kwuri towns were located on the coast. The principal town among them was *Kwuribue*. Other towns were *Barike, Gaen, Lee, Ilooloo, Keneke* and *Nokwuri*. The men did fishing as well as long distance trading by canoes along the coastal waters and on the rivers and creeks. They also practised some agriculture. The women traded in fish and various kinds of shell-fish. The women of *Kwuribue* in particular specialised in the making of fine pottery. *Kwuribue* potters supplied ceramic wares to the peoples of the hinterland as well as to the riverine peoples.

Immediately beyond these coastal towns were a group of inland towns located in the *Boue* area. Among the towns grouped in this area were *Baraboue, Kako, Keon, Gbamene, Kaboo, Toga, Uwegwere* and *Gbam*. The economy of these towns was mainly agricultural. They cultivated yams, cocoyams, aerial yams, peppers, plantains, oil palms, walnuts and a variety of vegetables, the best known of which were the fluted pumpkins (telfairia). Besides cultivating the minor crops, the women traded in smoked fish, foodstuffs, camwood and "industrial barks" (used for treating palm wine).

Kwuribue ruled all these towns and controlled their trade. Dapper described the role of *Kwuribue* by saying that it is the principal town in the area, having about eight or nine sub-towns under it, and ruled by a governor who boasted that he controlled the coastal trade as far as Sangama (Dapper, 1676:135; Jones 1963:35). Dapper's description corroborates with the oral tradition. For example, one oral source states:

> There were many great men in *Kwuribue*. Men like Gbenegarakara, Gbenetigina, Yokō, Gbenegōō, Ghenekarayoo, etc. Gbenegōō was from Kwuri. Those who founded towns and owned the ground were Gbenekarayoo who founded Tégō; Gbenegarakara who founded Éepie; Gbenetigina, who founded Kwaakwaa; and Gbenetibarakan, who founded Nobana (Inayo 33, tape 5, 7th Mar., 1984).

10.3(b) The Founding of Kónò Boue

During the sixteenth century, a long-drawn civil war broke out in Ogoni between the towns north of the Luubaara River and the towns south of it. In the south, this war was called the Baan wars.

The northern forces overran the south. Many southern towns were deserted, especially those towns which lay on the ancient route from the north. Even *Kwuribue,* the principal town of Boue and Kwuri, was severely threatened. Eventually, the war brought about the evacuation of the town to a new site in the Boue area.

One of the defence measures adapted during the war was the digging of deep trenches round the towns. According to Kpoko Kinanwii, every man and woman in Boue was tasked to dig the trenches and anyone who failed was fined heavily. From these reports, we gather enough hints that the natural defences of Kwuribue was badly inadequate. For example, there is the reference to being "in a mighty sea." It would appear that the low sea-level of the site of *Kwuribue* did not permit the digging of deep trenches for defence purposes.

10.4 The Causes of the Baan Wars

The oral traditions do not say much about the causes of the Baan wars, but a great deal has been remembered about how the wars were fought and about the great warriors who fought in them, in the northern towns, however, memories of the wars are almost non-existent.

10.4(a) Rumours of Assault on the Northern Women Traders

The oral tradition attributes the causes of the Baan wars to reports brought home by some northern women traders about sexual harassment by certain southern men when they attended the Nubien market in the south. The account explains that in those days because of long distance, it was not possible for the northern women traders to do their trading and return home on the same day. Accordingly, they had to sleep overnight in the south in order to do their trading the following day and return home in good time. Consequently, some southern men seized the opportunity to establish sexual relations with some of the northern women traders. Eventually, reports of such sexual relationships reached the ears of Baan people. Their elders, chiefs, and men became angry. They stopped their women from attending markets in the south and proceeded to declare war on the south.

Some versions, however, state that the actual cause of the Baan wars was a report of sexual assault on the northern women traders by some men, as they travelled from the Nubien market at Baraboue through Zaakpon territory to the north. Baan people waged a full scale war against Zaakpon; they attacked and overran their towns. Zaakpon people fled their towns and took refuge in Boue. Thereupon, Baan people declared war on Boue also. Thus the Baan wars spread.

The report about the Baan market women may have been a cause of the war, probably the immediate cause. But there were laws and taboos regulating sexual behaviour and sexual relationships and offences throughout Ogoni. For example, it was forbidden for lovers to have sexual intercourse in the bush. To do so was to desecrate the land; and it was an offence against the land deity. Such an offence was said to have serious repercussions not only on the offenders but also on the whole society, since it meant that the soil would withhold its yield, unless purification sacrifices were made. The penalty was therefore imposed and enforced by the co-operation of the whole society. Provisions also existed for settling offences of adultery, theft, sexual assault, etc. between citizens of different towns and communities through the joint action and co-operation of the chiefs and elders of the towns or communities concerned, who made sure that the offender was apprehended and punished according to the tradition.

On the other hand, it was possible that in the course of individual personal contacts between men and women through trade, certain persons in the group would fall in love with each other. Incidents of that kind were not considered socially abnormal, unless adultery was involved, for which there was also a means of redress on individual basis.

There was also the possibility that the alleged attack on the women traders was the action of some thieves. According to the oral tradition, the attack took place in Zaakpon territory which lay along the trade route from the south to the north (Map 4). The main motive for such an attack was probably to steal the luxury cloths purchased from the coast by these wealthy northern women long distance traders, who usually travelled in large groups. Such an attack was indeed a serious threat on the supply routes to the northern towns and could have provoked swift reactions from the north. However, the fact that the war quickly spread to all the coastal towns including Kwuribue, meant that there were other remote causes or grievances held by the north against the southern towns.

The most important of such remote causes or grievances was economic control by the south. We can understand how the method of economic control by the south became the major cause of the Baan wars by an analysis of the trade situation in Ogoni in the sixteenth and seventeenth centuries. One of the sources states:

> People from all the parts of Ogoni attended the Dukono (formerly Nubien) market with various items of trade. The Gokana brought yams and fowls; Tee people brought *geere* (old cocoyams), the

Sogho brought *tuu* (three-leaved yams); the Kwaa (Okwale) brought peppers; the Baan brought goats, sheep; the Kaani brought fowls; the Yeghe brought fowls; the Boue brought goats, sheep and fish; Kónò Boue (formerly Kwuribue) brought pots, fish, etc. People from parts of Northern and Southern Kana such as Kónò, etc. came to buy these things which they took back to their own places to sell. To them, it was like people go to the big cities like Port Harcourt today to buy goods, which they take back to sell in their own towns. People came from far and wide to buy Kónò Boue pottery, especially water pitchers which people who lacked drinking water during the dry season needed very much. People who lived in the drier areas used to say, I want to go to Du-Kónò so that I may buy some pitchers for storing cool drinking water for the dry season. For water stored in Kónò Boue pitchers remained cool for a long time even in the hot season.

Kónò Boue was the only place where pots were made for all Ogoni people and beyond. Moreover, at that time, the white man had not filled the whole place with different types of pans and pots. People from Gokana, Kónò, Bani (Bonny), etc, used to come to buy the pots and pitchers, including the special type used for palm wine tapping (Baedee 6, tape 22, 23rd Dec., 1983).

From the above passage, it is evident that the particular market, *Du-Kónò*, was a big centre of distributive trade in Ogoni. Before the Baan wars it was called *Du-Nubien*; and it was located in the Boue area in the town of Baraboue. There was another market on the sea coast in the Kwuri area. This seaside market was called *Du-Kwuri*, and it was controlled by Kwuribue. These two markets dominated the long distance trade of Ogoni in the sixteenth and seventeenth centuries. And the controlling town in this trade was Kwuribue, having replaced its predecessor town of Bangha which similarly dominated the eastern Delta trade in the previous century. Kwuribue controlled not only the coastal trade but also the overland trade (cf. Dapper, 1675:135; Jones, 1963:35).

10.4(b) Kwuribue and the System of the Coastal

Trade in the Sixteenth Century

The most important items of trade for the hinterland peoples apart from those goods brought by the Portuguese was fish or sea foods.

Although the coastal Ogoni towns were also fishermen, the bulk of the sea foods was brought by the Ijo peoples. The most important luxury item brought by the Portuguese was cloth (cf. Ryder, 1977:63).

The people living further inland regarded these sea foods as of extreme importance; and they not only highly desired these trade items but they actually craved or longed for them. For example, the idea of eating roasted fresh fish or lobsters or crabs in the southern towns was to them a dream which could only be realised by making the journey to Boue on one of the market days (i.e. on Deeko) when they could spend the evening before the market day in the house of a friend enjoying these treats. In those days of slow transportation, these items reached the hinterland peoples only in smoked state, sometimes badly deteriorated.

After the market on the following day, the northern traders carried home not only large quantities of smoked fish, shrimps, lobsters, etc. but also a great variety of shellfish which could remain alive and fresh for some days if properly packed, such as crabs *(aka)*, the big crab *(tuu)*, razor clams *(looli)*, murex and vase shells *(agboro)*, volutes *(Kónò)*, ark shells and cockles *(akoro)*, mussels *(ise)*, ceriths and winkles *(atuu)*, jingle shells (akpagara), etc. These shelled sea foods were highly prized by housewives not only because of their freshness but also for their economy and usefulness in the preparation of the staple foods. Besides these, they also bought other kinds of essential goods such as the assorted types of pots or ceramic wares brought from Kwuribue (and later from Kónò Boue). Other exotic goods were the imported red cloths brought first by the Portuguese and later by other Europeans (Ryder 1977).

Apart from obtaining these luxury goods, the hinterland peoples were also able to sell their own agricultural produce and domestic livestock as indicated in the passage quoted above. For the Boue market was also a great centre for the sale of agricultural produce while the Kwuri market *(Dukwuri)* at the waterside was the centre for the sale of fish and other sea foods brought by the Ijo peoples, who also bought the agricultural foodstuffs and other items from the hinterland. The Portuguese traders in their own period also bought large quantities of the agricultural produce, fish and livestock (Pereira, 1955).

The crucial aspect of the trading practice in these markets was that Kwuribue and all the Kwuri towns assumed the monopoly of both the land and the sea trade as middlemen to the disadvantage of both the riverine traders and the hinterland peoples. For example, the hinterland traders were only allowed to sell their goods at the Nubien market at Baraboue in the Boue area. Their goods were bought by Boue and Kwuri traders, particularly, the Kwuribue middlemen, who shifted the agricultural produce to the Kwuri market at the waterside to sell to the Ibani and to the other Ijo buyers, as well as to the Europeans.

They probably began this system of trading from the time of the Portuguese. Similarly, the Ibani and the other Ijo peoples were not allowed to sell or buy directly in the Nubien market. The Kwuribue and all the Kwuri traders bought the cloths and other goods brought by the Portuguese and the fish brought by the Ibani and the Ijo peoples to the seaside market. They then moved these goods to the Nubien market to sell to the inland traders.

Sometimes when a trader was unable to sell his trade goods, whether fish, agricultural produce or European goods, they counted the value of the unsold goods and handed them over to a middleman, who sold the goods, took his own commission, and rendered the account to the owner when he or she came again in the next two or three market weeks. It was an "offence" against the god of trade for the inland traders to visit or trade in the Kwuri seaside market. Similarly, the riverine peoples were not allowed to visit the Nubien market on the land for the same reasons. One source at Kwuri referred to this practice in this way:

> At the time of the Okrika war, the Ibani people were not there, they were probably in their own place at that time. But they used to come to Kwuri market *(Du-Kwuri)* though they had not come to our area. When they came to *Du-Kwuri*, they brought wine and spirits in casks, which they brought from the Europeans. They kept some in our compound where all Boue came to buy. Other things included tobacco, pipes, cloth, fish etc. There was no Port Harcourt at that time. I am older than Port Harcourt. The day the site of Port Harcourt was cleared, two persons were conscripted from our compound, Iparabari Nyiakpuru and Kpaama Imana.

They conscripted people from all Boue and from all Ogoni. The day they returned, not a penny was found on them (Barigwere, tape 10, 3.1.84).

This system of controlling 'external' trade appears to have been adopted throughout all entry ports of Ogoni in ancient times. An account of a similar practice was recorded at the fresh water port town of Ko (Opuoko) on the Imo River. The account states:

> There was a system of trade that existed at Ko river side market. When the Bani (Bonny) people brought their fish or other merchandise, the Ogoni would act as middlemen. They would buy these things from the Bani and take them to the main market on the land to sell. Similarly, the Ogoni traders would buy foodstuffs from the farmers and from the market women and move them to the riverside market to sell to the Bani people. The Bani were not allowed to buy directly from the producers in the market, or to sell directly to the buyers (Yomii, tape 24, 15th March, 1984).

By these methods, Kwuribue controlled and dominated the trade of the eastern Delta in the sixteenth century. This monopoly of both the luxury and the essential commodity trade by Kwuribue was bitterly resented by most inland towns and communities. That would explain why when the Baan people attacked the Zaakpon communities for the alleged assault on the northern women traders, the attack quickly spread like wildfire into a full scale war against all the south, particularly against Kwuribue and all Kwuri towns. This economic domination by the south through their monopoly of both the internal and external trade was a chief factor which united all the north against the south in the longest and bitterest civil war ever reported in Ogoni oral tradition.

MAP 6 - Inter and Intra Ethnic Trade Routes in Pre-Colonial Times

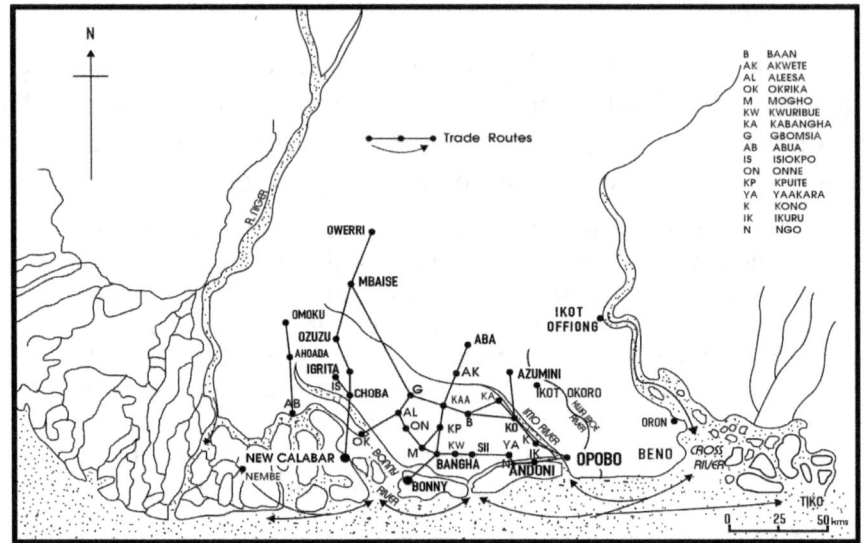

10.4(c) *The Course of the War*

The north overran the south. They sacked Zaakpon villages whose inhabitants fled and took refuge in Boue towns. They threatened Kwuribue, the principal town and trade centre on the coast.

Then the leaders of Kwuribue discovered that the site of their town was unsuitable for effective defence, they resolved to move the town from the coast to a site further inland in the Boue area. Three famous brothers were credited with taking the initiative to search out a new site for the town. These were Gbenekwerre, Gbenekote and Gbenetibarakan. The new town now located in the Boue area was renamed Kònó, meaning "The volute." According to the oral tradition, the new name meant that they were now hidden from their enemy like the volute does at the bottom of the sea. With the people of Kwuribue now settled in the Boue area as Kònó, the next step was to move the Nubien market from Baraboue to Kònó and to rename it Kònó market" *(Du-Kònó)*. From Kònó Boue, they began to prosecute the war. Despite all these changes, the war continued to drag on for a very long time.

Meanwhile, Baan people had attacked Kpong which was a vassal of Nama, apparently, because it refused to join the war. Led by Atee, a former fugitive from Baan-Goi in Tee who was received into the service of the king of Kpong, a coup d'etat was planned and the old kingdom was overthrown. King Gbeneakpong was killed and many of his chiefs and elders. Baan people moved swiftly across the Luubaara River and overran Luawii, the seat of Bariyaayoo and the administrative headquarters of the Nama kingdom. They also held Wiiyaakara, the crossing point on the Luubaara River and Baene on the Imo River to safeguard against any movements from the south.

In Boue area, under the leadership of Kònó Boue (formerly Kwuribue), they began a gigantic defensive project, that of digging deep trenches round their towns and at strategic points throughout the area. E.J. Gibbons, a colonial district officer who saw the remains of these trenches described them as a distinct feature of the Ogoni in their present home (Gibbons, 1932). This method of defence soon spread throughout the southern towns and later on, it became a common feature also in the north. For example, Kpong oral tradition describes this method of defence as follows:

> In those days when there was war, the deep trenches acted to prevent enemy forces from entering the towns. If you were a warrior, you would know your movements how you would do to overcome the enemy who crossed the deep trenches and entered the towns. You would know that you have cut them off and that they cannot get away. When they would turn back to escape, you ambushed them. They would not know that you have taken up positions in the places you previously selected outside the communities. It was for that purpose that the ancients dug the deep trenches round the towns. (Menewa tape 4, 21 Oct., 1981).

MAP 7A - Battle Sites & Millitary Strategies of the Baan Wars

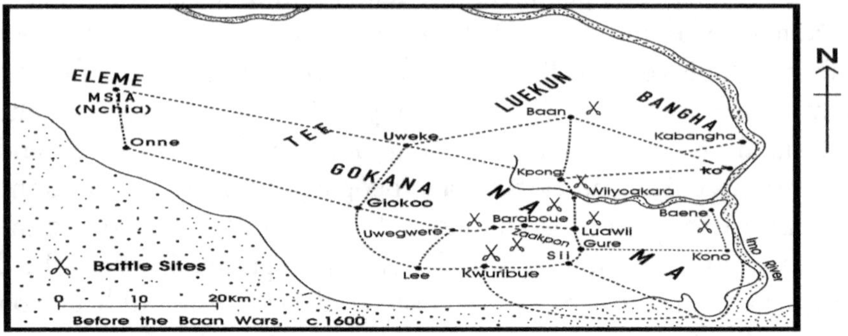

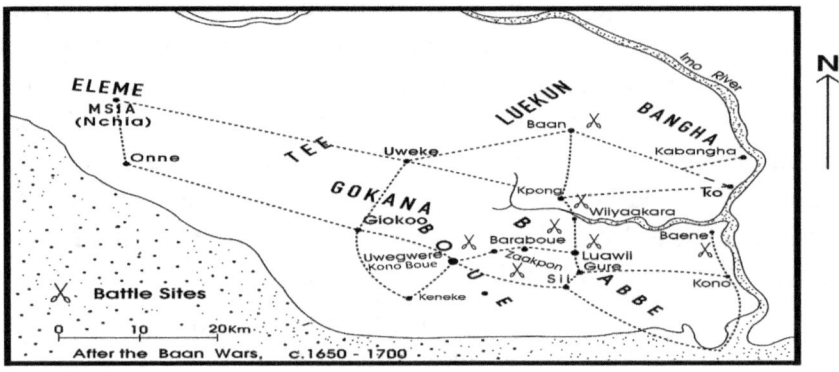

MAP 7B - Battle Sites & Millitary Strategies of the Baan Wars

Having completed these fortifications, Boue people, led by a warrior named Gbenekiri, began to take the offensive into the North. The combined Boue and Nama forces and finally forced the northern army out of Luawii but the war continued to drag on from that point for many years.

10.4(d) First Use of Firearms

While the war dragged on indefinitely without a decisive victory and without peace, news reached Boue through a Bonny trader at Kwuri market that the Europeans had introduced a new powerful weapon (firearms) at Bonny. A Kònó Boue warrior named Gbenebalikina, got the news from a Bonny friend at Kwuri market. He made arrangements to acquire the weapon. When the Bonny friend had brought the gun, they tested it on a goat and it killed the goat. Having seen this, Gbenebalikina bought the gun and thus became the first man to own and use the gun in Ogoni. Accordingly, although the Ogoni called the gun *naa(n)* (from the sound of its explosion, within the circle of hunters, it was fondly called *waGbenebalikina* (wife of Gbenebalikina).

Other sources state that while the Boue leaders were negotiating to acquire the firearms from Bonny, they also received information about a powerful medicine man at Bonny who was a priest of *Ikuba*. Three highest ranking warriors of Boue were sent to Bonny to bring the medicine man and firearms. The three men were Gbenekiri, Gbeneteebete and Gbenetaaduu. One source states that the medicine man whose name was Yobue, was a wizard and sorcerer who was expelled from Bonny for committing many murders by his sorcery. The elders of Boue took him into asylum because they thought that he would be useful in the war with his sorcery. Another account explains that when the medicine man, Yobue, was brought from Bonny, he was initially settled in the village of Keon. Later on, the elders of Boue came and took him from Keon to Kònó Boue where land had been provided for him.

Having introduced the new weapons into the war and having secured the services of a warrior-medicine man who would teach them how to use the firearms in battle, the Boue armies began a new offensive against the north. Baan people were decisively defeated and the war brought to an end. The Boue Kingdom emerged as the champions of the war and remained the most powerful and the leading state in Ogoni from the sixteenth century until the colonial conquest at the beginning of the twentieth century.

10.4(e) *The Change to Patrilineal Monarchy and Succession*

One of the most significant changes that took place in Ogoni as a result of the Baan wars was the change from matrilineal to patrilineal monarchy and succession. The fall of the Bariyaayoo dynasty at Luawii marked the dramatic climax of that change, which had begun with the elite practice of long distance marriages and ritual slave trade. The impact of the long civil war provided the practical experience and the setting for the dramatic change. Bariyaayoo was the heir and successor of Za. Her dynasty at Luawii rose to become the most powerful political institution in Ogoni during the sixteenth century. With the fall of Luawii, her power base eroded. The new kingdoms that emerged out of the war after her demise, such as the kingdom of Boue and the kingdom of Kpong, became male dominated and male-oriented.

Although later in the century, Gbenebeka, another female descendant of Za, appeared on the scene with a new dynasty at KaGwaara, her political role became mainly ritualistic but powerful. Her fame increased throughout Ogoni, not only on account of her royal descent but moreso because she was the glamorous associate of the great men of that time. For instance, she was said to have by arrangement of the elders of Boue, become the mistress of Yobue, the famous medicine man and warrior-guest of the kingdom during the Baan wars.

Owing to her glamorous character and association with the great men, she eventually received the *Gbene* title and thus became the third female ancestor of the Ogoni who got the *Gbene* title. The first was Gbenekwaanwaa, the first woman ruler of Ogoni; and the second was Gbeneyana, the founder of Ka-Gwaara.

Gbenebeka established herself at Ka-Gwaara on the legacy of Gbeneyana of Gwaara, from where she continued to receive the courtesy and the homage of the great rulers of Ogoni for ritual and spiritual blessings until her cult and shrine were destroyed in 1914 by the British colonial invaders.

10.5 The Kingdom of Gokana

The founding of Gokana, like that of Tee, took a certain dramatic turn quite different from the normal process by which most settlements and towns in Ogoni were founded. This was because Gokana was founded on the ruins of war. Gbenesaakoo was the acknowledged leader of the migrant "Khana armies" which conquered the territory. After the conquest, Gbenesaakoo became the dominant figure in the whole territory; and after building a war shrine at Giokoo, he established there as the first king of the Gokana people. The tenacity with which Gbenesaakoo ruled the Gokana kingdom comes out very clearly in the oral tradition. One of the methods he used was to ensure that no settler entered the territory without his permission. This practice was interpreted in Gokana oral tradition to mean that the founders of all the Gokana towns came from Giokoo, the dwelling place of Gbenesaakoo. An example from a testimony given in the town of Mogho will illustrate the point:

> According to what I heard from the ancients, two men on their journey came to Gbenesaakoo... He gave the land of Mogho to one and Kpoo to the other. Gbenesaakoo was the king of Gokana. He lived at Giokoo. All Gokana towns came from Giokoo before they were established in their different locations (Kpea, tape 27, 7th Feb., 1984).

10.5(a) Giokoo

Giokoo itself was not a town or settlement. It was a military base from where the leaders of the various Khana groups launched their attacks against their "Go" enemies during the wars of conquest in the area. Gbenesaakoo himself remained permanently at Giokoo, from where he directed and co-ordinated both the conquest and the settlement of the territory. There is no site in Gokana which might be called the site of Giokoo. What is called Giokoo, as far as this writer could see when he visited the place in 1984, is a small section of the town of Nweól, about fifty square metres where stands the palace of the Gbenemene Gokana. Behind the palace was another building which they said houses the shrine of Gbenesaakoo. Apart from that, there is nothing else at the place to indicate the component parts of a town. From what I could observe, it is clearly evident when it is stated in the oral tradition that Giokoo was not a town. According to one source, Giokoo was the meeting place of the great men of that time. It was the place where they met to discuss common problems and interests. Accordingly, the name was called Giokoo (ward or quarter for friends or comrades). Thus Giokoo was not the same thing as *Bue* (town). And Gbenesaakoo who lived there was their leader with whom they conferred. Perhaps a modern illustration which may help to illuminate the mystery of Giokoo is the United Nations Headquarters in New York, in the sense that the latter is only a section of the city of New York.

Major Arthur Leonard's description of Ogoni is thus shown to be completely distorted and incorrect. For example according to the Major:

> "One Ogbe-Saku, who was the first founder and king, lived in a town called Joko, which is of the southern half of the country. By this ruler, the latter was divided into sections or districts, which were named after the principal towns, viz Joko, We-o, Bewe and Boam; the first of these being the capital of N'galabia Ogoni; the second of Gogara branch, the third of Bewa, and the fourth of Boam; the people of the last mentioned locality being derived from Joko, while those of We-o and Bewa are related (Leonard,1906).

It is not the intention here to go into a debate with what the Major had written about Ogoni. All that a scholar needs to know is that the Major did not base his evidence on facts but on hearsay and on conjectures, as he himself also admits (Leonard, 1906:25,41).

At Bonny, the major came very close to Ogoni but he failed to visit the place to see things for himself. He was contented to rely on one of those preventive devices employed by Bonny people to scare away Europeans from venturing into Ogoni territory, which they had regarded as their economic preserve,

> ...but of the northern portion I was unfortunately unable to get any further information beyond the fact that the Ogoni are considered by the Ibani to be treacherous and excitable, and, in these respects especially, similar to the Ibibio in temperament and character. Unlike them, however, they are bad farmers and traders, and have the reputation of being the dirtiest people as well as the greatest cannibals in the Delta (Leonard, 1906).

All that may be said here is that Ogoni was a blue-collar society as opposed to the white-collar society of the Ibani, where Leonard lived. Perhaps the Ogoni were the "greatest" cannibals in the Delta but that by implication suggests that there were other great cannibal groups as well (see Jones, 1963:115,116). As shown in Chapter 11(Agricultural production), the Ogoni being farmers, knew how to determine who was a good farmer by the award of titles to successful farmers. Apparently, Leonard did not know about this. Apart from these few remarks, another thing that needed to be put right in Leonard's statement is the reference to a section of Ogoni which he called "N'galabia Ogoni. This is relevant because it concerns the Gokana area which is the subject of this discussion. The expression *"N'galabia"* is an Ibani idiom comprising several words compounded together. Rendered in full it would read *("M'naa gala bia")*, which means "I'm going and I'm coming back quick". Here, the idiom is used as an adjectival phrase to qualify a place, namely a "go-return" place; in our context that place being a particular part of Ogoni.

It is not at all clear why the Ibani should associate this particular expression with a part of Ogoni. But if one may attempt an explanation, it should be this. A glance at the map of the eastern Delta shows that the nearest mainland neighbour of Bonny is Ogoni, particularly the Gokana and Boue areas. Bonny traders could therefore attend markets in these parts of Ogoni by canoe and return on the same day, as against any other mainland market for which Bonny traders needed at least two days to be able to do the return journey by canoe (cf. Jones, 1963:38). It would seem therefore that through centuries of trade with the Ogoni mainland, this particular idiom had evolved in Bonny oral literature to identify that part of Ogoni where they could attend the markets for a quick trade and return home on the same day. Our context suggests that the Gokana area was that part of Ogoni. That is why Giokoo is said to be its "capital" and Gbenesaakoo its king.

10.5(b) Unitary State

Owing to the type of military discipline with which Gokana was founded, coupled with the personal charisma and dominance of Gbenesaakoo, who held together under his authority, every town in the area, Gokana began from the outset as a unitary state, unlike the other kingdoms such as Nama, Bangha, and Eleme, whose component parts consisted of several autonomous units.

According to one source, Gbenesaakoo was naturally a man of great power and popularity or charisma. Consequently, his name became more widely known than that of his father. The source further explains:

> All people who came from wherever they came, settled first at Giokoo. When they had found a place for themselves, they came to Gbenesaakoo who gave them "strength" (*ooge*) before they went to settle in that place. As each found a site suitable for settlement, each reported to Gbenesaakoo, who took the one round the place and vested him with authority to rule that place.... This method continued until all the Gokana towns were founded. That was why they named all the Gokana towns, 'Gokana-Saakoo' (Bagia, tapes 28/29, 19th Feb., 1984).

In Gbee, the oral tradition described the Giokoo connection in these words:

> The founder of Gbee was Gbeneyogbaa. He was the first man who settled at Gbee. He came from Giokoo. When the founders of Gokana first came, they gathered at Giokoo. The reason they called that place Giokoo was because all the founders who gathered there were friends and equals or comrades. From Giokoo, the people spread to the different places where they founded settlements and towns (Gia, tapes 27/28, 8th Feb., 1984).

The above testimonies show clearly that from the outset, Gbenesaakoo was acknowledged by all as the king of Gokana. Such acknowledgement extended also to the neighbouring states such as Bonny, as shown in the reference from Major Leonard quoted above. One of the sources quoted above confirms that all the Gokana towns are collectively called "Gokana Saakoo". That expression was a Kana/Gokana praise name, emphasising the fact that all Gokana was acknowledged as the "land (or the domain) of Gbenesaakoo. His authority and rulership was undisputably and unquestionably acknowledged.

Over the centuries, the magic of the name "Gbenesaakoo" has been the one factor that has continued to hold the kingdom together as a unitary state. No ruler in Gokana has succeeded in establishing a new dynasty without claiming or drawing his legitimacy on the legacy of Gbenesaakoo, the national hero and king of Gokana people.

Yet the name Gbenesaakoo was neither an eponym nor a patronym nor a spurinym, since his genealogy and paternal relations are known (see Henige, 1974; 1992:100). Moreover, the people of

Gokana did not practice positional succession as is done in some African states such as Yorubaland. For example, the king of Ijebuland was called "Awujale," which was a positional title quite distinct from the personal name of the incumbent of the office (Ogunba, 1973:92). In such a case, the positional title remained perpetual, where as some of the individual personal names of the various holders of the office might be forgotten (Henige, 1974). This was not the case with Gokana where the incumbent of the office of king (Gbanemene) retained his personal name. Yet the name of Gbenesaakoo appears to have remained permanent.

What seems to have taken place in the Gokana system is that every ruler who succeeded to the stool managed to identify himself with the name of Gbenesaakoo, without actually adopting this name for himself or as a title. But he nevertheless claims some kind of relationship with the famous charismatic founder and ruler of the Gokana kingdom.

10.6   The Kingdom of Tee

Like Gokana, the settlement of Tee was also by conquest. Indeed, it was in Tee that the Khana migrants first encountered the resistance of the "Go"peoples. Under the leadership of Gbenekuapie, the Khana migrants over-powered the "Go" peoples in Tee area, forcing a large number of them to migrate to the coast to settle in the area now known as Gokana. Gbenekuapie, the acknowledged leader of Tee people consolidated his rulership over all Tee people and became their first king. However, in the periods after the era of Gbenekuapie, certain units of Tee began to assert their own autonomy. Some units even claimed supremacy over Uweke, the capital town of Tee in the era of Gbenekuapie. One such units was the city state of Kaa, which came into prominence around the end of the seventeenth century, probably growing out of the Baan wars. Kaa became the most prosperous and powerful city-state in Tee in the eighteenth century.

It seems that its leaders engaged in long distance trade, especially the slave trade. Collateral evidence supports this. Moreover, Kaa was strategically located on a major trade route from the Igbo hinterland to the coast (Map 6). But Kaa was hated by her neighbours and subordinate towns. It is thought that this hatred grew out of jealousy because of her prosperity, or because of her oppression, or both (Dewhurst, 1936). The result was that a bitter war ensued in which all of Kaa's neighbours and subordinate towns joined together against her. In the end, Kaa was defeated and destroyed. Its inhabitants scattered to other places and some founded new towns. Kaa's agricultural lands and surrounding territory were occupied and shared out by the former subject towns and neighbours. The account recorded at the beginning of the colonial administration in Ogoni gives the story in a sketchy way thus:

> Long ago, an old town called Kaa inhabited the whole of this land. The people of that town disappeared and as a result many towns – Kpuite, Deke, Kani, Uweke, Yeghe, and Deeyo – shared out this land. The reason the town of Kaa was left by all the people was that Kaa had a war with another town and other towns joined in the war against them so that the people expected to be exterminated had fled away. This was before anyone now alive was born (Dewhurst, 1936).

Those towns which had fought against Kaa and had shared out the land which formerly belonged to Kaa became themselves embroiled in a dispute over that land. Evidently, some of the towns which had taken part in the war against Kaa had been cheated in the sharing of Kaa's land as this problem had become perennially recurrent during the periodic farming on that land. Some of those towns now sought to involve the colonial administrators whom they expected to adjudicate the matter.

After the fall of Kaa, Kpuite emerged as the leading town in Tee under the leadership of Yaa. According to the account, Yaa was a slave trader who had connections with the king of Ko (Opuoko) on the Imo River. The king of Ko himself was a close friend of the king of Bonny, with whom they carried on the trade in slaves. The king of Bonny brought firearms to the king of Ko who passed on some to king Yaa of Tee. The source described the connections as follows:

> One called Yaa was a ruler in Tee. He was a friend of the ruler of Ko. The Ko people and Bonny people were close friends, like two fingers of the hand together. The Bonny people passed many firearms to Ko people. Yaa obtained some of the firearms from his Ko friend. With

these, Yaa became powerful in Tee. People became afraid of him. Thus Yaa became a ruler in Tee, although the houses of the chiefs of the towns still existed (Ngito, tape 15, 17.3.84).

From the above testimony, it is evident that Yaa was not from a royal house in Tee. It suggests that Yaa was able to seize power because of his participation in the slave trade. But although Yaa had assumed the rulership, he nevertheless allowed the houses of the former rulers to survive. Apparently, this was because they no longer posed any threat to his rulership. It was also likely that they willingly surrendered the rulership to Yaa in recognition of the fact that it was he who possessed the means of defence. The account records that because of Yaa's influence and the firearms which he possessed, there was peace and protection in Tee. The result was that neighbouring towns and communities came to Yaa and pledged their loyalty in exchange for protection.

It will be recalled that the eighteenth century was the peak period in the trans-Atlantic slave trade. The distribution of the gun to agents of the trade presented a strong temptation to ambitious men who wanted power. In Ogoni, a number of such men were readily found, such as Atee of Kpong, Yaa of Tee, Igbara Abe of Boue, etc. With the gun in their hands, such men fomented troubles and victimised their opponents.

It might not be surprising if it was conjectured that the sudden overthrow of the city-state of Kaa in the middle of the night was the work of some ambitious slave kings or agents. And it would be even more surprising, if Yaa who had acquired these powerful weapons in Tee at this time, were to be ignorant of what happened at Kaa. As the oral tradition has indicated, the overthrow of Kaa was a well-planned invasion, most likely with the use of superior weapons such as firearms. One account records that the king and many inhabitants were killed in that night of the invasion, and that the surviving inhabitants who escaped from the town later founded other towns. Gbarakaa (lit. a man from Kaa) is mentioned as one of the notable escapees from the ill-fated city-state. He is credited with the founding of the town of Nwebiara in Gokana. Other towns founded by escapees from Kaa were Deeyo, Biara, Kaani (now a very large populous town north of

Bori township), etc. According to the account, the inhabitants did not return to the devastated city again because they feared a re-occurrence of the incident. But it could also be that a state of war existed in the area for a very long time after the initial fatal attack. Other sources mention the coastal market town of Kaa in Babbe as one of the towns founded by escapees from the ancient city-state of Kaa in Tee.

10.7   Bangha, Lueku and Eleme

Bangha, Lueku and Eleme, like Gokana and Tee were located on the trade routes from the hinterland (Map 6). Except Ko (Opuoko) in Bangha, Onne in Eleme, the political structure of those areas was based on autonomous villages and communities (cf. Ngofa, 1988:45). Consequently, their oral traditions do not mention any individuals or groups who emerged on the social scene more than a century ago to exercise wide powers capable of uniting the autonomous communities under one authority. However, because of their strategic locations on the major trade routes from the hinterland, their rulers participated in the trans-Atlantic slave trade, through which they gained prominence.

Accordingly, it will be appropriate to consider developments in these areas in Chapter 11, where matters of economic activities are discussed.

CHAPTER ELEVEN

ECONOMIC ACTIVITIES

11.1   Methods of Reckoning and Accumulating Wealth

The Ogoni are basically an agricultural people. The bulk of their wealth was derived from agriculture. But agricultural produce was difficult to preserve or store as wealth. Consequently, a large portion of their agricultural produce was sold off in order to convert the proceeds into other forms of property that could be preserved or stored as wealth, such as money.

From the account of Pereira and from Ogoni oral tradition, it is known that by the fifteenth century a flourishing trade in agricultural produce and other commodities was already in existence on the mainland fringe of the Eastern Niger Delta, for example, at the Bangha market in southern Ogoni (cf. Pereira, 1956). The agricultural produce traded in these markets were yams and other commodities from Ogoni and Ikwerre areas.

The archaic word for money *Kwiri,* now used only by spirit-mediums when possessed, was probably the common Ogoni word for the currency in use in the period before the arrival of white men in the eastern Niger Delta. Edward Kpea of Mogho, Gokana, gives the names of three kinds of currencies which existed in Ogoni in pre-colonial times, namely *Giaradaa, Nama-Kpugi* and *Ka-Kpugi.* According to him, *Giaradaa* and *Nama-Kpugi* existed from the time of the ancestors, but *Ka-Kpugi* was in circulation from pre-colonial to colonial times until it was withdrawn in 1949. The term *Ka-Kpugi* would therefore refer to the small manilas. On the other hand, the *Giaradaa* (lit. "Giant Teeth") would undoubtedly refer to the big manilas, which by the colonial times were no longer in circulation. In Khana area, these big manilas were called *Kporo*. From the above explanations, we may assume that the term *Nama-Kpugi* (lit. "Ancient money") probably referred to the money called *Kwiri* by spirit-mediums.

By the beginning of the sixteenth century, the Portuguese had introduced the large and the small copper and bronze manilas (Northrup, 1978:158; Ryder, 1977:40). The new money was now called *aan-Kpugi*. But these currencies were heavy and bulky when accumulated, and difficult to preserve from thieves. Some persons even tried to hide their wealth from thieves by burying their money in the ground, but burying money in the ground was very unsatisfactory and unsafe. Money so buried got lost completely when the owner died suddenly, or when a thief discovered its location. Moreover, it was found that wealth buried in the ground remained tied down and yielded no profit to its owner. For these reasons the early Ogoni found other ways and methods of accumulating wealth, which included investment in several areas of the economy, such as land, livestock, transport (canoes) and permanent tree-crops. I shall explain each of these methods of investing money in pre-colonial Ogoni in the subsequent sections.

11.1 (a) *Investment in Land and Livestock*

(i) *Investment in Agricultural Land*

Agricultural land offered the highest premium for investment in pre-colonial Ogoni. An individual whose crops yielded a bountiful harvest, who wished to save the increase from his crops, invested the proceeds on land. In pre-colonial Ogoni, agricultural lands were never sold out-right. If the owner of a piece of agricultural land was in urgent need of money, he could pledge his land to someone who was ready to give him the needed amount of money, provided the amount was commensurable with the size and quality of the land. Having paid for the land, the pledgee' was entitled to cultivate on the land as long as he wished until the amount pledged was paid back to him. The period the land was cultivated served as interest on the money invested. When the land was redeemed, the pledgee received the full amount pledged.

A hard-working, prosperous person could acquire several plots of farm lands in the different farming locations of a town or community. In some cases, the pledgers of agricultural lands were never able to redeem their lands. Such lands eventually became the permanent property of the pledgee. In post-colonial times, the sale of farmlands has become common. People have come to realise that the owner of farmlands could receive bigger amounts for his land if the land was put up for sale rather than to pledge, especially if the prospect of redeeming the land was uncertain. Farmland owners became aware that they could always buy another farmland in future provided one had the money. The more plots of farmlands a man or woman possessed the larger the size of his or her wealth in reckoning.

Certain conditions, however, governed the acquisition of farmlands by pledging. According to Chief Kiriki, one of such conditions was that all economic trees in a pledged farmland, such as oil palms (*Elaeisguineensis*), coconut palms (*cocosnucifem*), yagara (*Treculiaafricana*), etc., belonged to the pledger or owner of the farmland and not to the pledgee. The owner of a pledged farmland would still go into the farm to harvest his economic trees because the latter were never part of an agreement on pledged farmlands. However, when a pledged farmland has been put under cropping by the pledgee, the pledger or owner of the farmland was, by ancient convention, required to refrain from harvesting palm fruits in such a farm. But he could still harvest other economic trees in the farm. The informant explained that oil palms were the exception because:

> the cutting of palm fruits also involved cutting down some palm fronds which fall wild to the ground, often causing damage to crops. We perceive therefore, a convention which allowed the person whose crops were on the farm to harvest the palm fruits, so that if in doing so some damage was done to his crops, he would make no claims of anyone.

(ii) Investment in Livestock and Poultry

Livestock and poultry were another area in which the Ogoni invested their money. However, the Ogoni did not specialise in the keeping of livestock or poultry. Livestock and poultry were kept as subsidiary concerns to farming. The favourite livestock were cows, goats, sheep and fowls. Usually, an individual or family kept one type of animal, say cows or goats. Sometimes, a few fowls were added to the animals. A person interested in any of these brands of livestock might start with a few animals. A family or individual did not keep all the animals and birds in his stock under his personal care. As the animals multiplied, the young animals were given out to interested individuals in the village and in the neighbouring communities to raise on sharing basis.

It was considered a great favour and a token of love if the owner of livestock gave a young animal or bird from his stock to a person to raise on sharing basis. Such a favour was seen as a sure way for that individual to begin the accumulation of his own wealth. Thus the proverb was spoken:

O mue zaqara loo kome nam!
Dream you are surrogate owner of a cow!

The cow was the largest and most expensive livestock. To dream of oneself being the owner of a cow was like building castles in the air, a probability most unlikely to happen in reality. Because owning a cow entailed a great responsibility, the saying was spoken:

Kporo naa suqara kome nam.
The poor never accepts the 'gift' of a cow.

In the view of the society, the owner of a cow was definitely a rich man. The price of a cow was much more than the most expensive bride wealth. According to my informants, the price of a cow ranged from 2,000 to 2,400 manilas or more. Accordingly, a man who had several cows and bulls to his name was to that society as the millionaire is to the modern society. Thus, it was regarded as a grievous offence if any one did harm to a person's cow, or any valuable property. This was the basis of another proverb which says:

> *akato nam tage nyodee me a naa tan yie te-ere.*
> *The footprints of a cow may disappear from the road,*
> *but not from the heart of its owner.*

The dwarf cows were indigenous to the forest zone. They were among the animals domesticated during the Neolithic age. The oral tradition, however, suggests that they were naturally bred in the Eleme area. But Tee, Gokana and Eleme areas were settled by autochthonous peoples. From them, the Ogoni derived several cultural items, which probably included the dwarf cows and certain species of yam.

Before the owners of livestock gave out young animals to surrogate owners to rear on sharing basis, certain procedures were followed. The intending surrogate owner of animal must apply in person. If the indications were favourable, he would then formalise the application by buying a bottle of rum or gin and a calabash of palm wine and take them in company of a friend to the house of the owner of animal. At the home of the man or woman, he would present the drinks and say that he wished to be given a female issue of the mother animal for him to raise as surrogate owner. Once the drinks had been accepted and the libations poured in the presence of the friend who served as a witness, the owner of animal became legally bound to give a young female animal to the applicant according to the terms of surrogate services.

Once a surrogate owner was appointed, the sharing of animal followed a specific pattern. In the early times the sharing was in the ratio of 3:1. The owner of animal received the first three issues, while the surrogate owner received the fourth. In the second round, the owner of animal received the fifth, sixth and seventh issues, while the surrogate owner received the eighth. By that time, the mother animal was considered old and was either sold or slaughtered by the owner.

In a later period, the sharing was reviewed slightly in favour of the surrogate. The sharing in that period followed an initial 3:1 ratio. Thereafter the ratio was 1:1. In that case, the owner of animal received the first three issues, then the surrogate owner received the fourth. Thereafter the ratio of sharing was 1:1, until the mother animal was sold or slaughtered by the owner.

In still a later period, the number of first issues received by the owner of animal was reduced from three to two, and thereafter the ratio of sharing was 1:1. From about the 1950s, some surrogate owners have successfully pressed for equal sharing. Thus, during the last thirty years, the sharing between the owner of beast and the surrogate has been in the ratio of 1:1, the owner of animal receiving the first issue.

The condition for surrogate services for birds was slightly different. Application for surrogate service for birds did not require the payment of drinks. Application was made in person by interested persons. The giving of birds to surrogates depended solely on the goodwill of the owner. According to the oral tradition, the ratio of sharing birds has followed the same pattern as in the case of animals; i.e. progressively, the ratio has been 3:1, 2:1 and 1:1 from the earliest times to the present. However, in the case of birds, for each set of birds received by the owner the surrogate got one bird. In addition, the surrogate received all the birds when his turn arrived. This system of sharing continued until the mother bird was sold or eaten by the owner.

When the mother animal or bird was sold or eaten by the owner, the surrogate received a share of the sale money or a share of the meat, whichever was the case. If the animal or bird was sold, the surrogate received a certain amount which was about 6% of the sale price. This amount was called "Sweeping Money" or "Sweeping Fee" (*Kpugi Kpae Keto*). When the animal or bird was eaten; for animals, the surrogate received one foreleg and a piece of the heart; for birds, he received a breast.

Because cows produce only one issue in a year, the sharing of calves under the surrogate agreement was based on the number of years. Starting from the year the cow began to bear issues, the owner of the cow received a calf a year for three years, then the surrogate owner received his calf in the fourth year. However, under the modern surrogate agreement, a surrogate owner of a cow, got a calf every other year until the mother cow was sold or eaten.

Animals and poultry were not shepherded or kept in enclosures. They were allowed to roam about in the countryside or in the bushes surrounding the villages and homesteads, fending for themselves. Thus a man who invested in livestock ended up not caring for his animals alone, instead he distributed the caring among a number of families and individuals in several parts of the community or clan. His wealth was accordingly spoken of as spreading throughout the community or clan. Quite often, a person who started by investing on a few animals could raise a large stock in eight to ten years. During that period, all the male animals were killed for meat or sold to those who needed them for numerous sacrifices and rituals.

In 1950, the price of a big goat was about 160 to 200 manilas. One cow cost about 2,400 manilas, a cock cost about 12 manilas, and a hen 7 manilas. In 1699, a goat cost 1 bar of iron in the Niger Delta and a cow cost 10 or 8 bars of iron (Barbot, 1732).

Because the Ogoni viewed the acquisition of livestock and poultry as a business concern aimed at making profit and thereby increasing one's wealth, certain laws evolved which guided the relationship between the owner of livestock and the surrogate, so that no one of the two parties could be able to cheat the other without redress. For example, the application for surrogateship was made before the mother animal had actually produced her young. If before that happened, the owner of animal sold the animal or disposed of it in any other way, the owner of animal would be legally bound to buy a young female animal and give to the applicant to take care of under the terms of the surrogate agreement. If the animal died, the owner would be required to replace the animal and the applicant would be entitled to claim an issue of the replaced animal on the terms of the original agreement.

If none of the above happened but the animal had a stillbirth, the agreement became null and void. If the mother animal gave birth to a male, the agreement also became null and void, because male animals were never given out to surrogate ownerships. The applicant might be asked to make new application.

If an applicant was given an animal on surrogate ownership terms, if after the owner of animal had received his own share, the mother animal was sold by the owner or disposed of in any other way or the animal died, the owner of animal was legally bound to buy a young female animal and give to the surrogate as his own share.

If before the owner of animal had received his full share, or after the surrogate had received his full share, the animal became sick and died, the surrogate must return the carcass to the owner of animal or report the incident. If the animal was reported lost, the surrogate was required to replace the animal.

11.1(b)   Investment in Canoes (Transportation)

In pre-colonial times the only means of bulk transportation and movement for long distances was by canoes through the rivers and along the coastal waters. Possession of a large transport canoe was therefore a sign of wealth, as only a few wealthy individuals could afford to buy and own such transport canoes. Most long-distance traders who used such canoes could not afford to own their own canoes. Accordingly, prospective individuals who had money to save, invested on such canoes which were then let out to users on hiring basis at moderate charges.

In pre-colonial times, one such large canoe could cost about 1,200 manilas. Biiranee Gbenebai-kara of Ko (Opuoko), an expert canoe-maker, explains that the prices of canoes in pre-colonial and colonial times varied from £250.00 for the small fishing canoes to £650.00 for the large transport canoes. And Frank Mina informs us that in 1972, he sold a large canoe of about 52ft. long for £400.00, but adds that the price at that time was cheap for the size of the canoe. According to him, he did not haggle the price offered because the buyer was the then Governor of the Rivers State of Nigeria.

Some of the goods carried in such large canoes were pots, lumber, farm produce (such as yams, sugarcanes, plantains, fruits, etc); building materials (such as red earth, wattle, roofing mats, canes, piassava, poles, etc.), and certain red industrial barks used in palm wine production as flavouring and colouring agents. The paddlers were mostly hired men. The owners of the goods were usually one or two persons who did not have to own their own canoes. They hired or rented the canoes from the owners who might not be traders themselves.

At an early period, hiring charges on canoes were calculated on the basis of per trip, that is, each time the traders made use of the canoes, the owner charged a specified fee. The amount varied according to the distance of the market specified by the traders. In later periods, hiring charges varied according to the type of business the particular trader or traders were engaged in. In some businesses, the rents were changed per day, in others they were charged per week or per business trip. In this way, the canoe owners made reasonable profit on their investment. Because a canoe could last for many years without incurring major expenses on servicing or repairs, investment on canoes was usually profitable.

In the last forty to fifty years there has been a major shift in canoe investment in Ogoni. This shift has been occasioned partly by the opening of new roads and increased use of land transportation through the introduction of bicycles, cars, and lorries; and partly due to the decline of the pottery industry and pot-carrying trade, as a result of the introduction of modern ceramic wares, such as chinawares, aluminum pots, plastic containers and iron pots. These modern products forced the decline of the local coastal trade and transportation by canoes.

During that period, emphasis shifted from the large heavy carriers along the coast and in the rivers to the especially buoyant and fast-moving canoes for long distance trading and fishing between the Niger Delta and the island of Equatorial Guinea and between the Delta and the fishing grounds of Tiko in the Cameroons. Only the very wealthy could buy and equip this type of canoes, since it required upwards of £500,000.00 to equip and stock one of such canoes.

Often, the long-distance traders who stocked these canoes were different from the canoe owners, to whom rents were paid for the use of the canoes. The rents were usually paid for each return trip and commensurable with the type and value of trade goods carried on that route. On the Tiko route (fishing), the trip was once a year, from October to April. After that, the canoes were turned on to the Delta-Equatorial Guinea route for the rest of the year. On this route, the round trip took about three to four weeks. Bodo, Bomu, Dere and Baene are the best examples of Ogoni towns which specialise in this type of long-distance trading and fishing, involving the use of expensive canoes (cf. Scott, 1966).

This section was not intended to be a description of the canoe industry in Ogoni. Consequently, no description of the method of production has been considered here. This is discussed fully in chapter thirteen.

11.1(c) Investment in Permanent Tree-Crops and Plants

The most important tree-crops and plants in which the Ogoni invested their money as wealth were the oil palm, the raffia palm and the plantain. The Ogoni considered these permanent tree-crops and plants as high income-yielding concerns. Parents and the elderly often encouraged prosperous young men who had money to save to invest such money on those permanent tree-crops and plants.

Oil palm plots and bushes vary in sizes. Some oil palm bushes contain as many as a hundred, two hundred or more palm trees. But a bush containing any number of palm trees was regarded as permanent wealth. An oil palm bush was never sold outright. But the owner could pledge it for a sum of money. The oil palm bush reverted back to the owner when the amount pledged was paid back to the pledge. Since the last twenty or thirty years, owners of oil palm, and raffia palm bushes have adopted the system of selling seasonal crops, instead of pledging the palm bush for an unspecified period. By this method, the owners of oil palm or raffia palm bushes sell the entire crop for one or more seasons to the dealers for a lump sum of money. The dealers would then hire labourers to harvest the mature fruits during the season specified in the sale agreement. At the end of that season, the buyer's right to harvest fruits in that palm bush expired. In the case of raffia palm bushes, the owner of a palm wine bush contracted the tapping right to one or several palm wine tappers for a specified number of years, say three or four years, for a lump sum of money. At the end of the contracted period, the tapping right was terminated or renewed for another specified period. Usually with increased amount. In this way persons who invested on oil palm or raffia palm bushes made large profits on their investment.

In more recent times, owners of raffia palm bushes have discovered that they could still make higher returns on their investment if they sold the tapping right for individual matured raffia palm tree instead of contracting the whole bush for a number of years. Accordingly, in areas of high demand for palm wine, such as the Port Harcourt suburbs, Aba and Eleme areas, a matured raffia palm costs from $2,500.00 to $3,000.00, depending on the size of the tree. Thus, a person whose bush could produce ten large matured raffia palms in the same period could bag as much as $25,000.00 to $30,000.00 at one sale of tapping right. And the tapping period of matured raffia palm is three months; at the end of which the raffia palm is said to have died. By that time, a young replacement raffia palm had already been planted at the foot of each of the old raffia palm trees. In that way, the permanent state of the raffia palm bush was maintained. Thus, persons who owned plots of such permanent tree-crops were regarded as rich in the society.

The third category of permanent tree-crops and plants on which the Ogoni invested their money was the plantain. The plantain is one of the oldest food plants known by the ancient Ogoni. Together with yam, it was the principal ritual food used by the Ogoni in the worship of ancestral spirits. Apart from that, the plantain was always in great demand as a favourite staple. It could be eaten in several ways. It could be roasted and eaten with palm oil and fish; it could be boiled; it could be fried; it could be pounded – mixed with yams and eaten as foo-foo; it could also be baked and used as plantain chips; etc. The green plantain in particular contains a high level of natural iron and has little or no fat. For this reason, it was greatly demanded for feeding ante-natal women and nursing mothers, since it was known locally to increase the flow of breast milk and to hasten the replenishment of lost blood and energy after child-birth and during the monthly menses.

Thus in Ogoni as in most parts of West Africa, the demand for plantains was unlimited. Accordingly, prosperous individuals, especially women, who had money for saving, were always keen to invest such money on plantain groves. Like the oil palm and the raffia palm bushes, the plantain bush required very little caring. Moreover, it could increase its number by multiplying through its numerous sucker-system.

Like the oil palm also, the plantain plant or grove was never sold outright. This was because it was regarded as permanent wealth. When the owner of a plantain farm was in urgent need of money, he/she could pledge it. The plantain farm was redeemed when the owner paid back the amount pledged to the pledge. All the plantains harvested by the pledge during the period he held pledge to the plantain farm became the interest on his investment. Thus a person who held title to several plantain farms, raffia palm bushes and oil palm bushes, besides yam farms, coco-yam farms and cassava farms, was rated in the society as a wealthy man.

11.1(d) Acquisition of Manilla-Type Bronzes (Kporo)

According to the oral tradition, some of the wealthy men, besides investing in the various areas enumerated, after performing all the higher traditions, went a step further to save their reserves by acquiring the extra-large manila-type bronzes. Such manila bronzes were often displayed at conspicuous spots in their ancestor's shrines, where they remained to bear testimony to their wealth and serve as rare pieces of treasures or luxury items.

Professor Alagoa suggests that these bronzes originally entered the Niger Delta through long-distance trade contacts with the hinterland peoples (Alagoa, 1976). But their introduction into Ogoni may have been the result of trade relations with the hinterland during the era of long-distance marriage and during the slave trade. Ogoni was Bonny's nearest mainland neighbour; and during the period when Bonny dominated the slave trade, Ogoni acted more or less as second middleman between Bonny and other hinterland peoples. Accordingly, some of the European goods and firearms passed through Ogoni agents to places further away in the hinterland.

In those olden days, these large bronze manilas could not be stolen, since they could not be used in the ordinary monetary transactions, and they could not be found in ordinary houses. Those houses or compounds which possessed them were classified and well-known. From this system of 'saving', a proverb came into existence. Whenever it was noticed that a person was stingy or unwilling to spend his money, even on what was essential, the proverbial rhetorical question was asked, "Is it *Kporo*?" (*"Alu Kporo?"*). Kporo was the name given to these extra-large manila-shaped bronzes, and the term conveyed a sense of weight or massiveness, such that it would be unthinkable to expect anyone to attempt to lift or move it from its place.

One informant whose ancestral shrine houses one of these big manila bronzes explained how and why his ancestor acquired it:

> Because of much money which my ancestor possessed, when he had done all the things he wanted to do with money, he preserved this Kporo to remain so that his descendants might come to see it, saying, 'when they will come to see this Kporo in my own compound (*Be*), they will know that I was a rich man who had money.' He got this money after he had performed the *Yaanwii* tradition and all the higher traditions and had become a member of the ruling class *(Pya Kanee)*. As he still had plenty of money, he exchanged it into *Kporo* and preserved it. (Oodee, tape OG/SK/5, 30.12.83).

In more recent times, these manilla bronzes have become the object of thefts, but a few can still be found in shrines throughout Ogoni. In some cases, they have been hidden away by their owners. (See figure I, PP. 376-377).

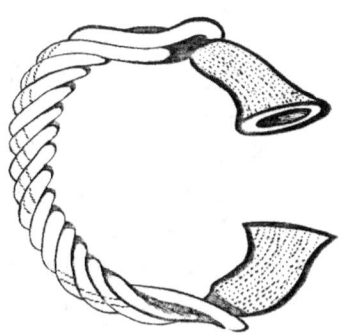

11.2 Agricultural Production

Ogoni tradition describes the yam, *Zia* (*Dioscorea Cavenesis or D. rotundata*) as the first indigenous crop cultivated by their ancestors. They speak of the yam crop as the first food that ever came into the world, and the first that men ever ate. This may have been a reflection of the important place the yam has come to occupy in their culture, which makes it an integral part of their ancestor worship.

Next in importance to yam were plantains (*Musa paradisiacal*) and the old cocoyam *geere* (*colocasia antiquorum* or *c. esculentum*). Jack Harlan notes that a well developed yam-based agriculture existed in the forest zone of West Africa before rice was introduced from the Savanna zone (Harlan, 1982). And Frederick Irvine has specified about seven species of wild yams in West Africa (Irvine, 1969). Recently, linguistic studies by Professor Kay Williamson has shown that the root of the word for yam can be traced back to Proto-Benue-Congo, and even beyond to Proto-Niger-Congo (Williamson, 1988:97). This implies that the yam was known to the speakers of the proto-languages of these areas, including the proto-Ogoni speakers. It is no coincidence therefore that over the centuries, yam cultivation in Ogoni has become a big institution. Every village has a yam shrine and yam priest. There was also a central shrine and a chief yam priest for every clan.

One of my informants, Deebari Igbug, claims that his own ancestor was the first man who domesticated the yam in Ogoni. He further claims that his ancestor also domesticated the plantain. But the tradition for the plantain does not appear to be as strong as that for yam. The plantain is, however, generally recognised as one of the ancient foods of the ancestors. Professor Kay Williamson suggests that the plantain is a member of the South-East Asian food complex (Williamson, 1988). It may therefore, be suggested that the tradition about the plantain probably developed out of its long association with yam in ritual services.

Yam cultivation gradually became the chief occupation of Ogoni people. Through it the citizens distinguished themselves in society. In Eleme area, titles in yam cultivation and production became the chief means of social recognition and political ascendancy. The number of large quality yams produced by a farmer at one harvest was recognised by the granting of titles.

The series of yam titles was graded from the least to the highest. The first in the series known as the "Two hundred" (*Aachu*) was achieved when the farmer was able to produce two hundred stakes of large smooth yams at one harvest. There were twenty-two such yams on each stake. Thus the total number of yams required for this first title was 4,400 smooth yams at one harvest. The second title in the series was the *Obo* title. An aspirant to this title was required to double the number of large smooth yams required for the first title. Accordingly the number of yams required for the *Obo* title was four hundred stakes or 8,800 smooth yams at the same harvest. For the third title in the series, the aspirant was required to double the number of yams for the *Obo* title. The aspirant to the third title known as *Obere Obo* title was required to produce at the same harvest, eight hundred stakes of yams or 17,600 large smooth yams. The last and highest title in the series was the "Four thousand stakes" (*Achu Ete*). Besides the four thousand stakes, there was in addition one hundred stakes of super-weight yams, known as *Ewo Achu Nsi*, which was used to form the front line staking in the barn arrangement. Thus, the total number of yams required for the *Achu Ete* title was 90,200 smooth yams at one harvest.

Only very few could attain the *Achu Ete* title in a generation. In recent times, however, a few modern farmers have attained this title but they have done so under very favourable conditions. One of my informants, Chief Hon. J.D. Osaronu, is among the few who have achieved this title in recent times. Farmers who had achieved from the *Obo* title up, were known as "Yam Chiefs". Those who attained higher titles occupied the top political positions as chiefs and rulers of the people.

Other crops the Ogoni produced were plantains, *ebue* (musa paradisiacal), peppers, *abege* (capasicum fratescens) maize, *kpaekpae, zia* (yams), vegetables, fruits, nuts, cocoyams, *geere* (colocasia antiquorum or c. esenlentum), *Ide* (Xanthosoma sagittifolium), oil palms (zoo), (Elaeis guineensis) raffia or raphia palms *Koe* (raphia hookeri), etc.

Somehow the banana, *ebue-bani* (*Musa sapientum*) and the cassava or *manioc ekpakuru* (*Manihot utilissima*), did not quite gain full acceptance in Ogoni society. The cassava in particular became an 'apartheid' crop. It was never planted in a farm in which yams and other crops were growing. It had to be planted on its own farm apart, usually on sub-grade farms. Its tubers, or flour (farina), garri, chips, etc. were never admitted in the main sections of the markets where yams were sold. It was a taboo to the elders and priests, and was never allowed to be borne through a town square. Similarly, but to a lesser degree, the banana, especially in the ripe state, was never eaten by an elder, a gentleman or lady. For an adult to pick up a ripe banana and eat it was unsavory behaviour, and smacked of worldliness and profanity. The best treatment that was given to the banana was to boil it green and eat it dipped in a vegetable salad.

A.E. Afigbo has made a similar observation among the Igbo with respect to the cassava and the banana (Afigbo, 1980).

The women's crops included several minor varieties of yams and other crops, such as water yam, *ya* (*Dioscorea alata*), aerial yam, *Sia* (*Dioscorea bulbifera*), three-leaved yam, *tuu* (*Dioscorea dumentorum*), etc. The women also had control of the maize or corn, cassava, vegetables, peppers, melons, *ikpeeton* (*colocynthis vulgaris*), fluted pumpkins, *nya-ee* (*telfaria occidentalis*), etc.

The old cocoyam was planted by both men and women. Indeed the old cocoyam was a favourite food of the elderly. Ritually, it was the food for the dedication of a new home, i.e. the first food to be cooked and eaten in a new home. In Ijo area, Kay Williamson has also observed that the Kolokuma used the old cocoyam as a special festival food (Williamson, 1970).

The old cocoyam could be eaten in many different ways. The finger-like suckers could be boiled and eaten with vegetable salad. The bulb-heads could be cooked, pounded and eaten as a soft foofoo. It could also be prepared as a soft oil-chop. The other type of cocoyam known locally as *Ide* (*Xanthosoma sagittifolium*) was traditionally regarded as of foreign introduction. Unlike the banana and the cassava, however, it has been fully accepted as a food by all classes of society. Nevertheless, the *Ide* could not be pounded and eaten as a *foofoo*, because it was hard and not as supple as the geere. Consequently, among the Ogoni, the new cocoyam (*ide*) was never eaten as a dinner or as the main dish of the day. Its main property, and attraction was that it could be roasted or boiled and eaten quickly while the main food for the day was being awaited.

Because of the high social and political reward which could be gained from success in yam production, most Ogoni farmers made yam their principal crop. Large quantities of yam and other agricultural produce were sold to their Ijo neighbours: in return, they imported fish and other sea foods, from the latter. Large quantities of yams were also sold to the Europeans through their delta agents, particularly Bonny, as part of the trans-Atlantic trade. The yams and other agricultural produce were needed to feed both the slaves and the ship's crew.

In 1699, James Barbot bought 60,000 yams for use during his voyage. He gives the price of the yams and other goods as follows:

King's yams	-	60 for 1 iron bar
Slaves' yams	-	160 for 1 iron bar
A goat	-	1 iron bar
A cow	-	10 iron bars
A calf	-	8 iron bars
A jar of palm wine	-	1 iron bar

(Barbot, 1732)

Barbot ordered for these quantities of yams and other goods through his agents at Elem Kalabari. Our knowledge of the trading system within the Eastern Niger Delta region suggests that there was trade contacts between Ogoni and Elem Kalabari, as well as between Ogoni and Bonny and other delta states more especially in connection with trade goods other than slaves. The indications are that Barbot's agents could have obtained the yams from any of the hinterland markets bordering the Eastern Delta, including the Ogoni markets. But to the Barbots themselves, all the hinterland bordering the Eastern Delta was Igbo. For example, a two-edged, curved sword engraved by Barbot (or his companion) is said to have been bought for him from an Igbo hinterland market by his agents. That knife has been identified by this writer as the Ogoni traditional knife called *Kobege*, which was used as the insignia of titled men who had performed the *Yaage* tradition (see Barbot, 1752:462, vol. V, Plate 26, item "E"). It is yet to be shown another people or ethnic group in the immediate areas which have a similar weapon or knife. An example of this knife is shown in Appendix IV.

Another indication that Barbot's agents probably bought some of their yams from Ogoni markets is shown by Barbot's classification of yams into "King's yams" and "slaves' yams" (Barbot, 1732). This classification is similar to Ogoni classification of the yam crop. What the Europeans called king's yams appears to be a reference to the *Mgwe*, which was the competitive elite crop planted by the yam chiefs for titles. This round variety was smooth, dry, tasty and absorbent in good palm oil. It was also easily digestible. Opposed to it was the hard, comparatively smaller and non-absorbent yams which were part of the women's crop. This was probably what they have called "slaves' yams". Perhaps this class of yams was reserved for feeding the slaves.

Although the Barbots gave their prices in iron bars, it is known that by the end of the seventeenth century, the most important currencies in the markets of the Eastern Niger Delta were manilas. However, evidence from the beginning of this century suggests that there were money changers in the market centres who exchanged money into the various local currencies.

Part of the income derived from the sale of yams was invested in farmlands, in oil palm and raffia palm bushes and in plantain farms, a part for marrying new wives, and a part for performing the higher traditions for more titles for greater social and political recognition.

Farm labour was organised somewhat on the basis of sex. There was a kind of division of labour between men and women. In the early times the distinction between men's and women's labour was clear-cut. The men cut the sticks for staking the yam vines. The women carried the sticks from the bush to the farms. The men did the staking of the yam vines, the women did the weeding. The men tended the yam vines, the women saw to the planting of the minor crops, such as the fluted pumpkins, maize, peppers, okra, melons, etc. around the farm and in-between the yam stakes. In later times, the division between men's labour and women's has become blurred. Men as well as women now cut the sticks; and both men and women do carry the sticks from the bush to the farms. However, men still do the staking of the vines, but it is not uncommon to see a woman staking the vines, especially the single women.

The heavy tasks like bush clearing, uprooting unwanted tree stumps, the circular-ploughing, etc. were done by hired labour, supplied by both local and migrant labourers. There are sufficient evidence in Ogoni oral tradition which indicate that hired labour particularly migrant labour was an integral part of labour organisation in Ogoni agriculture from very early times. The Ibibio and the Asa (*Pya Saga*) are mentioned in the oral traditions from a very early period. Other sources of labour were in-laws, relatives, *Yaa* patrons and pages, clients, and labour cooperatives or labour contributions. There is no mention of slave labour. This is probably due to the fact that slaves were incorporated and assimilated into families and households and did not exist as independent groups or as an institution.

11.3 Crafts and Manufactures

In addition to agricultural production, the Ogoni also specialised in a variety of manufactures. Pottery, canoe-making, salt-manufacturing, smithing, carving, and weaving were among the crafts and manufactures. The capacity of some of these industries, for example, smithing, depended on the sale of local demands and patronage. For others like pottery, salt, canoes and woven materials, the level of production was dictated both by local demand and by the demands of long-distance trade.

11.3(a)   Pottery

The oldest and most important industry was pottery. Finds excavated at Nama show that finely decorated pottery had been produced very early in Ogoni history. According to one informant, Ogoni pottery had undergone many changes over the centuries. Samples of different types of pottery have been found among the finds excavated at Nama. Samples of other types of vessels have also been found in old shrines (see Appendix V). Decorations appear to have been a common feature of Ogoni pottery in ancient times. In later times, however, the production skill appears to have been directed more and more towards the production of plain vessels for households and occupational requirements. This trend must have been occasioned by the demands of market forces. Production emphasis was therefore shifted from physical beauty to the basic requirements of quantity and utility, in order to satisfy the needs of the forces of demand. This condition must have developed in a situation where demand was consistently greater than supply, as a result of increased population without corresponding increase in production centres.

Evidence for this may be found in the fact that after the migration from the potting centres of Nama and Kugba, no other potting centre is mentioned in the oral tradition except the town of Kwuribue, and later the town of Kónò Boue. The migration of the people of Kwuribue to Kónò Boue as a result of the Baan wars increased the productive capacity of Kónò Boue, which became a large potting centre in the Eastern Delta area in the 18th and 19th centuries. From Kónò Boue, the potting industry spread to Kwawa, Buan and Luubaara. At a later date, a potting centre was developed at Ogu, about twenty kilometers to the west of Kónò Boue centres. But despite the new centre at Ogu, Okrika continued to import pots from the Kónò Boue centres until the late 1950s.

No archaeological excavation has been done at the Kónò Boue potting centres. Consequently, there are no potsherds from Kónò Boue for comparison with potsherds excavated at Okochiri and Ogoloma. However, archaeological excavations at Nama have revealed some early Ogoni pottery types. This writer has done a study of the Nama potsherds in comparison with Nzewunwa's detailed analysis of Niger Delta pot types (Nzewunwa, 1980). The study reveals no clear relationship between the Nama pottery and the Delta pots (Figure II: 1-28). The attributes compared in the study included rim forms, neck, body and decoration. Other attributes of comparison such as mean thickness, fibre/texture, colour, rim and body diameter, etc. were deliberately excluded at this preliminary stage for obvious reasons.

In the large majority of Nama pots, the rims are thin and incised or grooved into two thin lips'. The inner lip is generally incised with vertical or diagonal lines (Fig. II: 4, 5, 21). The necks are short and averted with a flare, such that the outside surface of the neck is turned away from eye-contact. The inside surface of the neck is thus brought to full view, and it is decorated. Where the inside surface of the neck is heavily decorated, the outside lip' of the rim is incised or grooved with Vertical' lines (Fig. II:3). Generally, in this variety of pot s, the outside of the neck is not decorated (Fig. II: 4,5,8,13,14,15). This is probably because it is not normally accessible to eye-contact.

As no whole pots were recovered, it is not possible here to describe how the shape of the pots looked like. The inside-neck decorations, of course, are various. Some appear in two, three or five deep incisions or grooves. The deep grooves are generally formed like concentric arc in slanting positions or in horizontal formations. In some cases the deep incisions are 'studded' with projecting knobs (Fig. I:9). Other forms of inside-neck decorations are sharp-angled wavy incisions in horizontal formations, obtuse-angled wavy incisions in vertical formations with the embossments punched with rounded holes at regular intervals (Fig. II:2,3,6). In others still, the deep incisions appear to be a representation of ferns (Fig. I:16). Where the outside surface of the neck is decorated, the necks are either vertical or semi-vertical (Fig. II: 12, 15, 17, 18).

Two samples of the Laadem, the Ogoni turn-table or 'potter's wheel' are shown in Figure II: 27, 28. Although they are partially broken, they none-the-less provide the evidence that this instrument had been in use at Nama. No other potting centre in the general area has shown evidence of using a similar device.

Body decorations vary from simple horizontal arc-shaped incisions to very sophisticated and articulate designs (Fig. II: 17-21).

Some of completely plain but very light potsherds were also observed; some with simple horizontal incisions and dotted with partial-punches or perforations (Fig. II: 23-25). A small, partially broken bowl picked up from the surface is shown in Figure II, 26. A heavy, solid, red-clay potsherd about 2.5cm thick is shown in Figure II, 22. This piece of potsherd is distinctly unique, and was recovered at a level of about 40 to 60cm.

Some potsherds found on the surface at Kugba, the traditional second settlement of Ogoni, show highly intricate and sophisticated decorations (Fig. II: 17, 18; cf. I: 19). Their sophistication indicates another stage in the potting industry. The rim form and decoration are distinctively different. One of the potsherds is perforated just below the neck (Fig. II:18). Excavation data for these potsherds, with detail of pit, level, location and date of excavation are provided in Appendix V.B.

Illustrations of pots and potsherds from Okochiri and Ogoloma and from other Niger Delta potting centres by Nzewunwa, have been carefully studied and compared with Nama potsherds. The Nama pots appear to be distinctly unique. For example, there are no inside-neck decorations in Ogoloma and Okochiri pots or indeed in the other Niger Delta pots. One of the distinguishing rim features of Delta pots as illustrated by Nzewunwa is "an external flange at the rim inclined downwards at an acute angle or further extended from a broad rim downwards in a bevel which gives a beak-shape when viewed in section" (Nzewunwa, 1980:208). Nama rim forms do not exhibit this characteristics (see Fig. II: 1-26). One simple conclusion that may be drawn from this study is that there was no material contact between the people of Nama and the people of Okochiri and Ogoloma, and indeed the rest of the Delta.

(i) The Laadem

One of the principal reasons for the dominance of the Kónò Boue pottery was the use of a mechanism called Laadem, which was a type of potter's wheel. As noted above, two samples of the Laadem have been excavated at Nama (Fig. I: 27-28). The implication is that the Laadem had been used in Ogoni for a very long time. The actual date will be known when the Nama potsherds are dated. The Laadem was shaped like a disc with a heavy knob at the bottom on which the disc rotated. The upper part was widened out and shaped like a saucer, so that its concave shape formed the bottom of the pot as it was being moulded by a slight tipping of the potter's big toe. The potter's hands were free to form the clay-coils one upon the other until the whole pot was formed. The potter sat on a stool but if the pot was a tall one, the potter stood on the ground or on a platform to mould the upper part of the pot, while the Laadem was kept spinning by the slight tipping of the potter's hand or big toe. Such tall pots included large water pitchers, palm wine storing pitchers, some ceremonial pots, etc. (Appendix V).

In terms of the technique of production, the Laadem put the Ogoni potting centres at Kónò Boue far in advance of any in the area. According to M.D.W. Jeffreys, the use of the Laadem was a considerable improvement on the potter's technique:

> In the scale of development which culminated in the potter's wheel, the Ladum (sic), turned by the foot, may be regarded as an improvement on the broken potsherd used by the Ibibio women (which involves continuous use of the left hand to keep it turning), and still more on the Igbo method, found in the Aboh Division, in which the potter walks round and round the pot (Jeffreys 1947).

This improvement in Ogoni pottery, which has been in use by the Ogoni from a very early period, was responsible for the wide extent of its market and high demand in Igbo, Ibibio and Ijo territories. A suitable clay was available locally at a place called Temaa.

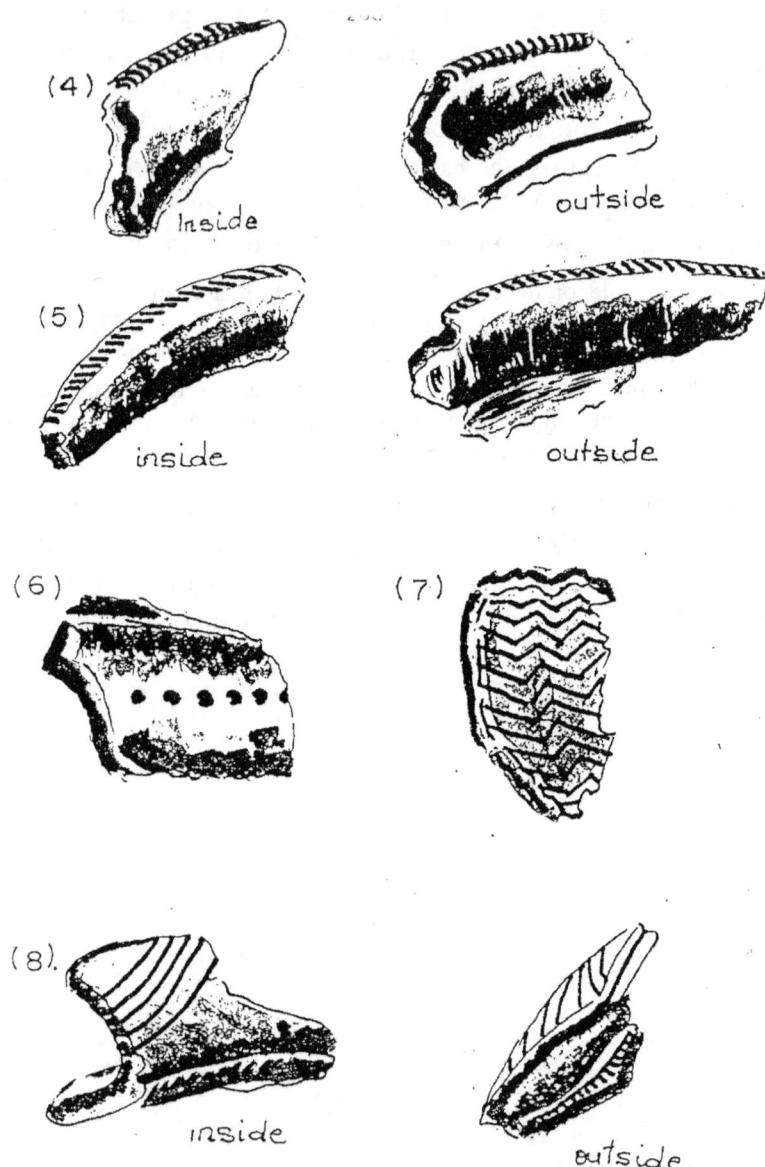

The rims are generally thin and grooved into two lips. The inner lips are incised with vertical or diagonal lines (Nos. 4, 5. 21)

Economic Activities 209

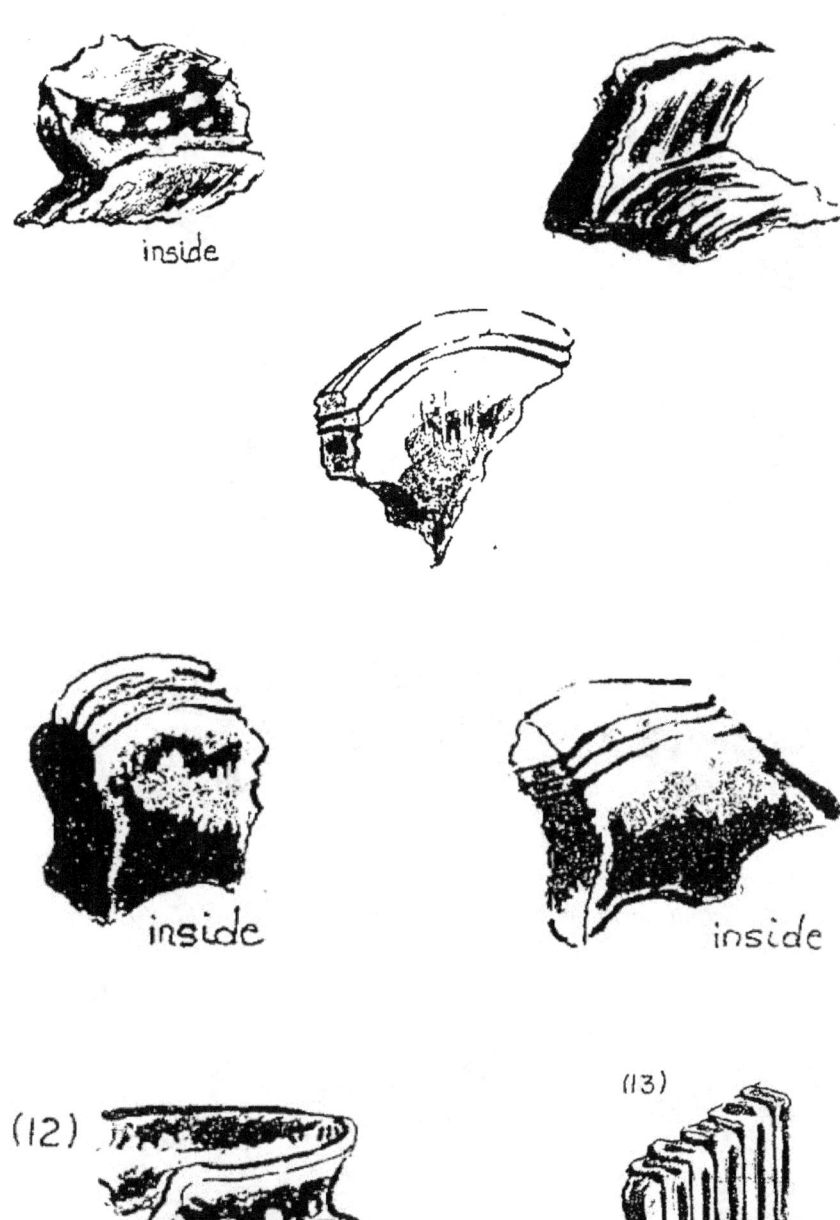

The necks are generally short and everted with a flare. The inside surface of the neck is heavily decorated with grooves and incisions (No. 3)

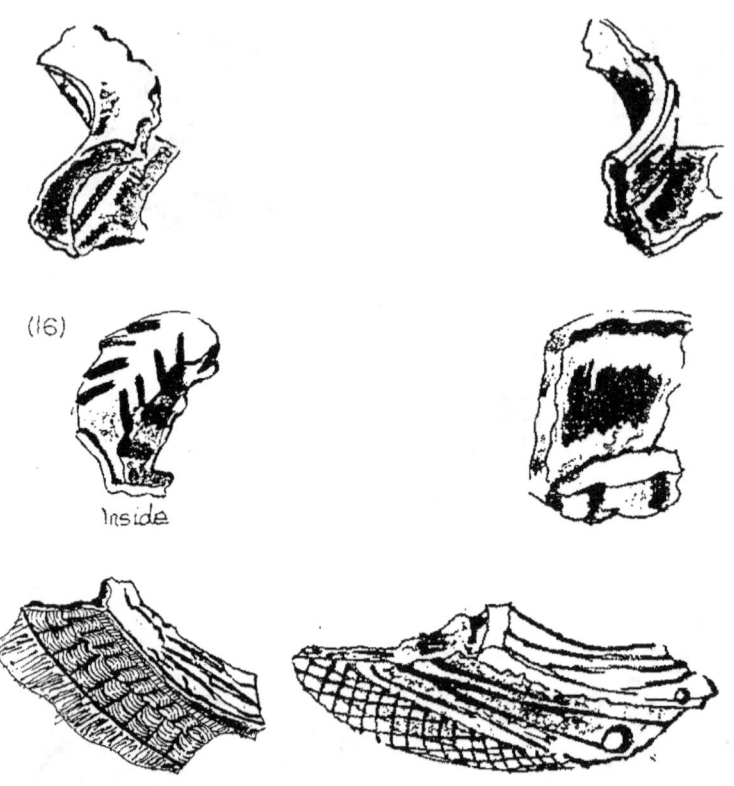

The outside surface of the neck is generally not decorated. This is probably because it is not normally accessible to eye-contact (Nos. 4,5,8,13,14,16)

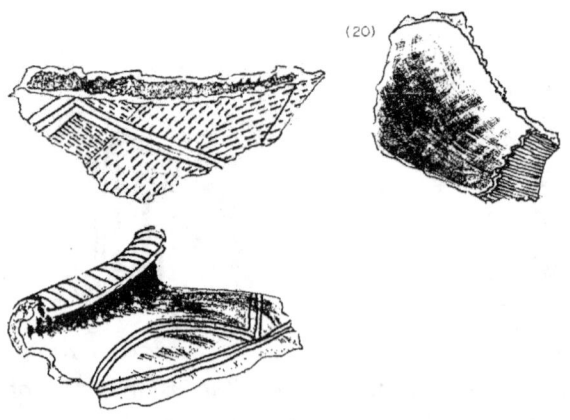

Potshered found on the surface at the site of Kugba, the traditional second settlement of Ogoni, exhibit a degree of sophistication in decorations (Nos. 17,18,19)

Two broken laadem (i.e Ogoni turn-table or potter's wheel) excavated at Nama (Nos. 27, 28).

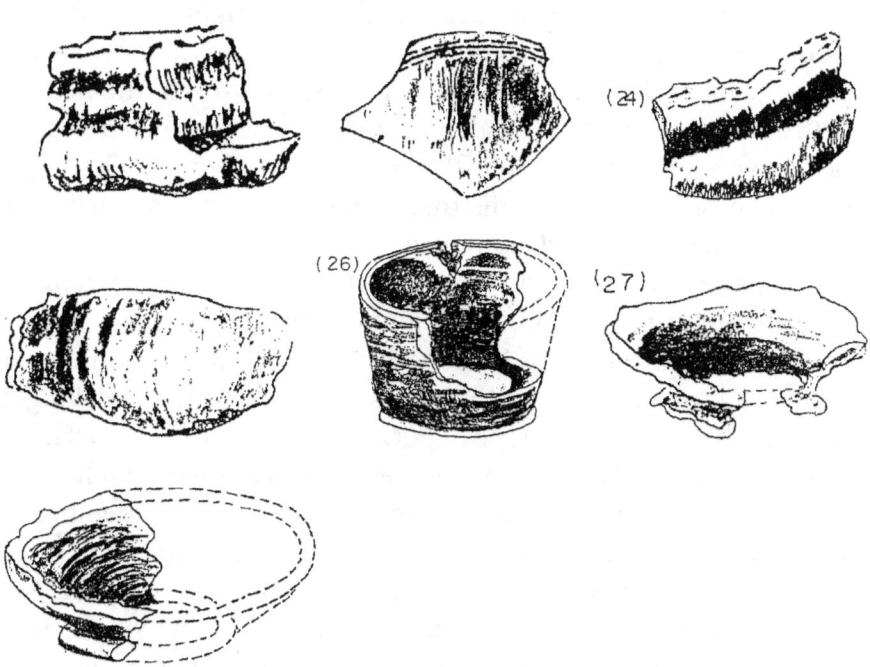

(ii) Organisation and Production

The Laadem increased the production speed and the output per potter per day. Like at Kwuribue, all the women of Kónò Boue specialised in pot-making, while the women of other Boue towns engaged in weaving. In Kwaawa, Luubaara and Buan, most women also specialised in weaving, while only a small minority of the women engaged in pot-making. Consequently, Kónò Boue became the main producers of pottery in the whole area. Demand for pots for both the local and the long-distance markets was therefore very high. With the aid of the Laadem, production was considerably increased to meet the high demand. One informant expressed the trend in a different way:

> In ancient times the people did not make as many pots as people did in recent times. The potters of today have been able to make larger numbers of pots than people were able to make in past times. They have also made new types which did not exist in ancient times. One of the new types is called Ikpu, another one is called Ibibiisi (Deezua, tape 16, Jan., 1984).

In modern times, a potter could make six to eight large pitchers in a day or ten to fifteen medium size pitchers in a day. The saucer-shaped Laadem also served as a pattern for standardisation, since the depth and diameter of the Laadem dictated the shape and size of the pot that was formed in it. And the potter knew the number, length and thickness of the clay-coils that would complete the particular size of pot that she intended to make.

Groups of women potters throughout the town organised themselves into pot-making contributions or potters' cooperatives called Lera-Ban. One day in a week they met at the home of a member and made pots for that member, each member making a given number of the same type of pot. The members did not all have to be at the same place. Some members stayed at their own homes, or chose to stay at the home of a friend who was also a member of the particular pot-making contribution or co-operative.

Once the name of the pot to be made was agreed upon, the members knew all the other details concerning that type of pot. With the details well-standardised, a potter could make the same type of pot irrespective of where she chose to stay to make them. The member for whom the pots were being made provided the clay already kneaded according to her quality of production, since the quality of a pot depended on the quality of the clay, the way it was kneaded, the texture and the proportion of "ingredients" or grit used. Such ingredients or grit included wood-ash, fine sand and ground potsherds.

"Sheets" of the kneaded clay were laid flat on the ground, measured, cut and rolled into soft "clay-scrolls". By measuring the clay, a potter could determined in advance how many pots of a particular type could be made out of one "clay-scroll." In this way, it was possible to know if a potter to whom a clay-scroll was sent cheated, that is, if she did not return the extra clay, or if she took some clay for her own use.

This was the cause of some of the problems which the members of a potters' cooperative had to contend with, since scrolls of kneaded clay were sent by the member receiving the pot-contribution to each member of the co-operative at the place she chose to stay to make the pots.

The Ogoni had about twenty-four names of different types of pottery wares. Because of the similarities of pottery types irrespective of the different potters who made them, the Ogoni devised a system of identification. This was the origin of the pottery "trade-marks" called *akuu-ban* (see Jeffreys, 1947).

When the pots of the same type were placed together, it was difficult to distinguish the pots belonging to the different potters. The use of the pottery trade-marks was therefore an attempt to solve the problem. Each household had a distinctive mark. A daughter used her mother's pottery trade-mark. A girl who was married to another compound adopted her mother-in-law's pottery trademark.

Some Ogoni Pottery Types

Source: Kote House, Kónò Boue

Source: Kónòboue

Source: Gbenekarayoo House

Source: Kpaankpaan Secret Society Kónò Boue

Source: Kónò Boue

216 *The Ogoni of the Eastern Niger Delta...*

SOURCE: YOBOUE HOUSE, KONO BOUE

Ogoni Pottery Trade Marks[1]

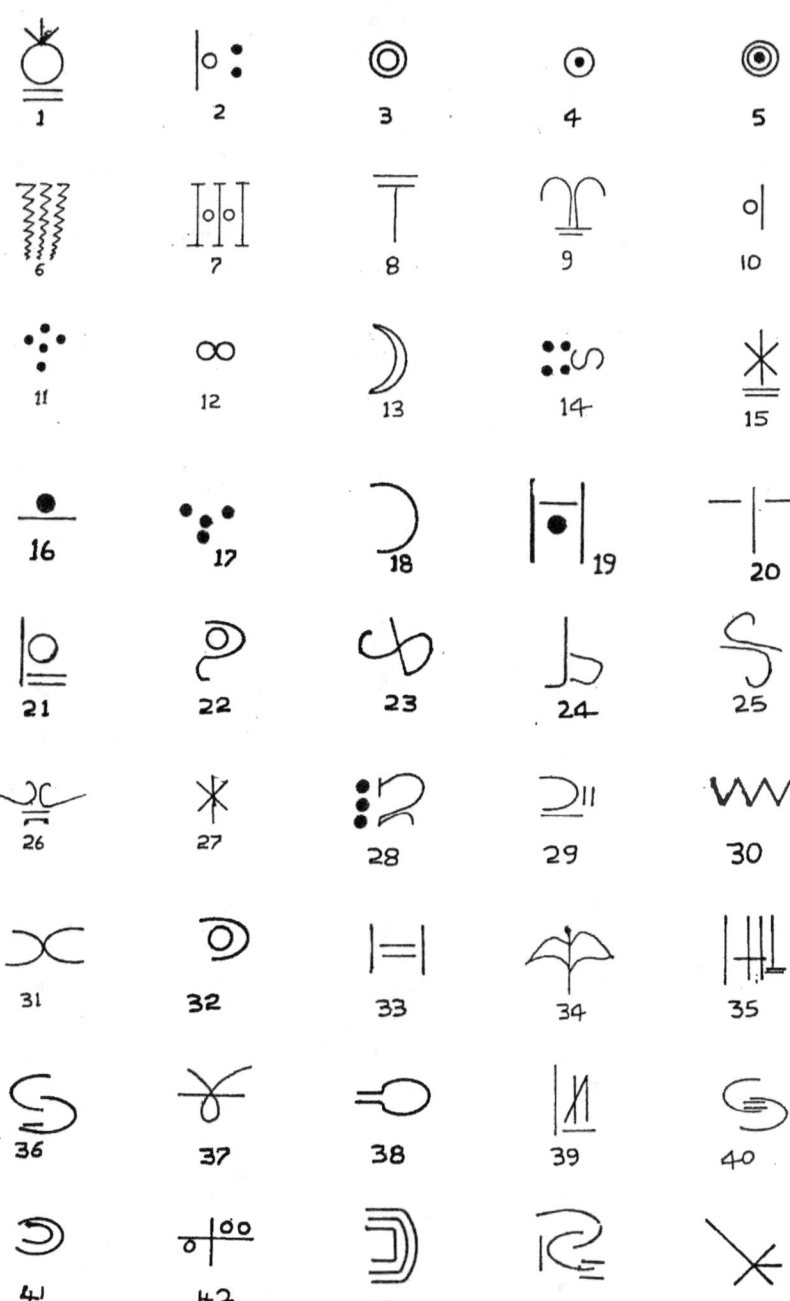

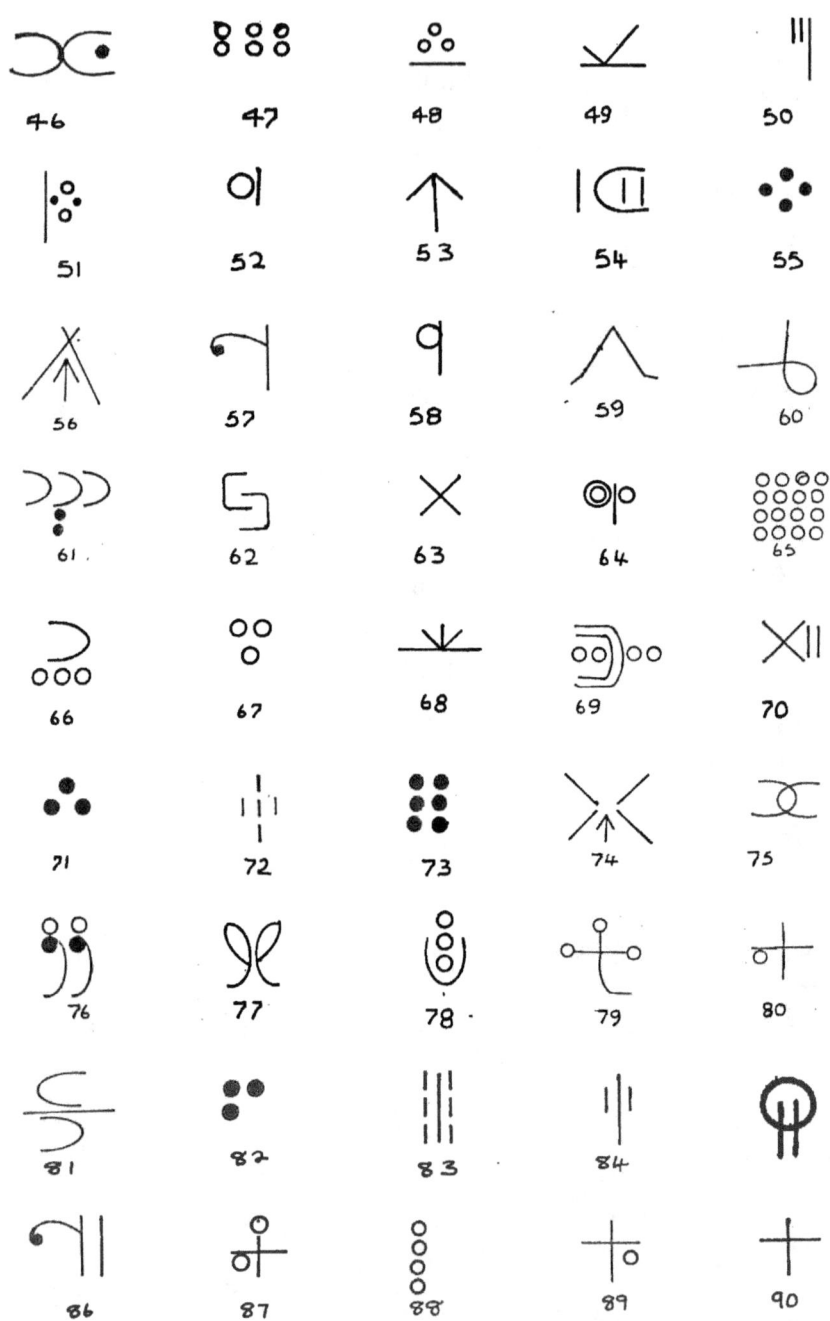

Economic Activities 219

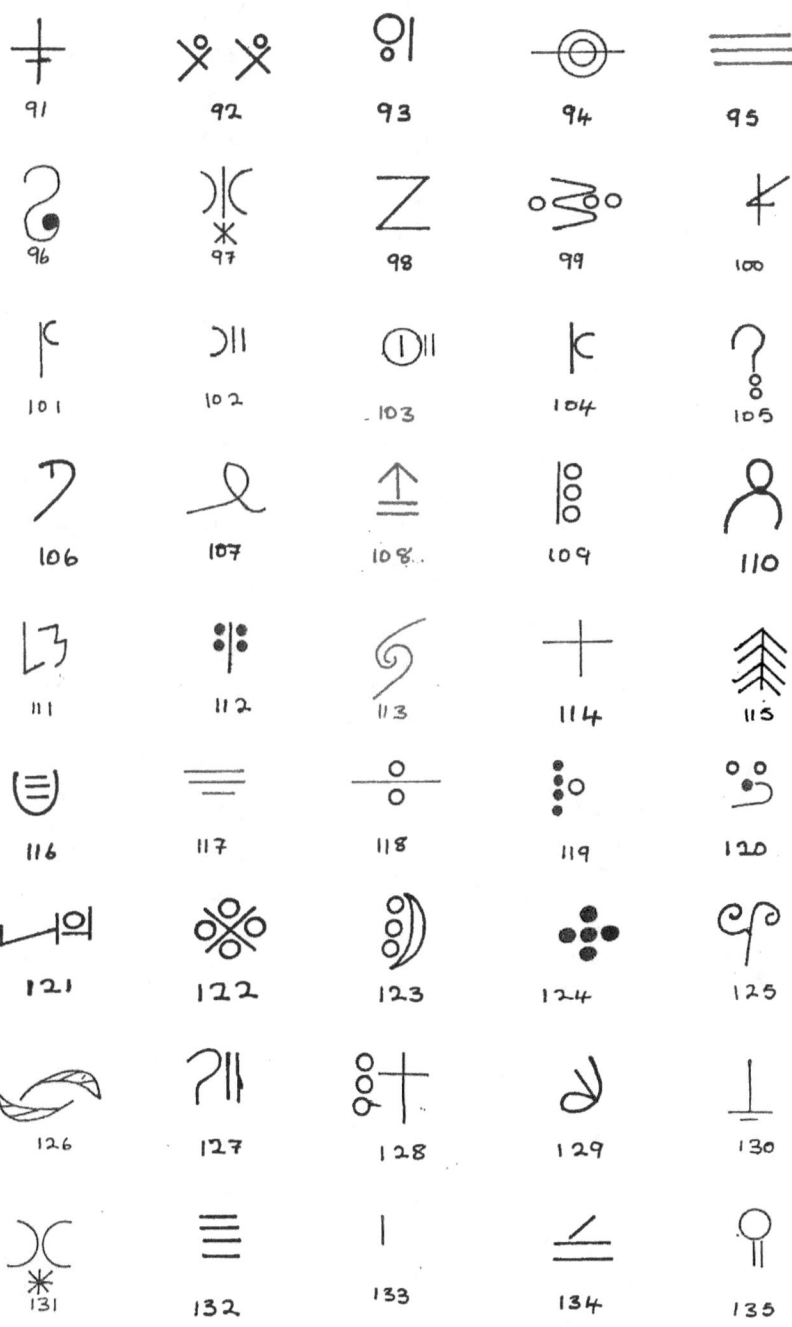

220   The Ogoni of the Eastern Niger Delta...

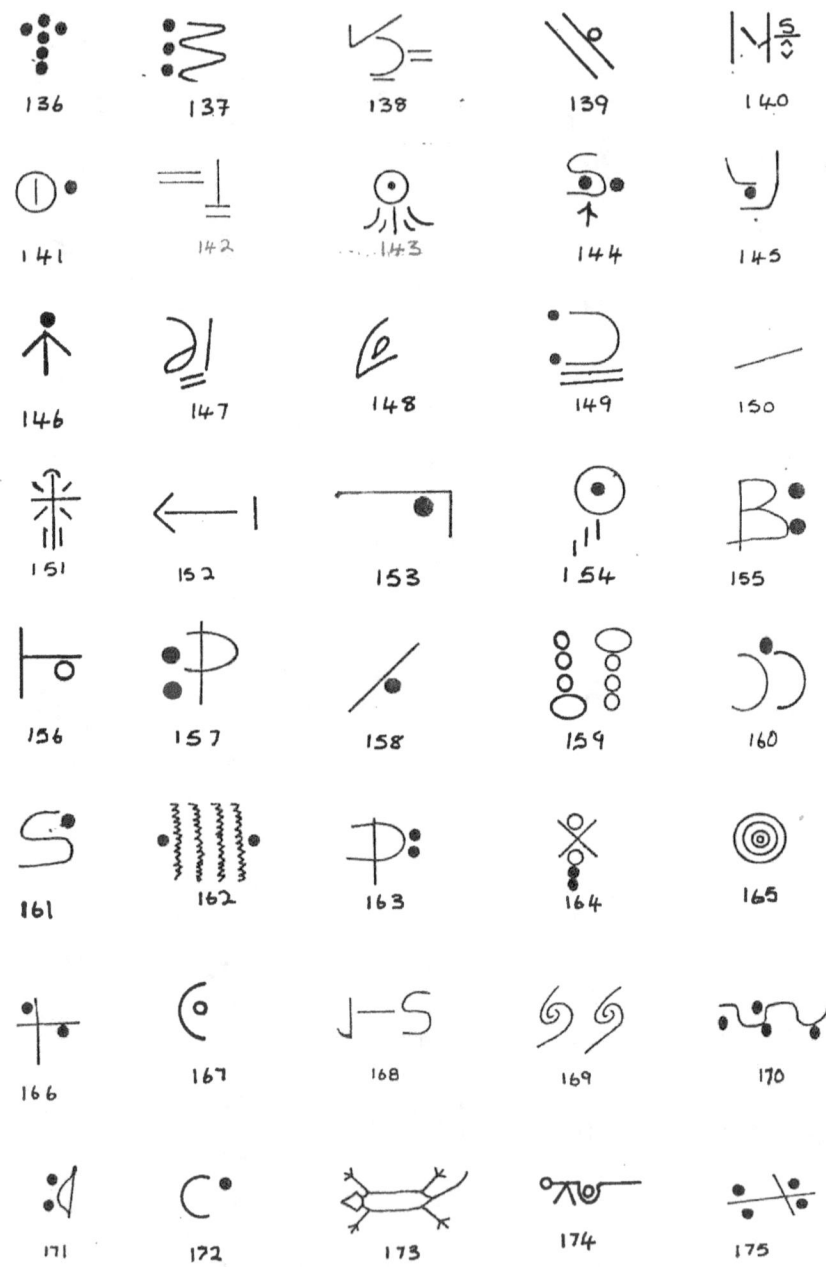

Economic Activities

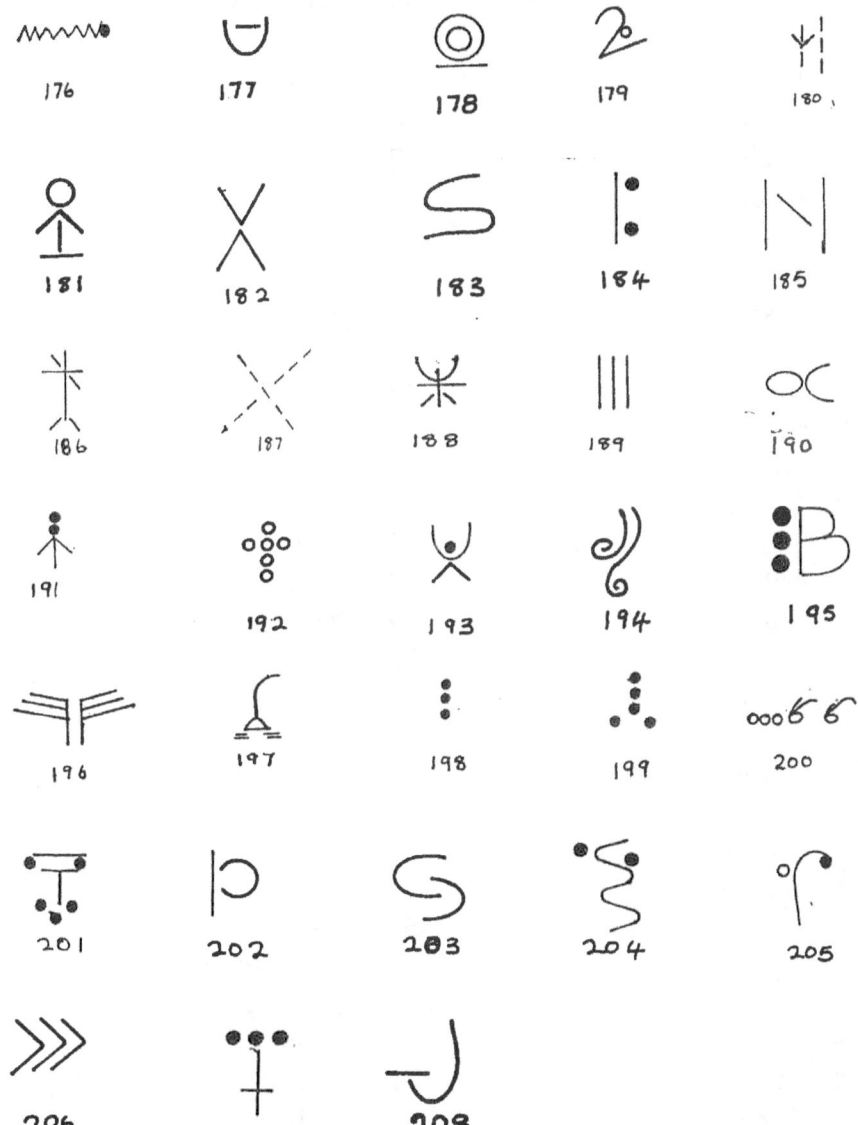

NAMES OF OWNERS OF POTTERY TRADE MARKS

1. Ipaan
2. Digbo
3. Gbibia
4. Gbonama
5. Iyo
6. Nwidae
7. Tekii
8. Zianu
9. Simee
10. Fade
11. Akpea
12. Naado
13. Inu
14. Nii
15. Piagbo
16. Kweneton
17. Ideele
18. Isogosi
19. Nwanade
20. Eeti
21. Barina
22. Toodee
23. Yaabue
24. Kpazoo
25. Kagbara
26. Tooue
27. Ideele
28. Soogbara
29. Nubiaga
30. Kiribia
31. Adoo
32. Neewaa
33. Naafo
34. Nyoone
35. Nyiazi
36. Naasua
37. Ogbonne
38. Keebia
39. Kiri
40. Nwiimaa
41. Legbo
42. Leton
43. Gbarato
44. Lesere
45. Ibom
46. Kirika
47. Wuubiloo
48. Ibakpo
49. Ideeko
50. Sonaatee
51. Fere
52. Nyazi
53. Kanee
54. Goneewa
55. Daewii
56. Noobekee
57. Kpuku
58. WaaKónò
59. Biiranwii
60. Naabo
61. Diidiwa
62. Yo'oh
63. Ibeanyie
64. Legbara
65. Iputu
66. Gbiwa
67. Ideeyo
68. Ibirayie

69. Gooni
70. Kpaadee
71. Deemua
72. Naabie
73. Kpakue
74. Toodee
75. Tabu
76. Ikinako
77. Deebom
78. Idadoo
79. Kirikawa
80. Ita
81. Ibaaga
82. Daeko
83. Kuebee
84. Leamua
85. Tonwe
86. Ikinako
87. Neewa
88. Toodee
89. Ikanee
90. Ipiagbo
91. Adamkue
92. Gbaadam
93. Kpakue
94. Kagbo
95. Kara
96. Piamaa
97. Ikoowa
98. Doonu
99. Titi
100. Logloo
101. Kpuruwa
102. Liwa
103. Komene
104. Anawa
105. Maagbo
105. Deeson
107. Ikinako
108. Baakawa
109. Ikoyaa
110. Kole
111. Kinanee
112. Nwidai
113. Mnaadu
114. Zoowa
115. Berewa
116. Kosi
117. Teezia
118. Kiiwa
119. Pabia
120. Adoo
121. Nyadu
122. Kpoga
123. Ikara
124. Bomwa
125. Nyaawa
126. Loere
127. Inyoone
128. Kpaadee
129. Anawa
130. Ba'ore
131. Neele
132. Daloo
133. Igbo
134. Iporo
135. Epwa
136. Biale
137. Ledee
138. Maako
139. Kodam
140. Bako

141. Gbabie
142. Nii
143. Yoronee
144. Siwa
145. Iko
146. Sine
147. Kawa
148. Tamwa
149. Akobawa
150. Maa
151. Dumwa
152. Tanee
153. Taade
154. Neenwaa
155. Muenee
156. Maa'ereme
157. Deezo
158. Anyaagbo
159. Nnaa
160. Naasue
161. Nukpugi
162. Kuwete
163. Maata
164. Deeko
165. Naanuuna
166. Akpogbara
167. Tigiri
168. Abanee
169. Kinanwii
170. Wereloo
171. Lenee
172. Barako
173. Berewa
174. Gbiyegee
175. Kiri
176. Yogbara
177. Taezia
178. Izuumia
179. Diginee
180. Tagaligi
181. Igolee
182. Gbian
183. Lewura
184. Yonwaatedoo
185. Katari
186. Neenia
187. Bianwaa
188. Uwega
189. Zianwa
190. Idudu
191. Yorosi
192. Kio
193. Daabaloo
194. Lemea
195. Kwenekia
196. Kpandee
197. Zuawa
198. Sosi
199. Naakue
200. Nyaanwaa
201. Irikien
202. Leneenwa
203. Bakoma
204. Ndidiwa
205. Nyaawa
206. Uenaakie
207. Kpadee
208. Aanesua

Pottery trade-marks were usually inscribed on the upper part of the pot at the junction of the body and neck. The marks were inscribed at three points so that an observer could see them from any angle; and they were inscribed just at the finishing of the pot when it was still soft. No marks were inscribed on pots "mass-produced" by the co-operative method, since they were not all made by the owner. Shortly before firing, the owner made her pottery trade-mark on all such pots by means of a brush-stick dipped in a yellow colour. The yellow colour turned orange after firing. Such marks also remained indelible on the pots but they usually became indistinct as the pot got older and its body darker through use.

(iii) Firing

There were five days in the Ogoni week. The fifth day was *Deeko* and it was the biggest market day. Usually, the dried pots were fired early in the morning of the *Deeko* so that the pots were ready for display at the *Dukono* market square at Kónò Boue by noon time. Later, it was found that the long-distance traders who had slept over-night in Boue in order to buy pots on Deeko were unable to do so until about noon. Because of complaints by the long-distance traders who desired to buy pots early and return to their own towns in time, a law was passed that the women potters should fire their pots on the day before the Deeko market.

An earlier law existed at Kwuribue where the women were forbidden to fire their pots within the town. They had to fire their pots outside the town at a place called Eresoo on the day before the market. Since the sixteenth century when the people of Kwuribue settled at Kónò Boue, that law had ceased to exist. The women had not only fired their pots within the town but they had also fired them on the market days. Most women potters had found this to their own advantage.

In 1950, however, an "amended" version of that old law was passed providing that women potters who could not fire their pots on other days could do so on Deeko days at a private bush. The relevant section of the law states as follows:

> There shall be no more firing of earthen pots in the market square on Deeko days, except on other days. Women who wish to fire their pots on Deeko days only may do so at a private bush at a corner

where their bare bodies may not be exposed before the crowd – as the women always neglect to cover their bodies while engaged in this work because of the heat of the fire. (Kónò Boue Local Laws and Customs No. 13: Firing of Earthen Pots, June, 1950).

The "crowd" in the above passage is a reference to the numerous long-distance traders and pot buyers who often arrived earlier, some from the previous evening, who usually spend the waiting time watching the firing of the pots. There were five major locations in the town, each of them firing about 2,000 pots, and all the five locations would be aflame at the same time every Deeko morning before the start of the market. The sight and sound of the huge fires and the tall flames and smoke going high up at various points in the town on a Deeko morning, usually aroused a curious excitement and a unique kind of feeling in the visitors.

There was also a local group of men pot-traders who used to buy the pots in bulk at wholesale prices from the women potters and carry them by large canoes to distant market to sell. On Deeko days, buyers from distant places used to offer the women potters higher prices than the local long-distance pot-traders. Consequently, there was usually a competition between them and the local buyers. For that reason, most women preferred to fire their pots on Deeko days. On Deeko days the women potters were able to sell all their stock of pots. Thus saving themselves the trouble of packing and storing until Deeko day. The big women potters who belonged to the big potting contributions usually have large numbers of pots to sell on wholesale basis. Thus, the presence of competitive buyers from distant places offered them their best opportunity.

(iv) The Activities of Long-Distance Pot-Traders

Long-distance pot trading by canoe provided employment for a sizeable proportion of the menfolk. This writer had the opportunity to travel with a number of men pot-traders to several places in the 1950s. On several occasions, he accompanied his elder brother, the informant, who himself was a long-distance pot trader and traveller. On those occasions, they traded at several markets in the Kalahari and Ikwerre areas, as well as at markets on the Obolo-Opobo Ibibio route through the Imo River system. During the same period, he also accompanied two other pot traders on different occasions on such journeys.

For these journeys, he was paid a hiring fee as a canoe boy to bail out the water from the centre of the canoe. These experiences made this writer familiar with some of the places on the routes described by the informant. From the following testimony, we can gather a good deal of information about the Kónò Boue long-distance pot traders:

> Some names of pot traders of Kónò Boue were Dugboo Kara, Naado, Dobu, Deebom Bira, Deebari Teenwaa, Gbeebe Kole, Naadole Ideme, Akiikpa Iguru, Obeye Kpone-Tonwe, Nwidae Gbege, Kobe Igbug, Pianee Barabe, Bogona Deebom, Porogbara Ikpoora, Kpugibue, Nnaapop, Piesu, Uwegbara Yokoo, Diginee, Obed Ana-ana, etc; and from Keneke Boue, Johnson Lewa.

We used to carry the pots in canoes to Okporoba market in Okrika and to Ahiaimunu market, also in Okrika. Another place we used to go to sell the pots was Port Harcourt. There, the markets were at Ahiagorogo and at Iwofe. But in Ikwerre proper, we used to trade at Ogbogoro, Akpor, Aluu, Choba, Isiokpo, Ibaa and Omagwa markets. Yet other places where we used to go to sell the pots were at Opobo and at Muma-Damboro as well as in the Akoro-Ete villages of Andoni.

When going to Okrika, we used to pass through Iyoba village, Bodo town and Boro before entering Okrika. In the case of Ikwerre, we used to pass through Port Harcourt, Ahiagorogo, Be-akoip and Iwofe. When going to Opobo, we used to pass through Unyeada, Nkoro and Kala-Ibiama before reaching Opobo Town.

At Okrika, the only customer I still remember by name was a woman named Ezinwayi. She was a woman from Okrika, and she was a bulk purchaser to resell by retail. Some canoes carried about 300 pots while others carried about 400 pitchers, depending on the size of the canoe.

In Kalahari, we used to trade in markets at Tombia, Osorgo, Asari, Abonema and at Owu-Sara.

When we travelled to Ibibio area, we used to pass through Egwanga (Ikot-Abasi) and trade at Urua-eka market in Mkpa, and at Esene, Urua-ete, Urua-Ugwa, Kefi, Ikparikpa, Urua-Dappa, Azumini, etc. All these markets were in Ibibioland (Kpone-Tonwe, 21 Nov., 1984).

The pot-traders carried pots needed for various purposes, such as water pitchers, palm wine-storing pitchers, palm wine tapping pots; pitchers for carrying water to the farms; cooking pots, bath pots, herbal pots, mini-pitchers for drawing water from wells, etc. After selling their pots, they also bought some food stuffs which they sold along the route on their return journeys.

The society in pre-colonial times did not have portable water; many still do not have it today. But in pre-colonial times, there were no aluminum buckets and plastic containers; there were no iron or aluminum pots; and no enamel wares. Pots were used for many purposes; and pots – of course, were breakable objects. Consequently, the demands for earthen pots was enormous. Accordingly, the people of Kónò Boue were producing about 5,000 or more pots per week, throughout the year and yet the market was never saturated.

Kónò Boue pots were particularly desirable, especially in hot weather conditions. They maintained a certain level of porosity which enabled the pots to send out warm air while at the same time sipping in the cool, thus keeping the water inside the pot cool and fresh all the time, even in the hot sun, provided it was under a shade. For this reason, Ogoni pottery from the Kónò Boue centres were not glazed, as glazed earthen pots could not act in this way. Glazing seals up the porosity of the pot, thereby trapping gases inside the pot. The gases warm up and cause the water to become dull and lukewarm; something undesirable in water in a hot climate. Housewives who understood the characteristics of Kónò Boue pottery usually bought several pitchers for storing water in the dry season, using them alternatively, allowing at least one pitcher to be empty over a period of time to let it dry over the fire place before putting it into use again. In that way, the pot retained its porosity which enabled it to keep water fresh all the time.

Other markets to which the Kónò Boue pots were carried were centred in Nembe and adjoining districts. Three men in the above list were well-known on this route; these were Dugboo, Naado and Johnson. These men were said to have prominent customers or wholesale buyers in the Nembe markets who bought the pots in bulk to resell in still distant markets in that area.

On the return journey, they bought other goods from that area. Dugboo and Naado were known to be bringing Lee, while Johnson brought lumber. Lee was the red bark of a certain tree, which was packed in hurdles of about 50kg. The Lee was ground and used in colouring and flavouring the palm wine. This product energizes the palm wine and gives it an attractive colour, a fragrant smell and a distinctively tart taste. Consequently, it was highly demanded in Ogoni by the palm wine tapers. After selling these goods, the men bought pots and set out again for the Nembe markets. These men used some of the largest canoes, and their return journeys took about three to four weeks.

11.3(b)   Smithing

In Ogoni, blacksmithing was both a closed and hereditary occupation (cf. Afigbo, 1980). Consequently, the practitioners of this trade were very few. They specialised in making the Ogoni traditional knives and weapons; which included the *Kobege* and the *Kuna* (Appendix VI). They also made other farm tools, such as the broad bladed digging hoe and the angular spear-shaped hoes used for sideway weeding by women and girls. They also fabricated door hinges and latches, kitchen knifes, razors, chisels and adzes used by canoe makers and sculptors and the special chisels used by palm wine tapers; hunting javelins and spear-heads.

Because of the specialist nature of this occupation and the small number of the practitioners, the demand on them was very high. The number of people bringing old tools for repairs were as large, if not larger than those placing orders for new tools. Innovations or inventions were few. Following the introduction of firearms in the sixteenth century, a new class of smiths emerged known as the "gun makers". They repaired the dane guns and eventually learned how to make an imitation model of their own using copper/brass pipes and other accessories. This group became the most respected class of smiths in Ogoni.

The source of the iron used by Ogoni smiths is uncertain. One informant, Bagia, reports that they obtained their iron from a place "farther away to the north", i.e. somewhere in the interior of Igboland. A.E. Afigbo explains that the Awka and the Nkwerre who were the leading smiths in Igboland, obtained their iron from the Agbada of Udi and from the Nsukka, both of whom mined and smelted their iron. The other group of Igbo smiths, the Abiriba, also mined and smelted their own iron (Afigbo, 1980). The Ogoni probably obtained their iron from the Nkwerre or from the Abiriba, the latter being the most likely. This is because, of all the Igbo national groups, the only group the ancient Ogoni knew by name were the Asa, whom they called Saga, who lived much farther north than where they are today, and the Eastern Igbo, whom they called "Mana", which includes the Abiriba. The rest they identified by the general name Gbon. Similarly, of all the Ibibio groups, the only group known to the ancient Ogoni by name were the Ibeno, whom they called "Ibono"; and they called the whole of the Cross River estuary "Ibeno Sea" (*Pene Ibono*). The implication is that the early Ogoni were familiar with the eastern peoples, including the Eastern Igbo. Accordingly, it is more probable that the early Ogoni obtained their iron from the Eastern peoples; perhaps from the Abiriba as well. According to Reverend H.M. Waddell, iron was obtained from the Qua Mountains in the period before the introduction of imported iron from England (Waddell, 1970).

In the nineteenth century, Nkwerre and Abiriba iron wares dominated Ogoni markets. New items like the kitchen tripod, the sickle-shaped hoe, etc. were introduced. Also in the nineteenth century, European swords and machetes appeared in the markets. By the twentieth century, the shovels had flooded the markets. These new iron products competed very strongly against the indigenous tools particularly the lighter European machete was preferred to the heavier Ogoni Kuna. By the 1950s, the Kuna had disappeared from popular usage, being replaced by the European machete. The locally produced hoes, however, continued to be in use side-by-side with the imported shovels. In recent years, however, both the men and the women have come to prefer the shovels to the traditional hoes. Thus, under these conditions, the role of the traditional Ogoni smiths has drastically declined.

11.3(c) Carving

(i) Carving for Secret Societies

Most Ogoni carvings had to do with secret societies. For this reason, the artists were not identified and their works were not publicised. Their masks and other carvings were simply regarded as mysteries or "spirits". For example, the puppets of the Amanikpo secret society were supposed to be mysteries, so were the *Gberegbe* mask, the *Akpo* mask, etc. and the various drums.

Although most Ogoni carvings have been destroyed by termites, whatever had survived the termites had also been stolen by thieves during the last one and a half decades, more especially since after the festival of African Arts (FESTAC 77) held in Lagos in 1977. Efforts by the chiefs to track down the suspects have not been very successful, as shown in the local police records.

(ii) Canoe-Making

In section 7.1(b), I described the use and sources of canoes in Ogoni and the Eastern Delta. I mentioned specific locations of production, sizes and prices of canoes in pre-colonial and in recent times. In this section, our focus is on organisation of production and methods of manufacture.

In early times, canoe manufacture was probably undertaken by the initiative of individual craftmen or by loose combines of several craftmen. During the last century, and especially in the beginning of the 20th century, canoe-manufacture in Ogoni appears to have been organised on the basis of what might be called "contract companies." According to Frank Mina, a canoe-manufacturing contractor, there was a definite procedure. First, an individual who had money and who was interested in canoe-making business, travelled to places having abundant timber to explore the forests searching for suitable trees for making canoes. Among the suitable trees were Tego, Degene, Yagara, Kpokpo, Gbam, Nyee, Gaete, etc.

Next, he negotiated with the owners of the forests and bought the trees. He might do the same in a number of locations along a particular river or within a particular forest area. Then he returned to *Ko* (*Opuoko*) to assemble together a number of expert canoe-makers, specialists, and labourers into an operational combine or company. He might organise several of such combines, depending on the number of locations on that route. Each operational company consisted of seven persons: five cutters, one fisherman and one cook. Of the five cutters, there were two experts, one responsible for shaping the bow and the other for shaping the stern; and three specialist tree-fellers who were also responsible for digging out the inside of the canoe and shaping the body.

The main tools were axes, knives and adzes. For digging out the inside of the canoe, no fire was used. According to my informants, the method of using fire was practised by Ijo canoe-makers, but they claimed that the method was too slow in that they often made three canoes while their Ijo counterparts were still on one. Moreover, the fire occasionally bore through the body of the canoe by accident. Dapper had also reported the use of fire to hollow out the canoe on the Gold Coast (Quoted by Smith, 1970).

Each operational company made sixteen canoes during an operational period of three months. The first two canoes made were sold and the proceeds used for feeding and for all allowances during the period in the bush. The canoes were rolled down from land to river on a pathway laid out with struts or logs, and then paddled to the canoe-yard at *Ko* (*Opuoko*) waterside, where the final stages of manufacture were completed.

At *Ko*, two specialist operations were performed by two groups of experts. The first group went over the whole body of the canoe getting it streamlined and making sure that the thickness was balanced or equal on all sides. The other group of specialists did the burning and expanding of the canoe. According to my informants, this was another highly technical operation, and only specialists could do it without splitting the canoe.

As soon as the canoes were brought to *Ko* from the locations where they were made, they were filled with sand and buried under water. When the buyers came, they were brought out from under water, emptied and displayed for sale.

Experienced buyers often bought the canoes before they were fired and expanded, because the prices usually went up by about 33% after firing and expanding. The canoes became so attractive at that stage that the buyers were often ready to pay almost any price.

The firing and expanding were done as follows. The canoe was fired upside down on a cross-bar of logs. A bonfire of dried raffia palm leaves was put under it. The flames burned the inside of the canoe. Long 'flags' of raffia palm leaves were used to fan the flames so that they did not concentrate on any one point for too long. The firing was regularly 'timed'. After a while the fire was put out and the canoe was turned upside up. At first, short struts were inserted across the mouth of the canoe to expand it. The firing acted on the dampness that had penetrated the wood to produce a steam or heat that caused the canoe to expand easily. As soon as it cooled, it hardened. Then it was turned upside down again and fired as before. After a while the fire was again put out and the canoe turned upside up. This time the expansion was much more, requiring longer struts, even twice as long as the first. This process was repeated several times until the canoe was expanded to a width that maintained a balance with its length and depth.

The outside of the canoe was also fired after placing the bottom of the canoe on a cross-bar of logs. When firing the outside, if the heat showed a tendency to cause a depression on the side of the canoe, a thick sheet of wet mud was used to plaster over the spot to keep it from reacting to heat.

The firing and expanding completed the process of manufacturing a dug-out canoe in Ogoni. The buyer of the canoe could then take home his canoe and hire his own carpenters to fix in it benches and other accessories for peddlers and travelers in the canoe to sit on.

11.3(d)   Weaving

Ogoni weaving covered a variety of items, raffia cloth, raffia bags, fruit baskets, fish baskets, fish nets, fish rackets, carrier baskets, fish traps, game traps, ropes, sleeping mats, bamboo mats, roofing mats, climbing ropes, masquerade dressings, etc. The weaving of raffia cloths, sleeping mats, fish rackets and ropes of cords, were women occupations. Fish traps, game traps, all kinds of baskets, climbing ropes, shoulder bags, masquerade dressings, etc. were done by men.

Women in towns along the coast and along the Imo River specialised in making sleeping mats, fish rackets, and ropes because the raw materials used for these products were obtained from the coastal vegetation and from the mangrove forests. In towns further inland, the women specialised in making raffia cloths, roofing mats and cords.

Woven materials, especially baskets, fish traps, fish rackets, racket-twines, sleeping mats, bamboo mats, etc. were highly demanded in the Niger Delta markets, where these goods were needed in bulk by both the regular and the migrant fishermen for use at their fishing locations. Thus, the men and women who engaged in weaving industries had ready markets in the coastal areas.

11.3(e) *Salt Manufacturing*

In all Ogoni, the Gokana were the only people who specialised in salt manufacturing. Salt manufacture was an occupation of both men and women. The salt was obtained by boiling the saline water or brine from the sea. The salt that remained in the pot after boiling consisted of large granules of salt. The granulated salt was therefore ground into fine salt by pounding in mortars. Water was then added to the ground salt and shaped in conical wooden vessels or cone-shaped calabashes into salt cones of various sizes. The moulded salt-cones were then placed on racks over the fire-place, where they hardened and became dry.

There were three sizes of salt-cones. The large size was about four inches high, the medium size about three inches, and the small about two inches. The large size was sold at the standard price of one manila each. The small and medium sizes were denominations of the large size; and they were not sold directly and did not have price tags of their own.

Because the common manila did not have smaller denominations, the small and medium sizes of the salt were used as currencies in buying goods of lesser value than one manila. Sometimes they were sawed into halves, thirds and quarters, and used in buying minor items like "snacks" and fruits. In times of slum, the smaller sizes were broken into pieces and added on top of the large salt-cones as discount sale values for the same price of one manila.

Gokana salt traders carried moulded salt cones to markets in all parts of Ogoni and beyond. Traders from farther away in the hinterland came to buy the Gokana salt-cones. The salt-cones were especially valuable and highly preferred by housewives because they were easy to preserve. They did not waste by watering or spillage. All that the housewives needed to do was to place them by the fire side or on the rack above the fire-place. Each time salt was needed, a little was chipped off or scraped from the salt-cone into the food.

The earliest reference to salt-manufacturing in the Eastern Niger Delta was by Duarte Pacheco Pereira in about the end of the fifteenth century. Pereira described a large village whose population he estimated to be about 2,000 households and noted that salt-manufacturing was the most important industry in the town, which attracted buyers from the hinterland as far as a hundred leagues away (Pereira, 1956). Ogoni oral tradition has identified the "Large village" as the ancient Gokana town of Bagha (map 8, p. 447).

One informant noted that salt-manufacture was an ancient industry in Gokana. During the Nigerian civil war (1967-70) when there was a scarcity of salt in the Eastern states as a result of a naval blockade of the Eastern ports by the Federal troops, the ancient industry was revived in Gokana, salt was, produced both for local consumption and for export to other parts of the Eastern states. According to my informant, the decline of the salt industry in Gokana was caused by the importation of cheap salt from Tiko in the Cameroons and from Europe.

11.4 Trade and Markets

11.4(a) Commodity Trade

Commodity trade involved various local and long-distance or foreign items. The local markets were divided into sections according to the type of commodities. In the section for foodstuffs, yams occupied a separate section, cassava and garri occupied another section. Fresh vegetables, fruits and fresh fish were sited close to this section, while plantains and cocoyams were sited close to the yam section. Another major section of the market was the smoked fish section. In the section for livestock, goats and sheep were the main animals. Next to these were the fowls in cages and a few tortoise tied to stakes.

Cows were never brought out into the open markets. They were sold and bought by order or by contract arrangement. When cows were seen in the precincts of markets, they were on delivery by agents to persons who had bought them.

Carved items consisted of wooden bowls and dishes, mortars, pestles, wooden spoons, carved doors, carved stools, etc. Masks were not displayed in the open markets. Most masks were treated as secret items.

Pottery was another important item of both local and long distance trade. The type of pots that were in great demand included cooking pots, water storing pitchers, palm wine storing pitchers, circumcision pots, palm oil storing pots, vegetable pots, ceramic dishes and bowls, etc. Ritual and ceremonial pots were made by special order, and only special potters could make them. The local demand for these varieties of pots was as high as the demand in the expert markets. The centre of the trade in pots was in Kónò Boue in the Boue area. It was here that people from all parts of Ogoni and from Bonny and Obolo came to buy their pots. Others in more distant places obtained their supply through the long-distance pot-traders, who travelled by canoes on the rivers and along the coastal waters.

In the salt trade, Gokana was the centre of distribution of the commodity. All the Gokana markets were distributive centres. The important markets were located at Kibangha, Bangha, Gbee/Mogho,

Dukono in Boue, Goi and Kisao at Bomu. Besides these markets, Gokana men and women carried dried salt-cones to distant markets beyond the Gokana area, and traders from Ndoki and Asa areas and from other parts of the hinterland were known to have travelled overland to the Gokana markets (cf. Afigbo, 1974).

The market for woven materials was widespread. Most towns in the inland areas engaged in the production of raffia cloths and bags, baskets of various kinds, ropes, cords, screens, sieves, game traps, fish traps, fish nets, bamboo seines, etc. Most of these manufacturers were in constant demand in an agricultural community.

Farm produce were packed and carried in baskets of various kinds. Shoulder bags for the hunters and farmers were made from animal skins as well as from raffia cloth. When cassava became a staple food, special raffia bags and finely woven sieve baskets were needed for processing the fermented cassava into cassava flour. Raffia bags and large strong cane-baskets (*Kpo*) were also needed for packing and carrying large quantities of palm fruits. Palm-frond baskets were essential for packing and for carrying lighter produce such as peppers, okra, bitter tomatoes (garden eggs), melon seeds, ogbono etc. from the farms or from the home to the market places.

The market for sleeping mats was large. There were several kinds of sleeping mats. The decorated type was for the elite, and they cost more. The elders, of course, used animal or goat skins, which lasted almost for a lifetime. The plain mats were always in great demand both for sleeping and for use by traders in the open markets to display their wares and for packing them at the close of sales.

The trade in bamboo mats was equally important. This article was in demand as portable shelter (canopy) from rain and sun; it was also used as roof and shelter over canoes. Traders used it to construct temporary sheds or canopies over their wares in the open market places. Market women used it to cover their market baskets, especially the fish and the *Lee* traders. While they used the bamboo mat to cover the mouth of the basket, they displayed only the samples of their wares on top of the mat to the view of prospective buyers. The bulk of the bamboo mats came from Ibibioland. The Ibibios were experts in the manufacture of this article.

Other woven products that were in great demand in the Obolo, Bonny, Okrika and Kalahari markets were fish rackets and racket twines. These products were needed in these markets for use in servicing fish catches.

Apart from these, the large heavy-weight cane baskets were also in great demand for storing smoked fish and lobsters or crayfish. The trade in fish traps, bamboo seines, piassava and other ropes and cords was also highly developed in these markets.

Other important items of trade were tools. As an agricultural society, Ogoni needed certain tools. Among these were the *Kuna* (i.e. the heavy, curved, double-edged iron tool for slashing the bush), the *Kobege* (the traditional elite insignia of status), hoe, hunting spears, bells (*mene*) for hunting dogs, game traps, knives, pointed iron rods (or javelins), household tools such as kitchen knives, and the kitchen tripod. These last-named items and certain types of game tarps were usually brought in by long-distance traders from Abiriba and Nkwerre areas.

11.4(b) *The City of Bangha as Centre of Long-Distance Trade*

The earliest reference to slave trade in Ogoni oral tradition were made in connection with long-distance marriages and with ritual sacrifices at Nama for the *Gbene* title. Given the historical origins of the *Gbene* title, it would appear that slave trade existed from very early times in Ogoni history. According to this tradition, part of the requirements for the *Gbene* title was the sacrifice of human victims at Nama. This requirement created a situation in which aspirants to the title and their agents had to go out searching for victims.

At that time in most hinterland areas, criminals were killed to rid society of unwanted elements. In extreme cases, this was the only option open to the authorities, as there were no public institutions such as prisons for the confinement of such elements. Offences included in this category were incest, sex before the *Yaa* tradition, witchcraft, murder/manslaughter, kidnapping/child stealing, theft, certain kinds of adultery, sexual intercourse in the bush (i.e. desecration of the earth or land deity), etc. Originally, persons accused of these offences were publicly tried and if found guilty were condemned to death and taken away out of public gaze to be killed at a place far from the town, usually on the bank of a river. This was done to avoid defiling the earth (soil) with their blood.

Through contacts between the hinterland and the coast, it became known that judgment victims could be sold. Accordingly, a trade in judgment victims between the hinterland and the coast began.

At Nama, besides the sacrifice of human victims, other requirements included the sacrifice of cows, goats, tortoise, etc. Cows and judgment victims were not sold directly in the open market. They were only delivered at the market point to the buyers or to their agents who had previously ordered for them and perhaps paid some money in advance. Usually the victims themselves did not know that they had been sold. Quite often, long-distance marriages were conducted in a similar way. The market point was the most convenient meeting place between the agents from the hinterland and the coastal buyers or their representatives. Thus in about the end of the fifteenth century, Duarte Pacheco Pereira reported the existence of this trade after visiting the Bangha market, which was located at a point east of the present town of Bomu and west of Kónò Boue (see Map 8)

In his description, Pereira stated that traders travelling in large canoes loaded with large quantities of yams, came from as far away places as a "hundred leagues, bringing many slaves, cows, goats and sheep" (Pereira, 1956). From Pereira's description, we notice that this trade existed prior to the introduction of commercial slavery in the area by Europeans. Thus it is observed that what Pereira had called "slaves" were infact condemned criminals or judgement victims sent away from their local communities (cf. Jones & Hull, 1949). At the coastal markets, they were delivered by agents to buyers who had ordered for them and paid some money in advance. Together with cows, goats and sheep, they constituted the set of ritual goods required for the *Gbene* title at Nama. But some of the human subjects were indeed would-be wives procured through these special agents by the same patrons (see Chapter three: "Later System of Marriage").

Accordingly, we may surmise that the Portuguese obtained their first slaves from this part of the Guinea coast by this method, using the same type of agents. Taking their cue from this internal trade therefore, the Portuguese eventually introduced the full commercial slavery and the slave trade in the area (cf. Page, 1969; Curtin, 1976).

11.4(c) Long-Distance Trade and the Trade Routes

One of the main overland trade routes came from western Igboland. This route linked long-distance trade from Onitsha, Awka, Oguta, Owerri, Mbaise, Nkwerre and Etche and thence into Ogoni on the coast. Another route came from central Igboland and from the fairs of Bende through Umuahia, Aba, Ngwa, Omuma and Akwete into Ogoni on the coast (Map 8).

Cookey has described how in 1880, Archdeacon D.C. Crowther discovered at Okrika an Igbo slave girl who had been kidnapped from her village in Umuoji near Onitsha and sold at a market in Ogoni, probably at the Alesa/Onne market, and was bought by Chief George of Okrika. According to the story, some years before her capture, the girl named Mgbeke, had seen Archdeacon Crowther in the Church at Onitsha. In 1880, after some years of captivity and enslavement, she saw Archdeacon Crowther again at a church service in Okrika and recognised him. Part of her story has been reproduced by S.J.S. Cookey, taken from the Archdeacon's dispatch to E. Hutchinson on 1st September 1880 (Cookey, 1972).

In her account, Mbgeke described the route through which she was taken by her captors until they brought her to the coast. First they took her to Mkpa, where they sold her to the Aros. The latter in turn took her to the large slave market at Bende. From Bende, her purchasers took her to Oloko (Umuahia), from Oloko to Akwete and from Akwete to Ogoni. From Ogoni, she finally ended up at Okrika in the home of Chief George.

The above testimony is a first-hand eye-witness account of the fact that major trade routes from the Igbo hinterland to the coast passed through Ogoni. As stated above, the Ogoni markets existed before the coming of Europeans. In the nineteenth century, the overland trade routes were still very much in use, as indicated by the above evidence. What is especially revealing is the fact that long-distance traders were able to move slaves through these routes from as far away places in the Igbo heartland as Bende on foot through Akwete into Ogoni territory. According to Professor Cookey, "the most significant aspect of Mgbeke's story was the information that Bende the great entrepot of Igboland could be reached from Okrika through Oloko (Umuahia), Akwete and Ogoni, without a major impediment, and that the route constituted an important commercial highway" (Cookey 1972).

In Ogoni, the slaves were not displayed in the market places like goods for sale. Except those captured, slaves on transit did not know that they were slaves; they did not even know when they were sold. Generally, they were treated like recruit-labourers for farm work to raise yam and cassava crops for overseas trade on payment of wages. They were lured with gifts such as new clothes and cloths for themselves and for their parents. Occasionally, gifts of money and cloth were "sent home" to living parents through the agents with messages purported to come from their sons and daughters, saying that the place was good and that they intended to stay a little longer in order to earn more money and goods. This trick succeeded in persuading other young men and women to want to go, and their parents to concede their release because of apparent benefits.

According to one informant, those to be sold were simply told that they were going "abroad" (*Kii-uwe*) for the better life. And another informant tells us that those who became slaves were recruited as free men and free women who were told that they were going to work on yam farms for payment of wages, to raise the special elite yams called *mgwe* for export to overseas.

Accordingly, on arrival in Ogoni, they were settled in camps from where they were taken to work on yam and cassava farms to raise food for their own feeding, for their masters, and some to be taken along when they were finally shipped abroad. In Eleme area, the largest camp was at Agbonchia. In the Gokana and Tee areas, the largest settlement or camps were at Kpoopie and at Bodo. There were others also along the water fronts. In Khana area, the most important camps/

settlements were at Ko/Buon (Opuoko/Kala-Oko), Baene and Kwuri areas.

But the transactions between the Bonny, Opobo and Okrika middlemen and the hinderland agents and the Ogoni chiefs and their agents, took place at the market points. In Eleme area, the markets were the Nchia and the Alesa/Onne markets. In the Gokana area, the markets were the Kisao market, the Mogho/Gbee market and the Goi market near Bodo. In the Northern Khana area, the markets were the Sii and the Yaakara/Kpean markets. In Boue area, the markets were the Kwuri and the Bangha markets. All these markets did not exist simultaneously, some of them were earlier and became extinct while others sprang up in their place.

Slaves arriving by the eastern routes through the Imo and the Azumini rivers from western Ibibioland and eastern Ngwa via Akwete and Ohambele, were taken to market points at Ko/Buon (Opuoko/Kalaoko), Baene and Yaakara/Kpean ports. Those arriving by overland routes were either taken to market points in Eleme area or to market points in Gokana and Boue areas. From these points they were finally taken to Bonny and eventually to overseas.

The towns which were located on the trade routes (Map 8) became important because of their activity in the trade. Their rulers such as Atee of Kpong, Yaa of Tee, and Deedam of Ko, collaborated with the chiefs of Bonny to provide slaves from the hinterland, while the Bonny traders supplied them with firearms, goods and money, which they had obtained from the Europeans.

According to the oral tradition, large numbers of the slaves released from the Eleme area later settled permanently at a place now called Oyibo, located to the north of Ogoni, on the bank of the Imo River. This followed a crisis which broke out between the Eleme citizens and the slave settlers, when it was noticed that the latter were trying to encroach on the citizens agricultural lands. Some of the slaves, however, became absorbed into Eleme society. Their descendants represent a sizeable group in Eleme society, whose surnames reveal Igbo roots.

Trade Routes from the Hinterland to the Ogoni Coast in the Era of the Slave Trade

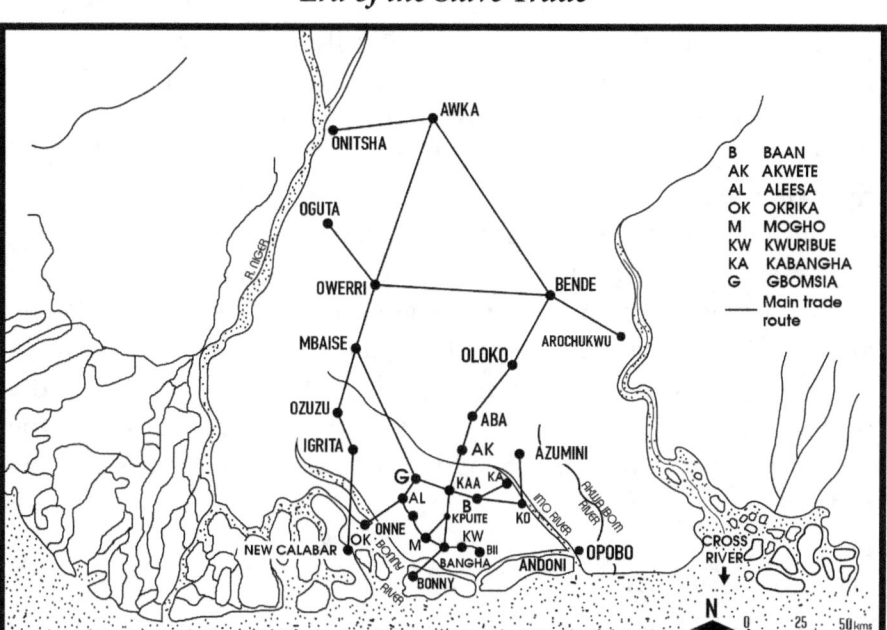

11.4(d) Impact of the Transatlantic Slave Trade

The most noticeable impact of the Atlantic slave trade on Ogoni was the appearance of some powerful individuals who wielded considerable influence and power over large sections of the territory. Among such individuals were Atee of Kpong, Yaa of Tee, Deedam of Ko (Opuoko), Igbara-Abe of Boue, Gbenedera of Bodo, and Michael Igwe of Alesa. These men rose to prominence as a result of their trade relations with Bonny, Okrika and Opobo in the Atlantic slave trade (cf. Alagoa 1980; 1976).

The most visible material benefit to the Ogoni participants was the gun which they possessed which enhanced their influence and political power over their areas. Because of their participation in the trade, the towns from where they operated became large population centres, due to the infusion of extra populations derived from the slave trade. Bodo for instance developed to become the largest and most prosperous town in Gokana, with a population of 14,257 (1963) census). Similarly, Kónò Boue, Opuoko, Alesa, etc. grew to become the largest and politically most dominant towns in their respective areas. Thus, in the nineteenth century, Bonny referred to Kónò Boue in the Boue area as the Big Town (Opu-Ama). In Eleme area, Alesa also became the largest and politically most dominant town, with a population of 4,428 (1963 census).

In Kpong, Atee did not concentrate the slave population in Kpong itself. Rather he distributed them to the peripheral towns. According to Pia'oo Menewa, Atee shifted large numbers of settlers to Baene and Beeri (Menawa 47, 1981). This pattern of slave settlement in the Kpong area may have contributed markedly to the size of the populations of Baene and Beeri, which are the largest towns in the area, with a population of 2,576 for Baene and 3,500 for Beeri (1963 census).

11.5 Conclusion

In Chapter 15, it will be shown that individuals who had accumulated wealth through hardwork in agriculture and participation in long-distance trade, applied such wealth in acquiring social titles and political power. Customarily, all adolescent young men were required to perform the *Yaage* tradition before they earned the recognition in society as members of an elite social category. But only wealthy parents could perform this social obligation for their sons. The ability to perform or failure to perform this tradition provided a basis for social and political distinctions from the grassroots.

CHAPTER TWELVE

THE CANOE INDUSTRY AT KO AND LONG-DISTANCE TRADE

12.1 Introduction

About ninety percent of the Niger Delta territory is water, only about ten percent is solid habitable land. Consequently, the movement of persons and goods, including fishing activities had to be done by canoes. Even the most essential chores, such as fetching firewood was done by canoes. This means that every household and every active individual needed to own a canoe in order to live successfully in the Niger Delta. However, while ownership of the small fishing canoes was a prerequisite for the survival of the average family or individual, possession of the large trade canoes remained the prerogative of the rich, because only the wealthy individuals could afford to own the large trade canoes. Thus, there was a high demand for both the small fishing canoes as well as for the large transport types. Because some of the wealthy owners of the large transport canoes rented them out to those long-distance traders who could not afford their own trading canoes, the market for this grade of canoes also continued to expand.

In this chapter, attempt is made to examine three fundamental propositions. First, that the emergent social and political superstructure in the Niger Delta during the eighteenth and nineteenth centuries, derived its being from the development of transport technology in the region. Second, that the canoe industry of Ko on the Imo River in the Eastern Delta provided a key to the genesis of this structural development. And finally, that a knowledge of the earlier developmental pattern can provide a sound basis for a wider economic development of the region.

12.2 Long-Distance Trade and Canoes

Alagoa has described two types of long-distance trade existing in the Niger Delta in pre-colonial times. One was a north-south trade between the Delta and the hinterland. The Delta peoples needed agricultural supplies for which they exchanged fish and salt. The other was a transverse trade across the Delta from east to west. According to him, this was little observed by the European visitors. The materials or goods involved was canoe and the Central Delta was the source of supply, with the Apoi as the main suppliers to both Eastern and Western Delta (Alagoa, 1970).

Another source of supply of canoes which both Alagoa and Robert Smith did not discuss, and which we shall take up later in this chapter, was the Ogoni region in the Eastern Niger Delta. However, in this section, and possibly throughout the chapter, we shall be looking at the canoe, not so much as an object of trade, but much more as a vehicle or carrier in long-distance trade.

Thus, we notice that in pre-colonial times the only means of bulk transportation and movement of goods and materials for long-distance in the Niger Delta was by canoes through the network of rivers and along the coastal waters (cf. Hopkins, 1973). Although every family in the Delta had its own little fishing canoe, possession of the large trade canoes was really an index of wealth, and only few individuals could afford to own such large trade canoes (cf. Horton, 1969). As most long-distance traders who engaged in such activities could not afford to have their own trade canoes, some wealthy individuals took advantage of this to invest on trade canoes which they then let out to users on hire at moderate charges.

From the evidence of Alagoa and Horton, it is uncertain whether the practice of owning trade canoes for the purpose of renting them out for profit was common in the Ijo communities. For instance Horton described the "canoe house" as a trading corporation under an independent trader as well as a military unit. According to him, besides being a piece of trading equipment, the "canoe house" was also a weapon of offence or defence which a house-head was expected to bring to the service of the community. Accordingly "possession of a war canoe became the criterion for establishing a new house" (Horton, 1969).

In Ogoni, however, the acquisition of a trade canoe was not the ultimate achievement to becoming a house-head. It was only one of the ways an individual could make his wealth by long-distance trade. The accumulation of such wealth made it possible for an individual to perform the required traditional rites which enabled him to become a titled chief and head of a "house".

Another point of comparison which deserves mention, was the variety of trade goods involved in long distance trade, as well as the extent of the market. Robin Horton explains that, because the Kalabari produced fish but not other food stuffs, they traded their surplus upstream in exchange for food stuffs. Consequently, economic interchange with neighbouring communities was low. This led to a high degree of social isolation of the individual villages (Horton, 1969). Alagoa also took notice of the same pattern of trade between the Delta and the hinterland, but in addition, he describes a "transverse trade" in canoes by the Apoi and the Arogbo of the Central Delta and in pots by the Itsekiri of the Western Delta (Alagoa, 1970). However, information on the extent of this internal market and on the variety of trade goods generated and distributed within the Delta communities is still very scanty.

In Ogoni, the coverage of inter/intra-ethnic trade was extensive and the variety of the trade goods generated and distributed was complex and voluminous because of its agro-based character. Consequently, there were many large, well-regulated and fully attended internal markets scattered throughout the communities in addition to a line of water front markets devoted for trade with their Ijo neighbours. Moreover, because the agricultural produce of the Ogoni were generally heavy or bulky commodities, and because the easiest way to move any quantity of such heavy or bulky goods in pre-colonial times was by water, the Ogoni also became big users of large canoes in which they conveyed their yams, plantains, calabashes of palm wine, pots of palm oil, sheep, goats, building materials, etc. to their water front markets to trade with their Ijo neighbours.

By the beginning of the sixteenth century, this type of long-distance trade by the use of large canoes had become well-developed, as shown by the report of the early Portuguese visitor, Duarte Pacheco Pereira. On his visit to the waterfront markets located in a Creek off the eastern arm of the Rio Real, called Bonny River, Pereira noted that the large canoes found in this area were the largest in the Ethiopia of Guinea. According to him, some of the canoes were large enough to carry about eighty men. "And they came from a hundred leagues or more up this river bringing yams in large quantities, which, in this country, are very good and nourishing" (Kimble, 1937).

The cost of one of such canoes in pre-colonial times had been estimated at about 1,200 manillas. An expert canoe maker at Ko, named Birranee Gbenebai Kara, explains that the price of canoes in pre-colonial times varied from £250.00 for the small fishing canoes to £650.00 for the large transport canoes. Another canoe expert, Frank Mina, a canoe-making contractor at Ko, recounts that in 1972, he himself sold a large canoe about 52ft long for £400.00. But he explained that that price at that time was very low for the size of the canoe. According to him, he did not haggle for much higher bidding because the buyer was the first citizen, Colonel Diete-Spiff, the first Military Governor of Rivers State of Nigeria, who personally came to Ko by an helicopter to inspect and bid for the canoe.

Further details about the goods carried in large canoes were pots, lumber, farm produce (such as yams, cassava, cocoyams, garri. plantains, sugarcanes, fruits etc.), fish, building materials (such as red earth, wattle, roofing mats, or thatches, canes, piassava, poles), and certain industrial barks used in palm wine production as flavouring and colouring agents. The paddlers were mostly hired men. The owners of the goods were sometimes also the owners of the canoes but generally they were non-owners, consisting of one or two men who combined to hire the canoes from their owners at a fee for a specific trading engagement or trip.

Long-distance pot trading by the use of large canoes provided employment for a large percentage of the Ogoni men folk of the town of Kónò Boue, where there was a big pottery industry (see Kpone-Tonwe, 1990). The territory and ethnic diversity which the long-distance pot traders traversed was vast. In fact, the people of Kónò Boue in Ogoni distributed their pottery products throughout the length and breath of the Eastern Niger Delta and beyond by means of canoes. They carried pots needed for various purposes, such as water pitchers, large palm wine storing pitchers, palm wine tapping pots, smaller pitchers for carrying water to the farms, cooking pots, bath pots, herbal pots, mini-pitchers for drawing water from the wells, etc. After selling their pots, they also bought some food stuffs and other products, which they sold along the route on their return journeys.

The society in pre-colonial times did not have portable water, many still do not have it today. But in pre-colonial times there were no aluminum pots, and no enamel wares:

> Earthen pots were used for many purposes, and pots, of course, were breakable objects. Consequently, the demand for earthen pots was enormous. Accordingly, on the basis of our findings, the people of Kónò Boue were producing upwards of 5,000 pots per week throughout the year, and yet the market was not saturated.

Ogoni pots from the Kónò Boue centres were particularly popular because of their characteristics in hot weather conditions. They maintained a certain level of porosity which enabled them to "breathe", sending out the warm air while at the same time sipping in the cool, thus keeping the water inside the pot cool and fresh all the time even in hot sun, provided it was under a shade. Glazing seals up the porosity of the pot thereby trapping gases inside the pot. The gases warm up and cause the water inside the pot to become dull or lukewarm, something undesirable in water in a hot climate, especially because the fridge or the cooler did not exist then. Housewives who understood the characteristics of Ogoni pottery from the Kónò Boue centres usually bought several pitchers for storing water during the dry season, using them alternately, allowing at least one pitcher to be empty over a period of time to let it dry over the fireplace before putting it into use again. In that way the pot retained its porosity which enabled it to keep water fresh all the time.

Other markets to which the Ogoni pots were carried centred in Nembe and adjoining districts. Three men among others, were well-known on this route, namely Dugboo, Naado and Johnson. These men were said to have prominent customers or wholesale buyers in the Nembe markets who bought the pots in bulk to resell in still distant markets in that area.

On their return, they bought other goods from that area. Dugbo and Naado were known to be bringing lee, while Johnson brought lumber. Lee was the red industrial bark which was packed in bundles of 50kg. The Lee was ground and used in colouring and flavouring the palm wine. This product energized the palm wine and gave it an attractive colour, a flagrant smell, and a distinctively tart taste. Consequently, the lee was a highly demanded commodity by the numerous palm wine tapers. There were women dealers who specialised on this product. To them the long-distance traders sold the product in bulk on their return, the women then retailed the product to the palm wine tapers. After selling these goods, the men bought pots and set out again to the Nembe markets. Similarly, other long-distance traders likewise set out with different kinds of goods, whether pots, yams, and material to their different distant markets along specific routes. These traders used some of the largest canoes known and their return journeys usually took three to four weeks.

As long-distance trading expanded, the prices of large canoes also increased; so also the hiring rates of such canoes. For example, at an early period, hiring charges for trade canoes were calculated on the basis of per business trip, that is, each time the traders used the canoes, the owner charged a specific fee. The amount varied according to the distance of the market specified by the traders. In later periods the hiring rates varied according to the type of business the particular traders were engaged in. In some business, the rents were charged per day, in others they were charged per week or per business trip. In the last fifty to sixty years, there has been a major shift in canoe investment in the Niger Delta, particularly in Ogoni.

This shift has been occasioned partly by the opening of new roads and increased use of road transportation through the introduction of bicycles, motor cars and lorries, and partly due to the decline of the pottery industry and pot carrying trade as a result of the introduction of modern ceramic industries, aluminum pots, plastic buckets, iron pots etc. These modern products forced the decline of the coastal trade and marine transportation by canoes.

As these declines set in, emphasis was shifted from the large heavy carriers along the coast and on the rivers to the especially buoyant and fast-moving canoes, which were then concentrated on the two most lucrative routes between the Niger Delta and the Island of Equatorial Guinea (formerly Fernando Po) and between the Delta and the fishing grounds of Tiko in the Cameroon. Again only the very wealthy could buy and equip this type of canoes, as it required upwards of ^500,000.00 to equip and stock one such canoes. Usually, the manpower on these canoes were labourers, who had little or no stake in equipping and stocking the canoes. But such labourers were under a leader or captain who controlled the manning of the canoes, while the real owners of the canoes or stock or both were resident in the Delta. On the Tiko route (fishing), the trip was once a year, from October to April. On return from the Tiko route the canoes were then turned on to the Delta-Equatorial Guinea route for the rest of the year. On this route the return trip took about three to four weeks. The centres of this organised trade were located in most of the big cities of the Niger Delta. In Ogoni, Bodo, Bomu, Dere, Baene, Ko, and Kabangha were the best examples of the towns which specialised in this type of long-distance trading and fishing involving the use of expensive canoes (cf. Scott, 1966).

12.3 Sources and Supply of Canoes

The predominant vegetation of the salt water areas of the Delta is mangrove forest, which did not yield suitable timber for making canoes. Alagoa explains that because of this, canoe-making technology became a specialised occupation among certain groups living in areas of abundant timber. Consequently, the canoe became an item of long-distance trade, the producing areas supplying the non-producing areas. According to Alagoa, one of the earliest groups who developed this technology were the Apoi of the Central Delta (Alagoa, 1970).

Another group who earlier developed the canoe-making technology were the Ko of Ogoni, who live on the Imo River. Oral tradition at Ko credits the development of the canoe industry in the area to a man called Gbenebai Kara, son of Gbenemenebere, the founder of Wiidaewii Town in Ko. The tradition records that at the time Gbenebai Kara began to fashion his canoe the Imo was a very small river and that its crossing at that time was done on light-weighted wood trunks fastened together and punted with poles. The reference to the young age of the Imo River implies that the canoe has been known in the area for a very long time. Therefore, it is likely that Gbenebai Kara's first canoe must have been produced at such an early period.

Over the centuries, canoe-manufacturing has become a big industry among the Ko people of Ogoni, with manufacturing locations spread over the Eastern Delta, the hinterland, the Cross River Basin and the Cameroons. Biiranee, a descendant of Gbenebai Kara, the traditionally held first canoe-maker of Ogoni, was reputed to be one of the greatest and best canoe-makers alive at the time of my field work. During an interview with him, he gave the names of thirty-four locations where he had worked making canoes, which span the Eastern Niger Delta, the Imo River Basin, the Cross River Basin and the Cameroons. The following are some of the places he named:

> *Along the Imo River Basin:* Ayama, Okoroma, Komkom, Miniwayi, Obuama, Ozuaba, Rumuebele, etc
>
> *Along the Atamini (a branch of the Imo):* Mbaise, Owerri Nta, Emekuku, Akarika, Egbu, etc
>
> *Along the New Calabar River (the Rio Real):* Ahia, Rumuola, Omoku, Okporowo, Ogbakiri, Choba, Aluu, Isiokpo, Abua, etc
>
> *Along the Cross River Basin:* Ikot Okpong, Iko, Okoroete, Ibano, Oron, Abana forest, Akpatat, Obenikan, etc
>
> *In the Cameroon:* Jankasa, etc

At Jankasa, the customers were mainly traders and fishermen from Duala and Tiko.

Robert Smith (1970), as well as Pereira and Barbot, cites the Eastern Niger Delta as the home of the largest canoes in West Africa. Smith described the size of the largest canoes as over 90ft in length (Smith, 1970). Earlier on in the seventeenth century, Barbot had given the size of some canoes in this area as "being 70ft in length and 7 or 8ft broad" (quoted by Smith 1970).

However, my most important informant on this subject, Gbenebai Kara of Ko, claims that the largest canoe he had made all his life as a canoe-maker, was thirteen and half his own outstretched arms sideways, measured from the finger-tip of one hand to the finger-tip of the other. And from the chest to the finger-tip of the hand was half measure. According to him, that was how they measured canoes in those days because there was no standard measurement such as the ruler or tape. I took a measurement of his extended arms, which I marked on a wall and it gave 73inch. I then multiplied 73inch by 13.5 which gave 82.125ft. Thus I realised that the largest canoe he had made was 82ft in length. (See Kpone-Tonwe, 1990:181 (n,i) notel). Moreover, Frank Mina, a canoe-manufacturing contractor at Ko, explains that in 1972, he sold three canoes to Colonel Diete-Spiff, the first Military Governor of Rivers State of Nigeria, the largest of which was 52ft long. And another informant, Friday Namene Oloka, also of Ko, gave the additional information, that the actual maker of that particular canoe was a man called Mumuu Adamkue also of Ko, and that the original place of manufacture was at Okoro-Agu in the Igbo hinterland, but the finishing stages were done at the Ko canoe yard on the bank of the Imo River.

Undoubtedly, these local evidence reinforced the validity of the reports of the early European travelers who visited the area in the sixteenth and seventeenth centuries, concerning the large sizes of the canoes found in this region. And as it will be shown forthwith the canoe industry at Ko in Ogoni, was the major source of these large transport canoes.

According to my informants, the market for the canoes produced at Ko and at other sites in Ogoni, included the traders and fishermen from Aba, Owerri, Omoku, Abua, Ogbakiri, Ikwerre, Kalabari, Nembe, Bonny, Gokana, Opobo, Andoni, Calabar, Oron, Duala, Tiko, etc. Because of the high demand, the prices of the large canoes kept rising. By the middle of the 1950s, the prices of the large canoes had risen from about £600.00 to £1,300.00 and those of the smaller fishing canoes from £200.00 to £400.00, depending on their quality and relative sizes. These were all pre-1973 prices. Nigerian currency changed from the pound (£) sterling to Naira (₦) in 1973.

From the foregoing, it is clearly evident that the canoe had been a very important, if not the most important factor in the economic development of the Niger Delta and the adjoining mainland territories. It is equally very compelling to discover that the Ogoni had played a very significant role in the manufacture and distribution of both the large transport canoes and the smaller fishing boats throughout the Eastern Niger Delta and its inland water ways, the Imo River Basin, the Cross River Basin, and the Cameroons.

So far we have discussed the historical, social, economic and commercial uses of the canoe in the Niger Delta. In the proceeding section, our attention will be focused mainly on the organisation and production processes.

12.4 The Ko Canoe Industry Organisation and Production Processes

In the early times, canoe manufacture was probably undertaken by the initiative of individual craftsmen or by loose combines of several craftsmen. During the nineteenth century and the early twentieth century, canoe manufacture in Ogoni appears to have been organised on the basis of small contracting companies. According to Frank Mina[2]:

> There was a definite procedure. First, an individual who had money and who was interested in canoe-making business, travelled to places having abundant timber to explore the forest searching for suitable trees for making canoes. Among the suitable trees were *Tego, DegeneYagara, Kpokpo, Gbam, Nyee*, (Kana names) etc.
>
> Next, he negotiated with the owners of the forest and bought the trees. He does the same in a number of locations along a particular river or

within a particular forest area. Then he returned to Ko and assembled a number of expert canoe-makers, specialists and labourers into an operational combine company. He might organise several of such combines, depending on the number of locations on that route. Each operation consist of seven persons: Five cutters, one fisherman and one cook. Of the five cutters, there were two experts, one responsible for shaping the bow and the other responsible for shaping the stern, and three specialist tree-fellers who were also responsible for digging out the inside of the canoe and shaping the body.

The main tools were axes, knives and adzes. For digging out the inside of the canoes, no fire was used.

According to my informants, the method of using fire was practiced by the Ijo canoe-makers, but they explained that the method was too slow in that they often made three canoes while their Ijo counterparts were still on one. Moreover, they stressed the fact that the fire occasionally bore through the body of the canoe by accident and that such canoes could be seen with a wooden patch over the hole. Dapper also reported the use of fire to hollow out the canoe on the Gold Coast (quoted by Smith, 1970).

Each operational company made sixteen canoes during an operational period of three months. The first two canoes made were sold and the money spent on food and as allowances during the period in the bush. The manufacture of the canoe was not completed in the bush at the site where the tree was felled. The stage in the bush consisted mainly of shaping the tree trunk into a rough canoe. The canoes were then rolled down from land to the river on a pathway laid out with logs and paddled to the canoe yard at Ko waterside, where the final stages of manufacture were completed.

At the Ko waterside canoe-yard, two specialist operation were performed by two groups of experts. The first group went over the whole body of the canoe getting it streamlined and making it symmetrically balanced by making sure that the thickness was equal on all sides. The second group of specialists did the firing and expanding the canoe. According to my informants, this was another highly technical operation and only specialists could do it successfully without uplifting the canoe.

As soon as the canoes were brought to the Ko canoe-yard from the locations where they were made, they were immediately filled with sand and buried under water. When the buyers came, they were then brought out from under water, emptied and displayed for sale. Experienced dealers often bought the canoes before they were fired and expanded, because the price usually went up about 33 percent after firing and expanding. The canoes become so attractive at that stage that the buyers were often ready to pay almost any price.

Firing and expanding followed a definite procedure. The canoe was fired upside down on a cross-bar of logs, A bonfire of dried raffia palm leaves was put under it. The flames burned the inside of the canoe. Long-flags of raffia palm leaves were used to fan the flames so that they did not concentrate on any one point for too long. The firing was regularly timed. After a while, the fire was put out and the canoe turned upside up. At first, short struts were inserted across the mouth of the canoe to expand it. The firing acted on the damness that had penetrated the wood during the time the canoe was under water, to produce a steam or heat that caused the canoe to expand easily. As soon as it cooled, it hardened. Then it was turned upside down again and fired as before. After a while, the fire was again put out and the canoe was again turned upside up. This time the expansion was much more requiring longer struts, even twice as long as the first. This process was repeated several times until the canoe was expanded to a width that maintained a balance with its length and depth.

The outside of the canoe was also fired after placing its bottom on a cross-bar of logs. When firing the outside of the canoe, if the heat showed a tendency to cause a depression on the side of the canoe, a thick sheet of wet clay or mud was used to plaster over the spot to prevent it from reacting to heat. The firing and expanding completed the process of manufacturing a dug-out canoe in Ogoni. Apart from causing the canoe to expand, the heat also produced a chemically smoothened and hardened surface both outside and inside the canoe to make it water-resistant. At the end of the firing, the buyer of the canoe could then take home his canoe and hire his own carpenters who would then fit in the benches and other fittings necessary for the sitting comfort of the paddlers and travelers in the canoe, as well as for the proper packing and safety of the goods carried.

12.5   Implications for Economic Development

This chapter has shown that the canoe had been an item of great dependency and development in the Niger Delta from the earliest times. The entire economic activity of the Niger Delta depended on the use of canoes. Even the least subsistence activity could not be done without the use of canoes. Yet the canoe was not a common product of the Delta as the predominant vegetation, the mangrove, did not yield suitable timber for making canoes. Consequently, the canoe-making technology was not developed in most areas of the Delta, except in areas where there was abundant suitable timber, such as the Apoi area of the Central Delta and the Ogoni region of the Eastern Delta.

The result was that the Niger Delta, which was an area most dependent on canoes, also became an area with the greatest demand for the supply of canoes. Accordingly, the canoe became an item of long-distance trade, the producing areas supplying the non-producing areas. Because the main economic activity of the Niger Delta was fishing, the type of canoes highly demanded in the area were mostly fishing canoes. This type of canoes were necessarily small in size, light in weight and fast in motion. These qualities were essential for easy maneuvering in the process of chasing and overtaking moving shoals of fish. Moreover, the occupation of fishing did not require too many people in order to avoid noise or disturbance in the presence of fish. One or two persons to a canoe was the ideal. Accordingly, the smaller the canoe the better for fishing.

Large canoes were required by relatively small number of people engaged in beach seine fishing to covey rolls of beach seine and heavy shafts for fastening them to and from the site. Such large canoes were generally idle during the long period the beach seine were in position at the site, until there was need for relocation. Some relatively large canoes were also required for deep sea fishing but this type of fishing was rare in pre-colonial times, because of lack of suitable equipment. Thus, it can be seen that in pre-colonial times, the type of canoes in high demand in the fishing communities, were generally small canoes. It can also be seen that during that period fishing was mainly a subsistence occupation, as Robin Horton clearly illustrated in the work already cited.

Moreover, Alagoa and Horton have both shown that long-distance trade from the fishing communities in pre-colonial times was limited in content and in scope. For example, because all the fishing communities produced fish, there was no need for one fishing community to carry its fish stock to another fishing community to sell. It was also less desirable to do so because all fish product constituted only one category of food requirement. It was therefore imperative for all the fishing communities to carry their fish upstream to trade and in exchange, they bought all kinds and varieties of food stuffs. For the same reasons, there were no effective redistribution centres in fishing communities, since practically all the fishing communities procured their foodstuffs and materials directly and more cheaply from source in the upland markets after selling their fish. These problems seriously limited the scope of the internal trade and considerable isolation of fishing communities.

The explanation then is that during this period of limited internal trade among the fishing communities, there was also little or no incentive for the use of long canoes by these communities. It can now be seen, as Robin Horton has also clearly demonstrated, that the use of long distance trade canoes by these communities began in earnest with the coming of the Transatlantic slave trade, which can be dated to the sixteenth or seventeenth century. Thus with the coming of this new trade, some of the fishing communities began to change from fishing to trading, and with the change, there arose the need for possessing the large trade canoes.

As stated above, about the beginning of the sixteenth century, Duarte Pacheco Pereira reported the existence of an already well-established trade by the use of large trade canoes, in an area east of the Rio Real or Bonny river. Pereira said that some of the canoes found here were so large as to be capable of carrying about eighty men, and that they were the largest he had ever seen in the Ethiopian of Guinea (Kimble, 1937).

Now, who were these traders? I have answered this question elsewhere. But let me briefly state here that the people described by Pereira were Ogoni traders. The data supplied by Pereira, from the goods they carried: "yams in large quantities", the language they spoke: "sheep are called *'bozy'* (Gokana language, bol)", the weapons they bore: "daggars" (Kana language, Kobɛgɛ), to the markets they attended (Bangha), have been identified as Ogoni (see Kpone-Tonwe, 1996).

Why had the Ogoni been using large canoes by that early date? There were many reasons. First, the Ogoni were familiar with use of large sea-worthy canoes from very early on in their history. In fact their oral tradition states that their ancestors landed at Nama, their first settlement in Ogoni in large sea-worthy canoes (Kpone-Tonwe, 1990:56). Second, their agricultural produce (e.g. yams), and their industrial output (e.g. pottery) were heavy, bulky goods, which needed transportation by large trade canoes. Third, more than half of Ogoni territory is surrounded by water. Fourth, the Ogoni were expert canoe-makers themselves, as it has been amply demonstrated by the Ko canoe industry.

In view of the foregoing analysis, it is argued that the Ogoni was instrumental to the emergence of long-distance trade in the Niger Delta with the Ogoni at the vanguard. The products of this early trade included agricultural goods such as yams, plantains, coco-yams, cassava, garri, maize, coconuts, sugarcanes, peppers, fruits, etc, and some low-level industrial goods such as pots, palm wine palm oil, industrial barks, lumber, fish traps, fish rackets, ropes, shafts, canoe paddles, red earth, wattle, thatches, poles, etc. With the coming of the Europeans, and by the middle of the seventeenth century, after the introduction of Transatlantic slave trade, the initiative began to shift from Ogoni to the Ijo communities, some of whom began to abandon fishing to participate in the new trade as middle men. The introduction of the slave trade and later the "legitimate" trade in vegetable oils, accelerated the growth of the Ko canoe industry, as the demand for the bigger canoe by the Ijo middle men began to have its impact. This increased demand led to the expansion of the Ko industry, as shown by the establishment of many locations beyond the Niger Delta into the Imo River Basin, and the Cameroons, in search of its raw material.

Evidence indicates that the industry continued to exist far into the second half of the twentieth century, as shown by the sale of three relatively large canoes (one of which was 52ft) to Colonel Diete-Spiff, the first Military Governor of the Rivers State of Nigeria in 1972. The Ko canoe industry finally declined, following the establishment of the Water Glass Boat Yard in Port Harcourt in the late 1970s, similarly, the Kónò Boue pottery industry also declined, following the introduction of cheap European iron pots, metal buckets and plastic vessels. One of the environmental benefits of these industries, as shown by age-long observation by the elders, was that the firing of their products used to produce huge volumes of vegetable smoke, which were found to be healthy to fruit trees and plants and yet harmless to humans, unlike the poisonous chemical releases into the atmosphere by the oil companies, which are dangerous to living things, including humans, vegetable plants, and marine lives.

12.6　Conclusion and Recommendation

In this chapter, we have shown abundantly the huge volume of economic activity that existed in the Niger Delta before the advent of Europeans. The question of unemployment did not exist, since every able-bodied man and woman was engaged in one type of productivity or another. The Europeans or colonialists studied the volume of economic activity in the area and the lucrative nature of the productivity, as well as the extent of the market and trade goods, and planned to introduce or import substitute products into the area to replace the traditional industries. Thus they forced the collapse of the traditional industries and occupations. The result was that whole communities were thrown into joblessness and unemployment. Large populations were thus reduced to poverty.

In view of the above, our recommendation is that the local and state governments and the environmental organisations, should encourage the communities which had indigenous industries by making the companies which had established substitute industries that replaced the traditional ones, to locate at least a branch of their modern or substitute industries in the communities whose traditional industries had been replaced. In that way, the economic skills and the prosperity of the communities would be recovered and restored.

CHAPTER THIRTEEN

EARLY USE OF MONEY AS MEDIUM OF EXCHANGE IN THE NIGER DELTA

13.1 History of Money in the Niger Delta

In this chapter, the emphasis is on Ogoni's perception of wealth and how the Ogoni went about accumulating wealth. From the very beginning the Ogoni had been an agricultural people. Although in many of their towns lying close to the coast there are numerous fishermen, the bulk of their total annual earnings came from agriculture. Because agricultural produce consists of perishable commodities, it was difficult to store as wealth. Consequently, a large part of their farm produce was sold off annually in order to convert the proceeds into forms of wealth that could be stored, such as land and money (cf. Hipkins. 1973).

From the account of Pereira and from the testimonies from traditional informants, it is known that by the fifteenth century a flourishing trade in agricultural produce and livestock was already in existence on the mainland fringes of the Eastern Niger Delta. The best example was centered in the very large town of Bangha, situated about 2km east of the modern town of Bomu on the coast of Ogoni (cf. Pereira, 1956). Other centres were the markets at Gbee near Mogho (Moko) in Gokana and at Kwuribue (Kuleba) in Boue (Bewa). At Mogho, the Europeans first saw indigenous iron money in circulation. Dapper described this iron money in 1669 and Barbot in 1699 (Dapper, 1676; Barbot, 1732). G.I. Jones has also noted the existence of indigenous currencies in the region during the eighteenth and nineteenth centuries (Jones, 1958). Latham says the existence of several different currencies in the region is proof of their indigenous originality, since if they had been introduced by Europeans, the tendency would have been for a common currency to develop (Latham. 1971). Similarly, A.G. Hopkins is of the view that the variety of currencies could easily have been, and probably were, developed in West Africa itself (Hopkins, 1973).

The agricultural produce sold for money in these markets was mostly yams and livestock from the Ogoni areas and Etche and Ikwerre hinterlands. The Ijo peoples from the salt water areas brought fish.

The existence of indigenous currencies in the region suggests that the trade was conducted on the basis of market principles through the application of a general purpose currency that was responsive to the effects of demand and supply as shown by the up-and-down movements of prices. If such was the case, it means that trade in the Eastern Niger Delta was significantly more advanced than the system which operated in parallel regions, such as the Upper Cross River Valley (Bohannan and Bohannan, 1968).

In the Eastern Niger Delta, trade was not a subject of moral judgment because of the existence of money as a common denominator for all types and classes of goods. Consequently, the movement of goods up and down the ladder of society was uninhibited.

The archaic *kwiri* (money), now used only by spirit-mediums appears to have been the name of the common currency circulating in the region during the period before the arrival of Europeans in the Eastern Niger Delta. Edward Kpea of Mogho (Moko) gives the names of three kinds of currencies which existed in Ogoniland in pre-colonial times, namely *Giaradaa, Nama-Kpugi,* and *Ka-kpugi.* According to him, *Giaradaa* and *Nama-kpugi* existed from the times of the ancestors but the *Ka-kpugi* was in circulation from pre-colonial to colonial times until it was withdrawn in 1949. If this report is correct, the term *Ka-kpugi* must refer to the copper wristlets which the Portuguese called manilas. But the *Giaradaa* (lit.

giant girth or gape) would undoubtedly refer to the large bronzes which by colonial times were no longer in circulation.

In Ogoni these large bronzes were called *Kporo*. From the foregoing it may be inferred that the term *Nama-kpugi* (lit. ancient money) probably referred to the money called *Kwiri* by spirit-mediums. This inference is based on the fact that the spirit-mediums speak an archaic language when they are possessed.

However, following the archaeological discoveries at Igbo-Ukwu by Thurstan Shaw, a debate has arisen concerning the origin of the manillas and the bronzes in West Africa. Could West Africa have possessed a sophisticated currency before the arrival of Europeans? Some scholars have expressed strong views that the manillas and the bronzes were of European rather than West African origin. Professor Lawal has been particularly sceptical about the view that the Igbo-Ukwu finds were the result of trade links with trans-Saharan commerce. According to him, Igbo-Ukwu was too far removed from any known trans-Saharan trade route. Also the Igbo-Ukwu manillas were so close to the European type that they could not have evolved from the kind of wristlets made by Hausa and Nupe Brassy Smiths, which were of northern origin (Lawal, 1973). Indeed, a type of *Kporo* which was the largest bronze currency supposed to have been used before the coming of Europeans can be identified among the Igbo-Ukwu finds (see Shaw, 1970, II: Plate 323 top). Jones did not think that the manillas originated in West Africa:

> Although the origin and age of the manilla in West Africa cannot yet be stated with any degree of certainty, all the evidence so far at our disposal suggest that it was a coastal phenomenon, and that it rose to "prominence both as a medium of exchange and ornament only after the fifteenth century (Jones, 1958).

Nonetheless, Jones acknowledges that there were several indigenous currencies in what is today southern Nigeria before the arrival of Europeans.

From the account of Arab travellers, al-Bakri in the eleventh century, and Ibn Battuta in the fourteenth, it is known that there was trade in copper from the Sahara and North Africa to black Africa before the arrival of Europeans in West Africa. Ibn Battuta gives a description of the mining of copper in sub-Saharan Africa through the use of women and slave labour, and of the making of copper rods, which were exchanged through black African traders for the gold mithqal and other goods (Hamdun and King, 1975; Ibn Battuta, 1953; cf. Triminghan, 1959). In veiw of these reports, David Northrop explained:

> The existence of markets and routes is one way of judging the sophistication of an economy; another way is its mode of exchange. Simple barter indicates a relatively primitive level of development... The use of a currency to facilitate exchanges indicates a more developed economy. A currency may operate simply as a standard of value or as a general purpose money able to measure, purchase and store wealth. According to Pereira, at the beginning of the sixteenth century, the Portuguese paid for all their purchases on the coast of Guinea... with copper wristlets or manillas, in contrast with the variety of items sold for gold on the Gold Coast (1978; cf. Pereira, 1956).

Professor Alan Ryder has suggested that the manilla was already being used by the Portuguese in Benin by 1515, but he gives no indication that the manillas originated in Europe. As for the cowries, Ryder shows clearly that the contract to introduce the Maldive cowries from India into West Africa was first signed on 26 March 1515, and that they did not arrive in West Africa until some years later (Ryder, 1959). However, using Pereira's reports (Pereira, 1937), Page explains that the Indian ocean cowries had reached Benin overland before the arrival of Europeans (Page, 1980).

13.2   Origin of the Manillas

From the foregoing observations, certain fundamental questions arise. If the manillas and the bronzes were of European origin, have their European prototypes been found in Europe? If they have, who were their manufacturers? What were they used for? Or were they also used then as currencies? Unless we can find some positive answers to these questions, we may tentatively assume that the Portuguese saw and adopted a prototype of the manilla in West Africa after they had arrived there in the fifteenth century. If this assumption is correct, the most likely place in West Africa was the

Eastern Niger Delta, particularly in the area east of the Rio Real, which in this case is east of the River Bonny, where the Europeans not only saw a well-developed market system and trading activity but also described the existence of indigenous iron money at Mogho (Moko) a market town on southern Ogoni (Pereira, 1956; Dapper, 1676; Jones, 1963). For this reason the cowrie currency which the Europeans imported from India and East Africa, was not accepted as a currency in the Eastern Niger Delta, except as an item of decoration (cf. Johnson, 1970; Ryder, 1959).

As further proof that the trade in this region was conducted on market principles with the use of money, this writer has done a preliminary survey of the names of money in the Eastern Niger Delta. The survey is based on Kay Williamson's earlier study of the names of food plants in the Niger Delta. In that study, Williamson proved that the names of food plants which were introduced into the area by Europeans jumped the linguistic boundaries, where as the names of food plants which were indigenous retained their linguistic roots.

The present survey revealed two facts. The first is that the peoples of the region were acquainted with the use of money in pre-colonial times and that such money was basically indigenous as the names of money showed no European influence. The second fact is that the Ogoni word for money (*Kpugi* had its root (Kp-) in the languages of the Eastern Niger Delta and Eastern Igbo, which also traded with Ogoni. This fact may be interpreted in more than one way. The most important, as far as this chapter is concerned, is that there was the use of money among the peoples with whom the Ogoni traded in periods before the fifteenth century (see Table A-E). The appearance of Europeans in the markets of the Eastern Niger Delta undoubtedly introduced a new impetus to the trading activities of the region. By the beginning of the sixteenth century the Portuguese had adopted the existing currency and re-introduced it as the 'new' manilla currencies (which the Ogoni called *"aan-kpugi"*) comprising both the large and small varieties (Northrop, 1978; Ryder, 1969).

The 'new' manilla (*'aan-kpugi'*) was also called 'genuine' money (*Kaana Kpugi,* short, *Ka-Kpugi*) in reference to its beauty and cuteness, while the former money was now colloquially called '*Kumbe'* meaning 'ugly' or 'uncute'.

The *Kaana-Kpugi* or *Ka-Kpugi* was the money Chief Kpea referred to above as existing from pre-colonial to colonial times until replaced by the British pound (£) in 1949. Although the Kumbe ceased to become legal tender, it was still exchanged for the *Ka-Kpuqi* at the rate of two to one. There were always money changers in the various markets who bought the *Kumbe* and resold them at a premium to the hunters, who cut them to use as bullet-chips, to the spirit-mediums, who used them for rituals to ancestral spirits, and to the blacksmiths, who melted them and used the alloy for various purposes.

With the acceptance of the 'new' manillas (*aan-kpugi* or *ka-kpugi*), the Portuguese began to control the economy of the Niger Delta, particularly the Eastern Niger Delta, until they were replaced by the Dutch and later by the British in the seventeenth and eighteen centuries.

However, because the *Ka-Kpuqi* or manillas were generally heavy and bulky when accumulated, and difficult to keep safe from thieves, some individuals tried to hide their wealth or savings from thieves by burying their money in the ground. But they also found out that burying money in the ground was unsatisfactory and unsafe, and that money so buried got lost completely if the owner died suddenly or when a thief discovered its location. They also discovered that money buried in the ground yielded no profit or benefit to its owner. For these reasons, the Ogoni found other ways of accumulating wealth by investing their money in several areas of the economy, such as land, livestock, transport (canoes) and permanent tree crops (cf. Hopkins, 1973).

Table IV: Indigenous Words for Money in the Niger Delta and South-Eastern Nigeria

Table IVA: Eastern Niger Delta

Linguistics Group/LGA	Word for Money
Khana (Ogoni)	Kpugi
Tee (Ogoni)	Kpugi
Gokana (Ogoni)	Kpege
Eleme (Ogoni)	Ekpii
Okrika (Ijo)	Igbigi
Kalahari (Ijo)	Igbigi
Bonny (Ijo)	Igbigi/ Ikpee
Opobo (Ijo)	'kpee
Andoni (Ijo)	kpok/Ikpoko
Abua (Abua)	kpuki
Ogbia (Ijo)	Igbogi
Nembe Brass (Ijo)	Igbogi
Sagbama (Ijo)	Okubo
Yenegoa (Ijo)	Okubo

Table IVB: Western Niger Delta

Linguistics GROUP /LGA	Word for Money
Warri (Edo)	Ogho
Okpe (Urhobo)	Igho
Sapele (Urhobo)	Igho
Ugheli (Urhobo)	Igho
Ethiope (Urhobo)	Igho
Oshimili (Delta Igbo)	Ego
Ndokwe (Delta Igbo)	Ego
Ika (Delta Igbo)	Ego
Asaba (Delta Igbo)	Ego
Bomadi (Ijo)	Okubo
Isoko (Ijo)	Okubo

An examination of Table IVA shows that the term *Kpuqi* (money) originating in the Eastern Niger Delta from the Ogoni area, and spreading outwards in the region. In the Kalabari area it assumed the characteristic 'i' augmentation or prefix of the Eastern Ijo. The Kp- stem or root became 'gb' owing to linguistic pronunciations. This augmented form spread westwards as far as the Nembe kingdom of Brass, which is the western end of the Eastern Niger Delta. The Nembe kingdom was also the area where Ogoni trading activities westward terminated in pre-colonial times (see Map 6). In Andoni the term *Kpugi* received a double modification, namely the 'i' augmentation of the eastern Ijo and the 'k' suffix of the Ibibio. (See Table IVA). But the kp- root of Ogoni was retained. In Bonny, both the Eastern Ijo form *Iqbiqi* and the Eastern Igbo form *Ikpeqe* were retained. This was because Bonny people speak a dialect of Igbo as a result of trade links with Eastern Igbo during the transatlantic slave trade.

In Table IVB (the Western Niger Delta) the term *iqho* (money) is derived from the Edo word igo (cowrie). According to J.D.

Fage, nowadays *igo* means money in general as well as cowries. It therefore seems tolerably certain that the Benin cowrie currency was not introduced by the Portuguese (Fage, 1980). From the above a pertinent question arises. Was the Igbo word *ego* (money) derived from the Edo word *igo* (cowrie)? Or vice versa?

In Table IVC the word for money (*Okuk*) is localised within the Ibibio linguistic group or territory. In Table IVD the Cross River area, the word for money is various and localised within each cultural group. In Ibiaku and Ibiono, which share proximity and trade relations with Eastern Igbo peoples, the word for money is Cross-cultural, as they adopt the Eastern Igbo form *Okpoqho*, having received their characteristic 'o' augmentation.

Table IVC: Akwa Ibom State

Linguistics GROUP/ LGA	Word for Money
Uruan (Ibibio)	Okuk
Ikot Abasi (Ibibio)	Okuk
Nsit-Ibium (Ibibio)	Okuk
Oron (Ibiobio)	Okuk
Ikono (Ibiobio)	Okuk

Table IVD: Cross River Valley

Linguistics Group /LGA	Word for Money
Ibiaku (Efikj	Okpogho
Ibiono (Efik)	Okpogho
Obudu (Obudu)	Ekpan
Ogoja (Ogoja)	Okwe
Odukpani (Efik)	Okun
Itam (Efik)	Ekit

Table IVE: Igho Land

TABLE IVE(I) EASTERN IGBO

Linguistics Group/LGA	Word for Money
Abam	Okpogho
Abriba	Okpogho
Afikpo	Okpogho
Arochuku	Okpogho
Bende	Okpogho
Ohafia	okpogha

Table IVE (II) South-Eastern Igbo

By Cultural Area/LGA	Word for Money
Ngwa	Ikpeghe
Asa	Ikpeghe
Aba/Abayi	Ikpeghe
Ndoki	Ikpeghe

Table IVE (III) Igbo Central/Heart Land

By Cultural Area/LGA	Word for Money
Nri	Ego
Awka	Ego
Orlu	Ego
Owerri	Ego
Nkwerre	Ego

Table IVE (IV) Igbo West and South/South-West

By Cultural Area/LGA	Word for Money
Onitsha	Ego
Oguta	Ego
Osomari	Ego
Ahoada	Ego
Etche	Ego
West Niger Igbo	Ego

13.3   Early Application of Money in Ogoni Economy

In this section attempt is made to demonstrate how the Ogoni applied the use of money to solve the problem of the perishable nature of their agricultural produce by selling off and investing the surplus income in selected areas of the economy, and how by so doing they sustained lively economic activity in the region through supplying the regional markets. Also, how as a result, every piece of land or forest in Ogoni became the property of individuals. Consequently, there is no community land in Ogoni, unlike in neighbouring or parallel communities.

13.4   Definitions

In this section, the term "pledge" is used frequently to describe the transaction involving 'temporary' transfer or conveyance of the right of ownership to land or landed property from one individual to another as a means of obtaining monetary benefits or loans. The term 'pledger' is used to refer to the owner of land or landed property who has offered to 'temporarily' transfer his ownership right in such land or landed property to any person prepared to 'give' him a needed amount of money, on condition that his ownership right to the land or landed property will be restored whenever he has paid back the full amount received, provided that at least one year has elapsed. The term 'pledgee' is used to refer to the individual who is prepared to advance his money to the owner of land or landed property in order to temporarily acquire the exclusive right to use such land or landed property, until such time as the amount advanced is repaid by the pledger or his representative, or by anyone else whom he may choose.

The term 'pawning' or 'pawnship' has been judiciously avoided, since by definition pawning or pawnship implies 'debt bondage' (see Falola and Lovejoy, 1994). This is because in Ogoni, pawning or pawnship was not practiced, and debt bondage was not a part of the economic system. Consequently the system described here, as I see it, was purely a method of providing access to monetary loans or land rights. But in the perception of the local people it was a means of profitable savings or investment, or a method of accumulating wealth.

13.5   Investing in Land

Agricultural land offered the highest premium for investment in pre-colonial Ogoni. An individual whose crops yielded a bountiful harvest, and who wished to save the increase from his crops, invested the extra income in land. In pre-colonial Ogoni agricultural land was never sold outright. If the owner of a piece of agricultural land was in urgent need of money, he could pledge (here) his land to someone who was ready to give him the needed amount of money, provided that the amount was commensurate with the size and quality of the land. Having paid for the land, the pledgee was entitled to cultivate the land as much as he wished until the amount pledged was paid back to him. The period the land was cultivated served as interest on the money invested. When the land was redeemed the pledgee received the full amount pledged. A hardworking and prosperous person could acquire several plots of farm land in the different farming locations of a town or community.

With this practice there arose some problems. One was that a person in urgent need of money often did not immediately know whom to contact or who might be ready to take his land. The second problem was that the individual in need wanted to keep his need private. Thirdly, the demand for agricultural land fluctuated widely, being very high immediately preceding the farming season and very low during the harvest season. To overcome these problems there emerged certain well-known individuals in the communities known as *pya tɛɛdɛɛ* (sing *nɛɛ tɛɛdɛɛ or atɛɛdɛɛ*) literally those who 'walk through', 'trace' or 'survey' the boundary between farmlands. These men acted as middle men or brokers between the pledger of land and the prospective pledgee.

With this class of men in the communities, all that a person who wished to pledge his land needed to do was to approach one of them and disclose his intentions. The *atɛɛdɛɛ nam* then took it upon himself to inspect the land, assess its value and assure himself that no one else was in possession of the land. After that he would 'pass on the word' (*yeege mue*) to prospective pledgees or he might decide to pay for the land with his own money and re-pledge it later at a premium. In that case the difference in the amount was borne by the would-be pledgee. Where the *atɛɛdɛɛ* was able to get a pledgee immediately the pledger paid him a fee for his services which was deducted or discounted from the amount pledged. But when the land was redeemed the pledger paid this full amount to the pledgee.

In some cases the pledgers of agricultural land were never able to redeem their land again. Such land eventually became the permanent property of the pledgee. In the colonial and post-colonial periods the sale of farmlands became common. People came to realise that the owner of farmland could receive more money for his land if the land was sold outright rather than pledged, especially if the prospect of redeeming it was uncertain. Farmland owners became aware that they could always buy other farmlands in future provided they had the money. The more plots of farmland a man or woman possessed the greater his or her wealth in terms of social reckoning. Thus a person's wealth was not reckoned merely by the amount of cash (cf. Bohannan, 1968).

13.6 Investing in Transport

From very early times, water transport was known to be the cheapest means of transporting bulky commodities over long distances. In the Niger Delta, the canoe was the only means of bulk transportation of goods for long distances through the network of rivers and creeks and along the coast. According to Hopkins, hundreds of such transport canoes were in use on the middle section of the Niger between Gao and Djenne from the thirteenth century onwards and probably earlier. Some of these canoes, according to him, carried twenty or thirty tons of merchandise, including foodstuffs, as well as the more luxurious items of long-distance trade (Hopkins, 1973).

In the Niger Delta, although the Ogoni are known to have used large war canoes by the time they settled in the region, because of lack of written records, the precise date when they began to use such large canoes for commercial purposes is unknown. However, in a paper entitled "Impact of Linguistics and Oral Traditional on the Origin and Identity of some Niger Delta Place-names: a Study of the Ogoni Region" (Kpone-Tonwe, 1996), I have argued on the basis of compelling evidence that the people described in the fifteenth century by Duarte Pacheco Pereira as operating large transport canoes in the Eastern Niger Delta were the Ogoni, and that the 'very large village' which he also described was their chief commercial town called Bangha.

Pacheco Pereira recorded his description in *Esmeraldo de situ orbis,* thought to have been published between 1505 and 1508. In the description he noted, at the mouth of the Rio Real in a Creek off its eastern arm (otherwise called River Bonny) the existence of a ' large village'. According to Mauny's translation, Pacheco Pereira said in part:

> At the mouth of the Rio Real, within the arm we have spoken about above, is located a very large village of about 2000 households... and in this place are found the biggest canoes ever known in the whole of Ethiopian Guinea and made out of a single tree trunk. The blacks of this area go about naked, around their necks they wear copper necklaces as thick as a finger... They are warriors who rarely live in peace (1956).

In George Kimble's translation, Pacheco Pereira continued:

> At the mouth of this river within the Creek above mentioned, is a very large village... where much salt is made. The people of this area have bigger canoes capable of carrying up to eighty men. And they came from a hundred leagues or more up this river bringing yams in large quantities... They also bring many slaves, cows, goats, and sheep. Sheep are called 'bozy'. They sell all these (merchandise) to the natives of this village for salt, and our ships buy these things for copper bracelets, which are here greatly prized more than those of brass... They carry daggers like those of the white Moors of Berbery. They are warlike and are rarely at peace (1937).

From the above references a few points become clearer. By the end of the fifteenth century Ogoni had become a populous and complex society, with many of its citizens engaged in salt-making, pot-making, canoe-making and long-distance trade, involving the use of large transport canoes.

But most of long-distance traders who engaged in such activities could not afford their own canoes. Consequently, wealthy individuals who had accumulated surplus money from the sale of agricultural produce, from domestic animals, from local salt production and from long-distance trade invested it in transport canoes, which were hired out to users at moderate charges. With increased demand for transport canoes, the canoe industry at Ko also grew and expanded to areas where there was abundant timber. Prices began to rise in response to increased demand.

13.7   Investing in Permanent Tree Crops and Plants

The most important tree crops and plants in which the Ogoni invested their money as wealth were the oil palm, the raffia palm and plantain. Like the Ikwerre and the Abua, the Ogoni consider these permanent tree crops and plants as high income-yielding concerns. Parents and the elderly often encouraged their prosperous young men with money to save to invest it in these permanent tree crops and plants.

Oil palm 'bushes' or plots vary in size. Some oil palm 'bushes' contain as many as 100, 200 or even more palm trees. But a 'bush' containing any number of palm trees was regarded as permanent wealth. An oil palm 'bush' was never sold outright. But the owner could pledge it for a sum of money. The oil palm 'bush' reverted back to the owner when the amount pledged was paid back to the pledgee. By the middle of the twentieth century, owners of oil palm and raffia palm bushes, have adopted the system of selling seasonal crops instead of pledging the palm bush for an unspecified period. This method has developed following the collapse of the colonial Marketing Boards, which usurped the producer initiative.

In this system the owners of oil palm or raffia palm 'bushes' sell the entire crop for one or more seasons to the dealers for a lump sum. The dealers would hire labourers to harvest the mature fruit during the season specified in the sale agreement. At the end of the season the buyer's right to harvest fruit in that 'bush' expired. In the case of raffia palm 'bushes' the owner of a palm wine 'bush' contracted the tapping rights to one or more palm wine tappers for a specified number of years, say three or four, in return for a lump sum. At the end of the contracted period the tapping right was terminated or renewed for another specified period, usually for an increased amount. In that way, people who invested in oil palm or raffia palm 'bushes' made large profits on their investment.

About the 1970s, owners of raffia palm 'bushes' discovered that they could make still higher returns on their palm 'bushes' if they sold the tapping rights in individual raffia palm trees instead of contracting the whole 'bush' for a number of years. Accordingly, in areas of high demand for palm wine, such as the Port Harcourt Suburbs, Aba, Eleme and Onne Port, a mature raffia palm tree costs from 1,000.00 to 5,000.00 naira, depending on the size of the tree. Thus, since the 1970s a person whose 'bush' could continually produce a minimum of ten mature raffia palms in the same period could earn as much as 1,000.00 to 50,000.00 naira at one sale of the tapping rights. The tapping life of a mature raffia palm is three months, at the end of which the tree would have exhausted its juices, and the raffia palm is said to be dead. Meanwhile, tapping rights in newly matured palms are constantly being sold. Before an old raffia palm dies a young replacement would have been planted at its foot.

In that way, the permanent state of the 'bush' was maintained. Thus those who owned plots of such permanent tree crops were reckoned in society as rich. The third category of permanent tree crops and plants in which the Ogoni invested their surplus income was plantains. The plantain is one of the oldest food plants known to the early Ogoni, second only to the yam. Together with yam, it was the principal ritual food used in the worship of ancestral spirits. Apart from that, the plantain was always in great demand as a staple. It could be eaten in many ways. It could be boiled and eaten with vegetables or pepper soup, it could be sliced and fried as *dodo*, it could be pounded with yams and eaten as *foofoo*; it could also be baked and used as plantain chips, etc. The green plantain in particular contains a high level of natural iron and has little or no fat. For this reason it was greatly in demand for pregnant women and nursing mothers, since it was known to increase the flow of breast milk and to hasten the replenishment of lost blood and energy after childbirth and during the monthly menses.

Thus in Ogoni, as in most parts of tropical West Africa, the demand for plantains was unlimited. Accordingly, prosperous individuals especially women who had money for saving were always keen to invest in plantain groves. Like the oil palm and raffia palm 'bushes' the plantain 'bush' required very little looking after. Moreover, it could increase in number by multiplying through its numerous sucker system. Like the oil palm also, the plantain plant or grove was never sold outright. This was because it was regarded as permanent wealth.

When the owner of a plantain farm was in urgent need of money he or she could pledge it. The plantain farm was redeemed when the owner repaid the amount pledged to the pledgee. All the plantains harvested by the pledgee during the period he held the pledge on the farm became the interest or profit (bii) on his investment. Thus a person who held title to several plantain farms, oil palm plots and raffia palm 'bushes', besides yam farms, cocoyam farms and cassava farms, was rated in the community as a wealthy man or woman.

13.8 Acquisition of the Kporo

Some of the wealthy men, after investing in various areas of the economy and after complying with the important traditions, went a step further and saved their extra financial reserves by acquiring the extra-large bronzes called *Kporo*. Such bronzes were often seen on display at conspicuous spots in ancestral shrines, where they not only bore testimony to the fact that those ancestors were wealthy but served as rare pieces of treasure.

One informant whose ancestral shrine houses one of these large bronzes explained how and why his ancestor acquired it:

> Because of much money which my ancestor possessed, when he had done all the things he wanted to do with money, he preserved this *kporo* to remain so that his descendants might come to see it, saying, "when they will come to see this *kporo* in my own compound (Be), they will know that I was a rich man who had money": he got this money after he had performed the *yaanwii* tradition and all the higher traditions and had become a member of *pya kanee* (the ruling class). As he still had plenty of money, he exchanged it into *kporo* and preserved it (Odee, 73, tape No. OG/SK/5, 1983).

13.9 Conclusion

An analysis of the various methods of conveyance, which were aimed at increasing personal wealth, showed that they were largely indigenous, as there is as yet no evidence of introduction from outside. The opportunity existed within the indigenous system for 'borrowing' or 'lending' money at a profit at relatively short notice through the system of pledging, repledging and redeeming. In the process no usable wealth or money was allowed to remain unprofitably tied down. Consequently, out of this system a whole body of customary law evolved, aimed at regulating and protecting the interests of the participants, without regard to sex, age or class.

From the foregoing analysis and discussion, it is also evident that there was a much wider degree of inter intra-ethnic contact in the region than hitherto imagined. Furthermore, it is significant that all these economic features combined to attest to the fact that there existed an active and growing market system in the region through the use of money. Thus the system was able to serve the basic economic needs of the people in the period both before and after the arrival of Europeans.

CHAPTER FOURTEEN

DIVERSIFICATION OF SOCIAL ORGANISATION

There is evidence that the Ogoni began very early in their history to develop a social organisation in which the youths were trained to fit well into society as respectable citizens. Two instances are reported in the oral traditions in which children born into the society were observed from childhood to the time they became responsible leaders of the society. One of such youths was Gbeneakpana the younger who was said to have been born at Kugba. The oral tradition records that as a youth he gave much trouble and headaches to the people. But it was also reported of him that he was very skillful in the use of the sword. As an adult, Gbeneakpana became a medicineman and a warrior and was one of those who achieved the *Gbene* (Great), which was the highest title in pre-colonial Ogoni. Accordingly, the name Gbeneakpana indicates that his pre-title name was *Akpana* but on achieving the *Gbene* he became Gbeneakpana meaning, Great Akpana. He is credited with the founding of the town of Kónò on the Imo River.

Another youth whose progress in life was followed from childhood in the oral tradition was Gbeneatekina. According to the oral tradition, Gbeneatekina was born at Wiisoro. He grew up to become a great leader having passed through the rigours of social ascendancy in the ancient society to attain the *Gbene*. This Gbeneatekina was mentioned as one of the principal participants in the ceremonies connected with the founding of the kingdom of Nama at Gure. On that occasion it is said that he was given the two highest offices after that of the king, both as the La-Bue and as the Land priest. These examples give us an insight into the social system of the early Ogoni society. It is clearly evident that the ancient society had a system of social ascendancy which enabled youths of ability to gain experience from lower positions before rising to the higher ones, our analysis for the rest of this chapter will focus on the system of these social organisations.

14.1 Social Stratification

The first major class division was between the rulers (*Pya bee hue*) and the ordinary citizens or commoners (*Pya Ke-bue*). Within each of these broad divisions there existed various distinctions. I shall devote the rest of the chapter to highlighting these distinctions.

14.1 (a)   The Rulers (Pya Bee Sue}

In early times the rulers consisted of the founder and co-founders of a town and of its component parts. This small, oligarchic group was called *Pya Te-Ere-Bue* or *Pya Mene-Bue* (lit. "The owners of the Town" or "The Rich" or "The Wealthy ones of the Town"). In Ogoni, wealth was reckoned in terms of ownership of land and livestock. Thus the name *Pya Mene-Bue* derived from the fact that the founders of a town or community were the wealthiest in terms of the land and, by extension, the livestock which they possessed in that town or community. Accordingly, the leader among the founders became known as "The Great Rich" or "The Great Wealthy One" (*Gbenemene*). This oligarchic group under the leadership of the *Gbenemene* constituted the government of a town or community. In a later period, it became necessary to bring into government some selected citizens who had distinguished themselves and attained high status in society by achieving titles, and by their exemplary performances at various levels of social activity. When such citizens became members of government, the term *Pya Mene-Bue* became inadequate as a reference to the class of rulers. Consequently, the term *Pya Kanee* (lit. "The Matured Men") was applied to embody both founders and non-founders.

Again, in still a later period when the functions of government and the task of controlling society became increasingly complex the ruling class began to recruit some mature and able men who had demonstrated some abilities in some area of society, to join in the task of government as junior partners or, as they used to say, as the "arm of the Elders." This group was called *Pya Zuguru* (the Lieutenants), and they constituted the reservoir from which the ranks of the Elders were filled. All these groups together constituted the Ruling Class (*Pya Bee-Bue*). We may illustrate the distinctions within this social class as follows:

i. *Gbenemene* - King or paramount Ruler
ii. *Pya Kanee or Pya Kabaari* - The Elders and Chiefs
iii. *Pya Zuguru* - The Lieutenants

14. 1(b)   *The Ordinary Citizens or Commoners [Pya Kebue]*

After the class of rulers, the next broad division of society was the ordinary citizens or commoners. The English word "commoner" or "ordinary citizen" does not reflect an exact meaning in the Ogoni languages. The Kana term *Pya Kebue* (translated into English as "commoners") literally means "people of the lower part of the town" or "country." The term is really a combination of two *Kana* words *Ke*, which means the "down or lower part of and *hue*, which means a "town" or "country." Accordingly, the term pictures the citizens of a town or country in tiers. Those occupying the upper tiers were the rulers (*Pya bee hue*) and those in the lower tiers were the ordinary citizens or commoners (*Pya Kebue*). Within the general framework of *Pya Kebue*, however, there were several class distinctions or categories. These were:

i. *Pya Gbara* - The elite or "Gentlemen"
ii. *Pya Kune nee* - The Commoners or ordinary free men
iii. *Pya Kporowa* - The unmarried poor
iv. *Zooro/Gbon* - Slaves
v. *Pya Saa nee* - The Strangers

In the following sections, we shall explain the origin and development of these social categories and distinctions and note the purpose they served in society.

i.   Pya Gbara (sing, Gbara nee]

The term *Pya Gbara* means "the elite" or "gentlemen." The term refers to those youths and adults who have performed or gone through the *Yaa* traditional experience. The first stage of the *Yaa* which every young man of consequence was expected to pass through was called *Yaa-ge*. The suffix *ge* means sword or machete. Accordingly, the *Yaa-ge* tradition was an experience in which the young men were taught to master the use of the sword or machete both as a working tool and as a weapon of war. Accordingly, it is to be observed that military training was a significant aspect of the *Yaa* tradition. Early in this chapter, reference was made to Nama oral traditions in which the youth *Gbeneakpana* was praised for his skill in mastering the use of the sword. Since this happened way back at Kugba, it suggests that the *Yaa* tradition is very ancient in Ogoni. The implication is that the social class distinctions which the *Yaa* tradition effected were equally as old. This is not to suggest that the traditions have remained static over the centuries, undoubtedly, many changes have taken place in these traditions especially in the social aspects of the traditions.

One important training in which the young man undergoing the *Yaa-ge* tradition was expected to gain experience, was the art of fencing. This was probably the essence of the term *"Yaa-ge."*

Other things learned in the traditional experience were spiritual fortitude, bravery, good character and good behaviour. Accordingly, all the young men who had performed this tradition were qualified to be listed into the town's fighting force as soldiers. Thus in Ogoni, age was not the main determinant of social classes. Rather it was the *Yaa* tradition. Consequently a youth of fifteen who had performed the Yaa tradition was more acceptable to the Elders than a man of fifty who had not, one informant explained the significance of the tradition in the following terms:

> Every male child must perform the tradition of *Yaage* before he could have respect in the society. A person who had not performed this tradition might not enter certain places or certain houses in the town. He might be excluded from certain groups. When such a person died, he was buried at the back of 'his' compound not in the front part (Teedee, tape 15, 18th March, 1984).

If a youth who had performed the *Yaa* tradition entered the presence of the Elders, he could be offered a drink by them without embarrassment. Such a youth was regarded as an "Elder in the making." He was considered spiritually alert and sound. Thus they were called *Pya Gbara* (gentlemen). Accordingly, the youths in this social class were exposed to various social activities, including the elite occupations such as yam cultivation or farming, palm wine tapping, and palm fruit cutting. Besides fencing with swords, other sports engaged in by the *Pya Gbara* were wrestling, judo, *kanikpo* and certain dances. They were encouraged to develop a capacity for hardwork and a desire to save wealth and money for the purpose of performing the higher traditions.

Although age was not a parameter for determining social classes in pre-colonial Ogoni, it was nevertheless a factor in social organisation for purposes of role performance. Social activities were organised by dividing the whole *Pya gbara* social class into activity clubs or associations known as *gbo*. The members were not necessarily of a uniform age-range. A leader of one of such activity clubs or associations which existed in the 1940s described the age-range of the members in these words:

> All the members were not exactly of the same age; some were twenty years old, some twenty-two years, some twenty-five, and some thirty years old. There were male and female members. Two leaders called Adue Gbo were appointed in each community to organise the club in that community. (Gbaratee, tape 20, 7th Jan., 1984).

Each social club or association performed public as well as private services for the association. Women were rated in the same social class as their husbands. Accordingly, they joined the same social clubs as indicated in above-quoted text. Nevertheless the admission of women into the social clubs must be seen as a modern innovation. The women members did not play the same roles as the men. Women membership appeared to have been conspicuous only on occasions of big ceremonies or dinners such as the performance of the feminine *Yaa* tradition or the *bogo* outing ceremony.

Each *gbo* had a specific name. The most popular social clubs were the "Three Horns" (*Gbo Taanuunu}* and the "Doers of Words" (*Gbo Ko Doo*). One informant described the "Three Horns" in these words:

> The "Three Horns" (*Gbo Taa-Nuunu"*) were a select group. They were powerful men; men of great strength in the area. Any town which needed this type of men for any difficult task, they used to come and hire us. For example, like the task of catching semi-wild bull alive for use in some ritual sacrifice. When there was a wrestling or judo tournament, whether within the community or outside, the members of the club were the men who used to do it. Next to the "Three Horns" were the 'Doers of Words' (*Gbo Ko Doo*). They were the able-bodied men, the doers of their words. They and the "Three Horns" were often hired out in any matter that required physical strength and power. (Legbara, tape 20, 5th Jan., 1984).

These groups engaged in public activities as well as in the activities of their respective clubs. In the public activities, each club tried to excel the other clubs of the same age range based in rival communities. Such rivalries were particularly strong in competitive sports like wrestling or judo (*kpurube*). Within each association or club, the members worked cooperatively to encourage their individual members to succeed in life by becoming financially and socially successful. For example, if during a particular farming season, a member could not plant crops on his farm because he could not afford to buy the seeds, the members of his *gbo* supported him by making it possible for him to plant crops on his farm that year. They also organised and financed the funerals of their deceased members.

The degree of a member's success was judged by his ability to perform the recognised traditions, by the number of wives he married especially those from "abroad" and by the number of elite yams (*mgwe*) he could produce during each farming season. When a man had distinguished himself in all these areas of life and was judged to be a capable leader, he joined the class of rulers (*Pya bee hue*).

(ii) Kune Nee (pl. Pya Kune Nee]

Apart from the slaves and the strangers, the next social category in Ogoni society were the ordinary free men (*Pya Kune nee*). This class of citizens were not placed in their class by any accident of birth or by any other cause. They remained ordinary free men because they could not perform the traditional rite of *Yaage*. The traditional rite of *Yaage* was the great differentiator of social classes in pre-colonial Ogoni.

The disadvantage was that persons who did not undergo the *Yaa-ge* traditional experience were said to be spiritually deficient, spiritually inactive and spiritually "unwise" (i.e. unwise in their spirit life). They were therefore incapable of leadership or of making decisions for others. Accordingly they were not listed as fighting men for the community; or as soldiers in time of war, because it was believed that in a time of emergency a man's spiritual soundness as a warrior was vital. They believed that a spiritually weak person could easily be led astray and "entrapped" by the enemy. Since the *Kune nee* lacked the benefits gained from both the spiritual and the military training which the *Yaa* tradition provided, they were considered deficient in the essential ingredients which equipped a man to fit well in an active society. For example if a community meeting was held to which all the citizens were invited, the *Kune nee* could attend such a meeting and listen from a distance. He could not join in the meeting or contribute to the discussions. One informant described this distinction thus:

> If an important matter occurred in the community and they wanted people to meet to discuss it, only those who had performed the Yaa tradition could enter the house where the matter was being discussed. Those who had not performed the Yaa tradition would sit outside and listen from outside. They could not be able to take part in the discussions. (Nii, tape 4, 29th Dec., 1983).

One problem is that the actual numerical strength of the *Kune nee* in comparison with the rest of the population is not known. But since most parents could only sponsor one or two of their sons at a time for the *Yaage* tradition, it may be speculated that the number which could not perform the tradition was quite substantial, and that they probably represented a silent majority.

(iii) Kporowa

A *Kporowa* literally means one who was "poor of a wife" or of a "woman." That is, a man who had not married a wife because he could not afford it. In Ogoni, the first responsibility of a mature man was to marry a wife. A mature man who had not fulfilled this social obligation was rated in the same social class as the man who had not performed the *Yaa* tradition; and the term *Kune nee* applied to both of them. If a man who had not performed the *Yaa* tradition was married, his wife was rated in the same social class as himself but he was higher in the social scale and commanded a greater respect in society than the man who could neither perform the *Yaa* tradition nor marry a wife. A *Kporowa* was therefore regarded as a worse pauper and an irresponsible citizen, since he was not responsible to a household or family. Hence he could not take part in any decision affecting the community. One informant in the Eleme area described the lot of the *Kporowa* in the following terms:

> In Eleme society, unless a person was married, he could not take part in important deliberations of the village or community. If there was a gathering of the community, and they wanted to select people who would form a committee for consultation, only persons who were married could be summoned to such a committee. If there was a community gathering and they wanted to appoint some people to make some findings, and report back, only those who were married could be appointed to the committee. (Osaronu, tape 8, 25th Feb., 1984).

(iv) Gbon

E.J. Gibbons has stated that there was no slave class in Ogoni society (Gibbons, 1932). That statement is true only to a degree. The fact is that in Ogoni society, slaves were assimilated into families and households as wives and concubines and absorbed into the larger society. A similar method was adopted probably on a much larger scale in the Ijo society of New Calabar (Horton, 1969). But in Ogoni, there was always in existence a sizeable number of slaves who were at various stages of transition into full assimilation. Such slaves, as long as they were still identifiable, formed the lowest stratum of society. Two *Kana* words were used to describe such slaves. *Gbon*, which means servant or slave, was used to refer to those slaves who were personal servants to individuals or to households. They performed the menial tasks. Thus in Ogoni, if "A" were to ask "B" in a rude manner to perform a task for him (whether menial or not), "B" might react by querying "A," "Am I your slave?" (*M lu o gbon?*). The word itself was never used in plural. When the plural form was required, this was indicated by the preceding personal pronoun. "Are we your slaves?" (*lu o gbon?*). If the word was preceded by the untranslatable *Kana* particle *Pya* i.e. *pya Gbon*, it meant the Igbo or Igbo people. Thus we have expressions such as *nee Gbon*, Igbo person/man; *wa Gbon*, Igbo woman; *nwi Gbon*, Igbo child. Accordingly, it would appear that the *Kana* term *gbon* was derived from the term "Igbo." It is probable that the term was derived in the period of long-distance marriages from the Igbo hinterland (see chapter 3: Later System of Marriage). It is to be noted, however that this class of slaves (*gbon*) were acquired only by the wealthy as a way of showing their prosperity and wealth.

(v) Zooro

The term *zooro* also means "slaves" but it carries with it the notion of bondage. It is the lowest form of servitude. While *gbon* was a form of luxury, *zooro* was something to be abhorred. The *zooro* were usually taken or captured in war. For this reason they were normally not owned by or attached to individual persons or households. Their assimilation was therefore very slow or almost impossible. Those of them not sold or dispatched as ritual victims were placed under the protection of gods and lived in isolation on the property of such gods. Neither the *gbon* nor the *zooro* could advance socially, as they could not perform the *Yaa* tradition. But once assimilation was complete, this problem ceased to exist.

(vi) Saa nee

The earliest strangers who settled on Ogoni land were Bonny people whom the Ogoni called *Ebani*, meaning "people from afar" or "from a distant place". Other early strangers who settled on Ogoni land were the Obolo (Andoni), whom the Ogoni called *Bono*. Still others were the Okrika, called *Kirika* by the Ogoni. With the possible exception of the Ibani who were said to have initially come to Ogoni territory overland, the oral tradition states that all these strangers arrived in Ogoni by sea in canoes (cf. Afigbo, 1974). Initially, they settled on Ogoni land along the coastal fringes and traded with Ogoni in fish and bought agricultural foodstuffs in return. All these peoples were regarded as strangers (*Pya Saa nee*) because they did not form part of the Ogoni society. They were not required to participate in Ogoni traditions, but they were expected to observe the laws of the communities in which they settled.

The other groups of strangers were the Igbo. Although the Ogoni had had contacts with the Asa (*Pya Saga*) who, in that early time, were not regarded as Igbo, in later times, Igbo traders settled in Ogoni communities, especially in towns along the trade routes. The Abiriba and the Nkwerre constituted the largest group of Igbo settlers in Ogoni land in pre-colonial times, yet they were not regarded as citizens of Ogoni society.

One favourable condition between Ogoni and these strangers was that they did not constitute a rival group with Ogoni on agricultural lands. In other words, they did not cultivate the land. The Ijo settlers engaged in fishing, while the Nkwerre and the Abiriba were mainly traders. Although the latter groups often owned vegetable gardens, such gardens were usually within the level of minor agricultural activity, which did not pose as a threat to the interests of the local farmers, as attempts to own plots of permanent tree-crops and elite yam farms would have done. Such an attempt would have created a situation of conflict between the stranger/settlers and the indigenous farmers over agricultural land. According to one informant, even among the Ogoni themselves, conflict over agricultural land was not completely absent.

Farmlands and raffia palm bushes were the major causes of trouble and quarrels among Ogoni people. It was illegal for somebody to plant a plantain plant on another person's land, or on land on which one was a temporary occupant. (Tonwe III 70, tape 26, 22.2.84). Thus the divergence of occupational interests between the settlers and the Ogoni farmers created a relationship of peaceful co-existence and mutual economic co-operation,

14.2 Evolution of Political Institutions

Information about the system of government at Nama and Kugba is sketchy, The oral tradition states that the founders of Nama and Kugba ruled with a council of chiefs. Another tradition states that the earliest rulers were women. The first to rule among them being a woman named Kwaanwaa or Gbenekwaanwaa. Tradition holds that she died at Gure, where a shrine supposed to have been erected on her grave exists till today. After her death, her first daughter named Za succeeded to the stool, but her son, Gbeneyaaloo, was in control of the government. Following the deaths of Gbeneyaaloo and Za, the succession passed to the latter's first daughter named Bariyaayoo, whose seat of government was at Luawii.

The Bariyaayoo dynasty is said to have continued until it collapsed during a civil war called "*Baan* wars" a war said to have been fought at a time when firearms were first introduced at Bonny. K.O. Dike dates the introduction of firearms to the sixteenth century (Dike, 1956). During the same period Boue; under the leadership of Gbenekiri, emerged out of the war as the leading state in Ogoni. Between the fall of Luawii in the 16th century and the colonial conquest at the end of the 19th century a number of political institutions evolved. References to such institutions are abundant in the oral traditions. The following analysis will focus on the developments during this period, highlighting the changes which occurred subsequent to their evolvement.

14.2(a) Social Organization and the System of Governance

Opportunities existed by which individuals could advance to positions of recognition in society. Included in such opportunities were membership of certain elite societies and social clubs, performance of acts of bravery and association with certain religious organisations.

Hunting for instance, was one of the means of social advancement; and it existed from very ancient times. Boys were taught the art of hunting from very early age. The ability to hunt and kill small animals by boys was regarded as a mark of manliness, diligence and responsibility. It was believed that a hunter was one who constantly practised the habits and character of a warrior. Thus the Ogoni dedicated two of their major annual feasts to hunting, namely the feast of *Yonwidam*, which took place in March and the feast of *Nubien*, which took place in August. The word *Yonwidam* is a combination of three *Kana* words, each having a distinct meaning, viz. *Yo* which means a "feast" or a "deity;" *Nwi*, which means a "child;" and *dam* (or *edam*), which means a "male." Thus *Yonwidam* literally means "Feast of the male child" or "of the virile youth" or "of the rugged male." This was the feast of hunting or of the hunters. The feast marked the opening of the hunting season. Usually by March when this feast began, the most difficult part of the year's farm work had been completed. There remained only the less difficult part of the work which consisted mainly of tending the yam vines and weeding by women. It was at this time that the men took off to engage in hunting. The hunting expeditions continued through the dry months before the rains set in. By June when the impact of the rainy season had increased, the hunting season was brought to an end.

The provision of bush meat was an important luxury in ancient Ogoni. The feast of *Yonwidam* was therefore an occasion on which men tried to provide plenty of bush meat for their wives and households for the celebration of this feast, one informant described the significance of the *Yonwidam* feast in these words:

> At the feast of *Yonwidam*, the men paid attention to their wives. Trappers, fishermen and hunters intensified their efforts in order to catch some big game, which they would use for the feast of

Yonwidam. They provided large resources of meat and food for the feast. They did this to please their wives.

(Tonwe III 7, tape 26, 22nd Jan., 1984).

One of the highlights of the Yonwidam celebration was the great war dance at the ancient town of Kako, near Baraboue. On the first day of the feast, boys armed with mock weapons and dressed like men with well-girded loins and bells on waist, went there to show their prowess in fighting, usually, among such groups of boys were some who considered themselves tough and powerful. They challenged similar groups of boys from other towns or parts of the same communities. The challenge often began by one group of individuals attempting to capture the mock weapons of the other group. Fifteen days after the boys' celebration the elders, warriors and some brave hunters went there to perform the annual war ritual known as the "dance" of Koogian. The word Koogian is a contraction of two *Kana* words, *Koo*, which means friend, mate, or comrade; and *gian*, which means bravery. Thus the *Koogian* "dance" was a dance by brave comrades. In 1984, I came across a type-written document dated June, 1964, by the late Gbenemene I of Babbe, Tonwe II, in which he and his Elders tried to write down these traditions in their order of occurrence and to state the major features of each of them. According to that document, one of the features of the occasion was the presentation of gifts to boys by parents and the wearing of special head-gears and outfits by the chiefs and Elders (Tonwe II, 1964:1). The importance of the document is that it clearly shows that hunting and war were regarded in pre-colonial Ogoni as closely related activities.

While *Yonwidam*, the men's feast opened the hunting season, Nubien, the boys' feast concluded the season. Nonetheless, both the men and the boys began the season from *Yonwidam* with the aim of preserving the meat produced against the end-of-year feast known as *Zua*, which was observed in August, and which coincided with the *Nubien* feast. According to one informant, the main aim of the *Nubien* was to train boys in the use of a simple contrivance in hunting small animals so that they could develop the resourcefulness which they would need in future to be able to provide meat for their families.

From the foregoing explanations, it is evident that the feast of *Nubien* was designed to encourage boys in the habit of hunting. Similarly, the feast of *Yonwidam* was designed to stimulate men in the same noble direction at a much higher level. The hunting expeditions became intensified throughout Ogoni soon after the *Yonwidam* feast. And the period became one of great excitement in many parts of the territory. Men tried to boost their masculinity and endeavoured to raise the expectations of their women. Wives, mothers and women in general looked forward with excitement and enthusiasm in anticipation of their men's success at the hunting expeditions. The names of those who succeeded in killing some big game spread like wild fire. Such men became popular with the Elders because their success had assured them of large supplies of meat. Their success had also vindicated the "powers" of the medicine-men who prepared the game charms which they had invoked on the animals before the hunting began. From these illustrations it will be shown in subsequent sections how hunting not only became an institution but also an avenue through which a man could rise to the higher levels of society.

Out of the whole lot of hunters, a small number of them became outstanding. These were men who were especially brave, who moved on from hunting the regular game to hunting the dangerous animals, like the leopard, the elephant, the python. etc. Any hunter who killed a leopard or any such dangerous animals, was awarded the title of *Damgian* (lit. Brave Male, or Brave Man).

When a hunter killed an animal like the leopard, the whole animal was carried to Yobue Square at Kónò Boue where the war shrine was located. There the Elders presided over the rituals. The killing of a fierce animal of this kind was treated in the same way as the killing of an enemy in battle or in a hand-to-hand fight, or in a war-like action such as a raid, in the case of a human enemy, it was the head of the enemy that was brought to the war shrine at Yobue Square. By tradition, it was illegal for any person to keep the head of a war victim in his house. The same law applied concerning the whole body of a leopard. At Yobue Centre, certain ritual purifications were performed on the body and hands of the warrior or hunter to release him from the power of blood, professor Nzimiro reports a similar practice among the Western Igbo (Nzimiro, 1972).

One of my informants who himself had killed three leopards and had on three occasions received the *Damgian* title, states that among other things, the purification sacrifice prevented the hands of the warrior from shaking so that he could drink from a cup without splashing his wine. Besides, the killer of a leopard must pay taxes for killing the animal. According to him, for each bullet hole found in the skin of the leopard, the killer was charged 3 manilas; and 6 manilas for each of the bullets that were fatal to the animal. (Gbarato, 1984). 14,2(b)

The Emergence of the House of Hunters

The history of modern hunting in Ogoni started with the introduction of firearms in the sixteenth century during the *Baan wars*. According to the oral tradition, the founder of modern hunting in Ogoni was Gbenebalikina, the man who introduced firearms into Ogoni during the *Baan* wars. The oral tradition states that he founded the Hunters' Society and a House of Hunters. Two words are connected with the history of hunting in Ogoni, namely *ton uwegbo* and *to uwegbo*. The term *uwegbo* is a combination of two *Kana* words viz. *uwe*, which means a bush and *gbo*, which means a dog. Thus *uwegbo* literally, means the "dogs' bush;" and that was the term for hunting. Accordingly, *Pya Uwegbo* literally means "people of the dogs "bush" or "hunters." Originally, the Ogoni hunted with dogs. A group of men armed with knives, spears and javelins, set game-traps at the opposite end of a bush or forest and waited to kill or catch the escaping animals. Then the hunters let loose a pack of well-drugged hunting dogs, each having on its neck several dangling bells and mini-gongs called *mene-gbo*. Inside each *mene* were fitted two small bars of iron or wood which produced jingling or clanging sounds as the dogs charged to frighten and chase out the animals towards the waiting men. Occasionally, some of the waiting men were killed, especially by the dangerous animals, such as the leopard or the python. That was why a man who killed one of these ferocious animals was honoured.

Now the words *Ton* and *to* are cognates but they also have very important distinctions. 'To' Simply means a "house". *Ton* is a contraction of *Keton*, which means a "home" a "resting place" or a "stable position." *Ton Uwegbo* therefore means the "home of the hunters" i.e. their resting place after the full day's hunt or the place where they regularly assembled to share out the meat according to custom. This was a square on the outskirts of the town. Evidently, *ton Uwegbo* was the older word which applied to corporate hunting in pre-colonial Ogoni. In the sixteenth century following the introduction of the gun to hunting by Gbenebalikina, hunting became highly institutionalised. A House of Hunters (*To uwegbo*) came into being. Gbenebalikina was accordingly credited as the founder of the House of Hunters. Another version of the oral tradition states that he was the first Ogoni man who used the gun to shoot an animal when he tried out the gun on a goat,

The Formation of the House of Hunters

With the knowledge that the gun was both a powerful weapon of war as well as for hunting, all the leading men of the state rallied round Gbenebalikina, with the result that an inner club was formed at Kónò Boue, known as the "Hunters' Society or Club" (*Pya To Uwegbo*), with Gbenebalikina as the head. His house became their meeting place. This society controlled and regulated all hunting in Ogoni. They also collected meat tribute on all game killed during the annual corporate hunting following the *Yonwidam* feast. Its membership was highly restricted and consisted of the very top men of the state. The following testimony gives an idea of the nature of this highly elitist society:

> The founder of professional hunting and the Hunters' Society (To uwegbo) was Gbenebalikina. He became the founder of modern hunting because he was the first man to introduce the gun into hunting in Ogoni. It was the Baan wars which made Gbenebalikina to acquire the gun. The Baan wars brought many new things and changes into Ogoni... Being the first person to use the gun in Ogoni, he became the 'Father of hunting' in Ogoni. People used to join the Hunters' Society like they used to join the House of Elders. If a man possessed a gun, he could go to a hunting expedition and if he

was able he might kill an animal but that did not show that he was a member of the Hunters' Society. (Tonwe III, tape 26, 22nd Jan., 1984).

Once the hunting season was declared open on *Yonwidam day*, the hunting continued throughout the season at the rate of one expedition a week on every *Deeson*. The founders of the House of Hunters who were also the leaders of the society, regulated the hunting procedure in such a way that each of the leading men of the age was honoured with a hunting expedition in the year as a kind of meat tribute for their forests and bushes. For example, there was one annual hunting expedition called *Uwegbo Yo Nobana*, which was dedicated to the honour of Gbenekiri and named after his *Gan* i.e. *Gan Nobana*. But because Gbenekiri was deified, the term was called *Uwegbo Yo Nobana*.

The five days of the Ogoni week are *Deemua, Deebom, Deezia, Deeson* and *Deeko*.

This was the Ogoni week of five days. *Deeson* was the fourth day of the week, It was the day of gathering in of agricultural produce against the fifth day *Deeko*, which was the principal market day and a day of rest for most Ogoni men. Usually the professional hunters from places like Gokana, Tee, Kpong, Baa, etc. did not return to their towns that *Deeson* evening. They spent the night in Boue at the houses of their friends drinking the palm wine. They returned home on the *Deeko* after a bit of shopping at the Dukono market.

Similarly, there was one hunting expedition called *uwegbo Gbenebalikina*, which was dedicated to the honour of Gbenebalikina, the founder of the society. There was one hunting expedition for each of the outstanding leaders/warriors who owned forests. Such hunting expeditions were done in the forests or bushes belonging to the person in whose honour the hunting was done. The only outstanding warrior who was similarly honoured but who did not have a forest of his own was Yobue because he was a refugee (*iyiinayo*). Thus on the day they gave a hunting expedition to Yobue, the hunting was done generally, in the bushes surrounding that part of the town where Yobue lived. It is pertinent to notice here that the House of Hunters came into being as a professional organisation before ever the Elders were organised into a political institution. Although the House of

Hunters was purely a professional society, because of the tight and elitist nature of its membership, it had in it the seed of a political development. As we shall see later, the emergence of the House of Elders had the House of Hunters as its antecedent.

This was clearly obvious because when Assobienee the son of Gbenebalikina became the founder of the House of Elders, Gbenebalikina was no longer alive, nor Gbenekiri his contemporary and first king of Boue after the Baan wars. This is indicated in the fact that the leaders of that time entrusted the task of organising the newly formed House of Elders into the hands of Assobienee instead of his father Gbenebalikina. The fact that his father was made the head of the House must be seen as a posthumous honorarium.

From the foregoing observations, we come to the following conclusions. First, hunting and hunters were important aspects of social organisation in pre-colonial Ogoni. Second, through success in hunting a person could rise to the higher levels of the social order, especially because hunting and war were treated as complementary activities. Third, the organisation of the Hunters' Society provided the necessary antecedents which gave birth to a series of political and constitutional changes in Ogoni from the sixteenth century onwards. We shall address the issue of these political and constitutional changes in the forthcoming sections.

14.3 The Formation of the House of Elders

Prior to the formation of the House of Elders, the king ruled with a small group of Elders called *Pya Kanee* or *Pya Kabaari*. The word *Kanee* is a combination of two Kana words *Ka*, which means "mother" or "fully grown" or "fully developed" or "well-matured;" and *nee*, which means "a man" or "a person." in this context the king ruled with a small group of well-matured men, otherwise called "the Elders" (*Pya Kanee*). The king and the Elders constituted the decision-making body as well as the highest judicial court in the land. The executive arm of this body was a select group of men in the age-range of about forty to fifty years. This group was known as *Pya Zuguru* (the Lieutenants). Originally, the king and the Elders met at the king's palace for all matters of governance. However, in the period after the Baan wars, there appeared to have been a 'revolution.' A separate House of Elders was formed, which was situated in a different location from the palace of the king. The highest authority in the land became the House of Elders (*To Pya Kanee*), instead of the king.

Prior to this period, however, the king was the highest authority in the land. Next to the king in the scale of authority was the *La-Bue* (lit. "Second son of the Town or Country" or "King's Deputy/' or "Chief Minister"), followed by the Elders, and lastly by the *Pya Zuguru* (the Lieutenants). However, in the period after the Baan wars, there were several changes. The evidence suggests that the king was confronted by a strong opposition from some of the leading warriors who had fought in those wars. In the face of such opposition the king conceded to some reforms. The result was that a House of Elders came into being as a separate institution from the palace of the king. Consequently, the power and authority of the king were considerably reduced. Glimpses of these developments appear in the oral tradition.

For example, King Gbenekote is quoted in the oral tradition as having said "I am the *Te-ere-Bue* (Father or owner of these towns) but I alone cannot rule them." His brother Gbenekwerre is also quoted to have said, "I am the *Te-ere-Bue* (Father/Owner of these towns) but I alone cannot judge them." The account concludes by saying that the result of these declarations by these rulers was that "They divided the functions of government piece by piece. They selected Igbara Abe's house as the House of Elders (*To Pya Kanee*). They decided that all the possessing ancestral spirits (*Zim*) and deities should be represented in that House," (Nuaka56, 1983).

The above testimony clearly points to the fact that there was a political struggle between the king and the other veterans of the Baan wars for the sharing of political power. The House of Elders appears to have been created out of that political struggle. On the basis of internal evidence, we may date this event to the sixteenth century.

14.3(a) Constitutional Changes and Membership of the House of Elders

As already mentioned in the preceding section, the work of organising the newly formed House of Elders was entrusted to Assobienee. The latter organised the membership of the House on the basis of the seven ancient lineages of Ogoni known as *gan*. Obviously, Assobienee did not make that decision on his own accord. We noticed in the above-quoted text, a decision that all possessing ancestral spirits (*Zim*) should be represented in the House of Elders. That decision provided the constitutional basis for representation in the House of Elders. In their view, the best way to represent all the original ancestors in the new House was to base the membership on the seven ancient lineages. They probably judged that on that basis government would be completely removed from total control by the king and that the seven ancient lineages provided the best formula for governance.

By the sixteenth century, however, the number of such *gan* must have increased. Nevertheless they still reckoned their judgment on the seven original lineages. In that way they effectively limited the membership of the House of Elders. Since the king was already a member of the House, the King's *gan* (or the founder's *gan*) was given one additional member of the House. Thus the total member of the House of Elders became eight. On that basis, the permanent membership of the House of Elders in the Boue Kingdom was represented as follows:

Table III:
Membership of the House of Elders - Boue Kingdom

S/No.	Name/Owner of Seat	Name of Gan	Membership
1	Gbenekwerre/Gbenekote	Taankaan	2
2.	Gbenebalikina/Assobienee House	Abere (Be-Abere)	1
3.	Gbenekiri House	Nobana	1

4.	Gbenebion/Gbenebaligboro House	Dookunu	1
5.	Gbeneguatee/ Gbenenaa House	Joko	1
6.	Gbenetigina House	Gbaabio	1
7.	Gbom/Gbenelakarakue House	Baraboue	1
8.	Gbenegaraa/Tigina House	Kono	1

It is noted here that all the seven ancient *gan* of Ogoni are found in every Ogoni group. However, since the last forty to fifty years most Ogoni people have forgotten or have not learned about their *gan*, due to a steep decline in the performance of the *Yaa* traditions.

The eighth *gan* named above was not one of the original seven ancient *gan* of Ogoni. According to the oral tradition, *Gan Kónò* branched off from *Gan Gbaabio* after a quarrel which occurred at a *Yaa* traditional ceremony. The quarrel resulted in a fight which caused a schism in *Gan Gbaabio*. Gbenegara Tigina led a dissident group from the original gan and founded a new *gan* known as *Gan Kónò*. Evidently, the new *gan* was named after the principal town of the Boue Kingdom, *Kónò*. Since Kónò Boue was founded in the sixteenth century during the Baan wars, it means that *Gan Kónò* probably came into being in the seventeenth or eighteenth century.

The oral tradition states that one member of the House with observer status was granted to *Gan Kónò* because a prominent member of that new *gan* named Nii Yeegboronwaa married a great-granddaughter of Gbenekote named Deedu. Deedu was a daughter of Gbenegaraa Naalo, who descended from Gbenekote.

Having achieved the *Gbene*, he branched from Gbenekote House and founded a separate house – Gbenegaraa Naalo House. This marriage associated the house of Nii Yeegboronwaa with the royal house. Since Nii was from *Gan Kónò*, they honoured the *gan* by granting it membership of the House of Elders. Since it is known that Nii died early in the twentieth century, it is most probable that the admission of *Gan Kónò* into the House of Elders took place in the nineteenth century.

Further reforms were said to have been made by a grandson of Assobienee named Igbara Abe. The source reports that Assobienee bequeathed the authority to organise and lead the House of Elders to his grandson Igbara Abe. One of the reforms for which Igbara Abe is remembered was the introduction of "nominal members" into the House of Elders. The nominal members were those members whose membership did not derive from the membership of their ancestors. Such members did not have their permanent seats in the House of Elders. The explanation for this was that at the time the House of Elders was created, a certain number of *gan* among those which were entitled to send one member, did not actually send their representatives to assume their place in the House of Elders.

Perhaps there were no qualified candidates in such *gan*, or that they did not support the political changes that took place. In time, those seats lapsed.

When Igbara Abe assumed control of the House of Elders he took practical steps to bring into the House the representatives of all the remaining *gan* who were not physically represented in the House of Elders. It is this that was referred to in the oral tradition that Igbara Abe introduced the "nominal members" into the House of Elders. Although he did not enlarge the membership of the House, he nevertheless made it possible for the full physical representation of all the *gan* that were entitled to membership. On the basis of our chronological scheme, Igbara Abe's reform may be dated to the eighteenth or nineteenth century.

14.3(b)   The Role of Assobienee

According to oral tradition, when the king was the sole ruler in the land and the palace of the king the highest court and centre of government, the king and the elders who supported him, made use of a group of physically strong and courageous men to enforce the laws of the government. Such men were usually easily identified and recruited from the towns and communities into the king's service.

Assobienee was a leader of such a group of men who did services for the king. The following testimonies explain:

> If a man was sued in the palace of the king, the king sent Assobienee to summon the accused person. If the accused was a strong man or if he was recalcitrant, Assobienee was ordered to arrest him and to bring him bodily to the king's palace, when the person struggled with Assobienee, the latter broke his limbs to disable him and did not care even if he died. (Tonwe III, tape 25, 22.1.84).

Another informant stated the account thus:

> The Elders employed Assobienee to be near them in order that he might watch over their interest. If anyone broke their law, he should arrest that person. Whenever the Elders settled a divorce case, they gave of the fees paid, three manillas to Assobienee... The Elders paid him this money as wages for his work for them. For it was he who used to ensure that their laws were enforced completely (Asoo tape 12, 12.1.84).

As stated earlier, Assobienee was the son of Gbenebalikina, the great warrior who introduced the gun into Ogoni and became the founder and head of the Hunters' Society.

Assobienee had such a great leader behind his back. Besides, Assobienee had his own outstanding qualities, strength and courage which earned him recognition and brought him into the king's service. Moreover, Assobienee came on the scene in a particularly critical period in Ogoni, the aftermath of the Baan wars.

It seems that the great warriors who fought in those wars came to realise that they all had made sacrifices to preserve the peace and the security of the state. They therefore felt strongly that it was time that they all joined hands together in the task of governance and that it was no longer the ideal to let the king alone to control the destiny of the people. The following testimony gives an indication of this:

> They decided that all the functions of government should not be vested in the king alone. For the king would not live alone in his town, even though he was the founder of the town. (Tonwe III, tape 26, 22nd Jan. 1984).

In the circumstances they got Assobienee, the strong man on their side; and there is little doubt that what took place was a grand coup d'etat. To ensure that the action was successful, they placed

Assobienee in charge to organise the new power structure. Thus the House of Elders came into being.

14.4 Functions of the House of Elders

The Elders were responsible for war and peace. In times of crisis such as war, epidemics or famine, the Elders were by ancient custom never to leave the town. To do so was tantamount to abdication. They were expected to meet constantly at their House to pour libations, prepare the rituals, sacrifices and medicines needed to bring the crisis to the desired end.

The Elders did not go to battle but they remained at home to strengthen the people. If a warrior was wounded in battle, the treatment of such a person was the responsibility of the Elders. If a citizen (usually an important citizen) was in a state of crisis, such as a coma or seizure, information was sent to the House of Elders, who on receiving such information sent one or two of their members to act as intercessors between the victim and the supernatural, pouring libations and speaking prayerful incantations to the Supreme God to spare the life of the victim. When the House of Elders sat as a court of justice, it dealt with only the most serious cases, such as murder, witchcraft, sorcery, and all cases concerned with the loss of human life. When one of such cases was brought to the House of Elders, it took seven sittings for it to be disposed of. The seven sittings could extend over two months or two years, depending on how urgent the circumstances of the case were. During that time the case went through prescribed stages. The court met always on the first day of the Ogoni week i.e. on Deemua only.

The cases that were dealt with at the king's court or at the palace were land cases, such as cases about farms, raffia palm bushes, oil palm bushes; adultery cases, divorce cases, affray, theft, slander, defamation etc. The king, the Elders and the *Zuguru* together took part in the settlement of such cases. But cases in the House of Elders were dealt with by the king and the Elders only. The *Zuguru* were not admitted to cases in the House of Elders.

14.4(a) The Qualifications of an Elder

Two Kana words conveyed the idea of Elder, namely *Kabaari* and *Kanee*. The older word, *Kabaari* referred to all the titled men who had risen to the top level of society irrespective of whether or not they were members of the House of Elders. The feminine of *Kabaari* is *Kabaariwa,* The term *Kanee* had no feminine. This was probably because women were not admitted to the House of Elders. *Pya Kanee* referred to that small group of *Kabaari* who were members of the House of Elders, and were therefore concerned with the work of governance. Very often, people used the two terms interchangeably without taking notice of this important distinction.

To become a *Kanee* one must necessarily be a *Kabaari*. The only difference between a *Kabaari* and a *Kanee* is that the latter knew by oral tradition that he descended from one of the seven ancient *Gan*, (or lineages) of Ogoni, and being qualified was selected by his House (Be) to represent them in the House of Elders. In theory, however, every free born Ogoni citizen who was not a descendant of a slave was believed to have descended from one of these ancient *gan*. However, only those who have been studying and practicing the traditions remember their gan. Philip Noss has described this attitude of studying the past as the attitude of the master-weaver, who before weaving a new mat, first "puts down the old one," and Professor E.J. Alagoa has stated that the vision of the man with a deep knowledge of the past is "as penetrating as the python's eye" (Alagoa, 1980; Noss, 1987). This then was the basic difference which set the *Kanee* apart from the general class of *Kabaari*. Accordingly, to become a member of the House of Elders (*To Pya Kanee)*, a man must be above fifty years old and must be the head of a House (*Be*). He must have performed the traditional rites of *Yaa* and *Yaanwii*. The traditional rite of *Kpa Bina* was not required because it was not easy to perform. The *Gbene* title therefore reserved only for people who have performed the rites of *Kpa Bina*. Nevertheless, a candidate for the House of Elders must be spiritually upright, and of unblemished character. He must be a married man with children and a property owner (i.e. owner of land). He must be physically strong, intelligent, and a good orator. (Mackenzie, 1933; Ngofa, 1988).

14.4(b) The Powers of the House of Elders

(i) The Elders were not Kingmakers

The Elders did not have the authority to act as kingmakers. If a ruler was installed or crowned the Elders were present as witnesses just like the other citizens. However, after the new ruler had been selected and installed, he then presented himself to the House of Elders according to tradition. This was the occasion on which he presented the traditional basket to the House of Elders (*Noo To Sia To Pya Kanee*). On that occasion, the Elders would perform a ceremonial "cleansing" of his hands. One of the actions performed on this occasion was that the new ruler presented traditional gifts to all the previous rulers who had sat on that stool, while the Elders recited their names. Assobienee or his priest or spirit medium presided and performed the ritual cleansing of the king's hands. Although the Elders were present when the new ruler was crowned and installed, it was only after this ceremony in the House of Elders that they recognised him and accepted him as king and ruler.

Usually the Elders did not recite only the names of the royal successors, they also recited the names of the founders of the separate villages and communities and the names of all other important personalities who have contributed in various ways to the establishment of the state.

One could see in this tradition a method by which the Elders 'forced' the king to make a *defacto* recognition of other 'founders' besides his own ancestors. Making this ceremonial ritual to the president of the House of Elders, the new king thereby acknowledged the House of Elders as the highest authority in the land. This tradition created an environment in which the king came to appreciate the importance of all the other personalities and architects of the state other than the royal lineage. It pointed back to the root cause of the coup d'etat' or constitutional reforms which created the House of Elders. The facts seem to suggest that this tradition was invented to safeguard the aims and purposes of that constitutional reform.

(ii) The Traditional Kingmakers

The traditional kingmakers were the members of Gbenekwerre House, Gbenekote House and Gbenetibarakan House. The members of these Houses were the persons who met to select a new king upon the death of the incumbent. During the selection period, the identity of the elect was kept secret, although the public could make their own guesses. The identity of the elect was released by a proclamation which also fixed the date of installation. By this time, all the traditional rituals should have been completed.

On the other hand, when a seat in the House of Elders became vacant, the Elders sent a notice or message to the member's house informing them that their seat in the House of Elders had become vacant and that they should send their representative to fill the seat. On receiving such a notice the members of that house summoned a meeting of that house in which they selected one of their most senior members to fill their seat in the House of Elders. The person selected was usually the most senior firstborn son (*Saaro*) who must also be qualified in other respects such as having performed the traditional rites and ceremonies and having achieved some titles. He then dressed the traditional basket (*no to*) to be presented to the House of Elders on an appointed date. With this he was introduced to the House of Elders.

(iii) The House of Elders as a Court of Final Reference

Before the Baan wars, the highest court and highest authority in Ogoni was at *Luawii*, the seat of *Bariyaayoo*. It was here that all cases pertaining to the taking of human life were referred. It was here too that persons condemned to death in all the towns and villages were sent for confirmation and execution. No other constituted body or authority could execute a criminal in any town, except the authorities at *Luawii*. It was also at *Luawii* that the Ogoni calendar containing the names of the days of the Ogoni week and the important feasts of the year was prepared as part of the reforms following the Baan wars. The Bariyaayoo dynasty declined but Boue emerged out of the wars as the leading power in the area. All cases of murder, witchcraft, sorcery, etc. were now referred to Boue. In Boue the trials were conducted in the House of Elders but the executions of condemned persons were done at Kako, which was the oldest village and war centre in Boue in the period before the Baan wars. With the emergence of Kónò Boue as the capital of the Boue kingdom, all matters were dealt with at Kónò Boue. A new war shrine with a 'house of skulls' was built at Yoboue Centre in Kónò Boue. Koobee Asoo reports that Assobienee, the leader of the House of Elders, and Yoboue, the head of the Boue army, went to Luawii and claimed Boue's rights. These rights included the right to settle the big cases, the right to administer capital punishment, and the right to transfer Boue treasures from Luawii to Boue (Asoo, 1984). Among the treasures claimed were Boue skulls. Skulls could be sold at very high prices in ancient times.

In Boue, the Elders at Igbara Abe House who presided over these matters dealt at two levels. At the first level, they dealt with matters which pertained to Kono Boue as a separate entity. At the second level, they incorporated representative Elders from all the Boue towns and they dealt with matters of wider consequences. These Elders had the power to order the execution or banishment of a condemned person. They could punish the leaders of any community or town if they arrogated to themselves the powers which belonged to the Elders at the centre. They could outlaw a community or town, if the inhabitants contravened the laws of the state. When that happened, a state of "war" was declared against that town or community. Under such circumstances the property of the community concerned, particularly their farms, plantations, goats, sheep, fowls, etc. were seized. The community was put under pressure until the leaders sued for peace and paid the prescribed fines.

Once the Elders had publicly pronounced the ban on the disloyal community, the execution of the ban was usually the responsibility of the *Zuguru*, who then planned the strategy for carrying it out. They might decide to mobilise all the *Kpaankpaan* secret societies in the loyal communities against the disloyal community. The aim was usually not to cause bloodshed or bodily harm to the people but to ravage property and to disrupt the social order in that community.

The following testimony explains:

> In ancient times, the *Kpaankpaan* was the political force of the authorities or powers that were. If any citizen was stubborn and the *Kpaankpaan* secret society was called upon to see to the matter, the *Kpaankpaan* society came with music and dance and took occupation of the man's house. Within a short time they deroofed the house and did irreparable damage to the man's property. They continued the occupation until the stubborn person begged for peace. It was the *Kpaankpaan* that had the power to discipline society. (Imene, tape 20, 28th Dec., 1983).

Membership of such powerful secret societies was one of the prerogatives of the elite classes such as the *Pya Gbara* and the *Pya Zuguru,* Thus when such a society was invited to punish a stubborn community or individual it was really this class of people who were in fact taking action. However, when they were on such a mission, they did not necessarily go secret or in masks.

They might decide to go in broad day light or at night, but either way all non-members must run away from their approach and shut themselves in behind doors. Moreover, the members were highly disciplined, so that under oath, they dared not reveal the actions of fellow members to non-members, or discuss them outside the inner circles of the society. Thus whatever damage they caused in their attempt to punish the stubborn person or community, was never blamed on any individual person or group of persons because, as they used to say, "it was the action of the *Kpaankpaan* and not of persons."

When the British colonial forces advanced on Ogoni territory at the beginning of the 20th century, it was in the Boue kingdom that they encountered the toughest resistance. It was there too that they first learned about the *Kpaankpaan* secret society. The following eye-witness account illustrates:

> On arrival in the Ogoni country and while passing through the friendly portion messages were sent on to the seven towns especially mentioned in my instructions as requiring attention. The seven towns however, absolutely refused to submit to the government, openly stating that they had no desire to be forced to obey its harassing laws. On enquiring it was found that these towns were the acknowledged leaders of the Akpakpa (sic) secret

> society of which the Apia juju (?) was the oracle. This secret society had branches in practically every Ogoni town.... The heads of Bewe (Boue) and Betem who were the heads of the Akpakpa (Kpaankpaan) secret society were.., captured and are at Egwanga (Ikot Abasi) awaiting investigation of their case (Smith, 1907).

The colonial invaders realised the tremendous power of the *Kpaankpaan* secret society as a well-organised and disciplined force behind the indigenous government throughout Ogoni. They therefore concentrated their efforts on these organisations to destroy them. They also took advantage of the Ogoni customary law which forbade the Elders to vacate the towns in times of emergency. Thus they lured the Elders of the Boue kingdom into negotiations and then seized them and deported them to Egwanga (now called Ikot Abasi) where they held them as hostages until their militant supporters laid down their arms and disbanded. Many of the Elders died in detention at Ikot Abasi. The foregoing analysis is a clear demonstration that the practice of governance began in Ogoni from very early times. It continued to develop with specific institutions until the colonial conquest. In the *Kpaankpaan* organisation which existed throughout Ogoni in pre-colonial times, we see a kind of 'standing army' already in being.

14.5 The Emergence of the House of Lieutenants

The word *Pya Zuguru* was a close synonym of *Pya Gbara*, which means gentlemen. However, while the latter conveyed the notion of youthful exuberance and drive, the former portrayed a sense of nobility, power and wealth. Thus *Pya Zuguru* might also be translated as "the gentry."

The term lieutenant was applied to them because they carried out the decisions of the House of Elders. They did not make laws or initiate policies on their own. The House of Lieutenants (*To Pya zuguru*) was therefore the executive arm of the traditional government.

According to the oral tradition, the House of Lieutenants was founded by a descendant of Gbenegoo named Biiragbara.

Gbenegoo House was one of the noble houses of Kwuribue before the Baan wars and before its evacuation during the Baan wars. From Kwuribue, they moved to Boue area and founded the new town which they re-named Kónò Boue. Gbenegoo, the ancestor of Biiragbara was one of the founders of Kónò Boue; and was therefore one of the landlords of Kónò Boue, the capital of the Boue kingdom. The significance of this fact is that it shows Biiragbara, the founder of *Pya Zuguru* organisation, as a man of a noble origin. His background therefore played a vital role in shaping the character and aims of the organisation. What is not yet clear is when he founded the House of Lieutenants. It is generally believed that the House of Lieutenants was founded sometime after the establishment of the House of Elders.

Another view is that the House of Lieutenants was founded before the founding of the House of Elders. This latter view is based on the fact that many of the functions which the *Zuguru* performed in society were functions which the leaders of the elite class called *Pya Gbara* performed in society from very early times, as explained at the beginning of this chapter. Such functions included the organisation of defence, organisation of social activities, such as sports and tournaments and the execution of public or communal services. Leadership of such youth groups, namely *Pya Gbara*, was the duty of noble gentlemen, like Biiragbara.

It would appear that the impact of the Baan wars infused a political dimension into many of these otherwise non-political organisations. The successful coup d'etat by a group of Elders led by the strongman, Assobienee, acted as a political incentive for the leaders of the *Zuguru*, who then drew on the example of the Elders and constituted themselves into a House of Lieutenants, most likely in the nineteenth century.

14.5(a) *The Functions of the House of Lieutenants*

The Lieutenants or *Pya Zuguru* acted as the executive arm of the Elders by carrying out the decisions made by the House of Elders. All projects and decisions made by the House of Elders were effectively carried out by the Pya Zuguru. The following testimony gives evidence to the kind of duties performed by the Lieutenants: effectively carried out by the *Pya Zuguru*. The following testimony gives evidence to the kind of duties performed by the Lieutenants:

> They applied force to the decisions of the House of Elders. The Elders made decisions in their House, then they announced these decisions at the public Assembly located at *Yoburubu* Square (*Ee-Yoburubu*). After the announcement at Yoburubu square, the *Teere Bue* then summoned a meeting of the *Pya Zuuru* in which they discussed the preparations and fixed a date for the start. Before the date arrived, a public announcement was made by the town crier by means of the royal drum (*Akere Bue*). The announcement carried the details of the task to be performed. All able-bodied men and women and young adults were expected to take part in such a communal task. On the set date those who failed to take part in the communal service were penalised by *Pya Zuguru* through the imposition of fines. All fines collected were presented to the Elders.
>
> If there was a fight or war between two towns or communities, it was the *Zuguru* who led the Boue troops into battle. The *Zuguru* were the warriors. It was in this connection that their real name was *Pya Edam Gbara*. (Lit. 'The Male Men' i.e. 'Manly Men' or Virile Gentlemen') (Tonwe III, tape 26).

We notice in the above passage that *Pya Zuguru* is used as a synonym of *Pya Gbara* in the context of war, which is an action-packed phenomenon.

14.5(b)   Qualification and Membership of *Pya Zuguru*

The first and foremost qualification of a *Zuguru* was popularity. A member of *Pya Zuguru* was a person who was well-known in society. He achieved this popularity by his outstanding participation in one or more of the important activities of the society such as wrestling or judo, fencing or sword-play or by being specially gifted in social organisation and community service. I have already referred to the case of Gbeneakpana who was very popular as a youth because he excelled in sword-play or fencing.

Apart from popularity, the *Zuguru* was expected to be a married man and a householder, a good farmer (producing bumper crops of elite yams (*mgwe*), a man who owned his own house, a good palm wine tapper, a lover of progress in his community, and a man of honour. When a man like that had been accepted as a member of *Pya Zuguru*, he was required to make certain traditional payments. These included a cock, some yams, a bunch of plantains, a bottle of gin, a large pitcher of palm wine; and 400 manilas. In a later period, probably in the nineteenth century or early twentieth century, the payments were increased to one thousand two hundred manilas, twenty yams, twenty rackets of mullet, a large pitcher of palm wine, a bunch of plantains, and a bottle of gin. They cooked these things and ate them together in a fellowship dinner in honour of the new member. After this, the new member was introduced to the Elders at the earliest opportunity.

14.6 Summary

Social organisation was practiced in Ogoni from a very early period. Internal evidence shows that the training of youths as part of an organised society was practised at Kugba during the time of the early ancestors. The *Yaa* tradition which became the chief factor of social stratification appears to have been started during that period.

Within the framework of the *Yaa* tradition, two broad social categories are distinguished in society, namely those who have performed the *Yaa* tradition and those who have not. The former constituted a broad class of social elites called *Pya Gbara*, while the latter fell back to a status equivalent to second-class citizens. From the class of elites or *Pya Gbara* mobility to higher social levels became possible through distinction in one of the recognised social activities, such as youth organisation, sports, farming, palm wine tapping, hunting etc; as well as membership of one of the secret societies. The holding of political positions such as house head, village head, etc, was the special preserve of titled men.

In the period from the seventeenth to eighteenth centuries three political institutions emerged, namely the House of Hunters, the House of Elders and the House of Lieutenants. The development of these political institutions have been traced to the introduction of the gun into Ogoni in the sixteenth century. The gun as a new powerful weapon, provided an effective leverage with which some leaders seized political power from the traditional rulers and constituted themselves into a political institution known in Ogoni as House of Elders (*To Pya Kanee*). By the end of the nineteenth century, political organisation in Ogoni had reached an advanced stage, with a well-organised judicial system.

Thus when the colonial conquest of Ogoni began at the beginning of the twentieth century, it was found that its militant organs, such as the House of Lieutenants and the *Kpaankpaan* secret society, were well-established in every village.

CHAPTER FIFTEEN

THE TRANSATLANTIC IMPACT (1800 -1900)

Ogoni at the End of the Slave Trade (1800-1900)

At the end of the slave trade in the nineteenth century, Ogoni's participation in external commerce steadily declined. Several factors were responsible. The first was the introduction of the 'legitimate' trade which was unfavourable to Ogoni. Although Ogoni territory lay within the major palm oil producing belt, it was not a major palm oil producing area. From very early times, the Ogoni did not allow too many oil palm trees to grow on their farms. This was because the yam crop which was the main crop of the Ogoni, did not grow well under the shade of palm trees. The yam needed plenty of sunlight before it could grow well to produce bigger and better tubers. For this reason, the Ogoni did not allow more than a few palm trees on each of their yam farms. Numerous palm trees, however, grew on lands which were unsuitable for yam cultivation but the quantity of palm produce coming from such lands was relatively small compared with the quantities coming from the other parts of the Imo and the Cross River valleys, (cf. Northrup, 1978).

Secondly, during the era of the slave trade, Ogoni was a major trade route for the overland trade from the hinterland to Bonny and Okrika. This brought a substantial part of the trading business to Ogoni. The coastal market towns of Ogoni provided the final resting place or depots for the slaves before they were finally ferried across the sea either to Bonny or to Okrika. This meant that there was a considerable amount of business activities for the Ogoni middlemen in these towns. With the introduction of 'legitimate' trade, the overland trade routes virtually closed, palm produce being a heavy and bulky commodity, it could only be transported by river in canoes. Thus the trading activities during the legitimate' trade were confined to river routes. The result was that Ogoni declined both as a trade route and as a supplier of the staple commodities for the new trade, namely the palm oil trade.

Thirdly, the shift from slave trade to palm oil trade resulted in a substantial fall in the farm produce trade of Ogoni. For example, during the slave trade, large quantities of Ogoni yams and other agricultural produce were exported overseas along with the slaves, yams, goats, peppers, etc., were required for feeding the slaves not only during the time they were kept at the depots but also during the journey across the Atlantic to the Americas. (Barbot, 1732:4).

Thus besides participating in the slave trade, the Ogoni also carried on a lucrative trade in the sale of yams and other agricultural produce. Following the end of the slave trade in the nineteenth century and the introduction of palm oil trade, Ogoni lost all these trading activities.

15.1(b) Trade Monopoly by the Delta States

Another factor which contributed very significantly to the decline of Ogoni in the nineteenth century was trade monopoly by the Delta middlemen. Although this monopoly provoked a trade war between the European firms and the coastal middlemen, the outcome of the struggle did not alter in any significant way the pattern of monopoly already set by the Delta traders. The Delta states had come to depend on the prosperity brought to them by their participation in the slave trade (cf. Jones, 1963; Alagoa, 1971). The wealth of these states and their social superstructure had depended on this trade (Jones, 1963). Fishing which was originally the principal economic mainstay of these states had receded to the background to be left in the hands of the poorer classes as a means of subsistence. With the abolition of slave trade, the economic superstructure of the Delta states was seriously undermined. K.O. Dike explains that the abolition simply threw the Delta middlemen into financial ruin (Dike, 1956). Meanwhile the European firms began to push their way into the hinterland oil markets. They were determined to bypass the coastal middlemen to trade directly with the hinterland producers. Obaro Ikime explains that by the 1850s, the firm of Macgregor Laird had established stations at Aboh, Onitsha and Lokoja. By the 1860s the push into the Niger valley had dramatically increased by the presence of such trading firms as the West African Company, Miller Brothers and Company, the Central African Trading Company, James Pinnock and Company, etc. (Ikime, 1977). K.E. Ume observes that the push by the British traders into the hinterland gathered momentum following the transfer of the British Consulate from Fernando Po to Calabar in 1872. According to him, the transfer encouraged many British firms to penetrate inland to the oil markets in armed boats. Notable among them were Messrs Miller Brothers and Company, who built some factories in the Qua Iboe valley between Opobo and Old Calabar, despite bitter opposition by Opobo. In this way they diverted a part of the inland trade from Bonny and Opobo. According to Obaro Ikime, the push by the British Companies into the hinterland was a threat to the very livelihood of the Delta traders and made them determined to obstruct any further penetration of the hinterland (Ikime, 1977; 1968). Eventually, King Jaja of Opobo and King Archibong of Old Calabar drove the European traders from the hinterland markets of their areas (Ume, 1980).

By opposing the principle of free trade both Jaja and Nana rejected Articles VI and VII of the Protection Treaty which they signed with the British in 1884. Article VI of the treaty provided for freedom of religion and free practice by Christian ministers, Article VII provided for freedom of trade by the subjects of all countries in every part of the territories of the kings and chiefs of the country. (Ikime, 1968). Although Ikime is of the view that Jaja and Nana were within their treaty rights when they refused free trade and sought to protect their own interests, the fact remains that while free trade might have been in the interest of British commerce, it would have also provided a basis for the development of the hinterland of the Oil Rivers. It is shown below that because of the trade monopoly mounted by the coastal middlemen, especially by Bonny and Opobo, Ogoni suffered not only severe economic set-backs but also social and political isolation by them and by the European traders, missionaries and the colonial administrators.

J.C. Anene describes an area defined as Jaja's hinterland markets in three directions. To the north were the Ndoki markets of Ohambele, to which oil producers from as far away places as the district of Bende and Owerri brought their palm oil to sell. To the north-east were the Annang markets of Essene, to which oil from the Annang districts was transported to trade. To the east were the Qua Iboe markets (Anene, 1966). Evidently, Jaja's northern and north-eastern markets were within easy reach of Ogoni through the Imo and the Azumini Rivers. In fact, Jaja had to pass through Ogoni to reach these markets. Nonetheless, the monopolistic policies of the delta middlemen gave no opportunity for free and fair trading, a condition which could only exist in an atmosphere of free and fair competition between rival trading firms.

This was disadvantageous to the hinterland producers. The absence of free trade and free competition gave Jaja a wide choice of sources of supply which discriminated against some hinterland producers such as Ogoni, even though the latter was an old market centre within the trading network of the Imo and the Azumini Rivers. Under free trade conditions, the Imo market towns of Ogoni like Ko, Kabangha, Baene, Kónò, etc., could have developed into fairly large collecting centres of palm produce from within Ogoni itself and from farther away in the hinterland, some rival firms could have taken advantage of the favourable location of these Ogoni towns, basing such decisions on their roles as centres of trade in the period before the nineteenth century.

Apart from the palm oil trade, the nineteenth century was also an era of great exploratory journeys by Europeans into the interior parts of West Africa. Up till the time of the abolition of the slave trade and the introduction of the legitimate trade, the condition of many areas in the interior of West Africa was still largely unknown to the outside world. To open up such areas in order to establish proper trade relations, as well as social and humanitarian or Christian contacts, attempts were made by European organisations, groups, and individuals to explore the hinterland districts, part of the monopolistic schemes of the delta traders was to prevent the Europeans from making such exploratory journeys into the hinterland.

The Reverend Hope Waddell gives an account of the reaction of the people of Bonny in 1850, when a small group of Europeans made such an exploratory journey via the Imo River to Ndoki land. According to Waddell, the king and the chiefs of Bonny were greatly alarmed and highly displeased with those Europeans for having intruded on their preserve. After the heated quarrel which ensued, it was finally resolved that trade should be resumed "provided the shipping did not attempt to open trade with the hinterland." Waddell further explains that this opposition to Europeans exploring the hinterland displayed at Bonny, was a common attitude of all the coastal states in the territory between the Niger and the Cross River, because they feared that their commerce would thereby be destroyed (Waddell., 1970). This was part of a policy adopted by the delta states against the hinterland peoples in the nineteenth century.

In the Eastern Niger Delta, Ogoni became the permanent target of this type of policy by Bonny and Opobo. From that time onwards, these states made sure that later exploratory journeys to the interior by European travellers, missionaries, and colonial agents, were strictly controlled. Such trips were personally directed by agents appointed by these states to the usual places of Ndoki, Aba, Bende, etc. In 1866, for example, W.E. Carew travelling from Bonny and stopping at Egwanga, visited Ndoki and nearby districts. A chief of Bonny, Oko Jumbo, was controlling and directing this trip (Isichei, 1977). Similarly, guided exploratory journeys were made to parts of Isiokpo and Elele by K. Cambell in 1892 and by A.B. Harcourt to Ndoki, Ngwa and Asa in 1896 (Isichei, 1977:21). In 1896 also Major A.G. Leonard, an official of the Niger Coast protectorate, journeyed from Opobo through Ndoki to Aba, and thence to Bende and Arochuku (Isichei, 1977). These journeys and contacts had their impacts and benefits for the people of the areas concerned, as they opened up a window on them to the outside world, professor Isichei conceded these points with regard to Major Leonard's journey through parts of southern Igbo land in 1896. "For all its ethnocentricity and arrogance, his account sheds much vivid light on southern Igbo culture at that time" (Isichei, 1977). Unfortunately, however, none of these European travellers visited Ogoni land, even though most of the journeys were made via the Imo River, and therefore through Ogoni. Consequently, no reports or descriptions were written about Ogoni to the outside world. Clearly therefore, we can see that the isolation of Ogoni from the outside world became a deliberate policy from the nineteenth century. This policy was later identified as the major factor responsible for the economic and political retardation which Ogoni was to experience from the nineteenth century through the colonial period. During the same period, this preventive policy against Ogoni was especially intensified with respect to the civilising activities of the Christian missions. Concerning this attitude of the delta states, the Reverend Hope Waddell complained in 1850 that such misapprehension on the part of the coastal peoples was a great obstruction to the advance of missionary operations into the interior (Waddell, 1970).

As early as 1842, the C.M.S. began work in Yorubaland under the pioneering initiative of the Reverend Henry Townsend at Badagry (Oduyoye, 1978:.2-39). In 1846, the Reverend Hope Waddell opened the Presbyterian Mission Field in Calabar (Waddell, 1970). Eleven years later, (1857), the C.M.S. began work at Onitsha under the supervision of Ajayi Crowther, who was ordained Bishop in 1864 (Kalu, 1978). Then in 1865 Bishop Crowther began Christian work at Bonny. In the same year, a Christian school was opened at Bonny (Tasie, 1978). By 1867, the Christian Church had spread to Nembe and Okrika (Tasie, 1978). A careful examination of the spread of these missions reveals that for more than half a century, the Church remained within the coastal areas except for a few inroads on the shores of the Niger River. Thus during all that period the hinterland peoples were excluded from the benefits of the Christian missions. J.G. Mackenzie notes that even though the Eleme of Ogoni and Okrika had been in touch for centuries through trade, the latter exploited the former and hindered the spread of Christianity and education to the area "for fear that it should bring their supremacy to an end" (Mackenzie, 1933). The same was true of Bonny and Opobo with respect to the rest of Ogoni. The Christian missions carried with them into those areas not only the civilising message of the Gospel but they also devoted their energies to the task of spreading literacy and education. Consequently an educated class of westernised elite emerged in those places (Ade Ajayi, 1965; Eke Chi, 1971; Waddell, 1970).

Christian mission work was not introduced into Ogoni until in the 1920s; when the primitive Methodist Mission based at Oron established a preaching station at Kónò on the Imo River. But real earnest work was not started until 1929, when the Reverend Paul Kingston acquired land at Kónò for the mission house and began building what he described as a "semipermanent house" for the mission residence (Kingston, 1929:1J7). One of the contributions of this mission was the translation of the Bible into Kana language. The first fruits of this work were the *St. Mark's Gospel* and the *Kana Hymn Book* which were published in 1930 (Ayre, 1930).

Then in 1968, the complete Bible in the Kana language was published by the Bible Society of Nigeria.

15.2 Ogoni at the Close of the Legitimate Trade

By the end of the legitimate trade i.e. the beginning of the colonial period, Ogoni had declined economically, socially and politically, to the level of a minor ethnic group in south-eastern Nigeria. The eclipse of Ogoni from the outside world continued unabated into the colonial period. Ogoni with her agricultural resources became the private preserve of her delta neighbours. The colonial agents and the missionary groups remained ignorant and indifferent about the internal conditions of Ogoni.

15.2(a) The British Colonial Conquest

In 1901 the British colonial forces invaded Ogoni territory from Opobo and established a foothold at Kónò, from where they proclaimed Ogoni as a British protectorate. (Gibbons, 1932). But that was not the end of the matter because after that proclamation, the British colonial forces withdrew back to Opobo. They failed to establish an effective presence in the area. The absence of an effective presence by the British gave the Ogoni an opportunity for resistance. They refused to submit to colonial rule. One of the main reasons was that the British blundered about the nature of Ogoni society. Being ignorant of Ogoni traditional system and social organisation, they appointed persons who were not socially recognised to represent their interest in the area: (cf. Afigbo, 1972). The Ogoni resented the appointment of such persons as rulers and would have nothing to do with them.

In 1905, the British launched a further attack on Ogoni territory. This time the attack was more systematic and more devastating, as indicated in this report:

> Four years later, a patrol was sent to enforce administrative control. This patrol travelled via Obete on the river Imo in the north to Soo (Sogho) and destroyed a number of villages chiefly in Gokana and Tai (Tee) country. (Gibbons, 1932).

Again this second patrol failed to 'pacify' Ogoni mainly because after destroying the towns and villages, the patrol withdrew from Ogoni to Opobo. Although these operations were officially described as patrols, by the scale of destruction they inflicted on the people and by the standard of African warfare at that time, they were nothing short of war (cf. Johnson, 1973). Locally, these operations were given various names, in the southern area, they were called Ikosi war. The term 'Ikosi' was probably a reference to the British Consul who was then stationed at Calabar. By analogy, the patrols were described as the "Ikosi type of warfare." As already explained, up till now the Ogoni were still ignorant of who or what the British and their intentions were. Later on the term "Ikosi" was identified with the colonial government in the sense that it was a government of the "Ikosi." The colonial officials and administrators were then referred to as *Pya Ikosi*, meaning the consul's people. In the northern parts, the war was called *"Kaani Teegbara war,"* *Kaani* being the name of the last battlefield in the north and *Teegbara* the name of the local hero in that war.

The clear identity of the British invaders was not known. As already explained, there had been no direct contact between the two peoples. But the indiscriminate burning of towns and villages was seen as wanton destruction of their shrines and sacred places. The destruction of such places provoked the people's anger and hardened their determination to resist the colonial administration. The latter could not effectively enforce its rule because, first of all, it was an absentee administration. Secondly, its local representatives were often men whose social status and character would not have passed as rulers. The absence of a permanent colonial presence made matters worse. Thus as late as 1913, there was still some resistance in Ogoni especially in the southern half of the territory, spearheaded by the rulers of Boue who now controlled the whole of that area.

In that year (1913), the British launched another attack on Ogoni, which finally broke the back of the resistance. They entered Boue and destroyed a number of towns and villages by burning and carried away the leading chiefs whom they deported to Ikot Abasi (then called Egwanga), where many died in detention. Chief Inee Barigwere recalls that he was a boy when the destruction took place throughout Boue.

According to him the incident occurred before the founding of the city of Port Harcourt. He named a certain man Tende, who was shot dead through his ribs as he was returning from the Kwuri market where he had gone to sell his palm wine. When the attack which was sudden occurred, the people fled and hid themselves in the creeks. He recalled that before that, an earlier attack by the same people had occurred when he was not yet born. At that time, they burned all the Boue towns.

The conquest of Ogoni was finally completed in 1914 with the destruction of the *Gbenebeka* shrine at Ka-Gwaara which was the chief religious centre of Ogoni at that time. A brief account of this incident is contained in the following report:

> After the departure of the 1913 patrol, an Assistant District commissioner (Mr. Lovering) was stationed in Ogoni country. In 1914, Major H. Webber, Assistant District Officer, was accompanied by a large police escort under Major G.H. Walker, D.S.O. They destroyed the shrine at Ka-Gwaara and re-opened the Soo (*Sogho*)

Native Court, which had been closed due to the disturbances which took place after Mr. Lovering's departure some months previously. (Gibbons, 1932).

With the destruction of the religious centre at Ka-Gwaara in 1914, the way was cleared for the reopening and the proper functioning of the first instrument of colonial administration in Ogoni, the Native Courts. But the question which anyone familiar with the situation would like to ask is this: Why did it take so long for the colonial authorities to complete the 'pacification' of Ogoni? The answer obviously lies in the haphazard manner the pacification of Ogoni was planned and executed. For instance, they underestimated the strength of the people in terms of population and their capacity for resistance. Consequently, they failed to plan the task of conquest adequately. Secondly, they were ignorant of the economic potential of the territory as a source of raw material for British industries and as a market for the distribution of British goods.

Thirdly the colonial agents failed to supply accurate information about Ogoni. Because of the absence of such information, the colonial administrators made the error of leaving the Ogoni to themselves. These problems largely contributed to the failure of colonial administration in the area.

15.2(b) The Aftermath of the Conquest: Ogoni Under Colonial Rule

The traditional rulers were deposed and replaced by commoners who knew little or nothing about the organisation and the working of the indigenous society and government. The new rulers were appointed purely on the grounds of their assistance during the conquest and because they could speak a major Nigerian language, particularly Igbo. (Gibbons, 1932; Ngito, 1984).

Such rulers not only lacked legitimacy among the people but they were also grossly ignorant of the traditional ethics and protocols. Consequently they became completely estranged from the people, especially because their rulership had no roots in the society.

Thus when the time came for the colonial administrators to write the "history" of the people in the Intelligence Reports, the new rulers could not produce the authentic information required. Accordingly the Intelligence Reports did not have any information or account on such important historical places as Nama and Kugba, and the names of towns like Luawii, Kónò Boue, Gure, etc., were simply mentioned in passing like ordinary villages without any indication that these were the headquarters of the erstwhile indigenous government. Clearly, a situation like that could not have arisen unless there was some form of estrangement between the colonial government and the authentic traditional authorities. It abundantly demonstrates that the people from whom the colonial administrators obtained their information were not the right sources of such information on the origins and systems of the indigenous establishments.

The complication became worse by the practice of the colonial authorities who created entirely new centres of government away and far removed from the familiar centres of the old indigenous systems. With the new rulers imposed from 'outside' and from the new centres the colonial government became completely alienated from the people. One inadvertent outcome of this situation was that the traditions in the old centres remained preserved, except for the destructions which took place during the wars of conquest. With that exception, the indigenous system in the old centres continued fairly normally as before the introduction of colonial rule.

However, in the new scheme of things, this state of affairs was not the best for Ogoni, since in the general forward march that was taking place among the neighbouring peoples, Ogoni was kept behind. In contrast to the conditions in Ogoni, new developments were taking place in all aspects of life in the states surrounding Ogoni. The citizens of those states were already being introduced to new ideas, including western education and the new enlightenment of the Christian missions. Thus there is no gainsaying the fact that the long and continued indifference exhibited by each subsequent colonial administration at Calabar and Opobo towards the deplorable conditions in Ogoni, contributed very significantly to the further decline of Ogoni during the period of colonial rule. The following report will add illumination to this view:

> British rule has penetrated so little below the surface of Ogoni organisation during the last thirty years that in many respects the country is more or less as it was before the advent of government. Lawlessness is to be found everywhere and there is little or no public spirit outside the confines of the villages, which in their outlook are as parochial as ever. The reasons for the foregoing are obvious, and Mr. Falk in the provincial Annual Report for 1930 is of the opinion that the absence of contact with civilisation has been a boom rather than the reverse. I now wish emphatically to reiterate the considered opinion of not only myself but of the other District Officers who have been in charge of the Opobo Division that no real success can attend to the administration of this large tribe until the local organisation, placed on proper. footing, is guided by a European officer of experience and stationed permanently in the area, to replace the haphazard method of occasional visits from Opobo which has hitherto been in force. (Gibbons, 1932).

The above is a graphic illustration of the fate of Ogoni during the first thirty years after the British colonial conquest of Ogoni. In actual fact the Ogoni suffered for a period of more than forty years in that condition of isolation and total neglect by the colonial administration. For as evidence shows, the plans recommended in the above quoted text were not implemented until 1948, when an Ogoni Division was finally created (Schofield, 1946).

After the overthrow of the indigenous system, it was expected that the new system would be introduced immediately to fill the vacuum created by the removal of the indigenous system. But nothing of the sort happened. There was instead a long period of inaction by the colonial administration during which the people of Ogoni were virtually left to themselves in a state of helpless stagnation in the trauma of the conquest. The vacuum created by the removal of the old system and its leaders without immediate and proper substitutionary replacement, created a fertile condition in which lack of direction, lawlessness and degradation thrived. The result was a state of general decline to a level worse than before the advent of colonial rule, as cogently noted in the above-quoted text.

In the meantime, the citizens of the delta states and other neighbours were receiving the benefits of western education being provided by the Christian missions and by the colonial administration. In these circumstances, Ogoni was bound to trail backwards especially when compared with her neighbours. For instance, the first Ogoni man to obtain a university degree, Mr. Timothy Paul Birabi, did so in 1948, forty-eight years after the colonial conquest and only twelve years before Nigeria's Independence from colonial rule. But Mr. Birabi got his chance only because of a stroke of luck, when his brilliance was noticed by a missionary pastor from Bonny during the latter's itinerant catechumen classes in the area. The Reverend Jumbo (later Bishop Dimieari) took him to Bonny where he first attended primary school. He later moved to Onitsha where he continued his education at the secondary level (Loolo, 1980). Despite these facts, two factors may have influenced British policies in connection with Ogoni. One was the geographical location of Ogoni which was far removed from the nearest anchorage of British trading ships. The second factor was crucial, that is, the very purpose for which the British were there at the coast and later in the country. Was it for the interest of Nigeria communities or for that of Metropolitan Britain? Accordingly remoteness from direct contact may be assessed positively as a factor protecting the Ogoni and other such communities from some of the ill-effects of colonial exploitative activity.

CHAPTER SIXTEEN

CONCLUSION

This book has discussed in some detail the history of Ogoni from settlement in about the 5th century BC. Through the British colonisation at the beginning of the twentieth century. During their long settlement in the Niger Delta, the Ogoni had spearheaded and introduced many changes in the region. The most recent example was the rise of the Movement for the Survival of Ogoni People (MOSOP) in the early 1990, which demanded from the Nigeria Government a share of the economic resources of their land. Today, that demand has become a nationwide demand of the Nigeria people on the Federal Government. We hope that when at last the Federal Government decides to yield, history will not forget to state that this effort was first started by the Ogoni of the Niger Delta.

Perhaps the most important social and political changes that occurred in Ogoni in the period from 1600 to 1800 were the evolution of the House of Hunters, House of Elders and House of Lieutenants. The oldest of these was the House of Hunters, which evolved following the introduction of the gun into Bonny and Ogoni in the sixteenth century. The emergence of the House of Hunters provided the antecedent for the formation of the House of Elders in the seventeenth century. The House of Elders became the highest political and judicial authority in Ogoniland. Further reform of the House of Elders occurred in the eighteenth and nineteenth centuries with the rise of *Igbara Abe* and *Nii Yeegboronwa* in Boue. By the first quarter of the nineteenth century, Ogoni's role as a trading partner of Bonny in the Transatlantic slave trade began to decline.

This followed the abolition of the slave trade and the introduction of the legitimate trade. The practice of trade monopoly by the Delta States, particularly Bonny and Opobo, further aggravated the decline of Ogoni. The decline reached its climax at the beginning of the twentieth century with the British Colonial conquest. After the conquest, Ogoni remained more or less in a state of stagnation until 1948, when an Ogoni Division finally came into being. Thus it was from 1948 that Ogoni truly began the tedious journey on the road to modernity.

In addition to this book, this writer has compiled a separate volume titled, *Ogoni Historical Traditions: Fieldwork Texts:* this volume contains lots of fieldwork materials which will be useful to scholars and students of whatever field of interest, especially, those in African history studies and cultures.

APPENDICES

APPENDIX 1
LEXICOSTATISCAL COMPARISON OF KANA, GOKANA TEE & ELEME BASED ON THE REVISED SWADESH 100 WORD LIST

S/N	English	Kana (Betem)	Gokana (Deeyo)	Tee (Nonwa)	Eleme (Alesa)	Cognagtion KG	KT	KE	GT	GE	ET
1.	Head	akobee	togo	akobee	ebo	-	+	-	-	-	-
2.	Hair	zia	jia	zia	jia	+	+	+	+	+	+
3.	Ear	ton	ton	ton	oton	+	+	+	+	+	+
4.	Eye	dee	dee	dee	adee	+	+	+	+	+	+
5.	Nose	bion	bion	bion	mbion	+	+	+	+	+	+
6.	Mouth	agan	gan	agan	onu	+	+	-	+	-	-
7.	Tooth	daa	daa	daa	adaa	+	+	+	+	+	+
8.	Tongue	adem	dem	adem	adide	+	+	+	+	+	+
9.	Neck	mee	men	mee	ome	+	+	+	+	+	+
10.	Hand	ba	ba	ba	obo	+	+	+	+	+	+
11.	(Finger) nail	pion	mbion	pion	mbion	+	+	+	+	+	+
12.	Breast	ma	ma	ma	mmima	+	+	+	+	+	+
13.	Heart	nyee	nyen	nyee	anie	+	+	+	+	+	+
14.	Belly	bu	gbaa	bu	egbaa	-	+	-	-	+	-
15.	Navel	bon	ooh	ooh	opun	-	-	+	+	-	-
16.	Leg	to	to	to	ooh	+	+	-	+	+	+
17.	Knee	beezun	dunu	beedhu	atun Nkpo-on	+	+	+	+	-	+
						14	16	13	15	13	13

S/N	English	Kana (Betem)	Gokana (Deeyo)	Tee (Nonwa)	Eleme (Alesa)	\multicolumn{7}{c}{Cognation}
						KG	KT	KE	GT	GE	ET
18.	Saliva	maasa	muukia	maasia	nta	+	+	-	+	-	-
19.	Blood	mii	mii	mii	mmi	+	+	+	+	+	+
20.	Bone	akpo	kpoo	akpo	ekpikpii	+	+	+	+	+	+
21.	Skin	akpa	kparo	akpa	ekpa	+	+	+	+	+	+
22.	Horn (on animal)	koo	koo	koo	nchoo	+	+	+	+	+	+
23.	Tail	zun	dun	dun	ojun	+	+	+	+	+	+
24.	Meat	nam	nam	nam	nna	+	+	+	+	+	+
25.	Fat	leg	duo	leg	ndo	-	+	-	-	+	-
26.	Feather	paan	paan	apaan	apaan	+	+	-	+	+	+
27.	Egg	ke	ken	ke	oken	+	+	+	+	+	+
28.	Fowl	kon	kon	nkon	okon	+	+	+	+	+	+
29.	Bird	anue	nnom	nwinam	eno	+	+	+	+	+	+
30.	Fish	bari	gian	bari	njira	-	+	-	-	+	-
31.	Dog	gbo	gbogo	gbo	ngbao	+	+	+	+	+	+
32.	Goat	pee	bol	pee	mbo	-	+	-	-	+	-
33.	Housefly	si	kin	sin	nchin	+	+	+	+	+	+
34.	Person	nee	nen	nee	nie	+	+	+	+	+	+
35.	Man	needam	nendom	needam	okundo	+	+	+	+	+	+
36.	Woman	Neewa/pyabia	pa-bia	Neewa/pyabia	Okunmba	+	+	+	+	+	+
37.	Child	nwi	nwin	nwi	onwi	+	+	+	+	+	+
38.	Name	bee	bee	bee	abee	+	+	+	+	+	+
39.	Tree	te	te	te	ete	+	+	+	+	+	+
40.	Seed	asuu	suu	ahiu	echere	+	+	+	+	+	+
						20	23	18	20	22	19

S/N	English	Kana (Betem)	Gokana (Deeyo)	Tee (Nonwa)	Eleme (Alesa	Cognation						
						KG	KT	KE	GT	GE	ET
41.	Leaf	apa-nya	pa-san	apa-hia	nsan	+	+	+	+	+	+
42.	Root	li	ni	li	nni	+	+	+	+	+	+
43.	Rope	azii	dii	azoo	ojiji	+	+	+	+	+	+
44.	Fire	mian	san	hian	nsan	-	+	+	-	+	+
45.	Smoke	soomia	kei	soohia	echeia	-	+	+	+	-	+
46.	Ashes	ton	buuru	ton	nton	-	+	+	-	-	+
47.	Stone	dem	dem	dem	nyade	+	+	+	+	+	+
48.	Sand	asaan	san	asaan	nsisan	+	+	+	+	+	+
49.	Ground	keneke	kunuke	koroke	nkike	+	+	+	+	+	+
50.	Road	dee	eere	egere	ogbere	-	-	-	+	+	+
51.	Mountain /hill	agu/kpoke	gu/kpakpagu	kpo	ekpo	+	+	+	+	+	+
52.	Sun	anaani	naani	nanno	naani	+	+	+	+	+	+
53.	Moon	anoo	en	anoo	oen	-	+	+	-	+	-
54.	Star	zina	gia-kaar	zina	suri-njira	-	+	-	-	+	-
55.	Night	uune/edee	uune	uune	nden	+	+	+	+	-	+
56.	Water	maa	muu	maa	mmu	+	+	+	+	+	+
57.	Eat	de	de	de	de	+	+	+	+	+	+
58.	Drink	on	on	on	wa	+	+	+	+	+	+
59.	Bite	dam	domi	dam	du	+	+	+	+	+	+
60.	Swallow	yogora/mee	soora/me	hrugara	mee	+	+	+	+	+	-
						14	19	17	15	18	15

S/N	English	Kana (Betem)	Gokana (Deeyo)	Tee (Nonwa)	Eleme (Alesa)	Cognation						
						KG	KT	KE	GT	GE	ET
61.	Roast	op	ovi	op	oh	+	+	+	+	+	+
62.	See	moe	mon	moe	mo	+	+	+	+	+	+
63.	Hear	da	da	da	da	+	+	+	+	+	+
64.	Know	sua	yima	sua	yan	-	+	-	-	+	-
65.	Sit down	egeteke	ieteke	ieteke	intite	+	+	+	+	+	+
66.	Lie down	make	make	make	makike	+	+	+	+	+	+
67.	Sleep	daa	daa	daa	jii	+	+	-	+	-	-
68.	Die	uh	uh	uh	uh	+	+	+	+	+	+
69.	Kill	fe	fe	whe	li	+	+	+	+	+	+
70.	Bury	li	li	li	li	+	+	+	+	+	+
71.	Bathe	bira	bira	bira	bira	+	+	+	+	+	+
72.	Give birth	mae	man	mae	ma	+	+	+	+	+	+
73.	Come	lu	du	lu	ju	+	+	+	+	+	+
74.	Walk	kia	kia	kia	chan	+	+	+	+	+	+
75.	Jump	pee	pee	pee	pee	+	+	+	+	+	+
76.	Give	ne	ne	ne	ne	+	+	+	+	+	+
77.	Say (something)	ko	ko	ko	tan mu	+	+	+	+	-	-
78.	Blow (of wind)	fuuri	uuri	whiir	oweiri	+	+	+	+	+	+
79.	Steal	yip	zip	yip	ji	+	+	+	+	+	+
80.	Big	kuin/gbene	pop	gbue/gbebe	egbere	-	+	+	-	-	+
						18	20	18	18	17	17

						Cognation					
S/N	English	Kana (Betem)	Gokana (Deeyo)	Tee (Nonwa)	Eleme (Alesa)	KG	KT	KE	GT	GE	ET
81.	Long	nyon-yon	beg	nyon	negebo	-	+	-	-	+	-
82.	Small	ikina	nkem	nkina	nkele	+	+	+	+	+	+
83.	Red	miimii	miimii	miimii	okponkpon	+	+	-	+	-	-
84.	White	eeh	eeh	eeh	ioro	+	+	-	+	-	-
85.	Black	biira	bira	biira	bibira	+	+	+	+	+	+
86.	Hot	aramia	arasan	arahian	ewara	+	+	+	+	+	+
87.	Cold	too	too	too	ajii	+	+	+	+	-	-
88.	Full	uma	uma	a-uma	anwa	+	+	+	+	+	+
89.	New	aan	aan	aan	ian	+	+	+	+	+	+
90.	Good	le	le	le	a kaa	+	+	-	+	-	-
91.	Dry	kagara	kaakaa	kagara	akai	+	+	+	+	+	+
92.	I	mda	nda	da	ame	+	+	-	+	-	-
93.	You	olo	oro	oro	a oh	-	+	+	+	+	+
94.	We	ili	beere	iri	ebai	+	+	-	-	-	-
95.	You (plur)	bolo	booro	boro	a bai	-	+	-	+	-	-
96.	One	zii	ene	zii	nne	+	+	-	-	+	-
97.	Two	bae	baa	bee	bere	+	+	+	+	+	+
98.	Three	taa	taa	taa	taa	+	+	+	+	+	+
99.	Four	nia	teni	yian	tale	-	+	-	-	+	-
100.	Five	òoo	woo	ooh	ero	+	+	+	+	+	+
					Total	18	20	18	18	17	17
					Total for all pages	84	98	77	84	83	74

338 The Ogoni of the Eastern Niger Delta...

APPENDIX II A

Kinglist/Genealogy of Nama Kingdom

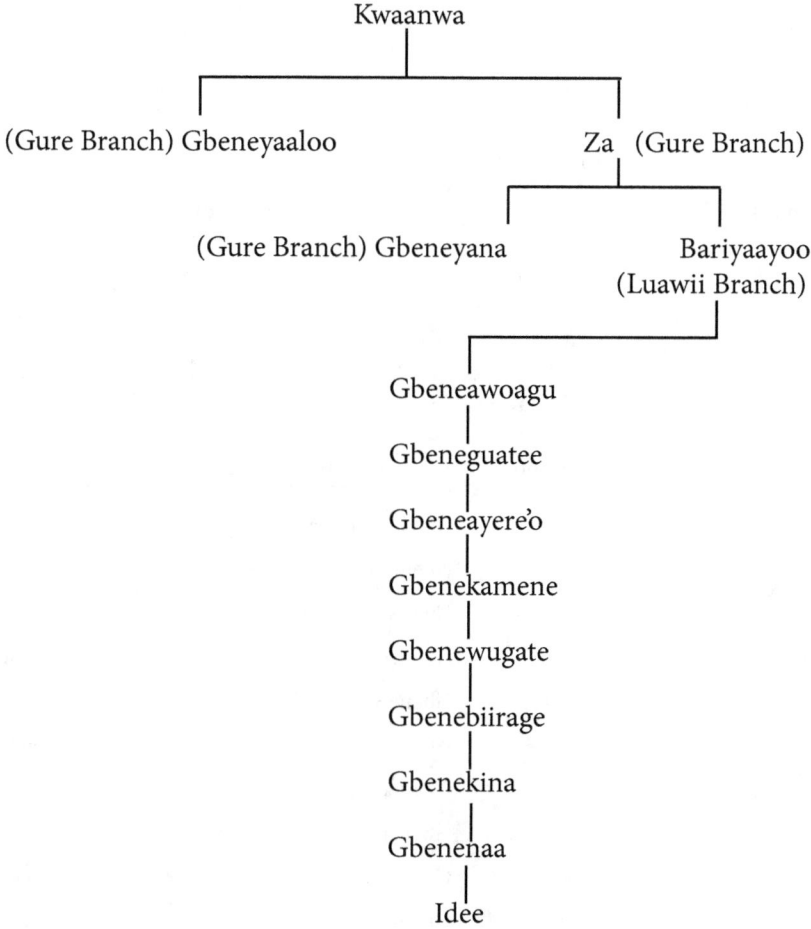

APPENDIX II B
KINGLIST/GENEALOGY OF GOKANA AND BOUE KINGDOMS

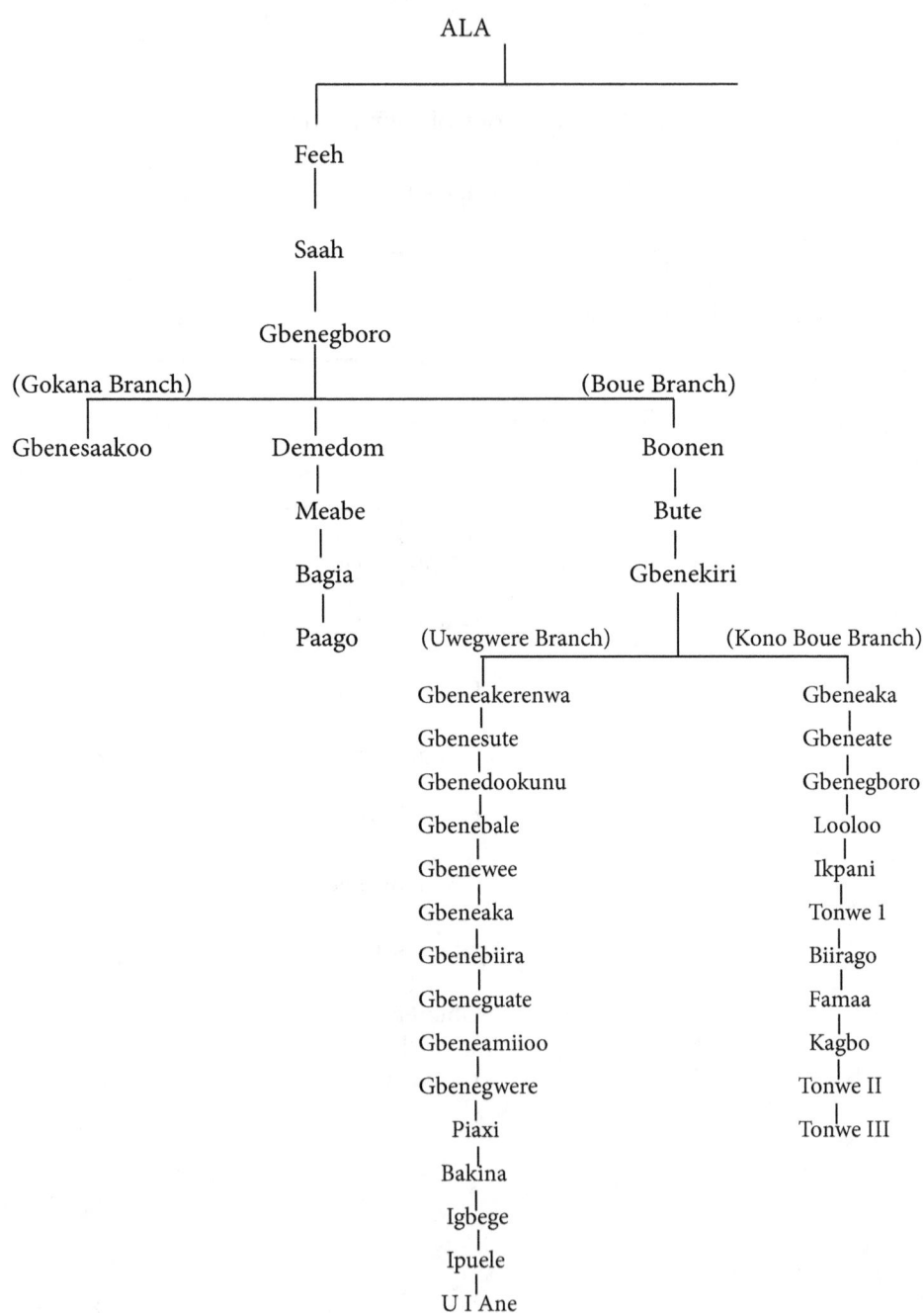

APPENDIX III SOME EARLY OGONI PLACE-NAMES[1]

EARLY FORM OF NAME	NEW-CORRUPTED[1] FORM OF NAME	TYPE OF NAME
Kwaa	Okwali	Place-name
Buon-Ko	Opuoko	Place-name
Goi	Kalaoko	Place-name
Leme	Eleme	Ethnic name of an Ogoni group
Tee	Tai	Ethnic name of an Ogoni group
Boue	Bewa	Ethnic name of an Ogoni group
Khana	Egane	Ethnic name of an Ogoni group
Teebaan	Taabaa	Place-name
Kpuite	Kpite	Place-name
Kaa	Ika	Place-name
Keneke[3]	Kereke	Place-name
Koloma	Okoloma	Place-name
Buduli/Bubu	Ebubu/Ibubu	Place-name
Gosi[4]	Ogosu	Personal name
Kpora	Ekporo	Place-name
Te'ol[5]	Eteo	Place-name
Msia[5]	Nchia/Ncha	Place-name
Agaele[7]	Ogale	Place-name
Aleesa[8]	Alesa	Place-name
Aleeton[9]	Aleto	Place-name
Kpajo[10]	Akpajo	Place-name
Boomu[11]	Bomu	Place-name
Boodoo[12]	Bodo	Place-name
Booli[13]	Bori	Place-name
Gbo-Msia[14]	Agbonchia	Place-name

See notes on Place-names P. 621

Notes on Place-Names

1. **Corrupted Ogoni Place-names:** Appeared mostly in the 18th and 19th centuries during the period of increased population movements from the Igbo hinterland to the coast as a result of the Atlantic slave trade. A few of them however, such as Opuoko and Kalaoko, appeared earlier during the initial contacts between the Ogoni and the Ibani ancestors.

2. **"Egane":** About the middle of the 19th century, W.B. Baikie recorded that Ogoni territory was called "Egane" by Bonny people but others (the Igbo) called it "Ogone". (Baikie, 1856:309). Evidently, the term "Egane" was Bonny's corruption of the name Ghana and the term "Ogone" was Igbo re-corruption of the term "Egane". The term "Ogone" was therefore a secondary corruption of the same word by the Igbo. From the evidence, it appears that in Igbo speech, the initial "E" in a "foreign" name was often changed into an "O". For example, Baikie records that the actual name for Bonny up till the middle of the 19th century was "Ebane".

According to him, while the Ijo of Kalabari pronounced this word "Ibani", the Igbo called it "Obane". (Baikie, 1856:438). From this evidence, two facts became relevant. The first is that up till the middle of the 19th century, the name Ghana or Khana applied to the entire Ogoni territory. This evidence corroborates with the data found in Nama and Boue oral traditions about the Ogoni-wide application of the name. The second fact is that the name "Ogoni" is of recent introduction, having come into usage in about the middle of the 19th century.

3. **Keneke:** This is the name of a town in Boue. The original name was *Keneke-Maala,* meaning "where land and sea meet" or "lands-end". According to Nnaa Kpugita, the founder described the settlement in this way because it was the last settlement of solid ground in the area, after which the vegetation and the geological structure changed into soft mangrove swamp and salt-water. The name was corrupted

to "Kereke" during trade contacts with Bonny in the 19th century, or during the early colonial period.

4. **Gosi:** Is a personal name of "Go" origins. It means "shyfaced". According to S.O. Laaka, the corrupted form of the name "Ogosu" was a common family name of the ancient Etabajo people. The implication is that the Etabajo migrated from "Go" in Tee, possibly during the time of war in Tee.

5. **Te'ol:** Is a Gokana word meaning "right inside bush". The name was descriptive of how the original village was situated.

6. **Msia:** Was the original name of the chief town of Eleme. According to tradition, Lene, the ancestor of Eleme people was from Gokana, but his wife bore twins. Faced with certain death, he fled from Gokana with his family. After many days of bush trek, he arrived there exhausted, so he soliloquized, "I will not run again; I will stay here. Where else should I go?" Gokana, "*Msi-an*?" Kana, "*Msia?*" He gave this name to his first son born there saying, "I said, "where else should I go?" "*Msia*". This son inherited his father's compound which eventually expanded into a town and bore the man's name. During the Atlantic slave trade (18th and 19th centuries), as a result of large influx of Igbo populations into the area and trade relations with Bonny and Okrika, the name was corrupted to "*Nchia*". Even today, one often hears these 'foreigners' pronounce the name "*Ncha*".

7. **Agaele:** Was the original name, and it means "It'll be well." It is the name of a community in Eleme. It was originally the compound of the first son of Msia, who gave the name to his son in memory of his father's strong faith in the future. Faced with the difficulties of settling among the autochthonous inhabitants of the area, the father was reported to have often told his neighbours, "It'll be well" "*Agaelee.*" The name was later corrupted to "*Ogale.*" In the corrupted form the original meaning of the name appears to be completely lost.

8. **Aleesa:** Is the name of another community in Eleme. It grew out of the compound of the fourth son of Msia. *Aleesa* is a

Kana/Gokana word meaning "It's well already." According to tradition, when people asked Lene, the ancestor of Eleme people, whether he thought that it would be well with him (in view of the fact that he did not submit to the custom of twin births), he replied, "It's well already" *"Aleesa."* Msia gave this name to his fourth son in retrospect of his father's proactive faith in the future.

In later times, the name was shortened or corrupted to *"Alesa,"* in which form it is extremely doubtful whether the original meaning of the name can be readily grasped,

9. **Aleeton:** Again this is another community in Eleme. The name derived from the Gokana word *Aleeton* which means "It is time for action," or "I'm ready." This was the name of the third son of Msia. According to tradition, Msia gave this name to his third son as a notice to his taunting autochthonous neighbours saying, "I will no longer be on the receiving end. I will act. With three sons, it's time (for action). I'm ready (to act or do something)," *"Aleeton."* In later times, probably in the 19th century or early colonial period, the name was shortened to its present form *"Aleto."*

10. **Kpaajo:** This is the name of the western-most town of Ogoni. The name derived from the circumstances in which it was founded. According to tradition, the founder of the town was banished from Aleto, having been accused of possessing some powerful 'medicines' which were considered by the elders as dangerous to the society. The name was later corrupted to *"Akpajo."*

11. **Boomu:** Is the name of a Gokana town, which derived its name from its location on the sea coast. It means "on water." That is, it was as it were built "on water." Over the centuries, the name has been shortened to *"Bomu."*

12. **Boodoo:** Is the name of another town in Gokana which was also derived from its location on the sea coast. It means "on the sea shore" or "on the shore". Through centuries of trade

contacts with the Ibani and the Igbo, the name has been shortened to its present form *"Bodo"*.

13. **Booli:** Was the original name of the locality where the administrative headquarters of Ogoni now stands. It was a low plateau. An ancient village which stood near the site derived its name from the fact of being located on a hill top. Hence its name was called *Booli*, meaning "on the hill" or "on the hill top". The name has a "Go" origin. In colonial times, the name was corrupted to *"Bori"*. As it is, the term *"Bori"* does not have any relationship with Ogoni culture and it does not have any meaning.

14. **Gbomsia:** Is the short form of *"Gboo-Msia"* which means the "gateway" or "open ground of *Msia*" or *"Msia* Square". The name derived from the location of the compound of the second son of Msia. This son's actual name is now unknown. According to tradition, his compound was located at or near the cross roads leading into Msia's settlement. Eventually, the compound expanded into a separate community. The name was later corrupted to *"Agbo-Nchia"* or *"Agbonchia"*.

APPENDIX IV
OGONI KNIVES

A Sheathed Kobege

The sheathed Kobege, strapped by a leather belt, was worn on the waist by men who had performed the yaa tradition as an insignia of social status.

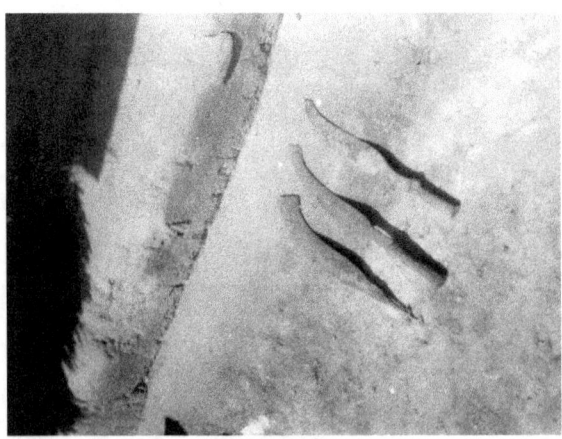

The Kuna

Appendices 347

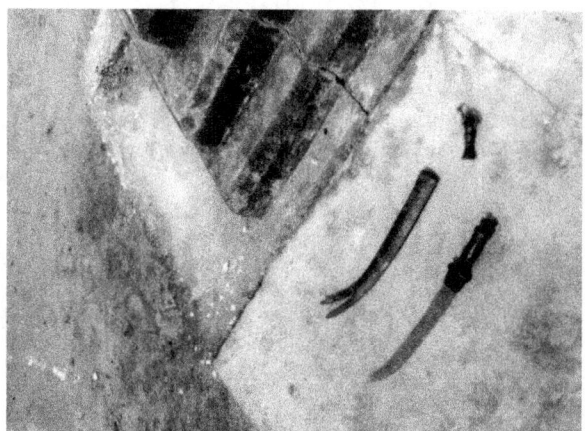

Unsheated Kobege

The *Kuna* was a common working tool used by both men and women. The bulged edge was used for every rough work and for brushing the farmlands, while the curved edge was reserved for cutting and for pruning the trees.

APPENDIX V
"MOKO" IRON MONEY[1]

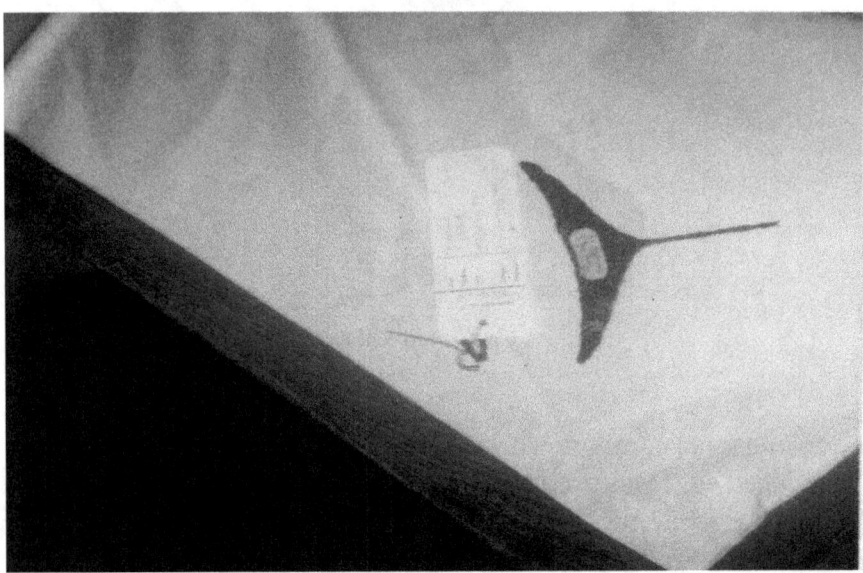

Source: Ethnographic Department Museum of Mankind, London

1. Dapper gives the geographical location of "Moko". According to him, the district of Krike (Okrika) is about twenty miles up the Rio real (i.e. its eastern branch of Bonny River) and borders on the north-west of "Moko", while the district of Bani (Bonny) borders on the south of "Moko" (Dapper, 1668, 1676: 135; Barbot, 1732:380; Jones, 1963:36).

By this geographical description, Dapper precisely identified Mogho, a southern Ogoni town in the Gokana area, whose seaside market was located at Gbee (Gia 26, tapes 27/B3/28. 8.2.84). It is hoped that archaeological excavations in the area will unearth samples of the iron money.

Some scholars, however, have suggested that "Moko" refers to Ibibio (Northrup, 1978:159; Noah, 1980:3); and others have suggested a part of Southern Igboland (Jones, 1963:36).

APPENDIX VI
REPORT OF RADIOCARBON DATING OF NAMA

REPORT OF RADIOCARBON DATING ANALYSES

Dr. Sonpie Kpone-Tonwe

Report Date: 8/8/2013

Material Received: 7/30/2013

Sample Data	Measured Radiocarbon Age	13C/12C Ratio	Conventional Radiocarbon Age(*)
Beta - 355377 SAMPLE : UPMN-SAD0001 ANALYSIS : AMS-Standard delivery MATERIAL/PRETREATMENT : (charred material); acid/alkali/acid 2 SIGMA CALIBRATION : Cal AD 1670 to 1780 (Cal BP 280 to 170) AND Cal AD 1800 to 1890 (Cal BP 150 to 60) Cal AD 1900 to 1950 (Cal BP 50 to 0) AND Cal AD 1950 to post 1950 (Cal BP 0 to post 1950)	140 +/- 30 BP	-25.0 o/oo	140 +/- 30 BP
Beta - 355378 SAMPLE : UPMN-SAD0002 ANALYSIS : AMS-Standard delivery MATERIAL/PRETREATMENT : (charred material); acid/alkali/acid 2 SIGMA CALIBRATION : Cal AD 1670 to 1780 (Cal BP 280 to 170) AND Cal AD 1800 to 1890 (Cal BP 150 to 60) Cal AD 1900 to 1950 (Cal BP 50 to 0) AND Cal AD 1950 to post 1950 (Cal BP 0 to post 1950)	190 +/- 30 BP	-27.8 o/oo	140 +/- 30 BP
Beta - 355379 SAMPLE : UPMN-SAD0003 ANALYSIS : AMS-Standard delivery MATERIAL/PRETREATMENT : (charred material); acid/alkali/acid 2 SIGMA CALIBRATION : Cal AD 1520 to 1590 (Cal BP 430 to 360) AND Cal AD 1620 to 1660 (Cal BP 330 to 290)	250 +/- 30 BP	-22.9 o/oo	280 +/- 30 BP
Beta - 355380 SAMPLE : UPMN-SAD0004 ANALYSIS : AMS-Standard delivery MATERIAL/PRETREATMENT : (charred material); acid/alkali/acid 2 SIGMA CALIBRATION : Cal AD 1470 to 1650 (Cal BP 480 to 300)	360 +/- 30 BP	-27.4 o/oo	320 +/- 30 BP

Dates are reported as RCYBP (radiocarbon years before present "present" = AD 1950). By international convention, the modern reference standard was 95% the 14C activity of the National Institute of Standards and Technology (NIST) Oxalic Acid (SRM 4990C) and calculated using the Libby 14C half-life (5568 years). Quoted errors represent 1 relative standard deviation statistics (68% probability) counting errors based on the combined measurements of the sample, background, and modern reference standards. Measured 13C/12C ratios (delta 13C) were calculated relative to the PDB-1 standard.

The ...ional Radiocarbon Age represents the Measured ...rbon Age corrected for isotopic fractionation, calculated using the delta 13C. On rare occasion where the Conventional Radiocarbon Age was calculated using an assumed delta 13C, the ratio and the Conventional Radiocarbon Age will be followed by "*". The Conventional Radiocarbon Age is not calendar calibrated. When available, the Calendar Calibrated result is calculated from the Conventional Radiocarbon Age and is listed as the "Two Sigma Calibrated Result" for each sample.

CALIBRATION OF RADIOCARBON AGE TO CALENDAR YEARS

(Variables: C13/C12=-25:lab. mult=1)

Laboratory number: Beta-355377

Conventional radiocarbon age: 140±30 BP

2 Sigma calibrated results: Cal AD 1670 to 1780 (Cal BP 280 to 170) and
(95% probability) Cal AD 1800 to 1890 (Cal BP 150 to 60) and
Cal AD 1900 to 1950 (Cal BP 50 to 0) and
Cal AD 1950 to post 1950 (Cal BP 0 to post 1950)

Intercept data

Intercepts of radiocarbon age
with calibration curve: Cal AD 1680 (Cal BP 260) and
Cal AD 1730 (Cal BP 220) and
Cal AD 1810 (Cal BP 140) and
Cal AD 1930 (Cal BP 20) and
Cal AD Post 1950

1 Sigma calibrated results: Cal AD 1680 to 1700 (Cal BP 270 to 250) and
(68% probability) Cal AD 1720 to 1760 (Cal BP 230 to 190) and
Cal AD 1770 to 1780 (Cal BP 180 to 170) and
Cal AD 1800 to 1820 (Cal BP 150 to 140) and
Cal AD 1830 to 1880 (Cal BP 120 to 70) and
Cal AD 1920 to 1940 (Cal BP 30 to 10) and
Cal AD Post 1950

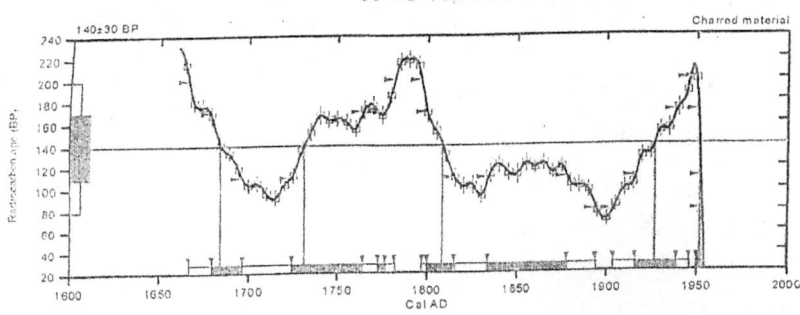

References:
Database used
INTCAL09
References to INTCAL09 database
Heaton,et.al.,2009, Radiocarbon 51(4):1151-1164, Reimer,et.al., 2009, Radiocarbon 51(4):1111-1150,
Stuiver,et.al,1993, Radiocarbon 35(1):137-189, Oeschger,et.al.,1975,Tellus 27:168-192
Mathematics used for calibration scenario
A Simplified Approach to Calibrating C14 Dates
Talma, A. S., Vogel, J. C., 1993, Radiocarbon 35(2): -322

Beta Analytic Radiocarbon Dating Laboratory

CALIBRATION OF RADIOCARBON AGE TO CALENDAR YEARS

(Variables: C13/C12=-27.8:lab. mult=1)

Laboratory number: Beta-355378

Conventional radiocarbon age: 140±30 BP

-2 Sigma calibrated results: Cal AD 1670 to 1780 (Cal BP 280 to 170) and
(95% probability) Cal AD 1800 to 1890 (Cal BP 150 to 60) and
Cal AD 1900 to 1950 (Cal BP 50 to 0) and
Cal AD 1950 to post 1950 (Cal BP 0 to post 1950)

Intercept data

Intercepts of radiocarbon age
with calibration curve: Cal AD 1680 (Cal BP 260) and
Cal AD 1730 (Cal BP 220) and
Cal AD 1810 (Cal BP 140) and
Cal AD 1930 (Cal BP 20) and
Cal AD Post 1950

1 Sigma calibrated results: Cal AD 1680 to 1700 (Cal BP 270 to 250) and
(68% probability) Cal AD 1720 to 1760 (Cal BP 230 to 190) and
Cal AD 1770 to 1780 (Cal BP 180 to 170) and
Cal AD 1800 to 1820 (Cal BP 150 to 140) and
Cal AD 1830 to 1880 (Cal BP 120 to 70) and
Cal AD 1920 to 1940 (Cal BP 30 to 10) and
Cal AD Post 1950

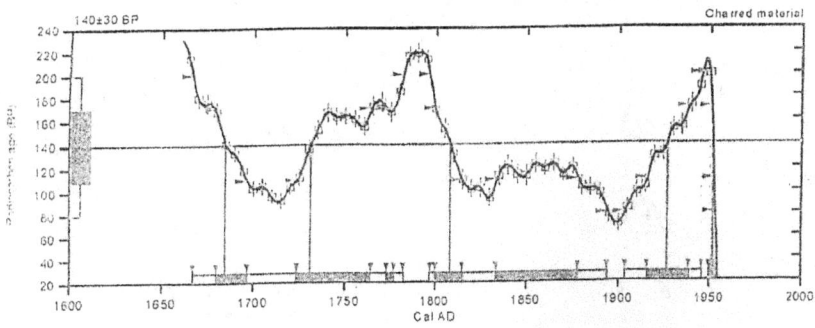

References:
Database used
INTCAL09
References to INTCAL09 database
Heaton, et.al., 2009, Radiocarbon 51(4): ... ...mer, et.al., 2009, Radiocarbon 51(4): 1111-1150.
Stuiver, et.al., 1993, Radiocarbon 35(1) ...eewhger, et.al., 1975, Tellus 27: 168-192.
Mathematics used for calibration scene
A Simplified Approach to Calib... using C14 Dates
Talma, A. S., Vogel ... 993, Radiocarbon 35(2): 317-322

Beta Analytic Radiocarbon Dating Laboratory

CALIBRATION OF RADIOCARBON AGE TO CALENDAR YEARS

(Variables: C13/C12=-22.9:lab. mult=1)

Laboratory number: Beta-355379
Conventional radiocarbon age: 280±30 BP
2 Sigma calibrated results: Cal AD 1520 to 1590 (Cal BP 430 to 360) and
(95% probability) Cal AD 1620 to 1660 (Cal BP 330 to 290)

Intercept data

Intercept of radiocarbon age
with calibration curve: Cal AD 1640 (Cal BP 310)

1 Sigma calibrated results: Cal AD 1530 to 1540 (Cal BP 420 to 410) and
(68% probability) Cal AD 1550 to 1550 (Cal BP 400 to 400) and
Cal AD 1630 to 1650 (Cal BP 320 to 300)

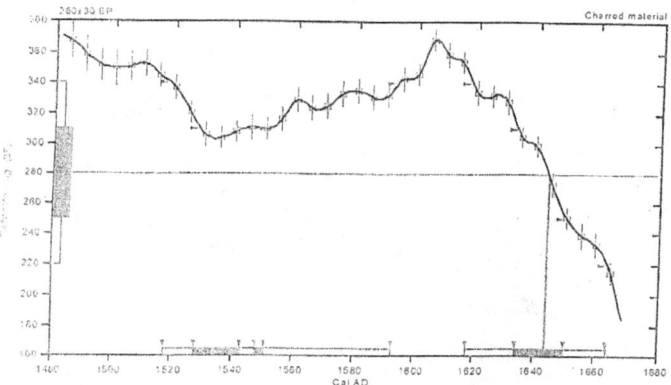

References:
Database used
INTCAL09
References to INTCAL09 database
Heaton, et al., 2009, Radiocarbon 51(4):1151-1164, Reimer, et al., 2009, Radiocarbon 51(4):1111-1150,
Stuiver, et al. 1993, Radiocarbon 35(1):137-189, Oeschger, et al. 1975, Tellus 27:168-192
Mathematics used for calibration scenario
A Simplified Approach to Calibrating C14 Dates
Talma, A. S., Vogel, J. C., 1993, Radiocarbon 35(2):317-322

Beta Analytic Radiocarbon Dating Laboratory

CALIBRATION OF RADIOCARBON AGE TO CALENDAR YEARS

(Variables: C13/C12=-27.4:lab. mult=1)

Laboratory number: Beta-355380

Conventional radiocarbon age: 320±30 BP

2 Sigma calibrated result: Cal AD 1470 to 1650 (Cal BP 480 to 300)
(95% probability)

Intercept data

Intercepts of radiocarbon age
with calibration curve: Cal AD 1520 (Cal BP 420) and
Cal AD 1560 (Cal BP 390) and
Cal AD 1630 (Cal BP 320)

1 Sigma calibrated results: Cal AD 1500 to 1500 (Cal BP 450 to 450) and
(68% probability) Cal AD 1510 to 1600 (Cal BP 440 to 350) and
Cal AD 1620 to 1640 (Cal BP 330 to 310)

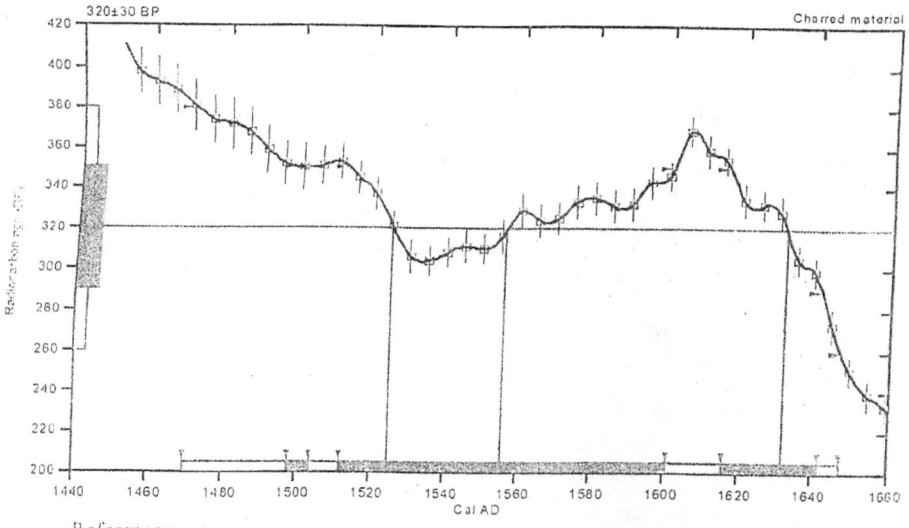

References:
Database used
INTCAL09
References to INTCAL09 database
Heaton.et.al.,2009, Radiocarbon 51(4):1151-1164, Reimer,et.al, 2009, Radiocarbon 51(4):1111-1150,
Stuiver,et.al,1993, Radiocarbon 35(1):137-189, Oeschger,et.al.,1975,Tellus 27:168-192
Mathematics used for calibration scenario
A Simplified Approach to Calibrating C14 Dates
Talma, A. S., Vogel, J. C., 1993, Radiocarbon 35(2):317-322

Beta Analytic Radiocarbon Dating Laboratory

APPENDIX VII

GEOGRAPHICAL DIRECTIONS IN OGONI LANGUAGES

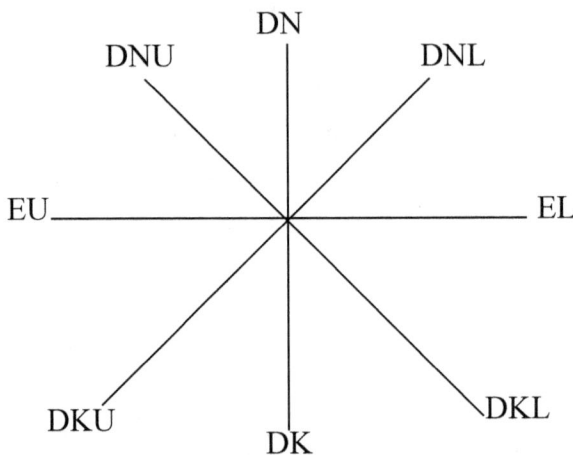

Deenyon (DN)   North (N)
Deeke (DK)   South (S)
Enaani Loole (EL)   East (E)
Enaani Unne (EU)   West (W)
Deenyon Enaani Loole (DNL)   North-east (N.E)
Deeke Enaani Loole (DKL)   South-west (S.E)
Deenyon Enaani Uune (DNU)   North-west (N.W)
Deeke Enaani Uune (DKU)   South-west (S.W)

APPENDIX VIII
LIST OF IMPORTANT TEXTS (ORAL INTERVIEWS)

S/N	NAME	TAPE NO.	DATE
1.	ADOOKON, Emmanuel	OG/SK/14	4 Mar. 1984
2.	AKEKUE, Mark Nuka (A) (B)	 OG/SK/1&2	21 Nov. 1981 21 Nov. 1981
3.	ALAWA, Innocent Lekie	OG/SK/33	11 Jan. 1984
4.	ASOO, Koobee	OG/SK/12	12 Jan. 1984
5.	AWALA, Oji	OG/SK/21	4 Mar. 1984
6.	BAEDEE, Eli	OG/SK/22	23 Dec. 1983
7.	BAGIA, J.P.	OG/SK/28 OG/SK/29	19 Feb. 1984
8.	BARIGWERE, Inee	OG/SK/10,11	3 Jan. 1984
9.	BIRANEE, Tuanee A.		18 Oct. 1981
10.	BONKOO, Pasi	OG/SK/32	11 Jan. 1988
11.	DEEMUA, Daasang D.	OG/SK/23	5 Dec. 1983
12.	DEEZUA, Koanyee	OG/SK/21	27 Dec. 1983
13.	DEEZUA, Nnaaduikie	OG/SK/5	16 Jan. 1984
14.	DUNWAA, Edward	OG/SK/24	15 Mar. 1984
15.	EJO, Dennis L.	OG/SK/30	25 Feb. 1984
16.	FOGHO, Doone N.		21 Oct. 1981
17.	GBARATEE, Deezua	OG/SK/20	7 Jan. 1984
18.	GBARATO, Aanee	OG/SK/27	5 Feb. 1984
19.	GBARATO, Adoo	OG/SK/5	18 Jan. 1984
20.	GBARATO, Gosi	OG/SK/19	22 Jan. 1984
21.	GBEGE, Abanee	OG/SK/22	25 Nov. 1983
22.	GBENEYAALOO'S Spirit Medium	OG/SK/17	12 Mar. 1984

23.	GBIGBO, A'ean	OG/SK/21	27 Dec. 1983
24.	GBORO, Zoraba	OG/SK/28	11 Feb. 1984
25.	GBOSI, Keenam	OG/SK/22,23	11 Jan. 1988
26.	GIA, Dirnkpa	OG/SK/27,28	8 Feb. 1984
27.	GININWA, G.N.K.	OG/SK/16	19 Mar. 1984
28.	GOOKINANWAA, Ibeyo G.	OG/SK/16	19 Mar. 1984
29.	IGBUG, Deebari	OG/SK/19	22 Jan. 1984
30.	IKPODEE, Goabere	OG/SK/19	15 Jan. 1984
31.	IMENE, Nwii	OG/SK/20	28 Dec. 1983
32.	INAYO, Inaatura (A) (B)	OG/SK/11 OG/SK/21	27 Dec. 1983
33.	INAYO, Teera (Prince)	OG/SK/6	7 Mar. 1984
34.	IPAAN, Tobina	OG/SK/20	9 Jan. 1984
35.	IWAGBO, John	OG/SK/18	24 Mar. 1984
36.	IWEREBE, Urane Frank	OG/SK/19	22 Jan. 1984
37.	IYORO, Dike	OG/SK/12	5 Feb. 1984
38.	KEEKEE, Dominic Anderson		24 Oct. 1981
39.	KINANWII, Kpoko	OG/SK/11,12	5 Jan. 1984
40.	KPEA, Edward Nwebon	OG/SK/27	7 Feb. 1984
41.	KPONE-TONWE, Obeye		27 Oct. 1984
42.	KPUGITA, Nnaa	OG/SK/10	2 Jan. 1984
43.	LAAKA, Solomon O. (A) (B)	OG/SK/7	21 Feb. 1984 6 Mar. 1984
44.	LEGBARA, Bakoba	OG/SK/8	5 Jan. 1984
45.	LOOLO, Godwin N.	OG/SK/20	25 Mar. 1984
46.	MENEWA, Pia'oo	OG/SK/3	21 Oct. 1981
47.	MKPEME, Christopher et al	OG/SK/4	3 Jan. 1988
48.	MPEBA, Mbaedee, Francis	OG/SK/32	10 Mar. 1984
49.	NAASA, Agbeebe	OG/SK/9	4 Dec. 1983

50.	NGITO, Leelee Naabee	OG/SK/23	17 Mar. 1984
51.	NGOFA, Obo O.	OG/SK/15	5 Mar. 1984
52.	NII, Isaanee (Prince)	OG/SK/31	28 Dec. 1983
53.	NNEKA, Emmanuel	OG/SK/4	16 Nov. 1981
54.	NTEYOO, Ndii	OG/SK/22	11 Feb. 1984
55.	NUAKA, Lemue (A) (B)	OG/SK/27	30 Nov. 1983 2 Dec. 1983
56.	NWIKOGBARA, M.D. (A) (B)	OG/SK/24	17 Oct. 1981
57.	NWILABBA, Teetee Edamni	OG/SK/16	15 Mar. 1984
58.	NWIMEA, Teewoo	OG/SK/24	18 Mar. 1984
59.	NWINEE, Deegbara		22 Oct. 1981
60.	NWINEEDAM, Michael et al	OG/SK/17	24 Mar. 1984
61.	NYONE, E.B et al	OG/SK/13	26 Feb. 1984
62.	OBUH, J.B.	OG/SK/24	15 Mar. 1984
63.	OPUSUNJU Na'ue L.		23 Oct. 1981
64.	OSARONU, J.D.	OG/SK/8	25 Feb. 1984
65.	TANEE, Kuenee	OG/SK/20	3 Jan. 1984
66.	TEEDEE, Frederick B.	OG/SK/15,16	19 Mar. 1984
67.	TIGIRI, John P.	OG/SK/14	
68.	TONGO, Tiitii	OG/SK/32	9 Jan. 1988
69.	TONWE III, M.A.M (A) (B)	OG/SK/25 OG/SK/26	21 Jan. 1984 22 Jan. 1984
70.	YOMII, Jim B. (A) (B)	OG/SK/24	21 Oct. 1981 15 Mar. 1984
71.	ZAGA, Baridon	OG/SK/19	22 Jan. 1984
72.	OODEE, J.T.	OG/SK/5	30 Dec. 1983
73.	KIRIKI, I. & KPONE-TONWE, O.		17 Feb. 1990

74.	MINA, F.M. & GBENEBAIKARA B.	OG/SK/34	24 Mar. 1990
75.	OLOKA, Friday Namene	OG/SK/34	24 Feb. 1990
76.	BEKANWAA, I & KAGBARA, T.	OG/SK/34	7 Apr. 1990

BIBLIOGRAPHY
PRIMARY SOURCES

A. Oral Evidence
List of Important Informants

Name	Approx. Age	Social Status	Place of Interview	Date
ADOOKON, Emmanuel	77yrs	Chief spirit	Luuyo Gwara	4/3/84
AKEKUE, Mark Nuka	58yrs	Medium	Kpuite, Tee	21/11/81
ALAWA, Innocent Lekie	76yrs	Chief	Bodo	11/1/88
ASOO, Koobee	120yrs	Chief	Uwegwere Boue	12/1/84
AWALA, Oji	55yrs	Chief	Ogale, Eleme	4/3/84
BAEDEE, Eli	55yrs	Chief	Eepie, Kono Boue	23/12/83
BAGIA, J.P.	70yrs	Gbenemene Gokana	Giokoo	19/2/84
BARIGWERE, Inee	98yrs	Chief	Ilooloo	3/1/84
BEKANWAA, Isaiah et al	68yrs	Mene Bua Luawii	Zako Luawaii	7/4/90
BIRINEE, Tuanee A.	53yrs	Chief	Sii Town	3/1/84
BONKOO, Basi	65yrs	House head	Mogho Town	11/1/88
DEEMUA, D.D.	62yrs	Mene Bua Boue	Gbam Boue	5/12/83
DEEZUA, Koanyee	87yrs	Ancestral Priest	Kono Boue	27/12/83
DEEZUA, Nnaadu	82yrs	Kabaariwa	Kono Boue	16/1/84
DUNWAA, Edward	58yrs	Former councillor	Buon Ko	15/3/84
EJO, Dennis L.	65yrs	School teacher, church councillor	Agbeta, Onne	25/2/84
FOGHO, Dooonee N.	70yrs	House head	Bara, Sii	21/10/81
GBARATEE, Deezua	65yrs	Former head of a social club	Tego Kono Boue	7/1/84
GBENEBAI-KARA, Biiranee	70yrs	Chief canoe-maker	Ko (Opuoko)	24/3/90
GBARATO, Aanee	110yrs	Elder	Lewe Gokana	5/2/84
GBARATO, Adoo	72yrs	Elder	Noobana Kono	18/1/84
GBARATO, Gosi	92yrs	Priest of Gbenekiri	Uwegwere Boue	22/1/84
GBEGE, Abanee	87yrs	Chief	Eepie Boue	25/11/83
GBIGBO, Aean	45yrs	Son of a priest of Yobue	Kwaakwaa	27/12/83
GBORO, Zoraba	67yrs	Priest of Bari-Gokana	Mogho Gokana	11/2/84

GBOSI, Keenam	87yrs	Lineage head of *Gan Ben* in Kpoo	Kpoo, Gokana	11/1/88
GIA, Dimkpa	75yrs	Chief	Gbee Gokana	8/2/84
GININWA, G.N.K.	58yrs	Gbenemene Tuatua Tee	Korokoro Tee	19/3/84
GOOKINANWAA, Ibeyo Gbenegbara	98yrs	Bearer of Gbene Title	Uweke Tee	19/3/84
IGBUG, Deebari	67yrs	Yam priest, Boue	Kono Boue	22/14/84
IKPODEE, Goabere	78yrs	Kabaariwa Tego	Tego Boue	15/1/84
IMENE, Nwii	64yrs	Head of Kpaankpaan Secret Society	Kwaakwaa Boue	28/12/83
INAYO, Inaatura		Head of Kote House Kono Boue	Kono Boue	27/12/83
INAYO, Teera	55yrs	A prince of the Royal House of Kote	Kono Boue	7/3/84
IPAAN, Tobina	63yrs	Head of Gbenebaara House, Kono Boue	Kwaakwaa Boue	9/1/84
IWAGBO, John	70yrs	Spirit-Medium of Nama deities	Nama & Kugba	24/3/84
IWEREBE, Uranee Frank	65yrs	Chief and Head of Gbenekiri house of Uwegwere	Uwegwere	22/1/94
IYORO, Dike	70yrs	President, House of Elders Boue	Noobana Kono Boue	5/2/84
KAGBARA, Teeh	65yrs	Chief	Luawii	7/4/90
KEEKEE, Dominic Anderson	53yrs	Chief	Kpong	24/10/81
KINANWII, Kpoko	87yrs	Chief & head of Gbenekarayoo house Tego	Tego Boue	5/1/84
KPEA, Edward Nwebon	89yrs	*Mene Bua* Mogho	Mogho	7/2/84
KPONE-TONWE, Obeye	58yrs	Head of Pot-traders Asso. Boue	Kono Boue	27/11/84
KPUGITA, Nnaa	55yrs	Chief	Keneke Boue	17/2/90
KIRIKI, Ipiagbo	70yrs	Lineage head	Tego Boue	2/1/84
LAAKA, Solomon O.	67yrs	Reverend Minister	Ekara Onne	17/2/90
LEGBARA, Bakoba	74yrs	Head of a social club	Noobana Boue	21/2/84

Name	Age	Role	Place	Date
LOOLO, Godwin N.	57yrs	Chief & director-Gen. Rivers State Govt.	Port Harcourt	6/3/84
NEMEWA, Noa'oo	85yrs	Priest, spirit-medium	Kpong	5/1/84
MKPEME, Christopher D.	65yrs	Chief	Sogho	25/3/84
MINA, Frank M.	54yrs	Chief	Ko	21/10/81
NAASA, Agbeebe	63yrs	Chief	Kwaakwaa Boue	3/1/88
NGITO, Leelee Naabee	99yrs	Elder	Tee	24/3/90
NGOFA, Obo O.	58yrs	Chief	Aleto, Eleme	4/12/84
NIL, Isaanee	95yrs	Chief	Eepie	7/3/84
NNEKA, Emmanuel	80yrs	Chief	Kpuite Tee	9/1/84
NTEYO, Ndii	65yrs	Lineage head	Lewe Gokana	24/3/84
NUAKA, Lemue	90yrs	Priest of Yobue	Tego	22/1/84
NWIKOGBARA, M.D.	57yrs	Chief	Sii Town	5/2/84
NWILABBA, T.E.	120yrs	Elder	Buon Ko	7/4/90
NWIMEA, Teewoo	87yrs	Priest of Bariyaayoo	Luawii	24/10/81
NWINEE, Deegbara	68yrs	School Teacher	Kono	5/1/84
NWINEEDAM, M.	35yrs	Member of Gbeneyaaloo house, Gure	Gure Town	7/2/84
NYONE, E.B. et al	67yrs	Chief	Lewe Gokana	27/11/84
OBUH, J.B.	72yrs	Chief	Kabangha	27/12/83
OLOKA, F.N.	43yrs	Craftsman	Port Harcourt	7/3/84
OPUSUNJU, Na'ue L.	72yrs	Priest, spirit-medium	Kono	9/1/84
OSARONU, J.D.	47yrs	Chief	Ogoloma Onne	24/3/84
OODEE, J.T.	55yrs	Chief	Kwaakwaa	22/1/84
TANEE, Kuenee	57yrs	Youth Leader	Kwaakwaa	22/1/84
TEEDEE, F.B.	43yrs	Head of Gbeneyaaloo house, Gure	Gure Town	5/2/84
TIGIRI, John P.	83yrs	Chief JP	Luuyo	7/4/90
TONGO, Tiitii	70yrs	Chief	Nyongo, Beele	24/10/81
TONWE III. M.A.M.	48yrs	Chief, Head of Tonwe House	Kono Boue	5/1/84

YOMII, Jim B.	58yrs	Chief	Ko	7/2/84
ZAGA, Baridon	60yrs	Chief	Uwegwere	22/1/84

B. Published Sources

BARBOT, James "An Abstract of a Voyage to New Calabar or Rio Real in the year 1699" in Churchill & Churchill (eds.), *A Collection of Voyages and Travels* Vol. V. (London; Thomas Osborn, Henry Lintot etc. 1732), pp. 455-465.

BARBOT, Jone, *A Collection of Voyages and Travels* Vol. V, (London: printed by Assignment from Messrs Churchill & churchill (eds.), for Thomas Osborn, Henry Lintot etc., 1732).

BAIKIE, V.B. *Narrative of an Exploring Voyage up the Rivers Kwora and Binue (commonly known as the Niger Tsadda) in 1854.* (London: John Murray, Albemarle Street, 1856).

DAPPER, Olfert, *Naukeurige Beschrijving der Afrikaensche Gewestern* (Amsterdam: Jacob van Meurs, 2nd ed. 1676 (1st ed. 1668) see *"Het Koningrijkvan BIGUBA"* p135.

LEONARD, Major Arthur Glyn, *The Lower Niger and Its Tribes* (London: Macmillan & Co. Ltd. 1906).

PEREIRA, Pacheco (Duarte), *Esmeraldo de Situ Orbis* (Vers 1506-1508) Tr. Raymond Mauny (Bissau, 1956).

WADDEL, Rev. Hope Masterton, *Twenty-Nine Years in the West Indies and Central Africa 1829-1858.* (1st edn. 1863). Second edn. With a New Introduction by G.I. Jones. London: Frank Cass & Co. Ltd. 1970.

_____ *Vocabulary of the Efik of Old Calabar.* Second edn. Revised and Enlarged. Edinburgh: Grant & Taylor, George St., 1849.

C. Archival Sources

Gibbons, E.J. *"Intelligence Report on Ogoni"* Opobo Division Calabar Province, 1932. N.A.E. File 28032 Cs026/3.

MACKENZIE, 3.G. *"Intelligence Report on Eleme"* Opobo Division Calabar Province. File E.P. 9595 CSE 1/85/4888.

N.A.E., R.P. 6378 "proposed Ogoni Division." Opobo Division Calabar Province.

N.A.E., R.P. 6402/vol. II "Ogoni Patrol Report, Ogodest, Opobo Division, Calabar Province.

PORTER, J.C. *"Intelligence Report on Okrika."* Degema Division; Owerri province, 1933, N.A.E. File 29004 CS026/3.

WEBBER, H. *"Intelligence Report on Bonny District"* Owerri Province, 1931. N.A.E. File 27226 CS026/3.

METHODIST MISSIONARY SOCIETY ARCHIVE, LONDON, AT S.O.A.S. LIBRARY, LONDON: Primitive Methodist Missionary Society, Nigeria 1897-1933 Eastern Nigeria: 1907-1933 2 Box 1163 1907-1929 6 Box 1167.

D. Secondary Sources

Afigbo, E.E. "Efik origins and Migrations Reconsidered" *Nigeria Magazine* 87, (Dec. 1965), pp. 267-280.

_____ "The Ndoki from the Earliest Times to 1901: An Introductory Survey" *Oduma* Vol. II, I (1971), pp.16-20

_____ *The Warrant Chiefs: Indirect Rule in South-Eastern Nigeria 1891-1929.* Longman Group Ltd., London, 1972.

_____ "Trade and Trade Routes in Nineteenth Century Nsukka" *J.H.S.N.* Vol. VII, I (1973), pp. 77-90.

_____ "Economic Foundations of Pre-Colonial Igbo Society" (in I.A. Akinjobin & S.O. Osoba (eds.) *Topics on Nigerian Economic and Social History* (Obafemi Awolowo University press, 1980) pp. 1-18.

_____ Ropes of Sand: Studies in Igbo History and Culture Nsukka: University of Nigeria press 1981.

ALAGOA, E.J. "Settlement of the Niger Delta: Ijo Oral Traditions." (Ph.D. Thesis, University of Wisconsin, 1965).

_____ "Oral Tradition among the Ijo of the Niger Delta" J.A.H. Vol. VIII, 3 (1966). Pp. 405-419.

_____ "Long Distance Trade and States in the Niger Delta" J.A.H. Vol. XI, 3 (1970), pp. 319-329.

_____ "The Niger Delta States and their Neighbours to 1800" in J.F. Ade Ajayi and Michael Crowder (eds.), *History of West Africa* Vol. 1 (London: Longman Group Ltd. (1st edn. 1971) 2nd edn. 1976), pp. 331-372.

_____ *A History of the Niger Delta.* Ibadan: Ibadan University Press, 1972.

_____ "Dating Ijo Oral Tradition" *Oduma.* Vol. 3, 1 (1976) pp. 19-22.

_____ "On the Python's Eye" The Python's Eye: Journal of the *History Students' Association* University of Port Harcourt, Vol. 1, 1 (1980), pp. 3-4.

_____ "Oral Historical Tradition in Africa" *Tarikh* Vol. 8, ed. E.J. Alagoa (Longman Nigeria Ltd., 1987), pp. 1-7.

_____ "GOD IS MOTHER: A Historical Review of Women in the Development of the Niger Delta Communities" (A Seminar Paper, Faculty of Humanities, University of Port Harcourt, 19th April, 1989).

ALAGOA, E.J. and FOMBO, A. *A. Chronicle of Grand Bonny* Ibadan: Ibadan University Press, 1972.

AKINJOBIN, I.A. "A Chronology of Yoruba History, 1789-1840," *Odu* Vol. II, 1 (1965), pp. 81-86).

ANENE, J.C. *Southern Nigeria in Transition 1885-1906.* Cambridge University Press, 1966.

ANOZIE, F.N. "Archaeological Research in the Rivers State." *Oduma* Vol. 1, 1 (1973), pp. 4-9.

_____ "Onyoma and Ke: A preliminary Report on Archaeological Excavations in the Niger Delta" *West African Journal of Archaeology* (WAJA) Vol. VI (1976), pp 89-99.

ARMSTRONG, R.G. "The Use of Linguistics and Ethonographic Data in the Study of Idoma and Yoruba History" in Vansina, Jan, Manny, R. and Thomas, L.V. eds.), *The Historian in Tropical Africa* for International African Institute (London: Oxford University Press, 1964). pp. 127-144.

AJAYI, F.F. ADE, *Christian Missions in Nigeria 1841-1891,* London: Longman Green and Co. Ltd. 1965.

ARDENER, E. 1968: "Documentary and Linguistic Evidence for the Rise of the Trading Polities between Rio del Rey and Camerrons, 1500-1650" in I.M. Lewise ed. *History and Social Anthropology*. London, Tavistock Publications.

BARCK, O.T. and LEFLER, H.T. *Colonial America* 2nd edn. London: The Macmillan Co. Ltd., 1968.

BIOBAKU, S.O. "The Problem of Traditional History with Special Reference to Yoruba Traditions *J.H.S.N.* Vol. 1, 1 (1956), pp. 43-47.

BRADBURY, R.E. "The Historical Uses of Comparative Ethnography with Special Reference to Benin and Yoruba" in Vansina, J., Mauny, R. and Thomas, L.V. (eds.) *The Historian in Tropical Africa* for International African Institute (London: Oxford University Press 1964), pp. 145-164.

COOKEY, S.J.S. "An Igbo Slave Story of the Late Nineteenth Century and the Implications" *Ikenga: Journal of African Studies,* (University of Nigeria, Nsukka), pp. 1-9.

CURTIN, Philip D. "The Atlantic Slave Trade, 1600-1800" in J.F.A. Ajayi and Michael Crowder (eds.), Vol. 1. (New York: Columbia University Press, 1976), pp. 302-330.

DIKE, K.O. *Trade and Polities in the Niger Delta 1830-1885.* London: Oxford University Press, 1956.

DEWHURST, J.V., "Report of Settlement of Land Dispute between the Communities of Kpuite, in Tee and Deke in Gokana under the Boundaries Settlement Ordinance 13 Oct. 1936, N.A.F. File 28032 CS026/3 Ogodist Opobo Div., Calabar Prov. Rp. 6401. Pp. 37-43.

EKECHI, F.K. Missionary Enterprise and Rivalry in Igboland, 1857-1914 London: Frank Cass & Co. Ltd. 1972.

EKEJIUBA, F.I. "The Aro System of Trading in the Nineteenth Century II" *Ikenga: Journal of African Studies* Vol. 1, 2(1972), pp. 10-21.

ERIM, O.E. "A Pre-Colonial History of the Idoma of Central Nigeria" (Ph.D. Thesis, Dalhouse University, 1977).

EVANS-PRITCHARD, E.E. *The Nuer* London: Oxford University Press, 1971.

EJITUWU, N.C., "The Obolo (Andoni) of the Eastern Niger Delta" (Ph.D. Thesis, University of Lagos, 1977).

FAGE, J.D., *A History of Africa.* London: Hutchinson University Library for Africa, 1985.

_____ "A Commentary on Duarte Pacheco Pereira's Account of the Lower Guinea Coastlands in his *Esmeraldo de Situ Orbis* and some other early Accounts" *History in Africa* Vol. 7 (1980), pp. 47-77.

_____ "Slavery and Slave Trade in the Context of West Africa" *J.A.H.* Vol. X, 3(1969), pp. 393-404.

GABEL, Creighton and BENNET, Normal R. (eds.). *Reconstructing African Culture History*, Boston Massachusetts: Boston University Press 1967.

GREENBERG, J.H. *The Languages of Africa* 2nd edn. Bloomington Indiana University Press, 1966.

HARLAN, Jack R. "The Origins of Indigenous African Agriculture" in *The Cambridge History of Africa* Vol. 1: from the Earliest Times to c.500 B.C., (ed.) J. Desmond Clark (Gen. eds.) J.D. Fage & Roland Oliver. (London: Cambridge University Press, 1982), pp. 624-657.

HARTOUNGH, J.C.C. "Report on Agricultural Development in the Niger Delta Area" (Port Harcourt: Niger Delta Development Board, 1966).

HENIGE, David, *The Chronology of Oral Tradition*: for a Chimera. Oxford: Clarendon Press, 1974.

_____ *Oral Histotriography* Lagos: Longman Nigeria Ltd., 1982.

HORTON, Robin, "From Fishing Village to City-State: A Social History of New Calabar" in Mary Douglas and Phillis M. Kabery (eds). *Man in Africa*. London: Tavistock Publication Ltd. 1969). Pp. 37-58.

HRBEK, Ivan "Towards Periodization of Africa History" in T.O. Ranger (ed.), *Emerging Themes of African History* (Nairobi: East African Publishing House, 1968, pp 37-52.

IKIME, Obaro, *The Isoko People*. Ibadan: Ibadan University Press, 1972.

_____ *Merchant Prince of the Niger Delta*. London: Ibadan Nairobi: Heinemann Educational Books Ltd., 1968

_____ *The Fall of Nigeria.* London: Lusaka, Nairobi. Heinemann Educ. Books Ltd., 1977.

INIKORI, J.E. *Forced Migrations.* London: Hutchinson University Library for Africa, 1982.

IRVINE, F.R. *West Africa Crops* Vol. 2. Oxford University Press, 1969.

ISICHEI, Elizabeth, *Igbo Worlds: An Anthology of Oral Histories, Historical Descriptions.* London: Macmillan Education Ltd. 1977.

_____ *A History of Igbo People.* London and Basingstoke: The Macmillan Press Ltd. 1976.

_____ *Varieties of Christian Experience in Nigeria* (ed.) London & Basingstoke: The Macmillan Press Ltd. 1982.

JEFFREYS, M.D.W., "OGONI POTIERY: A Note" *MAN* Vol. 47, pp. 84-102 (June, 1947), pp. 81-83.

_____ "The Umundri Tradition of Origin", *African Studies* Vol. 15, 3(1956), pp. 119-131.

JOHNSON, The Rev. Samuel, *The History of the Yorubas.* Dr. O. Johnson (ed.), London: Routledge & Kegan Paul Ltd., 1973. (Isr edn. 1921).

JONES, G.I., *The Trading States of the Oil Rivers: A Study of Political Development in Eastern Nigeria.* London: Oxford University Press, 1963.

_____ "Time and Oral Tradition with Special Reference to Eastern Nigeria"*J.A.H.,* Vol. VI, 2(1965), pp. 153-160.

JONES and HULHULL, H. "An Examination of the Physical Type of Certain Peoples of Southeastern Nigeria" *Journal of Royal Anthropological Institute* Vol 79, (1849), pp. 11-18.

KALU, Ogbu, "Protestant Christianity in Igboland" in Ogbu Kalu (ed.) *Christianity in West Africa*. Ibadan: Daystar Press, 182), pp. 308-320.

LAN David, *Guns and Rain: Guerillas and Spirit Mediums in Zimbabwe*. London: James Currey Ltd., University of California Press, Berkeley and Los Angeles, 1985.

LATHAM, A.J.H., *Old Calabar, 1600-1891: The Impact of the International Economy upon a Traditional Society* Oxford: Clarandon Press, 1975.

LEWIS, Herbert S. "Ethnography and African Culture History" in Gabel and Bennett (eds.) *Reconstructing African Culture History*. (Boston: Boston University Press 1967), pp. 25-44.

LLOYD, P.C. "The Portuguese in Warri" *Odu: Journal of Yoruba and Related Studies*. No. 4, (1957) pp. 28-33.

LOIELLO, John "Bishop in Two Worlds: Samuel Ajayi Crowther. (c. 1806-1891)" in Elizabeth Isichei (ed.) *Varieties of Christian Experience in Nigeria*. London: 1982). Pp. 34-61.

LOOL, G.N. "Timothy Naakuu Paul Birabi of Ogoni" in T.N. Tamuno and E.J. Alagoa (eds.), *Eminent Nigerians of the Rivers State*. Ibadan; Heinemann Educational Books (Nig. Ltd., 1980), pp. 125-134.

_____ *A History of the Ogoni* (Port Harcourt, 1981).

MCCALL, Daniel F. *Africa in Time Perspective: A Discussion of Historical Reconstruction from Unwritten Sources*. New York: Oxford Univ. Press, 1969.

MILLER, J.C. (ed.) *The African Past Speaks:* Folkestone Kent, England: Wm. Dawson and Son Ltd., 1980.

_____ *Kings and Kinsmen: Early Mbundu States in Angola*. London: Oxford University Press, 1976.

MEEK, C.K. *The Northern Tribes of Nigeria* 2 Vols. London: Oxford University Press, 1925.

MEILLASSOUX, Claude, *The Development of Indigenous Trade and Markets in West Africa.* Madison: University of Wisconsin Press, 1971.

MIERS, Suzanne and KOPYTOFF, Igor (eds.) *Slavery in Africa: Historical and Anthropological Perspectives.* Madison: University of Wisconsin Press, 1977.

MACEVEDY, Colin, *The Penguin Atlas of African History.* Harmondsworth England, Penguin Books Ltd. 1980.

MERRIAM, Alan P. "The Use of Music as a Technique of Reconstructing Culture History in Africa" in Creighton Gabel and Norman R. Bennett (eds.) *Reconstructing African Culture History.* (Boston, 1967), pp. 83-114.

NOAH, Monday, Efiong, *Old Calabar: The City-State and the Europeans 1800-1885.* Uyo: Scholars Press, Wig) Ltd., 1980.

NORTHRUP, David. *Trade without Rulers: Pre-Colonial Economic Development in South-Eastern Nigeria.* Oxford: Clarendon Press, 1978.

NDIOMU, A.M. "Development Strategy for the Niger Delta Basin" (Port Harcourt: Niger Delta Basin Development Authority (NDBA), 1980).

NGOFA, O.O. *The People of Eleme* (Rivers State Newspaper, 1988).

NZWUNWA, N. The Niger Delta Pre-Historic Economy and Culture: Cambridge Monographs in African Archaeology I BAR International Series 75, 1980.

_____ *A Source Book for Nigerian Archaeology.* Nigeria: Standard Printing and Publishing Co. Ltd.

_____ "Organization of Pre-Historic Research in Nigeria" *Kiabara* Vol. 4, 2(1981), pp. 203-215.

NZIMIRO, Ikenna, *Studies in Ibo Political Systems: Chieftaincy and Politics in Four Niger Delta States.* London: Frank Cass & Co., Ltd. 1972.

NOSS, Philip A. "The Perception of History Among the Gbaya of Cameroon" *Tarikh* Vol 8 (1987), pp. 24-36.

ODUYOYE, Modupe. "The Planting of Christianity in Yoruland, 1842-1888" in Ogbu Kalu (ed.). *Christianity in West Africa: The Nigerian Story.* Ibadan: Daystar Press, 1978), pp. 239-302.

OGOT, Bethwell A., *History of the Southern Luo* Vol. 1: Migration and Settlement, 1500-1900. Nairobi: East African Publishing House, 1967.

OGUNBA, Onyia, "Ceremonies" in S.O. Biobaku (ed.) *Sources of Yoruba History.* London: Oxford University Press, 1973.

OTTENBERG, Simon and PHOEBE, "Afikpo Markets" in Paul Bohannan and George Daston (eds.). *Markets in Africa* (North-Western Univ. Press, 1962 2nd Printing 1965), pp. 118-169.

ONWUEJEOGWU, M.A. "The Dating of Oral Tradition" *Tarikh*, Vol. 8, (1987) pp. 53-67.

POLANYI, Karl. Ports of Trade in Early Societies." *Journal of Economic History,* Vol. XIII, 1 (1963), pp. 30-31.

POLANYI, Karl, *et al* (eds.), *Trade and Markets in Early Empires* Glenioe, Illinois: The Free Press, 1957.

RICHARDS, Audreyi. "Social Mechanisms for the Transfer of Political Rights in Some African Tribes" *Journal of the Royal Anth. Institute* (1960), pp. 175-190.

ROBERTS, Andrew. *A History of Bemba Political Growth and Change in North-Eastern Zambia before 1900.* London: Longman Group Ltd., 1973.

RODNEY, Walter. *A History of the Upper Guinea Coast, 1545-1800.* New York & London: Monthly. Review Press, 1970.

_____ "A Reconsideration of the Mane Invasion of Sierra Leone" *Journal of African History,* Vol. VIII, 2(1967), 219-246.

RYDER, AFF. C. *Benin and the Europeans 1485-1897.* London: Longman Group Ltd., 1977.

_____ "The Trans-Atlantic Slave Trade" in Obaro Ikime (ed.), *Groundwork of Nigerian History* (Ibadan: Heinemann (Nig.) Ltd., 1980). Pp. 236-246.

SCOTT, J.S. "Report on the Fisheries of the Niger Delta Special Area" (Niger Delta Development Board, 1966).

SIMMONS, D. An Ethnographic Sketch of the Efik people" in Daryll Forde (ed.) *Efik Traders of Old Calabar* (for International African Institute London: Oxford University Press, (1956), pp. 1-26.

SMITH, M.G. Government in Zazzau 1800-1950. London: Oxford University Press, for International African Institute, 1960.

SMITH, Robert. "The Canoe in West African History" *J.A.H.* Vol. XI, 4(1970), pp. 515-533.

SMITH, E.H. Captain, "Extract of Aka and Ogoni Report to the Hon. Provincial Commissioner, Calabar, dated 14th March, 1907" in "Intelligence Report on Ogoni" Ogodist File R.P. 6402/Vol. II, Opobo Division, Calabar Province.

TALBOT, P. Amaury, *The Peoples of Southern Nigeria,* 3 Vols. London: Oxford University Press, 1926.

TASIE, G.O.M. *Christian Missionary Enterprise in the Niger Delta, 1864-1981.* Leiden, The Netherlands: E.J. Brill, 1978.

_____ "The Church in the Niger Delta" in Ogbu Kalu (ed.) *Christianity in West Africa: The Nigerian Story* Ibadan: Daystar Press, 1978, pp. 323-332.

TONWE II M.D.K. "Kono Boue Customary Laws" (Unpublished Manuscript dated June, 1950).

_____ "Some Festivals in My Clan" (Unpublished Type Written Document, dated 16th Jan., 1964).

UME, Kalu E. *The Rise of British Colonialism in Southern Nigeria 1700-1900.* Smithtown, New York: Exposition Press, 1980.

VANSINA, Jan, *Oral Tradition As History.* London: James Currey Ltd., 1985.

_____ *The Children Woot: A History of the Kuba Peoples.* Madison: University of Wisconsin Press, 1978.

_____ "Recording the Oral History of the Bakuba I: Methods" *J.A.H.* Vol. 1, 2(1960), pp. 257-270.

VANSINA, J. MAUNY, R. and THOMAS, L.V. (eds.). *The Historian in Tropical Africa,* London, for Ibadan, Accra: International African Institute. Oxford University Press, 1964.

WESCOTT, Roger W. "African Language and African Pre-History" in Gabel and Bennett (eds.) *Reconstructing African Culture History.* (Boston, 1967), pp. 45-54.

WILLIAMSON, KAY, "Languages of the Niger Delta" *Nigeria Magazine* No. 97 (1968), pp. 124-130.

_____ "Some Food Plant Names in the Niger Delta" *International Journal of American Linguistics* Vol. 36, 2(1970), pp 156-167.

_____ "Linguistic Evidence of the Pre-History of the Niger Delta" in E.J. Alagoa, F.N. Anozie and N. Nzewunwa (eds.) *The Early History of the Niger Delta* (Helmut Buske Verlag Hamburg, 1988), pp. 65-119.

WOLFF, Hans: "Synopsis of Ogoni Languages" *Journal of African Languages* Vol. III, 1 (1964), pp. 38-51

_____ "Niger Delta Languages T. Classification. "

INDEX

A

Aan-kpugi, 186, 267–68
Aba, 240, 254, 278, 321
Abiriba, 102, 230, 292
Abolition, 318, 320, 332
Abua, 252, 254, 269, 277
Accessories, 41, 229, 233
Activities, social, 284, 287, 313, 315
Adzes, 229, 232, 255
A'ean Gbigbo, 41, 97
Afigbo, 103, 109, 200, 229–30, 237, 292, 324
African societies, 2, 41, 69, 80
Agaelee, 142, 147
Agbonchia, 142, 146–47, 241
Agents, 51, 183, 201, 236, 238–42, 321
  colonial, 321, 323, 326
Agreement, 101, 120, 153, 187, 191
Agricultural lands, 51, 145, 182, 186, 242, 274–75, 292
Agriculture, 11–12, 50, 92, 101, 104, 114, 117, 151, 153, 164, 185, 244, 263
Akwete, 240–42
Alagoa, 1, 15, 79–80, 94, 141, 196, 243, 246–47, 251–52, 258, 307, 318
Alesa, 142, 147, 243–44
Alode, 142, 145–46
Ancestors, 2–3, 6, 15–16, 40–41, 58, 79–80, 97–98, 105–6, 110–12, 116–18, 120, 143–44, 157–58, 197–98, 280
  early, 29, 128, 315
  founding, 103, 106, 113, 126
  original, 98, 142, 156, 302
Ancestor worship, 15, 198
Ancestral spirits, 26, 29, 40, 155, 158, 195, 268, 279
Ancient times, 18, 102, 171, 203, 212, 294, 310–11
Ancient town, 44, 130, 295

Andoni, 9, 77, 79–80, 227, 254, 269–70, 292
Angle, 37, 51, 225
Animals, 12, 35, 38, 62, 70, 188–92, 236–37, 296–99
  domestic, 12, 53, 81, 277
  owner of, 189–92
Apoi, 246–47, 252
Application, 2, 189–91, 264
Appointments, 51, 152–54, 324
Area, producing, 251, 257, 317
Arms, 34, 37, 47, 56, 76, 276, 312
  executive, 300, 312–13
Army, 57, 108, 122, 160
Artists, 49, 71, 74, 231
Asa, 203, 230, 272, 292, 321
Aspirant, 34–35, 199, 238
Assobienee, 300, 302, 304–6, 308, 310, 313
Atee, 127–28, 138–39, 157–59, 161–63, 173, 244
Atee of Kpong, 183, 242–43
Atlantic slave trade, 127–28, 243
Attack, 37, 162, 167, 171, 177, 324–25
Attendants, 37–38, 63, 123
Authority, 30, 32, 40, 54–55, 70, 100, 120, 153, 179–80, 184, 238, 301, 304, 308–9, 311
  highest, 301, 308–9
Autochthonous peoples, 132, 134–36, 138–39, 145–48, 189
Autochthony, traditions of, 97–98, 111
Awka, 230, 240, 272
Azumini Rivers, 242, 320

B

Baan, 31–32, 106, 135, 138–39, 157, 160–62, 166, 168, 171, 173, 175
Baan communities, 161
Baan-Goi, 132, 134, 139, 161, 173
Baan wars, 93, 95–96, 138–39, 155–56, 159, 161, 165–68, 175–76, 293,

297–98, 300–301, 303, 305, 309–10, 313
Babbe, 4, 31, 103, 135, 154, 184, 295
Baene, 98–99, 127–28, 157, 159–60, 162–63, 173, 193, 244, 251, 320
Baikie, 74, 79, 102
Bamboo mats, 233–34, 237
Ban, 127, 157, 160–61, 310
Bananas, 12, 199–200
Bangha, 74, 78, 82, 84–87, 94–96, 129, 134, 138–39, 149, 164, 168, 184, 236, 238, 259
Bangha areas, 32, 129, 138
Bangha market, 85–86, 89, 149, 239, 242
Bani, 74, 82, 90, 168, 171
Bank, 98, 239, 242, 253
  West, 98–99, 141
Banquet, 60, 62–63
Baraboue, 85, 92, 98, 149, 164, 166, 168, 170, 172, 295, 303
Barbot, 76, 79, 81–82, 90, 95, 191, 201–2, 253, 263, 318
Bari, 14, 26, 107
Barike, 85, 92, 164
Bariyaayoo, 52, 126, 128, 151, 154–55, 175
  Seat of, 162, 173, 309
Bariyaayoo dynasty, 21, 120, 154–55, 175, 293, 309
Baskets, 234, 237
Battle, 43, 67, 146, 175, 296, 306, 314
Bearer, 15, 31–32, 100
Belief, 14, 26, 29, 52, 54
Bells, 62, 238, 295
Bende, 91, 240–41, 272, 320–21
Benue-Congo Branch, 13–14, 108
Berbery, 76, 83, 107, 277
Bight of Bonny, 75, 79, 95, 110
Birth, 118–19, 142, 191, 289, 300
Bodo, 12, 193, 241–43, 251
Bohannan, 264, 275
Bomu, 84, 193, 237, 239, 251, 263
Bonny, 74–82, 90–91, 94–95, 174–75, 178–80, 182, 196, 201, 242–44, 269–70, 317, 319, 321–23, 329, 331–32
  chiefs of, 163, 242, 321
  king of, 182
Bonny Island, 78–79
Bonny River, 12–13, 75, 77–78, 84, 90, 95, 248, 258
Bonny traders, 174, 179, 242
Boonen, 84, 103, 148–49
Boue, 2, 4, 21, 23, 31–32, 92–93, 139, 148–49, 156, 162–66, 168–71, 174–76, 299–300, 309–10, 325
Boue area, 92–93, 149, 164–65, 168, 170, 172–73, 179, 236, 242, 244, 313
Boue Kingdom, 31, 139, 175–76, 302–3, 310–13
Boue leaders, 94, 175
Boue towns, 172, 211, 310, 325
Boys, 26, 65, 67, 294–96, 325
Bozy, 76, 81–82, 259, 277
Branch, 26, 129, 137, 149, 156, 252, 261, 312
Brave, 41, 66, 133, 296
Bravery, 286, 294–95
Bride wealth, 22–24, 44, 54
British Colonial Conquest, 323, 328, 332
British colonial forces, 311, 323–24
Bronzes, 196, 265–66, 280
Brothers, 84, 98–99, 101, 103–4, 106, 117, 119, 123, 127, 130, 135, 141–43, 148, 151, 157
Buan, 125, 154, 204, 211
Building, 11, 26, 176–77, 323
Bulk, 5, 31, 53–54, 134, 137, 160, 169, 185, 226, 229, 234, 237, 250, 263
Bunu, 129, 138–39
Bush meat, 116, 294
Business, 95, 121, 191, 193, 250
  canoe-making, 231, 254

Index 379

Buyers, 171, 192, 194, 226, 229, 233, 239, 248, 250, 256, 278

C

Calabar, 88, 94, 96, 254, 319, 322, 324, 327
Cameroons, 13, 79, 112, 193, 235, 251–52, 254, 260
Camps, 102, 118, 124, 133, 241
Candidates, 33–35, 56–58, 117, 122, 307
Canoe house, 246–47
Canoe industry, 50, 194, 245, 247, 249, 251–53, 255, 257, 259, 261, 277
Canoe manufacture, 231, 254
Canoes, 11–12, 76, 79, 100, 105, 113, 115, 179, 186, 192–93, 226–27, 231–33, 236–37, 245–59, 276–77
  largest, 78–79, 229, 250, 253
  making, 231, 251–52, 254, 257
Capital, 86, 178–79, 310, 313
Carving, 11, 203, 231
Cases, 2, 5, 25, 28, 134, 160–61, 181, 187, 197, 205, 275, 306, 309–10, 312
Cassava, 12, 199–200, 236–37, 248, 259
Cause, 27, 87, 118, 146, 162, 166, 213, 228, 233, 249, 256, 289, 310
Central Delta, 80, 246–47, 252, 257
Centres, 63, 67, 77, 125–26, 148, 154, 156, 204, 206, 227, 236, 304, 310, 320, 327
  Religious, 115, 130, 325–26
Ceremonies, 2–3, 20, 38–41, 59–60, 117, 120, 130–31, 153, 283, 308–9
Charge, 53, 306, 328
Chief Iyoro, 39–40, 63, 65, 67
Chief Kiriki, 42, 58, 60, 63, 187
Chief Kpugita, 36, 39
Chiefs and elders, 4, 63, 152, 162, 167, 173, 295
Christian missions, 43–44, 322–23, 327–28

Circulation, 90, 185–86, 263–65
Cities, big, 84, 168, 251
Citizens, 40, 139, 153, 161, 167, 198, 242, 277, 283–85, 289, 292, 306, 308, 311, 327–28
City, 48, 73, 84–86, 108, 122, 164, 177
Civil war, 44, 53, 93, 105, 143, 146, 161, 171, 235, 293
Clan, 3, 52, 191, 198
Class, 22, 50–51, 55–56, 68, 200, 202, 275, 280, 284–85, 288–89, 291, 307, 311, 315, 318
  elite, 51, 311, 313
  ruling, 117, 197, 280, 285
Climax, 38, 59, 66, 332
Cloths, 11, 24, 53, 62, 64, 66, 169–70, 241
Club, 62, 70, 287–88, 298
Coast, 77–78, 84–85, 92–93, 95, 103, 108, 149, 164, 167, 172, 181–82, 234, 239–40, 263, 266
Coastal trade, 93, 165, 168, 251
Coastal waters, 92, 164, 192, 236, 246

Cocoyams, 60, 92, 164, 199–200, 236, 248
  Old, 66, 167, 200
Colonial administration, 44, 182, 325–28
Colonial administrators, 107, 182, 320, 326–27
Colonial times, 31, 185–86, 192, 264–65, 268
Colonists, 128, 151, 157, 159, 162
Colony, 139, 151
Commodities, 75, 185, 236, 263
Commoners, 55, 284–85, 326
Communities, 19, 22, 26–27, 30–34, 56–57, 138, 141–42, 153, 160–61, 258, 260–61, 274–75, 284, 287–90, 310–11
Company, 145, 189, 232, 255, 261, 319
Compounds, 51, 54, 67–68, 80, 111, 196
Comrades, 133, 177, 180, 295

Conditions, 24, 41, 142, 187, 190, 199, 204, 231, 273, 292, 320, 327–28
Confinement, 60–62, 238
Conflict, 129, 146, 292
Confusion, 43, 94, 96
Connection, 2, 75, 78, 90, 103–5, 111, 114, 116, 123–25, 154, 182, 201, 238, 314, 329
Conquest, 69, 87, 129, 132–33, 135, 139, 145, 147–48, 176–77, 181, 325–26, 328, 332
  colonial, 18, 31, 175, 293, 312, 316, 329
  wars of, 132–33, 147, 177, 327
Consultations, 131, 151–52, 290
Contacts, 4, 26, 85, 102, 115, 124–25, 136, 239, 275, 292, 321, 328
Context, 12, 14, 54, 91, 179, 300, 314
Cords, 234, 237–38
Cost, 57–58, 192, 237, 248
Country, 30, 52, 68, 100, 114–15, 178, 248, 285, 301, 319, 324, 328–29
Coup, 162, 173, 308, 313
Cowries, 266, 270–71
Cows, 12, 21, 27, 36, 40, 42, 76, 78, 188–90, 201, 236, 239, 277
Creeks, 75–76, 78, 85, 92, 164, 248, 276–77, 325
Criminals, 238, 309
  condemned, 21, 89, 239
Crisis, 21, 53, 106, 110, 156, 161, 242, 306
Crops, 5, 12, 50, 186–87, 194, 199–201, 274, 278, 317
  minor, 92, 164, 202
  permanent tree, 24, 268, 277, 279
Cross River, 51, 78, 94–96, 108, 230, 317, 321
Cross River Basin, 79, 252, 254
Crowds, 62, 66, 226
Culture, 2, 6–7, 14, 45, 50, 52, 69, 71, 74, 77, 83, 86, 111, 124–25, 138–40
Currencies, 185–86, 234, 264–67
Customs, 6, 34, 112, 124–25, 129, 143, 226

D

Daggers, 76, 83, 277
Dam yaa, 58, 60–61, 63–64
Dance, 64–65, 99, 131, 287, 295, 311
Dapper, 76, 79, 82, 88, 90–95, 165, 168, 232, 255, 263, 267
Date, 22, 36, 43, 54, 62–63, 69, 109–10, 118, 161, 163, 204, 206, 301, 309, 314
  earliest, 109–11
Daughters, 18, 20–22, 36, 44, 52–55, 68, 145, 151, 213, 241, 293, 303
  first, 52, 126, 128, 151, 154, 293
  firstborn, 53–55, 59, 66
Days, 5, 16–17, 19–20, 39–40, 60, 63, 69–71, 121, 166, 169–71, 179, 200, 211–12, 225, 298–99
  five, 17, 225, 299
Dealers, 127, 194, 256, 278
Death, 16, 27–28, 34, 42, 49, 52–53, 58, 120, 122, 151, 154–55, 239, 293, 309
Decisions, 131, 153–54, 290, 302, 312–14, 320
Decline, 12, 41–43, 48, 193, 235, 251, 328, 331–32
Decorations, 116, 203–6, 211, 267
Deeko, 17, 169, 224–25, 299
Deeko days, 225–26
Deemua, 17, 106, 223, 299, 306
Defence, 47, 125, 173, 183, 247, 313
Degree, 6, 137, 211, 265, 280, 288, 290
Deity, 62, 106, 121–25, 131, 157–58, 301
Delta, 53, 79–80, 178, 193, 206, 246–47, 251, 257
Delta states, 201, 318, 321–22, 328, 332
Depots, 163, 317–18
Depth, 1, 212, 233, 256
Descendants, 16, 27, 31–32, 34, 39–41, 123, 128, 144, 146–47, 149, 154, 242, 252, 307, 312

Description, 6, 50, 77, 90–91, 95, 111, 194, 239, 266, 276, 322
Destruction, 164, 324–27
Digging, 93, 165, 232, 255
Dike, 94, 293, 318
Distribution, 50, 183, 236, 254, 326
District, 57–59, 62, 74, 90, 137, 149, 178, 320–21
Divorce cases, 23, 305–6
Drinks, 40, 58–59, 61, 144, 189–90, 287, 297
Drums, 2, 40, 130, 156, 231

Duarte Pacheco Pereira, 21, 73, 86–87, 90, 235, 239, 248, 258, 276
Duties, 19, 23, 313–14
Dynasty, 126, 154, 157, 175
  new, 128, 161, 176, 180

E

Early European Travellers, 73, 78, 82, 86, 94
Earth, 14–16, 21, 28, 238–39
  red, 192, 248, 259
Earthen pots, 225–26, 228, 249
Eastern arm, 75, 95, 248, 276
Eastern Delta, 9, 171, 179, 201, 231, 246, 252, 257
Eastern Igbo, 91–92, 102, 230, 267, 270, 272
Economic Activities, 184–85, 187, 189, 191, 193, 195, 197, 199, 201, 203, 205, 207, 209, 257, 260
Economic development, 246, 254, 257
Economy, 48, 74, 92, 164, 169, 186, 266, 268, 273, 280
Education, 23, 322–23, 329
  Western, 44, 48, 327–28
Effik market, 95–96
Efik, 271
Ego, 270, 272–73
Egwanga, 228, 312, 321, 325

Ejituwu, 77, 79
Elders, 4, 24–25, 27, 33, 57–64, 69–70, 105–6, 151–52, 155, 166–67, 285–87, 295–96, 298–310, 312–16, 331
  council of, 23, 25
Elders of Boue, 23, 175–76
Eleme, 4, 13, 20, 31, 110, 135–37, 141–47, 154–55, 179, 184, 269
Eleme area, 145–48, 152, 160, 189, 195, 198, 241–42, 244, 290
Eleme society, 242, 290
Elites, 44, 56, 68, 237, 244, 285, 315
Emergence, 32, 135–36, 147–49, 259, 297, 300, 310, 312, 331
Emergency, 15, 33–34, 70, 289, 312
Emigrants, 124, 129, 138–39, 144, 149, 160
Enemies, 27, 33–34, 56, 67, 162, 172–73, 177, 289, 296
Energies, 42, 121, 159, 195, 279, 323
Environment, 41, 54, 85–86, 308
Epidemics, 15, 27, 85, 87, 306
Equatorial Guinea, 85, 193, 251
Era, 1, 128, 132, 156, 196, 317, 320
Escape, 87, 143, 145, 173
Establishment, 111, 119, 152–53, 156–57, 161, 260, 308, 313
Etabajo, 145–48, 160
Ethnic group, 31, 74, 81, 83, 201
Europe, 89–90, 95, 235, 266
Europeans, 77, 90, 94, 169–70, 174, 178, 201–2, 239–40, 242, 259–60, 263–65, 267, 320–21
  arrival of, 264–66, 281
European traders, 74–75, 319–20
European travellers, 79, 321–22
Events, 2–3, 19, 49, 89–90, 94, 108, 123, 158, 161, 301
Evidence, 21, 23, 51–52, 77–78, 80, 100, 102, 111, 114, 116, 125–26, 143, 157–59, 202–5, 314
  internal, 130, 133–35, 138, 301, 315
  linguistic, 81, 83, 108, 110, 112, 144

Evil, 26–27, 34, 131
Excavations, 110–11, 206
  archaeological, 109–10, 204
Exchange, 22, 78, 183, 247, 258, 266
  medium of, 263, 265, 267, 269, 271, 273, 275, 277, 279, 281
Execution, 42, 67, 309–10, 313
Exercise, 21, 29, 66, 151, 184
Exile, 142–43, 163
Expansion, 107, 117, 120, 126, 128–29, 137, 233, 256, 260
Expedition, 114, 117, 299
Experience, 21, 175, 284, 286, 322, 328
  traditional, 286, 289
Experiments, 33, 35
Expert canoe-makers, 192, 232, 255, 259
Experts, 70, 232, 237, 255
Export, 11, 51, 235, 241
Extinct, 11, 73, 115, 134, 242
Eyaa, 145, 147–48

F

Factors, 3–4, 6, 42–43, 48–49, 52–53, 69, 77–78, 111, 116, 124, 180, 287, 317–18, 329
Families, 12, 19–22, 42, 58, 63, 67, 77, 85, 87, 119, 143, 188, 191, 290, 295
  royal, 117, 119, 126
Famine, 15, 27, 306
Farmers, 12, 51, 62, 171, 178, 198–99, 237, 314
Farming season, 5, 51, 91, 275, 288
Farmlands, 84, 143, 148, 187, 202, 275
Farms, 5, 12, 48, 53, 127, 187, 192, 199, 202, 237, 248–49, 288, 306, 310, 317–18
Father, 3, 18, 31–32, 35, 53–54, 100, 106, 114, 121, 133, 179, 300–301
  Blood, 22, 53, 105, 114, 117
Feast, 2, 17, 38, 154–55, 157, 294–95

Feast of yonwidam, 2, 17, 294, 296, 298
Fencing, 61, 83, 286–87, 314
Festivals, 2–3, 15, 71, 231
Fieldwork, 1, 5–6
Fight, 43, 127, 303, 314
Firearms, 94, 174–75, 182–83, 196, 242, 293, 297
  Introduction of, 94, 229, 293, 297
Firing, 225–26, 233, 255–56, 260
Firstborn sons, 53–54, 58, 63
Fish, 13, 36, 62–63, 92, 116, 155, 164, 168–71, 195, 237, 248, 257–58, 264, 292
  Smoked, 92, 164, 169, 238
Fishermen, 12, 70, 169, 253–54, 263, 294
Fishing, 12–13, 50, 77, 81, 92, 164, 193, 251, 257–59, 292, 318
Fishing canoes, small, 50, 192, 245, 248
Fish rackets, 233–34, 238, 259
Fish traps, 233–34, 237–38, 259
Foodstuffs, 5, 92, 164, 171, 236, 258, 276
Foofoo, 200, 279
Forest, 11, 29, 38, 84, 100, 106, 115, 118, 120–25, 131–32, 144, 232, 254, 297, 299
  sacred, 40, 122–23
Fortifications, 3, 174
Founders, 58–59, 100, 102–5, 122–24, 126, 138–40, 142, 144, 176–77, 180, 284, 298–300, 305, 308, 313
Founding, 32, 104, 116, 118, 120, 123, 128, 132, 141, 158, 160, 176, 183, 283, 313
Free trade, 319–20
Funerals, 26–27, 32, 117, 122, 288

G

Gaen, 85, 92, 164
Gan, 54, 58, 143, 156, 299, 302–4, 307
Gan Kónò, 303–4
Garri, 200, 236, 248, 259

Gbam, 92, 164, 231, 254
Gbamene, 85, 92, 149, 164
Gbee, 90, 134, 143, 180, 263
Gbene, 30, 32, 34, 39-42, 47, 283, 303
Gbeneakpana, 32-33, 104-6, 114, 116, 118-19, 121-22, 124-25, 283, 314
Gbeneakpong, 157-58
Gbeneatekina, 119, 283
Gbenebai Kara, 248, 252-53
Gbenebalikina, 174-75, 297-300
Gbenebeka, 52, 59, 154-55, 176
Gbenegarakara, 93, 149, 165
Gbenegoo, 93, 149, 312-13
Gbeneitekina, 98, 106
Gbenekarayoo, 93, 149, 165
Gbenekiri, 3, 32, 149, 156, 175, 299-300
  Leadership of, 156, 293
Gbenekote, 172, 303
Gbenekuapie, 32, 130-32, 138, 181
  era of, 132, 140, 181
  time of, 131, 135
Gbenekwaanwaa, 114, 126, 151, 155, 176, 293
Gbenemene, 30, 32, 55, 152, 284-85
Gbeneoleghere, 100-102
Gbenesaagba, 32, 98-99, 140
Gbenesaakoo, 32, 103-4, 132-34, 148-49, 176-77, 179-80
  name of, 145, 181
Gbeneteenwaawo, 42-43
Gbeneteetagana, 43, 104, 123
Gbenetibarakan, 149, 165, 172
Gbenetigina, 93, 149, 165
Gbenetiginagua, 32, 119, 138-39
Gbene title, 3, 15-16, 21, 27-35, 37-45, 48, 89, 100, 111, 115, 117, 130, 176, 238-39, 307
Gbeneyaaloo, 104, 106, 113-14, 116-20, 122-23, 126, 151-56, 160, 293
Gbeneyaanwaaka, 104, 123
Gbeneyana, 154, 176

Gbeneyiranam, 105-6, 111, 114, 118, 120-23
Gbigbo, 34, 41, 98
Gboo-Msia, 142, 147
Generation, 2-3, 16, 27, 32-35, 70-71, 106, 119, 124, 136, 199
Gentlemen, 55-56, 83, 285-87, 312
Ghana, 75, 104-7
Ghana origin, traditions of old, 104, 111
Giaradaa, 185, 264
Gibbons, 52, 107, 173, 290, 323-24, 326, 328
Gifts, 49, 62, 65, 188, 241, 295
Gin, 11, 36-37, 189, 315
Giokoo, 84, 86, 129, 132-34, 176-77, 179-80
Giokpee, 142-44, 147
Goats, 21, 25, 27, 36, 40, 76, 78, 81, 168, 174, 188, 236, 239, 310, 318
God, 14-16, 26, 38, 49, 54, 67, 158, 291
Goi, 134, 138, 237
Gokana, 31, 34, 84-87, 91-92, 101-4, 129, 132-37, 139, 142-47, 167-68, 176-77, 179-81, 183, 185, 234-37
  coast of, 73, 86, 92
  founder of, 84, 132, 180
  king of, 32, 177, 180
Gokana area, 84, 90, 132, 134, 137, 145-48, 160, 179, 237, 242
Gokana kingdom, 176, 181
Gokana language, 13, 81, 85, 136, 147-48, 164, 259
Gokana markets, 236-37
Gokana origins, 86, 143
Gokana sources, 133, 143
Gokana speakers, 147-48
Gokana towns, 94, 133-34, 177, 180
Gold Coast, 107, 232, 255, 266
Goods, 21, 168-70, 192, 201, 229, 234-35, 241-42, 245-46, 248, 250, 257, 259, 264, 266, 276
  exotic, 89, 169

ritual, 12, 35–37, 239
Governance, 54, 294, 301–2, 305, 307, 312
Government, 31, 104, 152, 154, 284–85, 293, 304, 311, 324, 326–28
  colonial, 324, 327
  functions of, 151, 285, 301, 305
Governor, first Military, 248, 253, 260
Grave, 28, 111, 117, 293
Ground, 26, 119–20, 149, 153, 165, 186–87, 206, 212, 229, 234, 250, 268
Groups, 62, 85–86, 99, 123–24, 140, 145, 160–61, 229–30, 251–52, 285, 287–88, 292, 295, 300, 304–5
  small, 115, 118, 122, 124, 300, 307, 321
Guests, 38–40, 59
Guinea, 90, 248, 259, 266
Gun, 43, 174–75, 183, 243, 298, 305, 316, 331
Gure, 40, 52, 104, 116, 118–24, 126–28, 140, 151–52, 154–56, 162–63, 283, 293, 327
Gurete, 157–58, 163
Gwaara, 52, 120, 123–25, 155, 176

H

Harvest, 187, 194, 198–99, 278
Heads, 4, 37, 53, 59, 65, 80, 84–85, 247, 296, 298, 300, 305, 307, 310, 312
Heirs, 22, 42, 53, 68, 119, 175
Hinterland, 21, 76, 78, 163–64, 169, 184, 196, 201, 235, 237, 239, 242, 246–47, 317, 319–21
Hinterland markets, 201, 319
Hinterland peoples, 168–70, 196, 321–22
Hinterland producers, 319–20
History, 2–3, 31, 41, 47, 74, 77, 124, 158, 259, 283, 297, 327, 331
Home, 18, 20, 24, 35–36, 40, 59, 62, 64, 68, 212, 233, 237, 240, 253, 256

Honour, 33, 299, 315
House, 19–20, 28, 30–31, 57, 59, 64, 80–81, 87, 144, 183, 298–304, 306–7, 309, 311, 314–15
House-fathers, 48, 57–58, 60–64, 66, 69
Households, 76, 80, 203, 213, 235, 245, 276, 290–91, 294
House of Elders, 298, 300–304, 306–10, 312–16, 331
House of Hunters, 297–300, 315, 331
House of Lieutenants, 312–13, 315–16, 331
Housewives, 169, 228, 235, 249
Human victims, 21, 35–36, 38, 89
Hunters, 4, 99–100, 105, 111, 125, 175, 237, 268, 294, 296–300, 315, 331
Hunters' Society, 297–300, 305
Hunting, 34, 42, 104, 294–300, 315
Hunting expeditions, 294, 296, 298–99
Hunting season, 294–95, 299
Husbands, 18–21, 24–25, 53–54, 68, 287

I

Ibani, 74, 80, 136, 170, 178–79, 292
Ibibio, 69, 85, 91–92, 98–99, 102–3, 111, 178, 203, 237, 270–71
Ibibioland, 98, 100–103, 228, 237
Ibibio origin, 97, 101, 103
  traditions of, 98–99, 103
Ibn Battuta, 265–66
Identification, 73–74, 79–81, 83, 90, 213
Identity, 30, 73, 75–79, 81, 83, 85, 87, 89, 91–93, 95, 134, 142, 276, 309
Igbara Abe, 183, 304, 331
Igbo, 16, 50–51, 69, 74, 82, 136, 200–201, 207, 223, 230, 270, 291–92, 326
Igbo hinterland, 85, 181, 240, 253, 291
Igboland, 103, 230, 241
Igo, edo word, 270–71
Ijo, 15, 50, 69, 79, 232, 255, 259, 269–70

Ijo canoe-makers, 232, 255
Ijo communities, 246, 259
Ijo neighbours, 50, 201, 247–48
Ijo peoples, 169–70, 264
Ijo settlement, oldest, 111–12
Ikot Abasi, 271, 312, 325
Ikwerre, 85, 227, 254, 277
Immigrants, 125, 138, 143–45, 147, 149
Imo, 51, 242, 252, 317, 320
Imo River, 9, 12–13, 93, 95, 98–100, 103, 105, 118, 121, 160, 162–63, 171, 173, 252–53, 321–23
Imo River Basin, 252, 254, 260
Implication, 34, 80, 116, 119–20, 145, 164, 178, 206, 230, 257, 286
Inayo, 93, 149, 165
Incident, 18, 23, 43, 103, 105, 113, 118, 128, 142–43, 146, 167, 184, 192, 325
Individuals, 15, 70, 118, 184, 188, 191, 243–44, 246, 268, 273, 275, 291, 294–95, 321
Industrial barks, 92, 164, 248, 259
Industries, 159, 203, 260
    traditional, 260–61
Informants, 3–7, 35, 41, 98–100, 104–6, 187–88, 197–99, 226–27, 232, 235, 241, 253, 255, 288–90, 294–95
Information, 4–5, 20, 23, 34, 36, 70, 74–75, 78, 80, 86–87, 93, 104, 106, 306, 326–27
Inhabitants, 74, 77, 80, 84–85, 134, 163, 172, 182–84, 310
Inheritance, 52–53, 55, 68, 115, 159
Inland, 93, 119, 152, 169, 172, 234
Inland towns, group of, 92, 164
Insignia, 56, 67, 83, 201
Institutions, 15, 29, 34, 105, 112, 203, 293, 296, 312
    political, 176, 293, 299, 315–16
Instructions, 27, 61, 311
Instruments, 39, 62, 153, 205
Intentions, 25, 57, 178, 275, 324

Interviews, 5–7, 98, 252
Introduction, 43–44, 68, 73, 77, 193, 196, 251, 259–60, 298, 304, 315, 317–18, 320, 327, 331–32
Investment, 186, 188, 192–94, 196, 274, 278–79
Ipaan, 35, 41, 222
Iron, 191, 228, 230, 297
Iron bars, 191, 201–2
Isiokpo, 227, 252, 321
Islands, 77–78, 85, 193, 251
Isolation, 141, 258, 291, 322, 328
Items, 20, 24, 169, 233, 266

J

Jaja, 319–20
Jan, 23, 212, 287–88, 295, 299
Javelins, 114, 238, 297
Joko, 178, 303
Jones, 32, 76–77, 90–91, 93–95, 102, 165, 168, 178–79, 263–65, 267, 318
Journey, 36–39, 101, 105, 169, 177, 227, 318, 321–22, 332
Judo, 287–88, 314

K

Kabaari, 30, 34, 47, 49, 307
Kabangha, 82, 95–96, 100, 251, 320
Ka-Gwaara, 59, 176, 325–26
Kako, 85, 92, 149, 164, 295, 310
Ka-kpugi, 185, 264, 267–68
Kalabari, 74, 82, 85, 96, 247, 254
Kalahari, 226–27, 269
Kalbanges, 75, 82, 95
Kalbarch, 75, 82, 95
Kana, 85, 99, 137, 148, 161, 164
Kana language, 13, 98, 135–37, 140, 259, 323
Kana words, 291, 294–95, 307
Khana, 130, 135–37, 140, 144, 156, 160–61, 269

Khana area, 137, 140, 186, 241
Khana immigrants, 129, 134, 138, 145
Killing, 127, 144, 157, 296–97
King, 31–32, 81, 90, 152, 156–57, 161–63, 178–79, 181, 183, 284–85, 300–302, 304–6, 308, 319, 321
   first, 133, 176, 181, 300
Kingdoms, 31–32, 151, 153, 155, 157, 159, 161, 163, 165, 167, 169, 171, 173, 175–77, 179–81
   old, 156, 162–63, 173
   old Kpong, 140, 156, 158, 161
Kingmakers, 308
   traditional, 309
Knives, 232, 238, 255, 297
Knowledge, 2–3, 33, 86, 163, 201, 246, 298
Ko, 50, 98–99, 134, 140–41, 160, 171, 182, 192, 232, 242–43, 245, 248, 251–53, 255–56, 277
   founder of, 140
   king of, 32, 182
Kobɛgɛ, 83–84, 201, 229, 238
Ko canoe industry, 245, 259–60
Kónò, 32, 34, 44, 85, 104, 121–25, 137, 153–54, 156, 168–69, 303, 320, 323
   founding of, 118, 121, 124
   town of, 104–5, 114, 118, 121, 283
   traditions of, 124, 153
Kónò Boue, 87, 168–69, 204, 206–7, 211, 213, 215, 225, 227–28, 244, 249, 296, 298, 310, 313
Kònó Boue, 172–75
Koo, 98, 133, 163, 295
Korokoro, 129–32, 138–39
Kpaankpaan, 311–12
Kpaankpaan secret society, 310–12, 316
Kpa Bina, 40, 130, 307
Kpone-Tonwe, 31, 47, 50–53, 69, 79–80, 84, 86, 228, 249, 253, 259, 276
Kpong, 23, 106, 123, 126–29, 140, 149, 156–63, 173, 176, 183, 242–44, 299

   founder of, 127–28, 156–58
   founding of, 127–28, 157
   king of, 162, 173
Kpong areas, 32, 149, 244
Kpong sources, 127–28, 156–58
Kporo, 186, 196–97, 265, 280
Kugba, 38, 44, 100, 104–6, 110–21, 123–26, 128, 130, 151–52, 204–5, 283, 286, 293, 315, 327
Kuleba, 73, 75, 82, 88–95, 263
Kwaanwaa, 52, 108, 114–15, 118, 293
Kwuri, 92–93, 149, 164–65, 170, 242
Kwuribue, 78, 82, 85, 92–95, 149, 164–65, 167–73, 204, 211, 225, 263, 313
   role of, 93, 149, 165
   town of, 149, 204
Kwuri market, 169–70, 174, 325
Kwuri towns, 92, 164, 170–71

L

Laadem, 205–7, 211–12
Labour, 28, 91, 119, 202–3
Labourers, 194, 232, 251, 255, 278
La-Bue, 101, 152–53, 284, 301
Land, 22, 31, 39–40, 91–93, 98–101, 136, 144, 146, 170–71, 182, 186–87, 273–75, 284, 292–93, 300–301
   owner of, 273–74, 307
Land deity, 119, 125, 157, 166, 238
Land priest, 4, 101, 119, 158, 284
Language, 7, 13, 69, 81, 85–86, 109–11, 129, 132, 137–38, 146–48, 259, 267
Large canoes, 13, 50, 78–79, 192, 226, 239, 248, 250, 254, 257, 259–60, 276
   use of, 248–49
Laws, 166, 191, 225, 292, 296, 304–5, 310, 312
Leaders, 57, 104–6, 111, 113, 118–20, 122–23, 130–31, 134, 146–47,

151–52, 177, 287–88, 299–300, 310–11, 313
Great, 130, 283, 305
Leadership, 30, 33, 55–56, 62, 69, 104, 116, 120, 139, 151, 173, 181–82, 284, 289, 313
Leather belt, 37, 56, 66, 83
Lee, 85, 149, 164, 229, 250
Leme, 31, 135, 142, 154
Lenee, 141–43, 224
Leopard, 115, 296–97
Libations, 37, 58–59, 144, 157, 189, 306
poured, 20, 32, 36, 105
Lieutenants, 55, 63, 285, 300–301, 312–16, 331
Life, 25–27, 34, 48–50, 62, 69, 117, 163, 241, 253, 283, 288, 306, 327
spirit, 27, 61, 289
Lineage, 20, 22, 54, 100, 307
Linguistics Group, 270–71
Livestock, 31, 169, 186, 188, 191, 236, 263–64, 268, 284
Locations, 61, 94, 103, 117, 131, 163, 177, 186, 206, 231–32, 252, 254–56, 260, 268, 301
geographical, 9, 77, 90, 329
present, 77, 79–80, 110, 124, 141
Long-distance trade, 203, 238, 240, 244–49, 251, 253, 255, 257–59, 261, 276–77
Long-distance traders, 51, 192–93, 225–26, 238, 241, 245–46, 250, 277
Luawii, 41–42, 52, 120, 123, 126, 128, 135, 140, 151, 154–57, 159, 162, 174–76, 293, 309–10
Lueku, 129, 134, 161, 184
Lumber, 192, 229, 248, 250, 259
Luubaara, 157, 162–63, 204, 211
Luubaara River, 93, 126, 129, 140, 156, 158–59, 162, 165

M

Maize, 199–200, 202, 259

Manilas, 20, 22–23, 58, 110, 188, 191–92, 202, 234–35, 248, 264-68, 297, 305, 315
Manufactures, 11, 203, 231, 237, 253–55
Map, 9, 77–78, 85, 90, 103–5, 116, 126, 128–30, 132, 179, 182, 184, 235, 239–40, 242
Market days, 169, 225, 299
Markets, 77–78, 85, 90, 95–96, 154, 166–71, 179, 225–28, 230, 235–38, 242, 249–50, 259–60, 263–64, 266–68
distant, 226, 229, 237, 250
open, 236–37, 239
Marriage, 3, 18–24, 52–53, 68, 100, 107, 157, 239, 291, 303
long-distance, 21, 23, 196, 238–39, 291
previous, 24, 157, 159
Marriage system, 21, 42, 52, 111, 114, 119, 291
Marry wives, 99, 140
Machete, 83, 159, 230, 286
Materials, 2–3, 5, 7, 11, 49, 71, 246, 250, 258
Maternal uncles, 19–22, 53, 105, 114, 117, 119, 121, 163
Matrilineal, 52–53, 107, 111, 115, 175
Mats, sleeping, 233–34, 237
Meat, 190–91, 295–96, 298
Medicine, 4, 15, 35, 37–38, 40, 70, 105, 111, 115–16, 121, 124–25, 175–76, 306
Medium, 26, 29, 111, 115, 126, 265
Members, 22, 70, 74, 117, 119, 197–98, 212–13, 280, 284, 287–88, 299, 302–4, 306–7, 309, 311
Membership, 4, 42, 44, 54, 144, 288, 294, 298, 300, 302–4, 311, 314–15
Memories, 6, 98, 117, 138, 166
Mene, 31, 36, 238, 297
Mene Nama, 36, 38–39
Merchandise, 76, 171, 276–77
Mgwe, 202, 241, 288, 315

Middle, 18, 74–76, 136, 148, 163, 183, 254, 259–60, 275, 278
Migrations, 97–98, 112, 137, 143–44, 204
Mina, Frank, 192, 231, 248, 253
Mission, 161, 311, 322–23
Missionaries, 107, 320–21
Mogho, 78, 82, 84, 90–91, 94, 101–2, 185, 263–64, 267
  Town of, 91–92, 101, 177
Mogho-Mana, 91–92, 101–2
Moko, 73, 75, 82, 88–95, 263–64, 267
Money, 22, 50–51, 53, 58–59, 63–64, 185–88, 194–97, 239, 241–42, 254–55, 263–65, 267–71, 273–75, 277, 279–81
  amount of, 186, 273–74
  names of, 267
  use of, 267, 273, 281
  word for, 269–73
Monopoly, 170–71, 318
Moors,
  of Berbery 76, 83, 107, 277
MOSOP (Movement for the Survival of Ogoni People), 331
Mother animal, 189–91
Mouth, 37, 66, 75–76, 233, 237, 256, 276–77
Movement for the Survival of Ogoni People. See MOSOP
Movements, 2, 116–17, 123–24, 138, 160, 162, 173, 192, 245–46, 264, 331
Msia, 142, 145, 147
Mullets, 36, 62–63, 315
Murder, 42, 49, 154, 175, 306, 310
Mysteries, 73, 77, 177, 231

N

Naado, 222, 227, 229, 250
Nama, 15–16, 32–33, 35–40, 42–44, 100, 103–6, 109–17, 119–20, 126, 128, 130–31, 151, 153, 203–6, 238–39

kingdom of, 126, 137, 151, 156, 173, 283
priest of, 36–37
Nama-kpugi, 185, 264
Names, 74–76, 86–88, 91–92, 94–95, 98–103, 113, 120–25, 130–31, 134–36, 140–43, 146–47, 157–60, 179–81, 267, 308–9
  Praise, 114, 133, 156, 159
Nchia, 142, 145, 147, 242
Ndoki, 141, 237, 272, 321
Necks, 27, 76, 204–6, 209–10, 224, 276, 297
Nee, kune, 56, 289
Neighbours, 3, 74, 80, 136, 182, 328–29
Nembe, 228, 250, 254, 322
Nembe kingdom, 270
Nembe markets, 229, 250
Newcomers, 101, 130, 138, 161
New towns, 21, 39, 117–18, 121, 124–25, 138, 151, 153, 172, 313
N'galabia Ogoni, 178–79
Ngofa, 20, 22, 152, 184, 307
Ngwa, 240, 272, 321
Niger, 276, 321

Niger Delta, 9, 69, 73–75, 95–96, 111–12, 206, 245–46, 250–51, 254, 257, 259–60, 263, 267–69, 275–77, 331
Niger Delta languages, 13, 108
Nigeria, 12, 70, 192, 248, 253, 260, 323, 331
Nii, 83, 222, 224, 289, 303
Nkwerre, 230, 240, 272, 292
Nonwa, 129, 138–39
Nubien, 167, 294–96
Nubien market, 166, 170, 172
Number, 16–17, 30, 80, 137, 145–46, 190–91, 194–95, 198–99, 212, 232, 254–55, 278–79, 288–89, 302, 324–25
  small, 123, 160, 229, 257, 296

O

Obolo, 9, 77, 79, 236, 238, 292
Obudu, 271
Occasions, 15, 19, 38–40, 58–59, 62–63, 120, 144, 156, 226–27, 283, 288, 294–95, 297, 308
Occupations, 6, 12, 45, 50, 61, 74, 104, 111, 229, 234, 257, 260, 311
Offences, 25, 159, 166, 170, 238, 247
Ogoloma, 110–11, 204, 206
Ogoni, 9–32, 50–56, 74–88, 90–100, 102–18, 170–76, 178–80, 188–208, 228–36, 246–54, 263–70, 290–94, 296–300, 302–10, 314–29
  ancient, 100, 131, 195, 230, 294
  decline of, 318, 327, 332
  early, 55, 186, 230, 279
Ogoni ancestors, 62, 68, 107–8, 110, 112–13, 115, 151
  early, 105, 113
Ogoni area, 79, 86, 264, 270
Ogoni chiefs, 89, 242
Ogoni coast, 84, 96
Ogoni country, 311, 325
Ogoni culture, 29, 49
Ogoni Division, 17, 328, 332
Ogoni farmers, 201, 293
Ogoni history, 1, 7, 203, 238, 331
Ogoni land, 40, 43, 87, 92, 292, 322
Ogoniland, 50, 92, 331
Ogoni languages, 7, 13–14, 81, 107, 110, 285
Ogoni markets, 201–2, 240
Ogoni polity, 15, 30, 101, 153
Ogoni pots, 249–50
Ogoni pottery, 203, 207, 228, 249
Ogoni Region, 73, 246, 257, 276
Ogoni society, 15, 47, 51, 55–56, 68, 199, 289–90, 292, 324
Ogoni territory, 5, 97–98, 110, 112, 117, 178, 241, 259, 311, 317, 324

Ogoni towns, 12, 95, 99, 162, 193, 312, 320
Ogoni traders, 171, 259
Ogoni traditions, 4, 111, 197, 292
Ohafia, 91, 102, 272
Oil palm, 11–12, 50, 61, 91–92, 164, 187, 194–96, 199, 202, 277–79
  owners of, 194, 278
Oil palm bushes, 53, 194, 196, 306
Okochiri, 110–11, 204, 206
Okpogho, 271–72
Okrika, 80, 90–91, 94–95, 110, 204, 227, 240–41, 243, 269, 292, 317, 322
Old Ghana Empire, 107–8, 111–12
O'nee, 142, 145–46, 148
Onitsha, 240, 273, 319, 322, 329
Onne, 48, 142–48, 184
Opobo, 227, 243, 254, 269, 319, 321, 323–24, 327–28, 332
Opuoko, 98–99, 140–41, 160, 171, 182, 184, 192, 232, 243–44
Oral tradition, 1–3, 86–87, 107–10, 112–17, 124–26, 128–31, 133–35, 140–41, 143–44, 165–67, 171–73, 176–77, 183–85, 283, 303–4

Organisation, 55, 211, 231, 254, 300, 312–13, 326
Origin, 68, 73, 75, 87, 89, 92, 94, 97–98, 102, 107, 109, 111, 143, 147–48, 265–66
  Country of, 110, 115
Oron, 252, 254, 271, 323
Outlying Districts, 127, 129, 131, 133, 135, 137, 139, 141, 143, 145, 147, 149
Overthrow, 21, 139, 161, 183, 328
Owerri, 240, 254, 272, 320
Owner, 51, 170, 186–94, 196–97, 222, 225, 232, 248, 250, 254, 268, 274–75, 278–79, 301
  farmland, 187, 275
Ownership, 245, 273, 284

P

Pacheco Pereira, 73, 75–77, 81, 83–84, 276–77
Pah-yaa, 61, 67
Palace, 177, 301, 304–6
Palm fruits, 12, 50, 102, 144, 187, 237, 287
Palm oil, 74, 195, 202, 248, 320
Palm oil trade, 318, 320
Palm trees, 194, 277–78, 317
Palm wine, 11, 20, 36, 60, 63, 92, 189, 195, 201, 229, 248, 250, 278, 315, 325
Palm wine tappers, 4, 194, 278, 315
Palm wine tapping, 12, 50, 61, 168, 287, 315
Parade, 63–64
Parents, 3, 20, 22, 24, 26–28, 44, 48, 56–58, 60, 62, 65, 70, 241, 289, 295
Participation, 59, 68, 183, 243–44, 314, 318
Parties, 120, 191
Passage, 35, 68, 105, 158, 160, 163, 168–69, 226, 314
Patrilineage, 54, 58–60, 156
Patrons, 20, 63–64, 66, 239
Payment, 25, 58, 66, 190, 241, 315
Peace, 76, 174, 183, 276–77, 305–6, 310–11
Peppers, 12, 92, 164, 168, 199–200, 202, 237, 259, 318
Pereira, 21, 74–75, 77–81, 83, 85–87, 94–95, 169, 185, 235, 239, 248, 253, 258–59, 263, 266–67

Performance, 15, 33, 35, 38–40, 47–48, 55, 57–59, 61, 63, 67–68, 130, 288, 294, 303
  traditional, 58, 60, 64–66

Period
  colonial, 136, 156, 322–23
  early, 115, 132, 151, 192, 203, 207, 250, 252, 315
Permanent tree-crops, 186, 194–95, 292
Personal names, 31, 99, 181
Persons, 4–6, 23, 26–28, 31–32, 34–35, 60–61, 99–100, 121–23, 186–92, 194–96, 273–75, 287, 289–90, 305–6, 309
Piassava, 11, 192, 238, 248
Pilgrimage, 35–36, 38, 41, 55, 58, 115
Pitchers, 168, 227–28, 249
Place-names, 3, 73–75, 94, 96, 129, 135, 146–47
Plantain farms, 196, 202, 279
Plantain groves, 53, 195, 279
Plants, 19, 60, 194–95, 260, 277, 279, 293
Pledge, 51, 186–87, 194, 196, 273–75, 278–79
Pledgee, 186–87, 274–75, 278–79
Pledger, 187, 273–75
Plots, 143, 187, 195, 274–75, 277, 279, 292
Po, Fernando, 85, 251, 319
Poles, 11, 192, 248, 252, 259
Policy, 312, 321–22
Political power, 69, 153–54, 243–44, 301
Polity, 114–15, 151
Population, 9, 48, 51, 71, 77, 80, 85, 87, 116, 118, 128–29, 137–38, 149, 235, 244
Port Harcourt, 7, 9, 48, 85, 168, 170, 195, 227, 260
Portuguese, 69, 73, 89–90, 94–95, 107, 168–70, 186, 240, 264, 266–68, 271
  early, 85, 94–95

Possessing ancestral spirits, 30, 34–35, 301–2
Possession, 29, 33, 64, 122, 135–36, 144, 192, 245–47, 275

Pots, 12, 50, 60, 110, 168–69, 192, 205–7, 211–13, 224–29, 234, 236, 247–51, 259
 aluminum, 193, 228, 249, 251
Potsherds, 109, 204–6
Potters, 206–7, 211–13
Potter's wheel, 205–7, 211
Pottery, 92, 164, 203, 211, 213, 236, 259
Pottery trade-marks, 213, 224–25
Potting centre, 204–5
Poultry, 12, 188, 190–91
Power, 16, 23, 29, 35, 39, 43, 85, 117–18, 120, 133, 183–84, 288, 296–97, 301, 308–12
Pre-colonial Ogoni, 14, 31, 186, 274, 283, 287, 289, 295, 298, 300
Pre-colonial times, 30–33, 79, 185, 192, 228, 246–49, 258, 264, 267, 270, 292, 312
Prices, 188, 191–92, 201–2, 226, 233, 235, 248, 250, 254, 256, 264, 277
Priests, 20, 22, 32, 36, 38, 40, 105, 111, 115–16, 121–24, 126, 131, 139, 151, 155
Proclamation, 39, 155, 309, 323
Property, 24, 54, 185, 188, 200, 273, 291, 310–11
 landed, 273–74
Prosperity, 47, 141, 182, 261, 291, 318
Proverbs, 3, 49, 142, 188, 196
Pya bee hue, 284–85, 288
Pya Gbara, 56, 84, 285–87, 311–15
Pya Kanee, 55, 197, 280, 285, 300–301, 307–8, 316
Pya Kune Nee, 285, 289

Pya Zuguru, 55, 285, 300–301, 311–14
Pythons, 115, 296–97

Q

Qualifications, 49, 57, 136, 307, 314
Quantities, 116, 201, 204, 247, 317
 large, 76, 169, 237, 248, 277, 318
Quarrel, 142–43, 148, 293, 303

R

Radiocarbon dating, 109–12
Raffia cloths, 233–34, 237
Raffia palm, 11–12, 17, 50, 53, 70, 92, 194–95, 233, 256, 277–79
Raffia palm bushes, 194–96, 202, 278, 293, 306
Ranks, 32, 56, 67, 108, 117, 139, 160, 285
Reforms, 301, 304, 309, 331
Region, 74, 78–80, 83, 86, 94–95, 107, 112, 245–46, 253, 264, 267, 270, 273, 276, 280–81
Relatives, 19, 22, 24, 27, 59–60, 62, 65, 108, 203
Religion, 14, 132, 154–55, 319
Representatives, 63, 154–55, 239, 304
Requirements, 21, 35, 51, 89, 130, 238–39
Resistance, 69, 132, 134, 145, 181, 324–26
Return, 13, 17, 39, 67, 78, 102, 120, 179, 184, 192, 201, 212, 250–51, 292, 299
Return journeys, 179, 228–29, 249–50
Revenue, 23, 101, 153
Rio Real, 75–76, 90, 94–96, 248, 252, 258, 267, 276
Rites, 3, 47, 51, 56–57, 83, 115, 307
Ritual elements, 33, 35
Ritual foods, 155, 195, 279

Rituals, 2–3, 12, 21, 27, 29, 35–36, 38–39, 42, 51, 58–59, 61, 64, 67, 131, 296
Rivers, 27, 76, 92, 95, 98, 141, 192–93, 232, 236, 239, 246, 248, 251, 255, 276–77
Rivers State, 31, 192, 248, 253, 260
Rocks, 105–6, 113, 118, 120
Root, 7, 31, 45, 54, 135, 140, 146, 198, 267, 270, 326
Ropes, 11, 233–34, 237–38, 259

Routes, 38, 63, 65–66, 129, 137, 193, 227–29, 232, 240–41, 249–51, 255, 266
Rule, 43, 151, 153, 180, 293, 301, 325
　colonial, 43, 69, 324, 326–29
Rulers, 3–4, 30–31, 55–56, 100, 122–23, 139, 151, 153–54, 157–59, 178, 180–84, 284–85, 288, 308, 324–26
　new, 308, 326–27
Rulership, 32, 100–101, 126, 180–81, 183, 326
Rumours, 121, 124, 166

S

Saa, 127–28, 133, 157, 159, 163
Sacrifices, 3, 12, 21, 26, 35–36, 38, 42, 51–52, 58, 61, 117, 144, 191, 239, 305–6
　purification, 27, 167, 297
Sale, 169, 187, 195, 203, 233, 237, 241, 256, 260, 277–78
Salt, 76, 78–79, 203, 234–35, 246, 277
Samples, 109, 203, 205–6, 237
Saving, 195–96, 226, 268, 279
Scene, 134, 154, 176, 305
Scholars, 71, 78, 90, 178, 265, 332
Sea, 27, 67, 69, 85, 93, 105, 113, 117, 149, 172, 234, 292, 317
Sea foods, 92, 168–69, 201
Seasons, 70, 194, 278, 295, 299
Seat, 32, 128, 293, 302, 304, 309
Secret societies, 4, 43, 70, 231, 311–12, 315
Section, 133, 137, 156, 177–78, 194, 206, 225, 231, 236, 246, 273, 302
Services, 15–16, 19, 173, 175, 247, 275, 305
　king's, 162, 304–5
Settlement, 77–79, 100, 102–3, 109–17, 121–25, 127, 129, 131–33, 137–39, 141, 143–45, 147–49, 153, 176–77, 180–81

　early, 157–58
　first, 15, 103, 105, 259
　new, 116–18, 125, 139, 152, 164
Settlers, 99, 138–40, 149, 157, 163, 177, 244, 293
Seventeenth centuries, 19, 21, 42–43, 51–52, 78, 94–95, 167–68, 181, 202, 253, 258–59, 331
Sex, 26, 61, 65, 202, 238, 280
Shaping, 232, 255, 313
Sheath, 37, 56, 66, 83
Sheep, 12, 36, 76, 78, 81–82, 168, 188, 236, 239, 248, 259, 277, 310
Shrine, 3, 40–41, 51–52, 105, 176–77, 197, 293, 325
Sii, 43–44, 104, 106, 122–24, 126, 152–54, 242
　founding of, 104, 122–23
Sisters, 68–69, 123, 126
Site, 84, 86, 110–11, 116–19, 121, 132, 134, 140, 170, 172, 177, 180, 253, 255, 257
Sixteenth century, 52–54, 90, 93–95, 151, 155, 161, 165, 168, 171, 175–76, 225, 229, 266–67, 297–98, 300–303
Size, large, 234, 253
Slavery, 65, 127, 159, 163
Slaves, 21, 51, 76, 78, 81, 89, 128, 201–3, 239, 241–42, 277, 285, 289–91, 307, 317–18
Slave trade, 100, 181, 183, 196, 238, 240, 243, 259, 317–18, 320, 332
　trans-Atlantic, 51, 69, 81, 157, 159, 161, 183–84, 243, 258–59, 270, 331
Smallpox, 28, 85, 87, 149
Smallpox epidemic, 73, 95–96
Smith, Robert, 79, 246, 253
Smithing, 203, 229

Social classes, 55, 84, 285, 287, 289–90
Social Classification Title, 49, 51, 53, 55, 57, 59, 61, 63, 65, 67, 69, 71

Social clubs, 44, 287, 294
Social organisation, 283–85, 287, 289, 291, 293, 295, 297, 299–301, 303, 305, 307, 309, 311, 313–15, 324
Social status, 4, 6, 51, 56, 83–84, 325
Social stratification, 48, 57, 284, 315
Society, 2, 4, 14–15, 26–27, 34–35, 41, 47, 55–56, 167, 188, 195–96, 283–87, 290–91, 298–99, 311–15
  ancient, 283–84
  musical, 64
Sogho, 106, 168, 324–25
Soil, 9, 28, 167, 239
Sons, 22, 31–32, 34–35, 41, 44, 51–53, 56–58, 63, 65, 68–69, 142–43, 241, 244, 289, 293
Sorcery, 50, 100, 154, 175, 306, 310
Sound, 2, 91, 159, 175, 226, 287
Sources, 7, 77–78, 127, 129, 142, 153, 157–58, 175, 177, 179–80, 182, 184, 213–16, 230–31, 246
Southern Ogoni, 185, 267
South-west, 10, 91–92, 94
Specialists, 1, 232, 255
Spirit-mediums, 15, 26–27, 105–6, 111, 116, 185–86, 264–65, 268
Spirits, wicked, 26–27
Sponsors, 65, 70, 289
Sports, 45, 61, 287, 313, 315
Staking, 199, 202
Statement, 100, 127, 131, 142, 144–45, 158–59, 290
States, 103, 106, 149, 153, 175, 293, 295, 298, 305–6, 308, 310, 318, 321, 327–28, 332
  Unitary, 179–80
Stock, 188, 193, 226, 251
Stool, 151, 181, 206, 293, 308
Story, 27, 100, 105, 107–8, 127, 141, 143, 159, 182, 240
Strangers, 87, 285, 289, 292
Streets, 60, 63–64, 81

Subjects, 1, 6, 29, 32, 77, 119, 163, 179, 253, 264, 319
Sub-towns, 93, 95, 129, 165
Succession, 52, 55, 115, 122, 126, 128, 151, 154, 175, 293
Successors, 31, 42, 75, 128, 175
Sun, 17–18, 69, 81, 237
Supernatural, 14, 35–37, 39, 306
Supernatural confrontations, 37–38
Supreme God, 14–15, 26–27, 306
Surface, 113, 204–5, 209–11, 328
Surrogate, 189–92
Surrogate owner, 188–90
Surrogate services, 189–90
Survival, 68, 114, 245
Survivors, 85–87, 149
Sword, 37, 43, 47, 56, 66–67, 83, 119–20, 153, 159, 283, 286–87
Synthesis, 7, 147–48
System, 19, 22, 42, 126, 168, 170–71, 190, 194, 196, 264, 274, 278, 280–81, 284, 293–94
  indigenous, 280, 327–28
  religious, 115
  traditional, 120, 324

T

Taboos, 35, 139, 166, 200
Tape, 5, 7, 34–36, 39–41, 43, 65, 67, 90, 92–94, 105–6, 145–46, 171, 180, 287–90, 305
Tapping, 194–95, 278
Task, 19, 100, 108, 159–60, 285, 288, 291, 300, 305, 314, 323, 326
Technology, canoe-making, 251–52, 257
Tee, 4, 31–32, 127, 129–32, 134–40, 143–47, 154, 156–58, 160–61, 167, 173, 176, 181–84, 189, 242–43
  founder of, 130, 138
  towns in, 130, 138–39, 182
Tee area, 129, 131–34, 136–37, 140, 145, 147, 160–61, 181, 241
Tee-Baan, 160–61

Teenama, 105, 113
Teenama River, 105, 113
Tee sources, 129–30
Terms, 18, 52, 54, 56, 91–92, 102, 123–24, 135, 163–64, 189, 191, 273–75, 284–86, 290–91, 324
Territory, 9, 13, 29, 31, 100, 108, 111, 135–37, 141, 157–58, 176–77, 243, 319, 321, 325–26
Testimony, 1, 35, 83, 86, 143–44, 157, 160, 177, 180, 183, 298, 301, 305, 311, 314
Tetenwi, 143–44
Te-yaa, 58–60, 62–63, 67
Theft, 50, 167, 197, 238, 306
Thickness, 204, 212, 232, 255
Thieves, 167, 186, 231, 268
Threat, 134, 167, 183, 292, 319
Tiko, 193, 235, 251, 253–54
Timber, 11, 79, 231, 251, 254, 257, 277
Titles, 3, 6, 16, 29–31, 35, 37, 39, 41–42, 47, 49–51, 115, 139, 196, 198–99, 202
Toga, 85, 92, 149, 164
Tonwe, 3–4, 86, 223
Toodee, 222–23
Tools, 3, 19, 70, 77, 114–15, 232, 238, 255, 286
Towns, 30–32, 39–40, 84–87, 90–95, 99–102, 119–26, 133–34, 141–43, 149, 163–68, 172–73, 176–80, 182–84, 284–85, 309–12
  coastal, 77, 79, 92, 164, 167
  dominant, 244
  group of, 125, 163
  large, 149, 263
  northern, 162, 166–67
  oldest, 128, 130
  separate, 104, 122
  southern, 93, 162, 165, 167, 169, 173
Trade, 21, 75, 77–78, 165, 167–68, 170–71, 179, 182–83, 227–29, 236–39, 242–43, 246–48, 258, 264–65, 317–22

  commodity, 171, 236
  external, 171
  legitimate, 11, 259, 320, 323, 332
  long distance, 50, 168, 181, 236, 247
  new, 258–59, 318
  silent, 107, 110
Trade canoes, 246–47, 250
  large, 245–46, 258–59
Trade goods, 170, 193, 201, 247, 260
Trade monopoly, 318–19, 332
Trade routes, 167, 184, 240–42, 292, 318
  major, 181, 184, 240, 317
  overland, 240, 318
Traders, 62, 68, 78, 170, 178, 192–93, 235, 237, 250, 253, 259, 292
  slave, 138, 157, 159, 182
Trading, 166, 170, 246, 258
Trading activities, 78, 267, 318
Traditional rite, 16, 28, 307, 309
Traditional rulers, 4, 31, 145, 316, 326
Traditional society, 32, 44
Traditions, 2–4, 6–7, 41–42, 47, 56–58, 60–63, 83–84, 97–98, 103–4, 111–12, 129, 138–41, 196–98, 286–88, 307–8
  Yaanwii, 30, 48, 50, 57, 63, 197, 280
Tragedy, 58, 87
Transatlantic Impact, 319, 321, 323, 325
Transition, 21, 27, 40–41, 55, 90, 107, 291
Translation, 7, 27, 41, 323
Transportation, 5, 21, 192–93, 259
Transport canoes, 192, 276–77
  large, 50, 192, 245, 248, 253–54, 277
Traps, game, 233–34, 237–38
Treasures, 196, 280, 310
Trees, 11, 19, 26, 61–62, 67, 119, 195, 229, 231–32, 254–55, 278
Trenches, deep, 93, 165, 173
Trip, 192–93, 248, 251, 321
Twin mothers, 65, 141–44
Type, 4, 6, 19–20, 97–98, 100, 116–17, 151–52, 193, 203–4, 206, 212–13, 236, 250–51, 257–58, 264–65

U

Ughelli, 270
Umuahia, 240–41
Umuoji, 240
Upside, 233, 256
Uwegwere, 92, 149, 156, 163–64
Uweke, 129–31, 138, 160, 181–82

V

Values, 23–24, 41, 48–49, 71, 170, 193, 266, 275
Variants, 6, 99, 123, 127, 141–42
Vegetables, 12, 92, 164, 199–200, 279
Very large village, 73–81, 83–84, 86, 90, 95, 276
Victims, 238–39, 306
Villages, 5, 18, 39, 64, 73, 76–78, 80–81, 84, 137–38, 155, 157, 188, 191, 324–25, 328
  large, 76, 235, 276–77
  separate, 138, 141, 147, 308

W

Waddell, 78, 81, 230, 321–23
Waist, 37, 56, 62, 65–66, 83, 295
Walnuts, 12, 92, 164
War, 2–3, 67, 93–94, 123–25, 130–32, 137–40, 144–46, 160, 162, 165–67, 172–76, 182, 293, 305–6, 324
  time of, 33, 39, 56, 115, 131, 289
Warri, 82, 270
Warriors, 33–34, 36, 56–57, 105, 111, 115, 173–74, 276, 283, 289, 294–97, 299, 301, 306, 314
Water pitchers, 168, 228, 249
Wattle, 81, 192, 248, 259
Wealth, 51, 54, 57, 67–68, 185–88, 191–92, 194, 196, 244, 246–47, 263, 266, 268, 275, 277
  accumulating, 185–86, 263, 268, 274
  permanent, 48, 194, 196, 278–79
Wealthy, 22, 25, 31, 50–54, 57, 193, 196, 251, 279–80, 291
Weapons, 3, 56, 70, 83, 107, 114–16, 174, 183, 201, 229, 247, 259, 316
Weaving, 12, 203, 211, 233–34, 307
West Africa, 89–90, 95, 195, 198, 253, 264–66, 320
WHO (World Health Organisation), 87
Wife, 14, 20–21, 42, 100, 102, 175, 290
Wiisoro, 116, 118–22, 124, 126, 152, 283
Wiiyaakara, 106, 159, 162, 173
Williamson, Kay 7, 14, 108, 110, 138, 144, 161, 198, 200, 267
Wine, 34, 36, 40, 170, 297
Witchcraft, 26, 100, 154, 238, 306, 310
Witnesses, 189, 308
Wives, 21, 23, 42, 51, 53–54, 68, 84, 134, 140, 145–46, 239, 288, 290, 294–96
  foreign, 50–54, 68
Wolff, 13, 81, 108, 137, 140, 144, 161
Woman, 14–15, 18, 20, 23–25, 52, 55, 61, 108, 157, 159, 187, 189, 227, 290, 293
Women, 61, 65–66, 113–15, 145, 164, 166–67, 200, 202, 211, 225–26, 229–30, 234, 287, 293–94, 296
Women potters, 212, 225–26
Women traders, northern, 166, 171
Wood, 60, 233, 256, 297
Words, 7, 34, 81–82, 122, 130, 133, 135–36, 141–42, 179–80, 271, 287–88, 291–92, 294, 297–98, 307
Work, 2, 6, 44, 49, 69, 77, 79, 86, 183, 241, 294, 302, 305, 307, 322–23
World, 2, 15, 27, 48, 98, 154, 197, 320–23
World Health Organisation. See WHO
Worship, 32, 118, 195, 279
Wrestling, 287–88, 314
Writer, 1, 47, 49, 73, 79, 84, 87, 105, 177, 201, 204, 226–27, 267, 332

Y

Yaa, 20, 28, 44, 57–67, 83, 131, 145, 147–48, 159, 182–83, 286, 303, 307
Yaa father, 57–58, 60, 62–64, 66
Yaa-ge, 28, 83, 286, 289
Yaage, 34, 47, 287, 289
Yaage tradition, 33, 43, 51, 201, 244, 286–87, 289
Yaage tradition, 56–57, 63, 65, 68, 70
Yaakara, 158–59
Yaakaragute, 157–59
Yaa marathon, 65–66
Yaanwii, 34, 44, 51, 57, 307
Yaa tradition, 44, 47–50, 52, 54–56, 62, 65, 67–71, 83, 131–32, 148, 238, 286–87, 289–91, 303, 315
Yaa Tradition and Social Classification Title, 49, 51, 53, 55, 57, 59, 61, 63, 65, 67, 69, 71
Yagara, 187, 231
Yam cultivation, 50–51, 61, 198, 287, 317
Yam farms, 196, 241, 279, 317
Yam priests, 4, 51, 198
Yams, 17, 19, 40, 58, 60, 74, 76, 195, 197–202, 241, 248, 259, 279, 315, 317–18
King's, 201–2
Large quantities of, 51, 201, 239
Yam vines, 202, 294
Yeghe, 85, 149, 168, 182
Yiranwaa, 157, 162–63
Yogurezogomo, 106, 122, 125
Yomii, 34, 98, 171
Yonwidam, 17, 294–96
Yoruba, 2, 6, 139
Yorubaland, 181, 322
Younger, 105, 114, 118, 122, 283
Youths, 28, 33, 44, 47–48, 50–51, 56–58, 60, 65, 68, 70, 121, 283, 286–87, 314–15

Z

Za, 52, 114, 118–19, 123, 126–28, 151, 154–57, 175–76, 293
Zaakpon, 106, 154, 166
Zaakpon territory, 166–67
Zia, 51, 197, 199
Zim, 34, 40, 301–2
Zimbabwe, 15, 29
Zua, 17, 155, 295
Zua feast, 17, 144
Zuawa, 224
Zuguru, 306, 310, 313–14

www.ingramcontent.com/pod-product-compliance
Lightning Source LLC
Chambersburg PA
CBHW070804300426
44111CB00014B/2423